Cover photo acknowledgments where necessary:

The Roger Stevens, University of Leeds and Broadcasting Tower by Michael Taylor
Hyde Park Picture House by Betty Longbottom
Both Hands provided by www.mickaul.co.uk
Henry Moore, *Reclining Figure* (1951) by Solipsist
Sydney Opera House by Matthew Field
Lancaster bomber by Alan Barrow
Corinne Bailey Rae by Ludovic ETIENNE
Dolbadarn – a Hunslet Port Class locomotive from 1922 – by John Barrie
The Switched Reluctance Motor image by Vonvikken
Wave by Jo Lee
Parkinson Building by Louparry

Back Cover:

Daze of Future Past flyer by Steven Johna Johnson/soldierant
Malcolm McDowell by lukeford.net
Baroness Chapman image supplied by www.iconphotomedia.com
Chippendale Chinese desk by Jorgebarrios
Billy statue by Steve Swift
Malcolm McDowell by lukeford.net
Ricky Wilson (Kaiser Chiefs) by Andreas Nowak
Leeds and Country Liberal Club by John Grogan – johnnyg1955 on flickr.
Icon A.D. artwork by Craig A Sharp-Weir

How Leeds Changed The World
The World
Encylopaedia Leeds

Mick McCann

ARMLEY ~PRESS~

Published by Armley Press 2010

Proof and Copy Editor: Steve Swift

Layout: Ian Dobson

Cover Design: John Wheelhouse & Mick McCann

Thanks to Vicky Lesley Jackson for being my joint best mate. I love you with a....

Special thanks to John and Ali from East Leeds Magazine for digging me out of a cover design hole, Steve Swift for being completely and constantly on the ball and sometimes even making me sound smart. John Poulter for chucking over a couple of entries in his specialist field. Last thanks go to Richard C. Allen for helping me through my Hartley obsession.

Contact: <Twitter - @mickmccann01 or search for the book on Facebook>

ISBN 0-9554699-3-7

INTRO

What is this? I suppose it's a book bigging up Leeds. I can't do the city justice but I've given it a go. I've brought together many of the remarkable ways in which the city has contributed to the world through developments, discoveries, ideas, inventions, innovations, organisations, events and important and interesting theories over the centuries.. Where's y' boundary? The Leeds urban subdivision covers an area of 109 square kilometres (42 sq mi) and I've drawn my Leeds boundary around LS postcodes.

I like the idea of taking one of the major, industrial northern cities and documenting some of its achievements. Naturally I chose Leeds, it's my city, I love the city, I know the city or so I thought as I set out on this journey. I knew nowt.

It obviously can't be comprehensive, that would be a lifetime's work and you could even argue that I'd have to include every last person living in Leeds because that's the essence of Leeds, its people. Anyway, it's my decision and I've decided not to do an entry on everyone in Leeds, past and present, that'd be daft....it'd take me weeks. There will be some glaring omissions. I have, for example, completely forgotten to mention the time when Houdini nearly died here repeating a trick he'd performed hundreds of times. His almost fatal mistake? The cask he needed to escape from was filled with Tetley's bitter instead of the usual water. Harry was overcome by alcoholic fumes and the great man had to be rescued. I'm interested in stuff that'll make you go, 'Eh? Y'kidding?' If you find yourself thinking *I can't believe he didn't include....* (such as Marks and Spencer's Penny Bazaar) then I reckon it'll probably be quite well known, although I would appreciate an email about it. The book could go on forever, it's my piece of string and I have to stop and publish at some point. If I didn't now I never would. I know me, I'd constantly be ruminating, 'Ooh, I'll just do what-is-it, who-j-m-bob....ey, thingy-m-jig is interesting.'

I think of it as an Encyclopaedia due to its breadth of content and not the amount of entries or a daft idea of completeness – give me a copy of the Encyclopaedia Britannica and I'll find you 20 things that aren't in it in ten minutes. I also didn't go trying to rack up a number of entries, preferring to give some topics or people more attention than you would expect. I accept that occasionally I get a bit 'local history' which I shouldn't but we're none of us perfect. I've nothing against local history, it's fascinating, it's just that this isn't supposed to be local history-ish, it should have different tone and content. I've obviously read plenty of local history over the last 18 months and have often found myself thinking *I can't believe they didn't include....surely that's the most interesting aspect?* Anyway it's a good job it isn't too 'local history' as David Thornton's historical dictionary should be out any time now and, judging by his previous work and the scope of his new project, I'm expecting the most comprehensive historical study of Leeds ever written. Doubt I'd've been able to compete with that.

By the end I'm feeling quite overwhelmed and, looking at the scatter-gun nature of it (that I'm not sure I could have avoided) feel like calling it Some of the Ways in Which Leeds Changed the World but that's not as catchy. Hey-Ho, I nab some of the ones that got away if I do a second volume. Sometimes you have to publish and be embarrassed. Hopefully there's some good stuff in it and some extra light is shone on ambiguities or hidden gems. The nature of my printing process means that I can change the content at anytime so send any queries, corrections or exciting missed entries to: updateleeds@hotmail.co.uk – it may take me a few weeks to update as I'll collect them together and do them in tranches. I've also got many references not included, so if you need further background on anything email me and I'll have a gander. Feel free to post new info, check, correct and generally chunter on the facebook group or at Regdafish in the book section.

Ey, if this book seems quite slim to you, it's smoke and mirrors, at 129,202 words it could easily have been 400 pages. Just to explain, the page count of a book isn't always connected to the word count, with clever layout and a big enough font size you can turn a pamphlet into a book. I can show you local history books the same size as this that will run to around 160 pages yet be less than 30,000 words – I think I counted one at about 26,000. Applying that to the word count of this tome would give you a book of 800 pages, which may leave you with fantastic biceps but coupled with extreme arm ache and the need of a decent physiotherapist.

Last thing, if you're looking for a dry book on Leeds, this isn't for you, it can be a bit moist can this one. Right, I've finished chuntering.

A

The **Accent Revolt** of 1996. It was a bloody affair situated around Leeds central bus station. In January 1996 management, wanting to innovate and provide a 21st Century service to customers, introduced talking bus stops to give basic information. Their fatal error was to choose the ultra Received Pronunciation voice of Rowan Morton-Gledhill, the locals were up in arms, complaining and writing letters to the press, they wanted a 'normal' voice, not to be lectured to by some authority figure. Ironically, Ms Morton-Gledhill was born and bred in Huddersfield and her forebears had arrived there at the time of the Vikings....if only they'd taught her to 'talk proper'. Not to worry, Rowan went on to produce the documentary *Single British Muslim* and *Songs Of Praise*. See **Chris Moyles** for an irrelevant and overlong accent related rant.

For the oldest British flying **aeroplane**, built in Leeds by Leeds folk, see the **Blackburn Type D** and **Robert Blackburn.**

Adel parish church (The Church of St John the Baptist) is the oldest (still standing) church in Leeds built between 1150 and 1170, around the same time as Kirkstall Abbey, and it has been little altered since. St Mary's Church, Whitkirk, may give it a run for its money as far as age of church site goes. Whitkirk Church can trace its vicars back as far as 1185 and there appears to have been a church on the site before this date, although the current St Mary's Church only goes back to the 14th century, quite modern really.

Back to the almost thousand year old Adel church, it's one of the best, complete Norman churches in Yorkshire and grade I listed. It also contains grade II listed features and memorials but unfortunately some of the external material has been stolen.

The **Afar Rift** in northern Ethiopia is, according to Radio 4's **Material World** (9/7/09), the only place in the world where it is possible to observe rifting, with continents being pulled apart and ocean basins forming on land that, tens of thousands of years ago, was itself part of the sea. **Dr Tim Wright** from the School of Earth & Environment, **University of Leeds**, is Principle Investigator of the **Afar Rift Consortium** (search them online, it's fascinating) a multinational collaboration of Unis/academics that study the area, and the Leeds team is (with Bristol) the largest contingent in the consortium. They are increasing our understanding of the mechanics of the earth – truly groundbreaking work....get it? Groundbreaking?

The **River Aire** rises at Malham Tarn, flowing underground to Malham Cove (Aire Head) and according to Martin Wainwright's *True North* is the spawning ground for Charles Kingsley's *The Water-Babies*, in part, a tract against child labour. The River Aire and the central Leeds crossing have been pivotal in the growth of Leeds, rising in the wool producing Yorkshire Dales, flowing on into the River Ouse and out into the Humber Estuary.

A Kind of Loving is a novel written by **Stan Barstow** who grew up in **Ossett**, the iconic film of the same name was scripted by Leeds writers **Keith Waterhouse** and **Willis Hall.** The film stars Alan Bates, June Ritchie and Thora Hird. An early, dark and gritty 'kitchen sink drama' about getting on with life in challenging circumstances, steeped in realism. The novel is part of a trilogy, the others are The *Watchers on the Shore* and *The Right True End*.

Sir (Thomas) Clifford Allbutt, MA, MD Cantab (1836–1925) was the inventor of the clinical thermometer. Born in Dewsbury, he was Physician at the Leeds General Infirmary and member of the Council of the School of Medicine from 1864 to 1884 and twice President of the School.

Thomas Clifford Allbutt in 1919 by Sir William Orpen.

Before his 1867 invention of the clinical thermometer (as we know it today) it took 20 minutes to get an accurate reading and patients had to hold the foot-long thermometer in their hands. He also introduced the ophthalmoscope, weighing machine and microscope to the wards and developed an interest in the care of the mentally ill (he was a Commissioner for Lunacy in England and Wales between 1889 and 1892). Later, as Regius Professor of Physic (an archaic word for medicine) at the University of Cambridge, he edited his vast *System of Medicine* which was for many years the 'doctor's bible'. He was knighted in 1907 and was the first to separate 'hyperpiesia' (essential hypertension) from renal hypertension (1921).

According to the **Leeds Institute of Medical Education** (University of Leeds) website, "The novelist **George Eliot** described him as a 'good, clever and graceful man, enough to enable one to be cheerful under the horrible smoke of ugly Leeds,' and is regarded generally as the model for George Eliot's **Dr Lydgate** in *Middlemarch*." (This is also asserted by other sources.) 'Lydgate represented a new type of doctor emerging from the surgeon apothecary........ the forerunner of the enlightened general practitioner of today. He was motivated by the prospects of scientific advance and medical reform; his use of the stethoscope and his wish to conduct autopsies placed him in the avant-garde of his profession.'

Vic Allen is a retired Leeds Uni prof who allegedly spied for the East German Stasi secret police. He wasn't a proper spy and not accused of passing on state secrets in the manner of a classic spy but rather of being an 'agent of influence'. He was shown from material contained in the *Mitrokhin Archive* to possess the code name 'Barber'. He told BBC Two's *The Spying Game*: 'I have no shame. I feel no regrets about that at all.' He's retired to Keighley now but was a Professor of Economics at Leeds University. He was given a lectureship at Leeds University 1959 and became a professor in 1973.

Vic was the NUM's official historian and made a secret visit to Cuba in 1988 to meet with Fidel Castro. In another episode, on a sabbatical from Leeds University in Nigeria (his third visit), he was arrested in Lagos and charged with 'managing an unlawful society for the purpose of overthrowing the government by military means' – a charge that carried a seven year jail sentence. Detained in solitary confinement, he went on hunger strike for eight days. The charge was later downgraded and he was granted bail but was then caught trying to escape from the country disguised as a local tribesman, when the turban slipped off his head, revealing his white skin. He was finally sentenced to one year in prison with hard labour but served only four months. He's published widely, look up Victor L Allen on Amazon for books such as *Russians are Coming: The Politics of Anti-Sovietism*. He also spent many years working on exposing the hardship and inequality of the mining industry in South Africa. His book *The History of Black Mineworkers in South Africa* was published in 2003.

On a related note a student from Leeds, **Fiona Houlding**, was also recruited by the Stasi and given the codename Diana. She fell in love with an East German while studying in Leipzig in the 1980s and passed on information to the authorities.

Roy Alon (1942–2006) was a stuntman born in Otley, not any old stuntman but the world's most prolific stuntman. According to the ***Guinness Book of Records*** he holds the world record for performing the most stunts in cinema history stretching from his debut in *A Bridge Too Far* to his last film ***Exhibit A*** which was partly shot in Leeds. During his 36-year career he appeared in over 1,000 films including the James Bond, Superman and Indiana Jones films and doubled for actors from Peter Sellers to Sophia Loren.

Thomas Ambler (1838–1920) was an architect, living and working in Leeds who designed many landmark buildings. That Moorish looking building (St Paul's House) in Park Square is one of his and I've often gazed at it thinking, *Eh? But I like it*. If you're interested Wiki has a link to photos of some of his grand Leeds buildings. See **John Barran**.

The Archers' **theme tune** is called '*Barwick Green*', as in **Barwick-in-Elmet**. It was written by **Arthur Wood**, a composer from **Heckmondwike** in 1924. It was written as a 'maypole dance' in his suite *My Native Heath*.

Ark Royal aircraft carrier started (1587) and ended its life as the flagship of the Royal Navy. During WW2 various government-sponsored campaigns were mounted to encourage people to raise money for the war effort. One of these was Warship Week. In Leeds, Warship Week was to be held on 30 January - 7 February 1942. In November 1941 the city of Leeds, as an additional incentive for the week, decided to adopt the HMS Ark Royal. Just days later the ship was torpedoed and sunk in the Mediterranean.

The fund-raising objective for Leeds Ark Royal Week changed from a target of £3.5m for a replacement hull and some refitting to over £5m for a replacement ship. A huge march took place down The Headrow in the city centre, led by the Navy and followed by military vehicles and personnel. The grand total raised by Leeds was over £9m. Contributions included money sent by children to buy nuts and bolts to sums of £250,000 from businesses to purchase Fulmar naval fighter planes, which cost £5,000 each.

The association between Leeds and HMS Ark Royal stems back to World War II. The third Ark Royal aircraft carrier was adopted by the city in 1942. When launched in 1950 she was the world's first

HMS Ark Royal in the 1970s.

aircraft carrier to be commissioned with an angled flight deck. In October 1973 the Ark Royal was granted The Freedom of Entry into the City, giving the ship the privilege of marching through the streets of the city on all ceremonial occasions. The last time this right was exercised was in June 2008, although I reckon it'll have been the crew not the ship. HMS Ark Royal has both official and non-official affiliations. She is officially affiliated with the following Leeds organisations: Ceres Division Royal Naval Reserve Leeds, City of Leeds, Headingly Royal Naval Association, Leeds Chamber of Commerce, Leeds United Football Club, the Royal Armouries, Royal Naval Historic Flight Support Group, Leeds TS Ark Royal and Yorkshire Fleet Air Arm Association. I had an *Airfix* model of the Ark Royal and remember mi'dad proudly telling me, 'That's Leeds's ship, is that.'

Arkwright (Leisureco) were the originator of old fashioned **retro football shirts** and the nation's current liking of **baggy fashion shorts**. Although not originally called Arkwright, they placed an advert for 'full cotton, authentic 1970s football shirts as worn by Billy and Norman' in the second issue of *The Square Ball* (1990), the high-end Leeds United fanzine that they also produced. The response from fans was huge and the company soon realised they were onto something and quickly set up Arkwright, obtained the rights to Celtic, Rangers and a host of top English sides. With Leeds United, the deal for the rights had been a nominal percentage of sales going to a charity and, as none of the football clubs realised the value or potential of this new market, Arkwright easily obtained rights to produce high quality copies of team's classic shirts for very small percentages of sales.

To reach the national market with its 'authentic footy shirts' Arkwright struck up a reciprocal advertising deal between *When Saturday Comes* (a national football fanzine/magazine) and *The Square Ball*, whilst also placing (usually) small adverts in the national press. To spearhead the Arkwright marketing campaign they used a picture of *Arkwright, the legendary one-eyed footballer* who used to ply his trade in the **West Yorkshire Heavy Woollen League** during the 1920s and 30s. This character attracted some general and media interest but was in fact a myth.

Quickly winning a contract to supply their shirts to Topshop and through mail-order the company reached a turnover of more than £1 million within 18 months of their first ad in *The Square Ball*. Part of the attraction for the 'classic' shirts was also a factor in the decline in sales of replica shirts. The shirts meant that many fans did not see the need for constantly buying their club's new season, low quality replica shirt and companies like Umbro and Addidas soon cottoned on to this. Unfortunately, Arkwright had only acquired a two-year deal with each club and by the end of this period the big companies took the licences and dominated the market.

Almost simultaneously to the shirts, they started to produce big baggy 1950s football shorts to compliment the shirts – footballers at the time wore more figure hugging shorts. I was there in the late '80s and (in the UK, I don't know about elsewhere) people didn't wear big, baggy shorts. When I played 5-a-side with people we wore the baggy '50s shorts and in summertime they were comfy and cool enough to wear out and about. I'd say that this was where the fashion for baggy shorts, that has lasted until this day, started. In 1992 the band **New Order** commissioned Arkwright to produce a classic football style shirt to promote the band, which they themselves designed and endorsed. I'd say that Arkwright changed the face of British fashion/leisure wear.

Wilson Armistead (1819–1868) was a Leeds writer with a particular interest in the abolition of slavery, Christian thought and a leader of The Leeds Anti-Slavery Association. He was a Quaker businessman, a correspondent of Charles Darwin, but a man who othewise seems to have largely disappeared from history. His books on the abolition of slavery were mainly aimed at the US market where slavery was not fully abolished until the 6th of December, 1865. According to the BBC Leeds website, the **Leeds Anti-Slavery Association** was instrumental in helping to abolish slavery. I can see that his books may have been influential but doubt that level of influence of The Leeds Anti-Slavery Association, although that's just my opinion, and who am I to argue with the BBC?

The first book of his (I can find) is, *Memoir of Paul Cuffe – A man of colour – Compiled from authentic sources.* (Edmund Fry, London, 1840) but I thought I'd concentrate on his second, *A tribute for the Negro* (W. Irwin, W. Harned, Manchester, New York, 1848) – *being a vindication of the moral, intellectual, and religious capabilities of the coloured portion of mankind: with particular reference to the African race.* 'The purport of the present volume, in contradistinction to the idea of the Negro being designed only for a servile condition, is to demonstrate that the Sable inhabitants of Africa are capable of occupying a position in society very superior to that which has been generally assigned to them.' – from the Preface. First published in 1848, it serves as both an angry denunciation of the 'terrible institution' of slavery in the United States and a celebration of the survival and achievements of Africans in America in the pre-Civil War era. *A tribute for the negro,* explains the 'sin of slavery', refutes notions of the correlation of intellectual ability to skin colour, explores the history of slavery across the globe, discusses the 'pernicious influence of slavery', mounts an impassioned defence of African culture and offers numerous biographical accounts of slave life in America. An important document of the North American slave experience and of the abolitionist movement, it inspired people in the States and abroad. Reprinted in 2005, it is used extensively as an academic text in many US universities teaching about the abolition of slavery.

Here are more of his titles:

Calumny refuted by facts from Liberia, (C. Gilpin, W. Harned, London, New York, 1848) with extracts from the inaugural address of the coloured President Roberts; an eloquent speech of Hilary Teage, a coloured senator and extracts from a discourse by H.H. Garnett, a fugitive slave, on the past and present condition, and destiny of the coloured race. Presented to the Boston Anti-slavery bazaar, U.S., by the author of *A tribute for the negro.*

A memoir of Robert Barclay, the author of the "Apology for the true Christian divinity;" (W. Irwin, Manchester, 1850).

Select Miscellanies (C. Gilpin, London, 1851).

Memoirs of James Logan: A distinguished scholar and Christian legislator. (C. Gilpin, London, 1851)

The garland of freedom - a collection of poems, chiefly anti-slavery (W. & F. Cash, London 1853).

A "cloud of witnesses" against slavery and oppression - Issued with half a million Leeds anti-slavery tracts (William Tweedie - W. & F. Cash, London 1853).

Journal of George Fox: Being an Historical Account. (W. & F. Cash, London 1853, reprinted 8 Dec 2008).

Five hundred thousand strokes for freedom (lay the axe to the root of the corrupt tree) a series of anti-slavery tracts, of which half a million are now first issued by the friends of the Negro. Illustrated by numerous biographical sketches, facts, anecdotes, etc. (William Tweedie - W. & F. Cash, London 1853 – reprinted 17th of August, 2009).

God's Image in Ebony: being a series of biographical sketches, facts, anecdotes etc. – Demonstrative of the mental powers and intellectual capacities of the Negro race. (Partridge and Oakey, London, 1854)

Anthony Benezet - From the original Memoir (A.W. Bennett, Lippincott, London, Philadelphia, 1859) An American educator and abolitionist.

Tales and legends of the English lakes (1891 – published after his death by Simpkin, Marshall, London and reprinted in 2009).

Kenneth Armitage (1916–2002) was a Leeds born sculptor known for his semi-abstract bronzes. In 1952 he held his first one-man show in London. In 1953, he became Great Britain's first university artist in residence, at the **University of Leeds** (to 1956). In 1958 he won best international sculpture under age 45 at the **Venice Biennale** (a huge deal, Venice Biennale is like the Brits of the art world). One of his sculptures was included in the British section (as one of a group of young British sculptors) of the 1952 Venice Biennale, the programme notes said, 'These new images belong to the iconography of despair, or of defiance ... Here are images of flight ... of excoriated flesh, frustrated sex, the geometry of fear.' You can see one of Kenneth's bronze casts, the 16 metres high, bronze and light blue *Both Arms*, at the south end of Millennium Square and on the front cover.

The Tate website biog of him talks of, 'a new, anti-monumental, expressionist approach........ Armitage's preoccupation was with the human figure, combined with an interest in vertical and horizontal structure. He created small-scale figures, full of droll humour, with broad, flattened bodies, pinheads and sprouting, stick-like limbs....... In 1955–7 he changed to working in clay, and in the 1960s he employed wax, resins and aluminium, and his pieces became darker in mood and more abstract. In the late 1960s and early 1970s he made a series of disembodied limbs and 'furniture-figures'. He also experimented with drawn, screen-printed and photographic figural images on three-dimensional surfaces (e.g. Folding Screen, 1972; U. Nottingham A.G.). Between 1975 and 1986 he moved from the figure to nature in his series of sculptures and drawings of oak trees in Richmond Park, London.' Armitage was made CBE in 1969 and was elected to the Royal Academy in 1994.

The **Armley asbestos tragedy** involved the contamination of over 1,000 houses and the surrounding area with deadly blue asbestos dust produced by the factory of J.W. Roberts Ltd. (Turner &Newall now Federal-Mogul). For between 50 and 64 years the company had been pumping the dust out through their ventilation systems into the surrounding area and for 26 years had known of the danger to public health that this represented. The dust was so prevalent that one local woman said that an hour after cleaning her window sills 'there would be another layer of dust half an inch thick.' It was the only place in Leeds where during rain it looked like it was snowing and kids had toxic 'snowball' fights. The children played in and were covered in the dust on a daily basis. At its peak the factory had 250 employees who wore protection against the asbestos but at least 300 former employees are believed to have died from asbestos-related illnesses. Taking anything up to 50 years from exposure to diagnosis, no one knows how many locals died or will still die as a result.

In 1987, after hearing the British government reject calls from Leeds City Council and Leeds West MP John Battle for a public inquiry into the resulting deaths in Armley, John stated to the House of Commons: "I cannot believe that those who owned and ran Roberts can have gone in and out without seeing the dust everywhere on the surrounding streets and pavements. If they knew that their workers within had to be protected from the asbestos dust, how could they have ignored the position of their neighbours who lived with that dust outside? It was not rendered neutral or innocuous as it left their premises. If they knew, why did they knowingly continue to ask not only their employees but local residents for a generation to pay the price with their lives for the profits of continued asbestos production? ...Should not the company be responsible for that deadly legacy? The Armley asbestos tragedy cannot remain private and hidden because it is not yet over." Even after the Council had commissioned a report into the deaths from the Department of Public Health at the University of Leeds which found asbestos contamination still present in the houses, the Minister for Housing and Planning, Sir George Young, refused any funding saying it 'would not be a justifiable use of public funds.'

All along T&N were not forthcoming in providing information on the situation. In another Commons debate (8 July 1992) John Battle said 'The difficulty lies in seeking it out - discovering it - and, especially, forcing the company to disclose all that it knew and knows.'

After years of fantastic work by John Battle, the Yorkshire Evening Post and YTV a landmark court ruling in 1996 proved Battle's assertion that the company was culpable to be correct. The judge said, "There was knowledge, sufficient to found reasonable foresight on the part of the defendants, that children were particularly vulnerable to personal injury arising out of inhalation of asbestos dust.... Reasonably practicable steps were not taken to reduce or prevent inhalation of emitted asbestos dust."

Testing and decontamination was still going on as late as November 2008, when 610 more properties were tested and found to contain residual asbestos dust, and decontaminated at a cost of £9.3 million. See **June Hancock**

Armley Cheesecake, created by Sarah Howells and winner of the Gold Award (overall winner) at the 2009 **Charlie Cake Park** cake competition. Adapted from the twentieth century classic pudding, Armley Cheesecake is too good for fruit or cream, refining the traditional delicate cheesecake into a 'proper pudding'. Lacking the pretensions of cream or fruit it's a solid pudding, a proper pudding, an honest pudding, like the area it's named after, it's a down to earth, unpretentious and substantial pudding. Obviously the exact specifications of such an exciting food stuff is a jealously guarded secret but I can exclusively reveal that the base of an **Armley Cheesecake** contains ginger nut, syrup and ginger root. The top is divine but I will give no clues as to its content and you can't make me. Have you ever eaten a cheesecake too good for fruit or cream? Then you've never had Armley Cheesecake.

Armley Gaol. Finished in 1847, this Victorian prison originally had four wings coming out from the centre (a typical style known as radial). Two further wings were added in 1994, and a new gate complex opened in September 2002. Many of the older parts of the building were tarted up in 2003, the year when a study by the Prison Reform Trust showed it had the highest level of recorded drug use among prisoners in England and Wales. 28.3% of inmates tested positive for controlled substances.

From 1847 until 1961 it was a place of execution/hanging. The last hanging there was of Hungarian born **Zsiga Pankotia** who, during a bungled burglary in Roundhay, murdered the householder. He was hanged by **Harry Bernard Allen** who was one of the United Kingdom's last official executioners, officiating between 1941 and 1964. His granddaughter is comedienne and actress **Fiona Allen**, from *Smack the Pony*. Whilst on her first visit to her first boyfriend's house and trying to get in with his father she told him she wanted to be an actress, to which he replied, 'Going on the stage are you, lass? Well keep away from the trapdoor!' (Simon Edge, *Secrets of the last hangman*, Daily Express, 21st of October, 2008.)

Between 1995 and 2004, 25 inmates committed suicide at Armley, the second highest in the country. In 1967, glamorous, American actress Jayne Mansfield was pictured outside Armley Gaol clutching a couple of Chihuahuas. A famous inmate was English dancer, suffragist and arsonist **Lilian Ida Lenton** from Leicester.

Armley Mills, now the site of **Armley Mills Leeds Industrial Museum**, dates back to at least the mid sixteenth century and in 1590 there was a fulling mill on the site called Carson's Mill. Colonel Thomas Lloyd acquired it in 1788 and transformed it into the largest woollen mill in the world. According to the council website it's 'now one of the largest textile museums in the world' including locomotives and rolling stock, collections of textile machinery, railway equipment and a small 1920s working cinema that is often used during the I Love West Leeds Festival. The current main building was put up in 1805 by **Benjamin Gott** who bought it just after the old structure had been wrecked by fire. Over one hundred years later (1907) it was taken over by clothing manufacturers Bentley and Tempest and closed in 1969 to be re-opened as a museum in 1982 by Leeds City Council. It's well worth a visit and is easily accessible from the back of the Kirkstall Leisure complex, so next time you go bowling or to the cinema give yourself an extra couple of hours and go have a gander....lovely spot for a picnic. See **Benjamin Gott.**

Robert Arthington (1823–1900) was a Leeds **Quaker** millionaire who 'combined miserliness and philanthropy in an extraordinary degree'. Inheriting a large fortune derived from brewing, he spent nearly the whole of his life as a recluse in a villa in the suburbs of Leeds, 'which was scarcely, if ever, entered by a woman and, consequently, scarcely, if ever, swept.' (The New York Times, December 30th, 1900.)

He left £550,000 to Baptist and African missionary societies, the largest legacy left to foreign missions by a single man. He wanted 'everywhere in all Africa, in South America, in Central America, in Asia, in the South Sea Island and the Indian Archipelago all tribes and populations' to be given a bible in their own language. Living the last years of his life in Teignmouth, keeping his wealth secret, looking poor and old, he asked a boatman about lodgings. The boatmen offered him a room in his house where Arthington lived with a kind family who had no idea of his wealth. (W. D. Rubinstein, *Men of property: the very wealthy in Britain since the Industrial Revolution,* Croom Ltd., London, 1981.)

ASDA's formation and growth is a complex affair that stretches back in time through its constituent parts but much of it is based around the Leeds retail market. I've been in touch with Asda HQ to check if they have a company historian or archivist and drew a surprised blank. There doesn't seem to be a definitive history so I'm having to piece together the history from material I can find, with little opportunity for double-checking, so if there are errors let me know and make sure you can substantiate it. The most recent history includes the 1999 sale of the company to Wal-Mart (in 2010, the world's largest public corporation) for £6.7 billion. In 2009 Wal-Mart sold Asda for £6.9bn to a Leeds-based investment vehicle called Corinth Services Limited, who are now the parent company of Asda Group. Corinth has no staff, other than directors, and is owned by Wal-Mart.

The seed of Asda was scattered by technology – the development of milk pasteurisation leading farmers to form co-ops to build processing units – and a bunch of 'Yorkshire' farmers (can't find more specifics) who formed Hindell's Dairies in the 1920s. They processed and retailed milk and meat to an ever growing customer base, gradually expanding and diversifying, gaining more farms, processing dairies, abattoirs bakeries and shops.

Wiki says 'Asda Stores Limited was founded as **Associated Dairies & Farm Stores Limited** in 1949 in Leeds' which is kinda true. This was the coming together of Farm Stores Ltd. and Associated Dairies into a public company. The roots of Farm Stores are in Hindell's Dairy Farmers Ltd, which was founded by Arthur Stockdale with a subsidiary, Craven Dairies Ltd, and supplied milk to Leeds. Stockdale later formed a partnership with Fred Zeigler, opening a pork products business at 118 Kirkgate, the basis of Farm Stores a company set up in 1928. The dairy business expanded, taking over other businesses in and around Leeds, such as Provincial Dairies of Leeds and Harrogate. At this stage the name changed to Associated Dairies Ltd. So it appears to me that Arthur was involved in two companies, Farm Stores Ltd. and Associated Dairies Ltd. that didn't come together until 1949. Both companies continued to 'incorporate' other smaller businesses in Leeds and the surrounding area. For example (and to give a quick nod to some of these smaller family businesses gobbled up in the march towards globalisation) in 1961 Farm Stores took over the old Leeds pork butchers **Joseph Bradbury and Sons.** I don't know when 'Porky Joe' (as Joseph was known) set up his business, but I've tracked it back to at least 1918. When Farm Foods moved in it was a decent sized business with anywhere between 20 and 27 'The County Pork Shops' all over Leeds, probably what Farm Foods were after. The company also owned an abattoir, a bakery, employed a lot of people and had a fleet of vans. As well as selling through the shops to the folk of Leeds, Porky Joe and his company supplied restaurants and wholesale and in, a Leodis photo, there is a sign on the shop advertising *'Sausage, Polony and Brawn, Fresh Daily.'*

The combined Associated Dairies & Farm Stores Ltd. became known as Associated Dairies Ltd. in 1963, although the Farm Stores were still trading throughout Leeds.

Meanwhile, over in Pontefract, after a dark night in 1963, the Asquith brothers, Peter and Fred, opened the 'Queen's Supermarket', offering 'Permanent Reductions' and a shop that stayed open until 8pm on Fridays – a no frills supermarket which was so successful that queues lined the street and the founders found themselves working 18 hour days. They opened other shops at Edlington in 1964 and South Elmsall in 1965 but didn't have the finances to expand at the pace they wished. Now some call it a merger, some say Associated Dairies bought out the supermarket entrepreneurs, Peter and Fred Asquith, but retained them as joint Managing Directors. I think, looking at the size of the operations, the latter is most likely with the deal sweetened by shares for the Asquiths but, whatever; Asda Stores Ltd. was born through this deal in 1965. People often think that the name ASDA comes from the first two letters of the words Associated Dairies but no, it doesn't, that's wrong, it comes from the first two letters of the brothers Asquith's name and the first two letters of Dairy. Although I'm sure the negotiators from Associated Dairies wouldn't have missed the irony.

Asda Stores (the shops were known as Asda Queen's, although we just called it Queen's) had offices and shops all over Leeds. They weren't anything like you'd find at Asda today. Very few shelves and careful stacking, more pallets dropped on the floor with the cardboard cut off the top of the big boxes that the stuff came in. I can remember this at the Queen's in Whitkirk where my mother had an account. She'd shop there and pay it off (or as much as she could afford) at the end of the month. She also used to take the kids (probably before I was born or very small) to see the animals in the pens there, as it was previously a farmers market. Queen's at Whitkirk closed when the Killingbeck Asda opened. It's quite ironic, after this no fuss, stack-it-high supermarket model pioneered by Queen's and Asda Queen's that Asda has agreed the purchase of Netto Foodstores which are expected to trade under the Asda name from summer 2011. Netto has been acquired by Asda primarily to 'break' the Scandinavian and Northern European markets.

Around the time that Asda Stores Ltd. was formed – probably the previous year, 1964 – an American company GEM had come to the British market with the novel idea of out-of-town superstores, lots of separate well known shops housed under one roof (think smaller version of the White Rose Centre). They initially opened one in Crossgates and one at West Bridgford on the outskirts of Nottingham (I can't unravel the dates as to which was first) some cite these as Britain's first ever out of town, enclosed, shopping centres but I'm not so sure. They could be, but there was an example just over the road in Crossgates with The Arndale Centre which will have been built around the same time and was not the first Arndale in the UK. GEM's revolutionary idea didn't go down well with British shoppers and their UK holding was bought by Asda in 1965/6.

In 1968 Associated Dairies bought the Asquith's stockholding and dropped the Queen's part of the name for the stores, although we still called it 'Queen's'. Asda continued to expand and spread across the north during the 1970s and also bought Allied Retailers and some Gateway stores. In 1989 Asda bought ninety of the large Gateway Superstores for £705 million in an attempt to move into the south which stretched the company finances almost to breaking point, although they restructured and survived.

Asda House, the company Headquarters, was completed in 1988 and was one of the first of the new large office blocks to open as part of the redevelopment of Holbeck. It was built on the site of the first Quaker Meeting House in Leeds and the burial ground from 1699 and maintains the strong Leeds connection. In June 1999, just as it seemed ASDA was about to merge with UK retailer Kingfisher, it was acquired by Wal-Mart Stores Inc. (which Asda had modelled itself on for some time) for £6.7 billion. It's a shop eat shop world.

There's plenty more I could say about Asda such as how it's become Britain's second largest supermarket, has 346 supermarkets, with a further 193 smaller stores to be added with the purchase of Netto, has been winner of *The Grocer* magazine 'Lowest Price Supermarket' Award for the past twelve years, has 150,000 employees and has featured prominently in lists of 'Best companies to work for', but there's plenty online if you're interested.

Asian Express newspaper is Britain's largest ethnic newspaper. It started on Roundhay Road in 2002 and is now based in swanky new offices on Armley Road. It's a 'five-nation-newspaper' with Yorkshire editions bi-weekly and a national edition of a quarter of a million copies, which started as a monthly but is now also bi-weekly, reaching an estimated readership of one million. There's obviously a different focus to the Yorkshire and the national edition (from 'Glasgow to London') but it kinda mimics a red top in layout and content and both 'steer away from political pressures and religious bias.' The national paper has a page 3 'desi diva' (fully clothed although there's sometimes a topless hunk), Bollywood features and gossip (south Asian film), celeb culture, a motors, business and sports section, lonely hearts, star signs etc. Its content is interesting; outside the features it has 'community' stories but also some serious, bold and hard-hitting investigations. You can flick through the copies online, just search Asian Express.

Joseph Aspdin (1778–1855) was born and raised in **Hunslet,** the bricklaying son of a bricklaying father. I have no idea what his granddad did. In 1824, after much experimenting on the cooker (I'd guess range) in his small kitchen, he was granted a patent for a process of making a cement which he called **Portland cement.** His process was to heat the clay and limestone at a very high temperature and then cool, grind and mix it with water, producing a cement he envisaged using as a render. It's regarded as the first artificial cement and was much stronger than previous limestone cements. He named it after **Portland stone**, either because it dried as hard as stone or because he thought it looked like the stone, or both. It was a good move, as the white/grey stone was particularly popular, classy and used on prestigious buildings – see the Civic Hall, built much, much later. His son William saw a wider possible use, adapted it greatly until it became much harder, quicker drying and what we could recognise as the most common type of cement in general use around the world today.

William Aspdin (1815–1864) developed a significantly different product than his father's. Although his new material was more expensive to produce than existing cements, its huge improvements to the basic material went down an absolute storm. William did not patent it but instead he pretended that it was the same as his dad's and thus covered by the original patent, even though he'd moved to London and set up a new and separate company. The crucial factor in his decision was that he did not want to reveal his cement's secrets in the patent as he knew other people/manufacturers would simply copy it. Also, in order to throw the thieving cheats off the scent and protect his secret, each time the loaded kiln was about to be sparked up he would leave his office and ritualistically scatter handfuls of brightly-coloured crystals across his mix, chanting incantations and doing weird dances. Actually, that last bit's an exaggeration (although he might have) but the scattering of coloured crystals every time the process of making the cement started is right. Anyway, this ruse largely worked and it was two years until someone finally worked out the formula and copied it. William was integral in the forming of **Blue Circle Cement** that went on to become the largest producer of cement in the world.

There's a back story, between father and son, that I can't quite pin down but there's stuff that makes me suspicious of some kind of excitement. In 1841 William left after arguments with his Dad, who posted notices that William had left and that the company were not responsible for his debts, and the same year the eldest son James went into partnership with his Dad. At this point William had already developed the new, improved cement but it is not known if he produced any at his Dad's place. The following year William returned to Yorkshire, from London, to get married but none of his family attended.

In 1853 William Aspdin did a runner to Germany, apparently to avoid his creditors. Now, obviously, I didn't know William and I don't know his version of events but I reckon he liked the 'high life.'

Some sources claim that William supplied the cement for Marc Isambard Brunel's **Thames Tunnel**, the world's first tunnel under a navigable river, but others claim that it was a clever sales ruse by William – and Brunel's diaries say that the cement used was 'Roman cement' provided by a company called Francis and Whyte. I know which I'm inclined to believe, although I wouldn't be surprised if the cement used was ripped off William's breakthrough cement anyway.

Herbert Henry Asquith (1852–1928). Born in Morley and educated at **Fulneck School** (Pudsey), a general good egg and social reformer who laid many of the foundations of the welfare state. Representing the Liberal Party, he was, until Thatcher turned up, the longest serving Prime Minister of the 20th Century but was replaced during The First World War as he appeared to go to pieces under the pressure.

It was during the pre-war peace time that Asquith achieved. Working with, amongst others, David Lloyd George and Winston Churchill, he passed legislation setting up free school meals, unemployment insurance, ending sweatshop conditions, and introducing old age pensions. They introduced more rights for children, medical inspections and, later, medical treatment, laws against neglect, sending kids out begging, imposing bans on children buying alcohol, tobacco, fireworks and introduced a juvenile criminal system in which borstals and juvenile courts took children out of the adult system.

The National Insurance Act (Part I – 1911) gave workers (making a small contribution) the right to sick pay, free medical treatment, sickness and maternity benefit. Part II of the Act, passed the same year, provided for unemployment benefit.

This was all against severe (sometimes barely legal) resistance from the Conservative Party who fought the 'People's Budget', through their majority in The House of Lords and against tradition, which systematically raised taxes on the rich, especially the landowners, to pay for the welfare programmes. The Conservatives had also previously used their majority in The House of Lords to stop the Liberals from granting Irish Home Rule in 1893. Asquith introduced the Parliament Act 1911 to limit the legislation-blocking powers of the House of Lords. Lloyd George later claimed that 'the partisan warfare that raged around these topics was so fierce that by 1913, this country was brought to the verge of civil war.'

Amongst Asquith's   descendants are writer **Princess Elizabeth Bibesco** *née* **Elizabeth Asquith** (daughter) – it is said that Elizabeth and her brother Anthony would throw things from the third floor windows of 10 Downing Street at the suffragettes shackled to the railings below; **Anthony Asquith** (son) a leading English film director, amongst his films are *The Winslow Boy* (1948) and *The Browning Version* (1951), *The Importance of Being Earnest* (1952); poet, novelist and lawyer **Herbert Asquith** (son); writer and politician **Violet Bonham Carter** (daughter); the actresses **Helena Bonham Carter** (great-granddaughter) and **Anna Chancellor** (great-great-granddaughter).

William Astbury (Bill Astbury, 1898–1961) made ground-breaking **X-ray diffraction** studies of biological molecules, according to Prof ACT North (see below) his work in Leeds, 'was seminal in developing our belief that the innermost secrets of living things may be explained from a knowledge of the structures and properties of their constituent molecules.' His pioneering work at the **University of Leeds** also took the first X-ray images of **DNA**, the breakthrough that eventually allowed the structure of DNA to be identified. His one 'failing' was that although he did much of the groundwork for many scientific breakthroughs it was largely other people who realised them. According to the **BBC**, he did coin the phrase '**Molecular Biology**'. Except he probably didn't, **Professor ACT North** (Leeds Uni's Astbury Professor of Biophysics from 1972 to 1996) reckons that 'the first recorded use of the term 'Molecular Biology' seems to be in a report by Warren Weaver, director of the Rockefeller Foundation's natural sciences programme, in 1938.' But, whatever, he did lay many of the foundations in the field of structural molecular biology and in *Nature* (190: 1124), 1961, described molecular biology as,

'not so much a technique as an approach, an approach from the viewpoint of the so-called basic sciences' with the leading idea of searching below the large-scale manifestations of classical biology for the corresponding molecular plan. It is concerned particularly with the forms of biological molecules and [...] is predominantly three-dimensional and structural— which does not mean, however, that it is merely a refinement of morphology. It must at the same time inquire into genesis and function'

In 1928, Astbury began his lectureship at the University of Leeds (where he stayed until his death in 1961) and where he studied the properties of fibrous substances such as keratin (from wool) and collagen (the protein of tendons and the matrix of bone and skin, which he classified) with funding from the textile industry on which Leeds was largely built. In the early 1930s he discovered and proposed that unstretched protein molecules formed a helix that he called α-form (**alpha helix**) and, when stretched, the β-form (**Beta sheet**). Although the α-form was incorrect in its detail, Astbury's models were correct in essence and represented a huge molecular breakthrough and correspond to modern elements of secondary structure of bipolymers, such as proteins and nucleic acids (RNA, DNA). Through the α-helix and the β-strand, Astbury's nomenclature was retained.

He isolated and classified the *k-m-e-f group* which shared these properties: **keratin** (the protein of wool, hair and silk), **myosin** (one of the principal muscle components), **epidermin** (a skin component) and **fibrinogen** (the blood clotting agent). He noted a third form of structure which he named 'cross-beta' found most relevantly in fibres produced from denatured proteins – proteins that change structure due to external stress, e.g. heat. Astbury's X-ray studies of many proteins (including myosin, epidermin, and fibrin) deduced that the molecules of these substances were coiled and folded. According to Thackray Museum website some of the research into treatments for diseases such as Alzheimer's is based on his pioneering work – I think based on his third form of protein (cross-beta)....but don't quote me on it.

In 1937 many experts had thought that the DNA chain was short and the bases repeated in a fixed order until William Astbury produced the first X-ray diffraction patterns that showed that DNA had a regular structure and he thought it might be feasible to deduce it. Astbury reported that DNA's structure repeated every 2.7 nanometres and that the bases lay flat, stacked, 0.34 nanometres apart, pointing out that the 0.34 nanometre spacing was the same as amino acids in polypeptide chains. The currently accepted value for the spacing of the bases in B-form of DNA is 0.332 nm (he was 0.008 nanometres out......close enough for me) and the structure repeats every 2.2 to 2.6 nanometres (again, 0.1 of a nanometre isn't exactly a football pitch) and the bases do indeed lie horizontally, stacked as Astbury had first deduced 'like a pile of pennies'.

Astbury's work provided stepping stones for the work of the outstanding American chemist **Linus Pauling**, one of only four people to win multiple **Nobel Prizes** and (with Marie Curie) one of only two people to win a Nobel in different fields. He almost won a third for the full 'discovery' of the structure of DNA but used Astbury's insufficient data to decide that there was a third helix (opposed to Astbury's double helix) and cited this insufficient data and a lack of quality in Astbury's images for his mistake. I'm sure he won't have bitched too much as he received the **Nobel Prize in Chemistry** the following year 'for his research into the nature of the chemical bond and its application to the elucidation of the structure of complex substances' work with its foundations firmly in Leeds. In 1931, Astbury was the first to propose that mainchain-mainchain hydrogen bonds contributed to stabilizing protein structures. His insight was followed up enthusiastically by a number of scientists, including Linus. Astbury's earlier work on keratin was the platform for Linus Pauling's discovery of the **alpha helix,** crucial in bonding, and which confirmed Astbury's1930's thesis.

I don't feel bitter that this Leeds lad built platforms from which others reached up and grabbed **Nobel Prizes** (Pauling, Watson and Crick) and didn't get one himself. I'm sure those standing on his platforms were smart cookies who worked hard and isn't that simply the nature of science, improving and building on the work of others, maybe even the nature of life/humanity? Perhaps Astbury didn't deserve one, maybe he didn't even want one – Bowie didn't want a knighthood. I'm sure it wasn't as bad as that Irish lass **Jocelyn Bell Burnell** who, as a post grad student, through hard work, determination and extreme intelligence found the first **radio pulsars** only to watch her bosses get the **Nobel Prize** and her work ignored. Tell you what, when I hear her speak about science even I understand it, and that ability to communicate is worth more than any daft prize. In my opinion she's gone on to prove who was the brains behind that particular operation. On this issue see **Melody Blackburn**. Did you see that? I digressed. Obviously Leeds Uni's Astbury Centre for Structural Molecular Biology is named after Bill Astbury, better than a Nobel Prize in my book.

James Henry Atkinson invented the classic mouse trap in 1897 and the patent for his 'Little Nipper' came through in 1899. James was an ironmonger from Leeds who dabbled in inventing and had a few goes at the mousetrap before he came up with the classic ***Tom & Jerry***, spring loaded mousetrap with a bar and trip to release it after you've temped a mouse on to it with a morsel of food. The 'Little Nipper' was manufactured by Procter Bros. in Garforth and, I'm guessing, launched their pest control products in which they are a market leader to this day.

Alfred Austin (1835–1913) was a Headingley born poet, who was appointed Poet Laureate in 1896 after the death of Tennyson.

Automatic is a word created by **David Hartley**, who spent many of his formative years in Armley, Leeds, Yorkshire, England. It seems a small jump from the nouns (automata, automaton) of the time to the adjective automatic but it was not. It was the starting point in adventure and intrigue, a leap into a controversial theory at the very heart of human nature, of how you function. Over 260 years ago, this seemed dangerous so it was misrepresented and pilloried as simplistic and then largely ignored through the defence mechanisms of the hegemony. Ironically, these 'persecutors', through religious and socio-political concerns, replaced it with theories whose conclusion could only be a theoretical dead end, and deliciously, through the lack of the theory that started with the **automatic**. At a time when we didn't even have a recognised Western, field of psychology Hartley was proposing something more akin to neuroscience, neurophysiology or cognitive science.

We don't know the man but we know his word, something that functions on a basic level, in and of itself....it just happens, like the beat of heart, automatically. **Automatic** was the first step in a theoretical journey (a complex philosophy of how we learn and function) to another word he made up, **decomplex**. See **David Hartley** and **Decomplex**.

Avro. During WW II the aircraft manufacturer created a 'shadow' factory just to the north of **Yeadon Aerodrome** making significant improvements to the airfield with two new runways, taxiways and extra hangarage leading to it becoming an important site for military aircraft testing and production. The factory was huge, employing 17,500 workers when the population of Yeadon was 10,000. It's output included over 4,500 of the **Anson** multi-role aircraft, 695 **Lancaster** heavy bombers (see The Dam Busters film and Airfix model), 25 **Lincoln** heavy bombers, 45 **York** transport aircraft and 250 **Bristol Blenheim** light bombers which also had an Airfix model. The factory produced the last ever batch of Lancaster III bombers after the end of the war. With so many Lancasters being built in Yeadon and the Lancaster being such an iconic plane it got me to thinking about the life expectancy of the crew of these bombers. I had a quick search looking for info and if you search *Lancaster LM658* there's an absolutely fascinating website that follows the fate of a Leeds built Lancaster. Alan Barrow, the webmaster, sent me the shot of a Lanc that I have used on the front cover and answered my question on life expectancy which hit home the true meaning of bravery:

'Taking Bomber Command as a whole during 1944, it was generally accepted that a figure of 13 ops (operations/trips) was an average...but this went as low as 6 ops.. (a tour of ops was at first 30 but went up to 35 later on in 1944)...which when averaged out was a life expectancy of about 6 weeks as an operational crew! Of course these were just figures, some men lasted months, some weeks, some just days, many lasted time that could be measured merely in hours, but the inescapable fact is that almost 56000 men lost their lives serving with Bomber Command out of a total force of 125,000, the highest attrition rate of any British fighting unit in WWII.'

The German bombers were after the factory, supposedly following the railway lines from Hull and looking for **Yeadon Tarn** which was certainly drained to guard against this. The main body of the factory was built in such a way that soil was stacked up against the side of it and seeded, giving it the appearance of a hill and some reports say that the roof had grass on it, others that it was painted. From photos it looks like grass, although it's inconclusive, but all reports agree that the roof had fake cows placed on it – which were either wooden or papier-mâché.

You can still see signs of the factory; in fact you can still see the factory. It's the industrial units right next to the airport (reclad in the 1980s), with some of the sloped soil still present and the old taxiway from the factory to the runway still evident. Anti-aircraft sites and bunkers are still visible (near to Carlton Hall Farm, just off the Old Otley road) and an old white square building just over the road from Yeadon Airport Industrial Estate, within a parking area, is the old ROC Group Headquarters (Royal Observer Corps) for inland aircraft tracking and reporting.

Jodie Aysha went to Lawnswood and had a number 2 in the UK charts with her R&B/Bassline house track **Heartbroken** which she wrote when she was 11. The track, a collaboration with Leeds's own **T2**, is the most requested track ever on **BBC Radio 1Xtra** and I've just checked YouTube, where it has a total of over 9 million hits – it'll have more by the time you read this obviously.

B

The legendary **Back to Basics** is Britain's longest running club night, set up in 1991 after 'the death of the acid house scene' by Dave Beer and Alistair Cooke. The pair were involved in a car accident 18 months later that killed Cooke and his partner. According to DJ Johnny Nelson 'within weeks [of the club opening].... hundreds were being turned away at the door' Lower Briggate often suffering gridlock as the revellers filled the road trying to get in. The top floor had been the Chocolate Factory which they renamed The Music Factory – and in my day Primos, where I spent many a giddy Friday night. People would travel from all over the UK to the club, Pete Tong found his handful of sets daunting and described it as 'a great honour', the club press were all over Back to Basics often invited and not let in and some of the clubs iconic flyers have even been sold in Sotheby's. They stuck to their roots, turning down the corporate stuff and multi-city thing taken up by people like Ministry Of Sound and Cream but the club has always been able to attract the world's best house music DJs. I don't think I've captured how 'streety'/honest/principled Dave and his club are, he started off working as a roadie for bands liked The Sisters and his passport reads Occupation: The Purveyor of Good Times....brilliant.

Bagel Nash (a play on the Yiddish word nosh, meaning to snack or eat) is a chain of bagel fast food restaurants founded in Leeds (1987) when Karen and Uri Mizrahi (from Jerusalem via California) opened one of the first bagel shops in the UK. After initially getting the bagels from a local baker, they started making their own, which they also supplied to local coffee shops, they were, and still are, one of the few dedicated bagel producers in Britain.

Opening their first delicatessen in Moortown, they noticed that the bagels were very popular, even though, at first, (non-Jewish) people thought they were doughnuts or didn't know how to pronounce the name. They were voted the region's best sandwich shop in the Yorkshire Post. They expanded to supply multiple, national, retailers and frozen food distributors. In 2003 the company expanded and has 12 branches: seven in Leeds, one each in Huddersfield, London, and York, and two in Manchester. I have it on good authority that the left-back of the Leeds United title winning team, **Tony Dorigo**, invested money in Bagel Nash. They produce 27 different flavours of bagels, claim to be one of the fastest growing bagel producers in Europe and export their bagels to 20 countries worldwide. In 2006 they were producing 250,000 bagels a week.

Florrie Baldwin. Born in 1896, Florrie became Europe's oldest woman at the age of 114. At the time of her death the lass from Hunslet was the second oldest person in the world after Eugenie Blanchard who lives on a Caribbean island. She experienced three different centuries. Just to hammer that home, electricity had been available to the city for over a decade but would not have been widely used around the city. Florrie would have watched the more widespread introduction of electricity to the city of Leeds, as she lived by gas light. She would then have seen the first man land on the moon and watched her grandkids play video games. She would have watched the car and van replace the horse.

Bands. While I was playing, in the mid-eighties, someone had calculated that there were 500 bands active in Leeds, now obviously I can't remember them all, neither would I want to. But here's a completely non- definitive list of Leeds bands, past and present.

Abrasive Wheels
Age Of Chance
Agony Column
Black Wire
The Bridewell Taxis
Christie
Chumbawumba
Cud
Dead Disco
The Dead Vaynes
Delta 5
Dinosaur Pile-Up
The Dope Smugglaz
Dorian Gray
Duels
Edward's Voice
Enuf Said
The Expelaires
Factory
Flowers For Agatha
Forward Russia!
Gang Of Four
Girls At Our Best
The Grumbleweeds
Guns On The Roof
Hadouken!
Hang The Dance
Hood
Icon A.D.
I Like Trains
The Isles
Judies Dream
Kaiser Chiefs

Little Chief
The Magnificent 7
The March Violets
The Mekons
The Mission
The Music
Music for Pleasure
Nightmares on Wax
Pale Saints
The Parachute Men
The Pigeon Detectives
Pink Peg Slacks
The Prowlers
Pulled Apart By Horses
The Rose of Avalanche
Red Lorry Yellow Lorry
The Rhythm Sisters
Rouge/2TV
Salvation
Saw Throat
Scritti Politti
The Sinister Cleaners
Sisters Of Mercy
Soft Cell
Spacehog
Stateless
Sunshine Underground
The Three Johns
The Ukrainians
Utah Saints
The Voltz
Wild Beasts
The Wedding Present

The Bank of England has its only subsidiary office based in Leeds at Bank House on King Street.

Bariatric surgery, or weight loss surgery, is a type of procedure performed on people who are obese, for the purpose of losing weight. Now I had a tip-off from a Leeds-based medic that this surgery was performed in Britain for the first time by Mr **Stephen Pollard** in Leeds. This shadowy character left me with the words, 'search online, it'll be well documented,' and disappeared into the mist-smudged night. Fired by caffeine and nicotine I searched well into the morning and found many sources claiming the same but none with the required authority to allow me wrap up the case. The press said that 'Leeds is [was] the only centre doing the surgery in substantial numbers', The Independent (19 September 1999) reported that he 'pioneered the gastric bypass in Britain'; an undated article in the Daily Mail said, 'Mr Stephen Pollard, consultant surgeon and director of the obesity surgery programme at St James's Hospital, Leeds, is believed to be the only surgeon in Britain to carry out gastric bypasses.' This would also mean he was the first, but the journalist took the lazy route with the phrase 'believed to be' and contaminated the crime scene.

What I know for sure is that in 1993 Pollard and his surgical team went to Richmond, Virginia to learn the surgical technique of the gastric bypass procedure and commenced a Leeds clinical programme in 1994. I can prove that as well as running the most active obesity surgery programme in the UK, he is also **Director of Liver and Intestinal Transplantation** in Leeds, and runs one of the largest and most successful intestinal transplant units in Europe. I know and can provide the evidence showing that he was one of the founder members of the British Obesity Surgery Society (BOSS).

I believe that Steve Pollard was the first UK surgeon to perform the RNY gastric bypass technique but can I make it stick, will it stand up in court....who knows? He probably carried out the procedure in broad daylight (under intensive lights) but will the witnesses have the guts to come forward or will this case end up in the file cabinet marked 'inconclusive'? This is life and death, we never knew when it started but we'll sure as hell witness the ending. Talking of life and death, his mortality rate for this surgery is 0.3% compared to the average 1%.

Robert Barnard is a writer and lecturer who lives in Leeds and was the winner of the 2003 CWA Cartier Diamond Dagger Award for a lifetime of achievement – a big deal. He's written 46 books, mainly crime.

Barnbow was the nation's first national shell filling factory (*Old Barnbow*) situated between Garforth and Cross Gates. At the outbreak of the World War I there was a dire need of munitions and under the guidance of the Leeds Munitions Committee Armley's Leeds Forge Company was, by 1915, filling 10,000 shells per week with following works at Hunslet and Newlay (Horsforth). The government had, in 1914, set up a committee of six Leeds citizens to solve the munitions supply problem, with **Joseph Watson (Soapy Joe's)** as Chairman. Soon the construction of Barnbow was underway. Building the factory on the 313 acre site (later expanded to 400 acres) was a massive logistical feat. For example, platforms of over 800 feet were added to the nearby railway station to transport workers on 38 trains a day and railway tracks were laid directly into the factory to transport the materials and munitions. The newly installed water main delivered 200,000 gallons of water per day and a 300,000 gallon storage reservoir was built.

In December 1915 shell filling operations commenced and between that time and 1918 Barnbow was Britain's top shell factory, producing a total of 566,000 tons of ammunition for the war effort, including the completion of 36,150,000 breech (rear) loading cartridges of all sizes – just pause a sec, that's over 36 million – 24,750,000 shells were filled and 19,250,000 shells were completed with fuses and packed. Due to the deployment of men abroad 93% of the Barnbow workforce was women and girls known as the 'The Barnbow Lasses'. The factory even adapted farm buildings to house 120 cows, which produced 300 gallons of milk a day. The women were nicknamed 'The Barnbow Canaries', due to their yellow skin. They worked constantly with cordite and contact with this propellant caused the skin to turn to yellow. The antidote was to drink plenty of milk, hence the cows.

The factory was also the site of what was apparently Leeds' largest number of fatalities in one incident when an explosion killed 35 of the women and girls on Tuesday 5 December 1916. There's a memorial just before the roundabout with the 'crossed gates' with a plaque to each girl who died and a further five workers who died in separate explosions. One of the things that struck me about this story was that as soon as the dangerous section was re-opened they were inundated with women and girls volunteering to work in it.

To check out some of the less well documented, more recent info I searched for months to find a knowledgeable ex-employee to quiz and it wasn't simply that one of my mates (Ali) said, 'Ooh, my uncle worked at Barnbow for years, he was quite high-up.' That simply didn't happen, but after the months of trawling records; I came up with a name, John Thirlwell, who, spookily, is the uncle of my mate Ali. John worked at Barnbow for around 30 years, starting in 1969 as a metallurgist in the lab and working his way up to Unit Leader. As well as his memory John had an unpublished pamphlet *From Munitions to Main Battle Tanks* by Lieutenant T. J. Roy of REME Corps (Royal Electrical and Mechanical Engineers). Anyway the 'Old Barnbow' factory closed down after World War I and a new factory – based on the Woolwich Arsenal in London – was built in Cross Gates/Manston at the beginning of the Second World War. Initially the factory (ROF Leeds/Barnbow) produced gun barrels and breach blocks – 6, 17, 25 pounders and 3.7 inch howitzers – for the army and navy but in 1944 started to adapt tank hulls to take 17 pounder barrels.

In 1944 it was decided that the factory would produce the Centurion tank and conversion started in 1945 with production of the new tank following 18 months after the initial decision. After over 15 years of service the tank was a radically developed and redesigned (with early work at Leyland) and in the early 1960s the first Chieftain prototypes were produced at Barnbow. Early in the 1980s the Chieftain was reworked at Barnbow producing the Challenger 1 tank – Barnbow initially producing 240 for the MOD – which was Britain's main battle tank from 1983 to the mid 1990s until it was superseded by the Challenger II. Vickers started to develop the new Challenger the same year they acquired Barnbow – 1986.

Other things that Barnbow built were the Fox (and Vixen) armoured car (reconnaissance vehicle) introduced into service in May 1973 and withdrawn in 1993/4; medium girder aluminium bridges that could be assembled by troops and the cab of a (European collaboration) multi-launch rocket system. The site was closed in 1999. Lastly I should mention that, soon after leaving school, I used to clean the toilets at Barnbow and under the strict guidance of my line manager spent happy hours playing hide and seek in and around the tanks. My last lastly is that the factory was never hit during the World War II Nazi bombing because the children of St Teresa's Primary School prayed for it every day. I know this because an old nun from the school told me on numerous occasions that it proved the power of prayer.

John Barran (1821–1905) was a pioneer in the manufacture of ready-to-wear clothing, who, after witnessing a band saw used to cut wood veneers in 1858, introduced its use for cutting cloth, a major innovation. He founded the firm of **John Barran and Sons**, clothing manufacturers.

In 1842 he moved to Leeds and soon opened his own tailoring shop at 30 Bridge End South. By 1851 he'd moved to Briggate and in 1856 he had a factory with 20-30 sewing machines. By the 1870s he had 2,000 machines, and in 1904 employed 3,000 people and was known for employing Jewish refugees which was why Michael Mark, of **& Spencer** fame, moved to Leeds. In 1895 he was created a Baronet of Chapel Allerton Hall and St Mary Abbots, in Kensington, London.

Julian Barratt (born 1968) is a comedian, musician, music producer and actor who's best known for playing the character of Howard Moon in the cult comedy *The Mighty Boosh* which he also co-writes with Noel Fielding. They took the name for the show from Fielding's brother Michael, who, as a child, had really big hair which a friend called 'the mighty bush'. Julian also does the music, which is extremely eclectic, for the show and used to play with **Little Chief**, an old Leeds band who I really liked (very interesting sort of ska/reggae with a lot to it) and played on the same bill as loads of times. Although he'll obviously remember me, I don't remember him. He's recently directed his first feature film, a dark comedy called *Curtains* about a Punch and Judy man. Mr Barratt's done plenty of other TV in character but he avoids doing personal appearances on comedy quiz-type shows saying he'd 'rather be at home with a book'. Julian is, apparently, quiet, shy and puts himself down for comic effect – that'll be more of that Leedsness I keep banging on about. He lives with comedian **Julia Davis** and they have twins together.

Stan Barstow grew up in **Ossett** and was born just up the road from there. Now Ossett isn't strictly Leeds but it's only four miles from the outskirts and there's more....he's best known for his 1960 novel *A Kind of Loving* which he adapted with Leeds writers **Keith Waterhouse** and **Willis Hall** for the iconic film of the same name. An early 'kitchen sink drama' and part of the movement that changed the face of film making/drama by giving a more realistic portrayal of the working class.

Stan's obviously done load of other stuff but – although he's not strictly from Leeds – I thought I could cheat a bit and shoe-horn an entry on him in on (try saying the last eight words really fast, five times) the back of the two Leeds writers working with him on the film script. I can include him anyway cos in his autobiography (*In My Own Good Time*) he says, 'The first money I earned by writing was for readings of my short stories on air from the BBC Studio in Woodhouse Lane, Leeds in the middle 1950s. Some years later I was led into radio drama at that same studio by the legendary **Alfred Bradley** who directed almost everything I wrote for the medium over nearly thirty years.' Stan has written 12 radio plays (one of five episodes), 18 books and has had lots of his stuff adapted for TV. Search his name, there's a website and everything. See **A Kind of Loving** and **Alfred Bradley**.

Barwick-in-Elmet is one of the oldest known inhabited places in Leeds dating back over 2000 years to between 200 and 600 BC. With Sherburn-in-Elmet it is one of only two places in the area to be explicitly associated with the ancient Celtic kingdom of Elmet. It appears as if Scholes became sometimes known as Scholes-in-Elmet at a later date. The village attracts many visitors for the raising of its maypole which at 86ft is one of the tallest maypoles in Britain and is raised every three years (2011). See **Elmet** and *The Archers.*

Mary Bateman the 'Yorkshire Witch' (1768–1809) was born in **Asenby** near **Harrogate** but it was during the 20 years she spent in Leeds that she gained her reputation as a witch. To quote *The Newgate Calendar* (a fascinating 18th/19th Century, monthly bulletin of executions), 'Mrs Bateman resided at Leeds, and was well known at that place, as well as in the surrounding districts, as a 'witch', in which capacity she had been frequently employed to work cures of 'evil wishes', and all the other customary imaginary illnesses, to which the credulous lower orders at that time supposed themselves liable. Her name had become much celebrated in the neighbourhood for her successes in the arts of divining and witchcraft.'

The contemporary accounts are damning (aged five she 'exhibited....sly knavery'). She was certainly a bit of a scallywag and became a murderer (probably a multiple murderer), but it's difficult, so far removed, to understand how hard it must have been for a woman – often alone – to survive in the late 18th Century/early 19th Century. It's also hard to imagine the brutality and 'dog eat dog' nature of these poor parts (The Bank) of the fledgling city of Leeds. (For a description of the state of the housing conditions in The Bank 40 years later see **Friedrich Engels**.)

From the age of twelve she worked as a servant in Thirsk for seven years until some 'peccadilloes' led her to flee to York. After less than a year her mistress detected some pilfering (or so said the gossip) and she ran off to Leeds where she remained until her trial and execution in York. For her first three years in Leeds she worked in a mantua (women's gown/robe) shop and then met John Bateman. Three weeks later, in 1792, she married him. Within two months of the marriage she was found guilty of a series of frauds and the couple had to keep moving to avoid arrest, which did John's head in, and he eventually left her to join the supplementary militia leaving her to fend for herself.

The Newgate Calendar says, 'unable to follow any reputable trade, she in the year 1799 took up her residence in Marsh Lane, near Timble Bridge, Leeds, and proceeded to deal in fortune-telling and the sale of charms.......she had acquired a manner and a mode of speech peculiarly adapted to her new profession.' Her act was very successful and many people fell victim to her 'fraud and deceit', her 'impudent and heartless schemes' and she became a celebrated witch. Her divine hen, which laid eggs (after payment of a penny) marked with the words 'ChrisT is coming' was reported in the *Leeds Mercury.* The *Leeds Intelligencer* later reported on the cruelty involved in pushing an egg back into a hen.

Here starts her downfall. Mrs Perigo of Bramley was suffering from a 'flacking' or fluttering in her chest. Her doctor could do nothing and told her she had been cursed, needed sorcery to gain a cure and Mrs Perigo's niece knew just the woman. Mrs Perigo and her husband went to Mary Bateman for help. Mary contacted Miss Blythe of Scarborough, who was better qualified to deal with this particular 'diabolical charm' and the treatment involved sending objects or money to obtain the cure. Miss Blythe wrote letters giving instructions and each letter contained directions to burn the letter in specific, ritualistic manners as all involved were in danger of death. Early on in the treatment Miss Blythe instructed Mary Bateman to take the four guinea notes she had sent her to the Perigo's, stitch them into a silken bag and then sew them onto the four corners of the bed, where they should remain for 18 months.

The treatment continued and each time a silken purse was sent with notes or coins in, to be sown onto the bed, the Perigos would refund the money. Other treatments were ordered by Miss Blythe and, amongst many other things, the Perigos gave Mary 'half-a-dozen of your china, three silver spoons, half-a-pound of tea, two pounds of loaf sugar, and a tea canister to put the tea in', 'a camp bedstead, bed and bedding, a blanket, a pair of sheets, and a long bolster must come from your house', 'a small cheese about six or eight pound weight'. To save the lives of all, Miss Blythe supplied powder for Mary Bateman to put in puddings and honey that the Perigos should take in a prescribed manner. After almost two years of treatment Mrs Perigo died and, although it was the surgeon's clear opinion that she had been poisoned, no action was taken. Mr Perigo stayed in communication with Mary, getting new demands from Scarborough where Miss Blythe asserted that Mrs Perigo had died due to her not following instructions 'and for this reason, she will rise from the grave, she will stroke your face with her right hand, and you will lose the use of one side, but I will pray for you. I would not have you to go to no doctor, for it will not do.'

Five months after the death of his wife Mr Perigo decided that the treatments were not working – he'd not been taking full amounts due to the unpleasant taste and feeling ill. He went to get the money from the corners of the bed and found 'the notes and gold had turned to rotten cabbage-leaves and bad farthings'. He contacted the authorities and Mary was tried, convicted of murder and hanged. Miss Blythe of Scarborough did not exist, Mary had written the letters herself. After her execution, her body was put on public display with strips of her skin sold as magic charms to ward off evil spirits.

Mary's body was 'sent to the General Infirmary at Leeds to be anatomized. Immense crowds of persons assembled to meet the hearse in which it was carried, and so great was the desire of the people to see her remains, that 30L were collected for the infirmary, by the payment of 3d. for each person admitted to the apartment in which they were exposed.' Meaning that 2,400 people paid their thrupenny bit to see the body. After her death, three different booklets were produced, one selling 10,000 copies when the population of Leeds and surrounding areas was 60,000 – if I sell this to 1 in 6 of the population of Leeds I've just retired. Mary Bateman's skeleton is on display to the public at **Thackray Museum** in Leeds. **David Thornton**'s *Great Leeds Stories* has an excellent chapter on her.

The **Battle of Seacroft Moor**, on 30 March 1643, was a decisive loss for the Parliamentary forces during the First Civil War. It took place near Seacroft, north east of Leeds and the battle reportedly turned the Cock Beck red with the casualties' blood for several days.

The **Battle of the Winwaed** (*Maes Gai*) was fought on November 15, either 654 or 655, between King Penda of Mercia and Oswiu of Bernicia, ending in the Mercian's defeat and Penda's death. No one is certain where it took place just that it was on the banks of a river named the Winwaed which is thought most likely to be the **Cock Beck** (east Leeds), in the ancient kingdom of **Elmet**, at a time of flood.

There'd been rucks between these kingdoms for a while, Mercia (the Midlands-ish) against Bernicia (Northumbria and a bit of Scotland) with Mercia having the upper hand. King Penda got his mates from East Anglia and Wales to come and help him but the Welsh abandoned him and the East Anglians stood back and watched the battle. It looked like the battle had been averted and Penda was on his way home at the time of the attack from Oswiu of Bernicia and although he had a much bigger force many of his men deserted or drowned in the beck and Penda was defeated and decapitated. His death is thought to have led to the naming of **Penda's Field** but also effectively marked the end of Anglo-Saxon Paganism and its last king, from now on Christianity ruled. **The last Anglo-Saxon Pagan king probably died in east Leeds.** There's something symbolic about the last pagan king losing his head in east Leeds but I'm going to ignore it.

I'd clocked **Zygmunt Bauman** quite early in writing this encyclopaedia but the depth and quantity of material on him made my head spin and I was lured away by more straight forward topics, with every intention of returning. Then, with weeks to the deadline, I received a text from academic John Poulter who teaches Cultural Analysis at Leeds Trinity University College asking if I'd included Zygmunt Bauman. My heart sank. I fired up the computer, did a quick search, became completely overwhelmed, turned off the computer and sat in the garden crying to the moon at three in the morning. The following day, having regained my composure, I left a message on his mobile, which, punctuated by heavy sobs, said, 'I can't handle any more complex topics, my brain's a mush of scrambled egg with too generous a squirt of tomato sauce. I know he's a top lad but my kids have disowned me, my wife's about to leave me and even my 80-year-old mother walks past me in the street without acknowledgement. PLEASE, PLEASE, will you do him? I'll give you my mint, 1969 copy of Ragazzo Solo, Ragazza Sola. – I lied, I'd lost it along with all my possessions in 1991 – 'Pleeeeeeeease....Right that's it,' I breathed, 'if Ziggy isn't in, it's your fault, you'll have to see if you can live with yourself if Leeds' greatest sociologist isn't in mi'book. IT'S ALL YOUR FAULT.' Pleased that I'd not let the pressure show and maintained my professionalism I took the return call in which John simply said, 'Yeh sure Mick, how much do you want?' That's the thing with academics they forever over complicate things, anyway here's John's entry:

Zygmunt Bauman is arguably the world's most influential living sociologist. Born in Poznan in Poland in 1925, his family fled to Russia to escape the invading German army at the start of WWII. Zygmunt subsequently served in the exile Polish Army during the war before turning to an academic career. In 1968, having lost his position at Warsaw University because of an anti-Semitic purge, he moved to work in Tel Aviv but left three years later to become Professor of Sociology at the University of Leeds. He has lived and worked in the city ever since. 'Retirement' in 1990 merely gave him more time to work! Since then he has written more than 25 books to add to his already considerable output. In common with all sociologists he sees his task as gaining a better understanding of society in order to be able to improve it. He is most well known for his argument that in the latter half of the 20th Century the certainties of Modernity, or 'solid modernity' as he calls it, gave way. As he pointed out in his work on the Holocaust, some of the results of the march of science, industrial and social organisation and 'reason' were anything but 'progress'. He argued that we now experience 'Liquid Modernity'. This liquidity demands constant flexibility and adaptability from individuals in the face of an increasingly complex and globalising world in which the pace of change can be bewildering, uncertainty the norm, social bonds increasingly temporary and in which consumerism and capitalism dominate the stage. His analyses attempt to answer the question 'How should we live?' In the course of this discussion he addresses a host of aspects of our lives including individual responsibility, justice, identity and even, and yet, of course, love. As a speaker he remains, even in his mid-80s, engaging, challenging and inspirational. In 2010 **The Bauman Institute** was opened at the University of Leeds.

The Bear Pit on Cardigan Road (Burley/Headingley) is all that remains of the Leeds Zoological and Botanical Gardens, a not very successful Victorian venture. It was built in 1840, but the planned plants, birds and wild animals didn't fire the popular Leeds imagination so more sensational attractions were introduced such as a woman walking a tightrope over the lake as exotic fireworks exploded around her.

It closed to become a pleasure garden retaining the bears which were displayed in a circular pit and the public viewed them from the tops of the turrets, one of which has a spiral staircase (the other probably had one as well.) The pleasure garden also held the annual Leeds Gala featuring laughing gas, a centrifugal railway whilst retaining the death defying tightrope and fireworks combo. The Leeds Civic Trust restored it in 1966.

Be-Bop Deluxe/Bill Nelson's Red Noise – Although Bill and **Be-Bop Deluxe** were from Wakefield and Bill settled in Selby (at one point next door to my girlfriend's dad) they played around Leeds a lot during their early career. I know for sure that they used to play at The Staging Post in Whinmoor and there was also talk of them playing at The Fairway in Gipton. Anyway, if you haven't heard any of the stuff, do do.

Edmund Beckett, Q.C. (1st Baron Grimethorpe 1816–1905) was an architect, lawyer and amateur horologist who designed the mechanism for the clock at Westminster responsible for the chimes of Big Ben. He also designed the clocks of Leeds Town Hall, Leeds Parish Church and St Chad's Church in Headingley. I can't quite nail where he was born (Wiki says Nottinghamshire) or lived but his granddad had been twice mayor of Leeds, his uncles and cousins were educated, and he worked (Beckett & Co Bankers of Leeds) and was buried in Leeds. It looks like his dad was Leeds-based and probably went to Leeds Grammar School and his son was born in Roundhay.

Beckett Street Cemetery (opposite **Jimmy's**) opened in 1845. The population of Leeds had almost trebled in the first four decades of the century, death rates were rising (see **Engels**) and space was tight for the burial of dead bodies. For example the graveyard of Leeds Parish Church (St Peter's) was being stacked well above ground level, and during heavy rain it would resemble a horror movie. Bodies were often disturbed to squeeze more in and the water supply was contaminated by the rotting bodies.

Originally known as **The Leeds Township Cemetery**, Beckett Street Cemetery was founded by the City of Leeds to provide a burial ground for all religions and classes and was one of the earliest publicly funded cemeteries in England. The 16 acre cemetery was split into two sections to accommodate Dissenters and Church of England/Anglican, as neither wanted to be buried with the other. There were separate entrances, chapels and lodges, the chapels being demolished by the council in the 1960s.

Leodis (search term below) reckons that in 1842 Leeds local authority had got the Leeds Improvement Act through Parliament and, at the same time, introduced the **Leeds Burial Bill** which allowed the council to collect rates to support the payment of burials for the first time in the country. Quoting the ***Leeds Mercury***, '...a precedent for providing Burial Grounds in all parts of the Kingdom for persons of all religious persuasions on equitable terms, protecting all just rights, without inflicting injury on any denomination.' (July 2 1842) The later 1850s Act of Parliament allowed local authorities to establish cemeteries at public expense.

There were different 'standards' of burial ranging from the paupers/common grave (big hole with lots of unrelated people in, no markers) up to the private grave and it was 'up to'. The richer you were the further up the hill you were buried. There was the innovation at Beckett Street, that seems to be a purely Leeds thing, of the **Guinea Grave** (Inscription Grave). Over the following 150 years approximately 180,000 people were interred at the cemetery in some 28,000 graves until the cemetery closed for business in 1992. Nine months old Thomas Hirst was the first to be buried there; his mother followed him (becoming the eightieth) less than a year later. Search 'the friends of Beckett Street Cemetery' for more detail or '*The One Certainty of Life*' where **Leodis** has an excellent section on the site as well as young Thomas's burial.

Alan Bennett. You don't get any more down to earth than Alan Bennett. He's a bit of a hero of mine.....bet he's a hero of most Leeds writers, it's not like we copy him, no, that wouldn't do. Top, top writer, proper writer, First Division (in old money) although I can hear him saying, 'You can't classify writers like old football teams they all have their different strength, cept for you Mick, you're rubbish.' I think he pretty much created his own genre of writing, look him up online, maybe YouTube and search *Talking Heads*, there's loads out there and he's fantastic. See 'essay' on **Leeds Social Realists/writers.**

Richard Bentley (1662–1742) was the founder of historical philology....don't ask me, all I know is it isn't philosophy or physiology......maybe you need to buy a proper book.

John Berkenhout (1726–1791) Appears to have produced the first lexicon/dictionary of plants in the English language, perhaps (I'm guessing) influenced by Michel Adanson, a French contemporary writing in French – Berkenhout was multi-lingual. He started work on ***Clavis Anglica linguae botanicae: or, A botanical lexicon*** in 1760 after returning from the war between Britain and France.

Leeds born, he was a physician, naturalist and miscellaneous writer who was educated at Leeds Grammar School after his Dutch parents had settled in the area. He served in the Prussian (becoming a Captain) and English armies and as a British agent in the colonies during the American Revolution. He was sent by The British Government to 'negotiate' with the Americans but was told not to travel further than New York. He sneaked to Philadelphia where the Congress was assembled and seems to have stayed there for a while before being arrested under suspicion that he was up to no good, sent by Lord North, the British Prime Minister. I don't know how long he was in prison for, or how he got out, but he later returned to Britain from New York.

He published several works on natural history and it was Berkenhout who named the brown rat as the Norway Rat ("Rattus norvegicus") thinking the rat had come over from Norway, stowed away on ships in 1728. Although it's still known as this today the common rat did not travel from Norway. They weren't even present in Norway at the time. Now, fair enough, he made this mistake but at the time nobody knew where the brown/sewer/common rat had originated from and it seems to me that he did some very important work towards our understanding of the natural world. His *Clavis Anglica Linguae Botanicae* was 'a book of singular utility to all students of botany, and at that time the only botanical lexicon in our language.' (*The Biographia Leodiensis*, 1865.) So do we have the first lexicon/dictionary of plants in the English language?

Some of his books:

Three original poems: being the posthumous works of Pendavid Bitterzwigg, Esq. Berkenhout, T. Carnan, 1750.

Along with Carl Gustaf Tessin, Gustaf III (King of Sweden), he contributed to, *Letters from an old man to a young prince, with the answers.* R. Griffiths, 1756.

Clavis Anglica linguae botanicae: or, A botanical lexicon; Berkenhout, T. Becket & P. A. de Hondt, London, 1764.

Pharmacopoeia Medici, Berkenhout, T. Becket et P. A. de Hondt, London, 1766 – 2nd edition expanded and published 1768.

Outlines of the natural history of Great Britain and Ireland: containing a systematic arrangement and concise description of all the animals, vegetables, and fossils which have hitherto been discovered in these kingdoms. Vol. 1. Comprehending the Animal Kingdom. Berkenhout, P. Elmsly (successor to Mr. Vaillant), London, 1769.

Biographia literaria: or a biographical history of literature: Berkenhout, J. Dodsley, London, 1777. – *The Biographia Leodiensis* (1865) says of this book 'and the author occasionally introduces sentiments hostile to religious establishments and doctrines, which could not be very acceptable to English readers.

Lucubrations on ways and means. Berkenhout, H. Payne, London, 1780. *Symptomatology*, Berkenhout, R. Baldwin, London, 1784.

Synopsis of the natural history of Great-Britain and Ireland. Berkenhout, T. Cadell, London, 1789. – 2nd edition of his 1769 work

First lines of the theory and practice of philosophical chemistry. Berkenhout, 1788, Cadell, London.

He also updated, to 1779, the book Lives of the *British admirals: containing an accurate naval history from the earliest period.* By John Campbell

Leeds born **George Bilson** worked in Hollywood and produced 76 films and five episodes of the 1950s TV series *Captain Midnight*. He also wrote the screenplay of 14 films and worked as the head of the trailer department at **RKO Pictures** and married screenwriter **Hattie Bilson.** His son, **Malcolm Bilson,** is a concert pianist and professor of piano at Cornell University. George is less well remembered than his other son **Bruce Bilson** who directed some episodes of classic American 1960s/70s/80s TV serials, including: *M*A*S*H - The Brady Bunch - The Six Million Dollar Man - Alias Smith and Jones - The Odd Couple - Bonanza - Hogan's Heroes - Hawaii Five-O - Bewitched - Mary Tyler Moore - Bonanza - Get Smart - The Partridge Family - Wonder Woman - Private Benjamin - Dynasty - Dallas - Sledge Hammer!* (I loved a few of these, particularly *Sledge Hammer!*, but maybe because it's more recent. It was a bit like *Police Squad/Naked Gun.*) **George** is the great grandfather of actress **Rachel Bilson** and producer, writer and director **Danny Bilson** who also worked on video games *The Sims* and *Medal of Honor: Frontline*

Bi-metallic spring/strips were invented almost 300 years ago by **John Harrison** and are still used today in thermostats, thermometers, time-delay relays and as miniature circuit breakers in all sorts of electrical appliances. No doubt the principle of using two different metals to convert a temperature change into mechanical displacement through the different temperatures and rates at which the metals expand is used in many other ways.....ask a physicist or engineer, you must know one. See **John Harrison**.

The Bingley Arms in **Bardsey** is the oldest pub in Britain, going back to at least 953 AD and evidence suggesting it could date to 905 AD. This fact is obviously argued over but **The Bingley Arms** has the oldest proven date (and a listed landlord) and until someone proves an earlier date for somewhere else it's the oldest pub in Britain, simple.

Bite Yer Legs, a production company with a spin-off sister company called **Sniffer**. London based but with names like that you do start to wonder, don't you? Well I didn't just wonder, I checked and received a couple of very helpful emails from one of the Company Directors, **Isobel Williams**, and I cut and paste; 'Of course there is a connection - we are Leeds fans and proud!' Apparently her hubby was at the centenary cup final when '**Sniffer Clarke**' scored the winner. They've made films or TV series for the BBC, ITV, Discovery, Sky and The History Channel and are 'a key supplier to BBC Network Radio' where I've repeatedly heard the name and wondered. By the way Isobel if you ever expand, come to Leeds and I'll write you a drama, also, should I send you a copy of *Nailed – Digital Stalking*? The fast moving, gritty drama based in real life, that loads of TV types right like but never do anything with.

Melody Blackburn is a particularly sharp PhD Student in the **Leeds Quantum Information Group** (School of Physics and Astronomy, University of Leeds) who designed a portable **magnetometer** solving a problem that had troubled medics for years. See **Heart monitor** and **Magnetometer.**

Robert Blackburn OBE, FRAeS (1885– 1955) was an aviation pioneer and the founder of **Blackburn Aeroplane & Motor Company** which concentrated mainly on naval and maritime aircraft during the first part of the 20th century. Born in Kirkstall, he attended Leeds Modern School and graduated in engineering at the University of Leeds, built his first monoplane in April and May 1909 using materials such as wood, brass, steel, fabric and string and flew it at Filey. He gave regular demonstration flights for crowds at **Roundhay Park**, and went on to found a company which on his death became part of **Hawker Siddeley** before being

Blackburn CA 15 C monoplane of 1932

incorporated into **British Aerospace**. Blackburn became a major aircraft supplier to the British government during the First World War, the principal aircraft being the Blackburn Kangaroo, a twin-engine bi-plane adopted by the Royal Naval Air Service (RNAS) for use in anti-submarine operations based in the North Sea.

Flight and AIRCRAFT ENGINEER Obituary 23rd of September, 1955 "All of us," continued Mr. Turner, "are very proud that the oldest British aircraft still flying is Robert Blackburn's, much of it built with his own hands. It was he who built the first British all-metal aircraft and it was his aircraft which gave the first demonstration of wireless telegraphy. I do not think there is any aspect of aviation which at one time or another did not benefit from Robert Blackburn's vision, enterprise, ability and unflagging determination. He built every conceivable type of aircraft, as well as piston engines, gas turbines and propellers. Robert Blackburn was one of the first in the world to run a flying school and to see the possibilities of commercial aviation. It is getting on for 40 years since he formed a company to carry freight and passengers across the North Sea. He was undoubtedly one of the greatest men in the history of aviation."

Robert Blackburn built the first working British planes, like his 1909 **Monoplane No 1** at **Thomas Green & Son Ltd.** where his father was manager. It flew for about a minute in 1910 before it crashed, resulting in, 'no personal injuries other than bruises and cuts but with the total wreckage of months of laborious work' – Blackburn's words. His **Second Monoplane** hit the sand at Filey during its maiden flight (whilst attempting to turn) but was fixed and used to teach people to fly. Wiki lists it as the **Blackburn Type D** (his sixth built) as the first British plane, perhaps because it worked well enough to carry the *Yorkshire Post* from Leeds to York for three days running.

Blackburn took over a failed flying school in Filey, successfully running **Blackburn Flying School** before the First World War, which is way older than the only reference to 'first' flying schools I can find on Wiki, which – a little digging through German sites showed – actually began in 1924. **Blackburn Aircraft** built over 60 different planes and that's not including all the variants of certain models. On the 22nd July 1914, Blackburn inaugurated **the first scheduled service in Britain** with flights every ½ hour between Roundhay Park and Bradford.

There's a blue plaque on the wall at Tesco's, Roundhay Road, which says: 'THE OLYMPIA WORKS **Robert Blackburn** - aviation pioneer – built aircraft here including over a 100 BE2C army and navy biplanes and the famous Kangaroo, Swift and Sopwith Baby planes. He test flew the BE2C's on Soldiers' Field and from there, in 1919, operated passenger flights to London and Amsterdam.'

Jessica Blackburn was the woman behind the man, most often to be found out front. She was crucial to the development of the company. Unlike her quiet and retiring husband, Jessica was sassy, outgoing and confident. The wedding to Robert released her large inheritance which, with Robert's father, she used to invest in getting **Blackburn Aeroplane & Motor Company** up and running, a task she took on with vigour. During the wedding reception her husband received a telegram from **Winston Churchill** with their first government contract; the honeymoon was postponed to attend a meeting at the Admiralty the following day, although they spent the night together on the journey down to London.

She was one of the first women to fly in a British monoplane when in 1915 she flew as co-pilot from Roundhay Park. She later flew competitively in the King's Cup air races of 1922 and 1928 but it was in the company's marketing and sales that she excelled. She entertained many of the 'great and good' of aviation at **Gledhow Lodge** and later **Bowcliffe Hall** in **Bramham**, such as aircraft pioneers, media proprietors, local financiers, RAF and Fleet Air Arm officials and national politicians like Churchill. One interesting visitor and friend was **Amy Johnson** and don't tell me that a sassy, ground breaking woman aviator, from the previous generation, who flew her first plane when Amy was only 11 or 12 – competing against men – wasn't an inspiration to Amy. Amy went on to be the first woman to fly solo from Britain to Australia. With her co-pilot she became the first pilot to fly from London to Moscow in one day and set a record time for flying from England to Japan etc. etc. etc.

Anyway, **Jessica** and **Robert Blackburn's** lives took a turn for the worse when, after Jessica had spent almost two years nursing a seriously ill son in Switzerland, their older son was killed in a freak accident and within the year the couple had divorced, ending 23 years of marriage. Jessica married a couple of more times but each was brief and ended in divorce.

Blackburn Type D was an airplane built in Leeds by **Robert Blackburn** for Cyril Foggin in 1912 and is the oldest flying British **aeroplane**. Foggin then sold the aircraft on to Montague Glew who crashed it in 1914, leaving the wreck where it lay. In 1938 the plane was discovered and after the War it was restored by engineers mainly from its original parts. It is now part of the **Shuttleworth Collection** in Bedfordshire where it still flies on quiet days. The Type D is not to be confused with **Blackburn's** previous plane, the **Mercury II**, currently on display at the **Yorkshire Air Museum** which is a full-scale non-flying replica made for the **YTV** series *Flambards*.

John Blenkinsop (1783–1831) was born in **Rothwell** and managed the **Middleton Colliery**. He was also a mining engineer and inventor who, due to the need of the colliery, became involved in the design and building of the first practical railway locomotive in the world. A previous attempt by **Richard Trevithick** (a brilliant, visionary inventor who died alone, a pauper) had been abandoned due to the weight of the locomotives being too much for the track. Blenkinsop worked with **Matthew Murray** and made his engines lighter. There was a concern that these lighter locomotives would struggle with the incline to Leeds so Blenkinsop invented and patented a rack and pinion system that is still used today on many mountain railways. The teeth on the wheels linked to a rack by the track and, rather than the estimated ability to carry four times the weight of the locomotives, Blenkinsop's five ton engines regularly hauled 90 tons. **Blenkinsop** and **Murray** drastically changed **Trevithick's** design, (introducing two-cylinders, geared wheel, losing the flywheel) and built four locomotives for the line *Prince Regent*, *Salamanca*, *Lord Willington* and *Marquis Wellington*. These locomotives caused a great deal of interest, were sold to other areas of the UK, copied in Germany and visited/studied by people who would move the technology forward such as **George Stephenson** (who based his first locomotive on *Salamanca*) and **William Hedley**.

Bradford is Leeds's brother city. I'm sure there's a line on a map where one begins and the other ends but the sprawl of each city merges into each another and it's less than ten miles from city centre to city centre. I can't do Bradford justice here and it deserves a compendium all of its own. Bradford is the 13th largest city in Britain and the **City of Bradford** (local government district) is the fourth most populous metropolitan district which at 501,700 has 37,000 more people than **Manchester**. I put a thread up on the onemickjones internet forum suggesting that Leeds and Bradford merge into one city called Ladford or Breeds or Ladford Breeds.....it didn't go down that well.

Alfred Bradley. I can't really find much out about this guy – and I've asked Radio Leeds – but know, through **Stan Barstow**, that he was a radio drama producer who was either based at or did a lot of work at Radio Leeds. Anyway, there's a BBC award for new Northern radio writers that carries his name, **The Alfred Bradley Bursary Award**, which was established in 1992. It is a biennial award in commemoration of Alfred's life and work which aims to encourage and develop new radio writing talent in the BBC North region. It's the most prestigious radio drama prize, run in collaboration with BBC Radio 4 and has a prize of a bursary of £5,000, the winners work produced on BBC Radio 4, a six month mentorship with a Radio Drama Producer and the opportunity to develop future commissions.

Sir William Henry Bragg (1862–1942), physicist, chemist and mathematician, occupied the Cavendish chair of physics at the University of Leeds from 1909 to 1915, where he laid the foundations of X-ray crystallography as a method for the determination of the structures of materials. Early in his career he took on an apprenticeship at an instrument makers to make equipment for his classes/lectures. During his time in Leeds he created the **X-ray spectrometer** (for determining the electronic structure of materials by using x-ray excitation) and with his son, **William Lawrence Bragg** (1890–1971), then a research student at Cambridge, was responsible for founding the new science of X-ray analysis of crystal structure. He and his son (the youngest ever recipient) shared the 1915 **Nobel Prize in Physics**, the only time a father/son combo has ever won it. Previously, in 1912, they also derived the arrangement of atoms in NaCl (sodium chloride/salt) and KCl (potassium chloride) and for ages chemists refused to accept the fact that NaCl contains no NaCl molecules, the crystals contain just an alternating array of sodium and chloride ions – in 1927 it was described as 'not chemical cricket' and 'the worship of false gods'. He also thought that X-rays were particles and not waves but, due to their short wavelengths, in medical applications X-rays do act more like particles than waves. Search *Braggs and Astbury* and have a look at **Prof ACT North's** top stuff on **The Astbury Centre for Structural Molecular Biology** website.

From 1914, with the start of World War I, he worked on submarine detection. Their work led to numerous, important 'laws', terms/states and tools in physics that carry their name such as **Bragg's law** (the son's), **Bragg diffraction, a distributed Bragg reflector (DBR)**, and **fiber Bragg grating (FBG)**. In 1930 William Henry received the Copley Medal 'for his distinguished contributions to crystallography and radioactivity' and William Lawrence received it 36 years later – the mineral Braggite is named after the father and son. See **Chemical Compounds.**

Bridgewater Place, nicknamed **The Dalek**, is a Leeds office and residential skyscraper. It is the tallest building in Leeds and the tallest building in Yorkshire, and has held this record since being topped out in September 2005. It is visible at up to 25 miles (40 km) from certain areas.

Bridgewater Place has a height of 110 metres (360 ft) to roof level. Originally the tower was to have had a spire which would have extended the height of the building to 137 metres (450 ft), however this was never built. It has 32 storeys (the Gherkin, London 40 storeys) and 40,000 square metres/430,560 square feet of floor space and the atrium hosts the 17.5 metre column sculpture called 'Hello Friends' by artists Bryan Davies and Laura Davies, which is the tallest sculpture in Yorkshire. The building's shape appears to be accelerating winds in its immediate vicinity to the extent that pedestrians have experienced severe difficulties walking past. These winds have led to some of the entrances to the building being closed for safety reasons. To rectify these design issues the building may require the addition of 'vertical fins' to its facade. It is said that, on a clear day, you can see York Minster from the building and, apparently, Look North featured someone base-jumping from the top.

Mrs Helen Currer Briggs founded the **Leeds Poor Children's Holiday Camp Association** in 1904 when she was the Lady Mayoress of Leeds. Since that date the serving Mayoress acts as the President of this registered charity. The camp was established at Silverdale on Morecambe Bay, near the Cumbrian border to allow children, most of whom had never left the city, to experience the open spaces, fresh air and holiday activities of the seaside.

The Association has been renamed **The Leeds Children's Holiday Camp Association** and each year around 200 seven to eleven year-olds are taken to Silverdale for five days and even now it is the first trip out of Leeds for some and their first sight of sheep, cows and the sea. 18 children from Chernobyl recently used the camp. The camp has featured in two books by **Frances McNeil**, *Now I am a swimmer: Silverdale Holiday Camp, the first 100 years* and *Sixpence in her Shoe* and **Matthew Lewis** (Neville Longbottom in the *Harry Potter* films) is its patron. **Mrs Currer Briggs** became a wealthy widower who continued to do good deeds and was one of the founders of the Leeds Maternity Hospital.

Broadcasting Tower is that newish, rusty, higgledy piggledy building that is behind the old BBC broadcasting building (which was also the site of Louis Le Prince's workshop, where he projected the world's first movie), on the way to Woodhouse Moor from town. It was completed in 2009 and I love it, and mainly see it, up close, from the inner ring-road, according to a seven yr-old I know it is 'like crazy dominoes out of control'. I particularly like the way the building changes shape drastically as you move passed it or see it from different angles. I'm apparently not alone. In a recent **Ee Po** poll readers voted it as Leeds's third favourite building, behind **Leeds Town Hall** and **Temple Works/Temple Mill**, the only one of the top three less than 150 years, and the only one shortlisted by a living architect. It's won various industry awards but the **Ee Po** one is the one that matters to me and I find it remarkable that a thoroughly contemporary building has entered the hearts of the citizens of Leeds so quickly. Anyway, the international Council on Tall Buildings and Urban Habitat voted it the best tall building in Europe and it now goes up against one's from around the rest of the world, including the world's tallest building in Dubai, to try to win the world's best in a final hosted in Chicago. Mindst you it'll have happened by the time you read this. Did it win? Yay, it won, I'm dead chuffed. Broadcasting Tower, officially, **the best new tall building in the world**.

The tower itself is part of **Broadcasting Place** that services 300 staff and 5,000 students and is a new academic complex for Leeds Metropolitan University hosting the Schools of Contemporary Art and Graphic Design, Architecture, Landscape and Design, Cultural Studies, the Department for Social Sciences, and the office of the Faculty of Arts and Society. The Tower has 241 student rooms, 22 of them single student studio apartments and the rest are in the form of five-bedroom student flats which include a kitchen and lounge shared space, like a student house in the sky.

It's officially 23 stories tall – to me it looks a few stories taller although why would they get that wrong? Can someone count them for me? Ta. I've enjoyed watching it rust and am interested in how far that rusting will go until it settles down. This rusting is caused by the Cor-Ten steel cladding which is obviously part of the design but also rather cunningly removes the need to paint or treat a huge building. Actually, it isn't technically rusting. That's part of the nature of the steel alloy – to weather and give the appearance of rusting when it's a 'stable' non-corrosive process. The special steel will rust if the design hasn't included the need for water to run off it (standing water will rust) and you need to be careful that the weld-points weather at the same rate as the other materials but I reckon they may have thought of that. I bet they haven't thought about the damage that salty air can do to the steel alloy though, bloody typical, and the seas around Leeds can blow up a proper gale sometimes.

Anne Brontë - drawing in pencil by her sister Charlotte, 1845.

The Brontë sisters; Anne, Emily and Charlotte. (Like many great writers – 'Ahem' *coughs* – Irish descent). Yes I know they weren't from Leeds but they went shopping there. Their father brought back the box of toy soldiers from Leeds that in a roundabout manner got the sisters writing. Leeds is portrayed as 'Millcote' in *Jane Eyre* and in one of Charlotte's other novels *Shirley* she used a report from the *Leeds Mercury* on the Luddite attacks on Rawfolds Mill, near Cleckheaton, as part of her research. And their first hint of success was when the *Leeds Intelligencer* (and Fraser's Magazine) published one of Anne's poems under her pseudonym, Acton Bell. Lastly, Charlotte worked in Leeds as a governess in Rawdon.

Anyway, you can look up this lot y'self, way too well known and easy to find for me to get into – you can watch the films f'God's sake, Charlotte's *Jane Eyre*, for example, has had at least 35 adaptations (25 film -based) and don't get me onto Emily's *Wuthering Heights*. In fact shut your eyes, stick y'fingers in y'ear, walk around like that for the next 20 years and you'll still hear about **The Brontë sisters.**

Anne, Emily and Charlotte are very 'important' authors and were born in Thornton, near Bradford but are more associated with Haworth where they grew up. Haworth is near **Keighley**, part of the **City of Bradford** and twelve miles from the outskirts of Leeds. You can't really sum up the three sisters' life-times work in a simple sentence, unless you're a bit daft......ooh, that means I'm perfectly qualified. Powerful, gothic, dark, romantic dramas often using the Yorkshire Moors/Pennines as a stark backdrop. Recommended stuff.

James Brown (born1965) is a journalist and print media guru/entrepreneur. Starting young as a writer in fanzine culture, he moved on to work for *Sounds* and the *NME*, eventually becoming Features Editor and the *NME*'s youngest ever senior editor. Since then he has written for many of Britain's leading newspapers and magazines (*Sunday Times*, *The Observer*, *The Independent*) and is currently writing for *American Playboy*, *Men's Health*, *Glamour*, *Readers Digest* and *Esquire*. He's a big Leeds United fan and set up **Leeds Leeds Leeds** the club's official mag as well as the internet forum **onemickjones**.

He conceived and launched **Loaded** magazine and **Jack** (a magazine that my brother loved), edited the British *GQ*, taking flagging sales figures up, until he was fired for including Field Marshal Rommel in a feature on style icons. I thought by now, everyone simply accepted that the hideous Nazi murderers had very good dress sense.....an SS uniform anyone?

His stuff is sharp, pithy and witty coming at the material from unexpected angles but he also has a fantastic business and new concept head on him. As a print media guru he has revamped various titles, sections and supplements such as *The Sport*, *The Independent's* Media Section and changed *The Mail On Sunday's Night and Day* supplement to *Live! Magazine*. If his career shows one thing it is that he knows what readers want and I'd have thought that's fairly useful in his industry. He has recently launched the web based **Sabotage Times Syndication,** an extremely interesting online mag with some fantastic writers and articles. I think the "syndication" bit is like an agency for feature writers and articles where other publications can access quality and interesting material. This new venture shows he's retained the energy, drive and vision that got him so high in the industry at such a young age.

Melanie Brown 'Mel B' was known as **Scary Spice** by her fellow **Spice Girls** and the press due to her blunt 'say it as it is' Leeds attitude and accent. The Spice Girls were earth shatteringly successful, *Wannabe* reaching number-one in 31 countries. Their first album sold more than 23 million copies (more than *(What's the Story) Morning Glory?* or *Parallel Lines* for example) and was the best-selling album by a female group ever; their second album also sold 20 million. Since the breakup of the Spice Girls Mel has done a range of celeb type stuff, hosting the MOBO Awards twice and Pure Naughty (a weekly black music magazine show on BBC2), *Bo' Selecta*, *MTV Cribs*, *A Bear's Tail* etc and came second in the US *Dancing with the Stars* show. Her first solo single went to number one in the UK, her third and fourth going to number 4 and 5 respectively.

Although she's gone out with normal folk, Mel has also done that celeb thing of going out with celebs such as Peter Andre, Max Beesley and Eddie Murphy. Eddie is the father of her second child, although there was a paternity battle after which Mel described him as the 'Beverly Hills Cock'. She is now married to film producer Stephen Belafonte.

In 1903 **Buffalo Bill** brought his *Buffalo Bill's Wild West and Congress of Rough Riders of the World* show to Cardigan Fields, apparently staying at the Cardigan Arms. It was the second time he'd brought his show to Leeds (the first probably in 1891) and was a huge event, including 800 men and 500 horses. It was dramatised on Radio 4, (9th Feb 2010) in *Buffalo Bill and Little Matty Dyer* by Peter Spafford. The blurb said, '1903 Cardigan Fields, Leeds. Buffalo Bill, slayer of the Lacota (sp, should be Lakota), the most famous American in the world, disembarks at

Sitting Bull and Buffalo Bill, Montreal, QC, 1885. Library of Congress Prints and Photographs Division Washington. D.C

Armley station with his Wild West show. They will stay in Leeds just five days, but that is long enough to change the life of 15-year-old Matty Dyer.'

An exhibition – *Buffalo Bill's Wild West* – ran at the **Royal Armouries** in the summer of 1999, May 29 to September 5.

Actress **Nichola Burley** was born in 1986 in Harehills. She attended **Intake High School** and started her screen career in the love story across the racial divide film, *Love + Hate*. She's has had many major TV roles in dramas such as *Born Equal*, *Drop Dead Gorgeous*, *Goldplated* and returned to film in the British made *Donkey Punch* released in 2008. Her time at the **Northern School of Contemporary Dance** set her up well for the 2010 released ***Street Dance*** in which she starred with Charlotte Rampling.

Sir Montague Maurice Burton (1885–1952) is quite well documented so I'll keep this snappy. Monty thought that 'good clothes develop a man's self-respect.' Born in Lithuania he came to England in 1900 on his tod and set up in Chesterfield (1903) selling readymade suits bought from a wholesaler. By 1913 his manufacturing in Leeds supplied his five men's tailor shops and at the start of World War I he switched to uniforms and clothed nearly a quarter of the armed forces. Burton employed 16,000 people by the 1920s at the largest tailoring factory in Europe. The company went public in 1929 and at the time had over 400 shops, factories and mills. By World War II Burtons clothed a quarter of the male population of Britain and sources say that during the war Burton's made a quarter of all British military uniforms and a third of the de-mob clothing. The de-mob clothing comprised a three piece suit (jacket, trousers, waistcoat), a shirt and underwear and became known as 'The Full Monty' which is a possible source of the expression. That one quarter figure for both world wars worries me slightly, the World War I stat comes from the Burtons website, but both could be true.

Montague died in 1952 while speaking after a dinner in Leeds, the funeral being held at the Chapletown Synagogue and at the time of his death the company was the largest multiple tailor in the world. In 1967 Arcadia became the new corporate title for the House of Burton and in 2002 Philip Green acquired the Arcadia Group, delisting it from the Stock Exchange and thus becoming the first sole owner since Sir Montague Burton himself. The **Arcadia Group Limited** currently owns Burton, Dorothy Perkins, Evans, Miss Selfridge, Topman, Topshop, Wallis and Outfit. Couple of quick things to finish with, Burtons supplied the suits for the 1966 World Cup winning team (and various other England teams) and the website says 'The House of Burton played a major role in creating the United Nations Association.'

C

Caged roller bearings were invented over 250 years ago and are used all over the place today; from roller skates to the technology that has taken us into space. See **John Harrison**

Beverley Callard (born1957, Morley) best known as **Liz McDonald** in *Coronation Stree*t and also Floella Henshaw in the always shown never watched, *Two Pints of Lager and a Packet of Crisps*. Bev made her television debut in 1983 as Angie Richards in Emmerdale Farm. In 2009 she took five months off Corrie with serious depression and spoke openly and at length to the media about it, brave lass, although she did write a book, *Unbroken: A Story of Survival* – is there anything worse than flogging authors? He says, blushing.

It looks like the **Cardigan Centre** on Cardigan Road, have created the world's biggest cardigan (get it?) measuring 16ft by 15ft. They created it with the help of the local community as part of the centre's twentieth anniversary and at the time of writing were waiting for confirmation that it was indeed the world's largest. Also I'll chuck in a bit of related info I picked up whilst living in Burley for 10 to 15 years. Apparently **Lord Cardigan**, who owned a lot of local land prior to building, was a tea-totaler who only donated the land on the understanding that it would not be used to build a pub. So stretching north, east and west from the Haddon Hall, towards Headingley, the Royal Park and Kirkstall there's a huge publess section of Leeds. Is this the largest urban area in Britain without a pub? It's a huge area. About a mile to the Royal Park, a mile (northish) to The Skyrack and 1.2 miles to the Old Bridge Inn in Kirkstall. Are there closer pubs on those sides of the Haddon Hall?

Cards – see Laminated playing cards and **Playing cards**.

Leeds Caribbean Carnival is the second biggest and second oldest in the UK, a couple of years younger than the Notting Hill Carnival. Also called The Leeds Carnival and the Leeds West Indian Carnival, Wiki describes it as 'the longest running West Indian carnival in Europe.' Held every August bank holiday, the three day event attracted 150,000 people in 2009 and since 2005 it has been covered nationally by BBC 1xtra.

Carey Films is based in **Yeadon** and produces feature films. Owen Carey Jones spent 25 years as a successful banking professional until in 1998 he started a two year MA in Screenwriting (Fiction) at the **Northern Film School** at **Leeds Met**. Sounds the like the classic story of taking a look at your safe life, your established career and breaking out to follow a risky dream to me. He shoots and produces his films in and around Leeds.

Baby Blues, 2001 feature film (writer/producer/director Owen Carey) which by 2005 had been seen by more than 30 million people in countries on four continents.

The Next Victim, short film (producer/director) 2003, worldwide distribution as part of a series of short film compilations produced for network television in the USA and elsewhere, also selected for the York International Film Festival, Belize International Film Festival, Final Cut Short Film Showcase.

In 2004, due to his work as a film producer and director, Owen became a member of the British Academy of Film & Television Arts (BAFTA).

A Mind Of Her Own, 2005, (writer/producer/director, Owen Carey) which screened in the Marche du film at Cannes in 2005 and was subsequently invited to screen at the London UK Film Focus. This film has received a coveted **Crystal Heart Award** from the Heartland Film Festival and two angel awards from the Monaco International Film Festival.

The Spell, 2009, was screened at the Marché du film in Cannes and was screened in the UK through Vue Cinemas following its world premiere in Leeds. If you like the idea of a film industry in Leeds, go and search **Carey Films** online and buy some DVDs from the website.

Ann Carr (1783–1841) was a Revivalist Society preacher.

Carr Manor in Meanwood, was, at different times, home to two eminent Leeds surgeons and was built for **Sir (Thomas) Clifford Allbutt** and then later occupied by **Berkeley Moynihan** who became Baronet of Carr Manor in 1922.

I'm so sad that I have to ignore **Castleford** with its Wakefield postcode. As an east Leeds lad it seems potty that Cas hasn't a Leeds postcode when Ilkley has – but them's the geographical/ bureaucracy gone mad breaks. I grew up with Castleford on the front of buses taking me home and passing through where I lived and in the 1980s had some good friends from there – got to meet loads more from doing miners benefit gigs – and played the town a few times in my old band. I was regularly shocked that, especially as I dressed in an unusual manner, the people of Cas gave Leeds people a run for their money in the friendliness stakes. It was at a gig in Cas that a friendly punter uttered the immortal words, 'it's a pity you didn't publicise this more in Allerton Bywater, the place would have been rammed, you're *Big In Allerton Bywater*. Anyway, all this talk of buses and Cas has reminded me of my old dad, so I'll lift a bit out mi first book, *Coming Out As A Bowie Fan In Leeds, Yorkshire, England*, in honour of the man that I still miss to this day. Ooh, but before I do, look up Cas online, it has a rich history and could easily have been 'the big city' of West Yorkshire but I like it just the way it is. Note to self, don't sue yourself for copyright infringement, that'd be daft and costly......and you'd probably lose and maybe win. Second note to self, don't do anymore notes to self, they're really poxy.

'My parents used to live opposite the No.165 bus stop going to Castleford. The bus only came, at best, every 30 minutes, you miss it, you got no option, you're waiting. As you waited for the bus there was no shelter and nowhere you could shelter in the safe knowledge that you would catch the bus, should it come. In rain or cold, if my dad noticed someone arrive at the bus stop just after the bus, he would put on the kettle, put a little bowl of sugar on a tray, make a tea or a coffee; apparently, with years of experience, he could spot a coffee drinker,

'You can't trust coffee drinkers.'

He'd then take these across the busy road and say, 'How many sugars?'

When I could, I used to watch the people's reactions, they were priceless and I never saw anyone who was anything but genuinely grateful. One time when it was bouncing it down, he lent them a brolly. If they tried to engage him in conversation he'd say, 'Can't stand and chat, it's freezing.'

'What shall I do with the cup?'

'Either leave it on the wall, or take it with you, I've got loads.'

He had a garage full of cups and mugs, his stock for the market store, and they always got the seconds. If there were a few people, he'd take a few cups of tea or coffee, if someone else arrived while he was passing over the beverage he'd take their order.

It was funny watching the reactions as people passed a group at the bus stop, sipping from china cups.'

Brilliant, I've done an entry on Cas that I shouldn't have done **and** said nothing about the town.

Cement is one of those materials we rarely think about but it is the material that bonds together much of the man made, physical world and Leeds made three major contributions to its development through **John Smeaton**, later **Joseph Aspdin** and more importantly, his son **William Aspdin**. Although Smeaton's independent and extensive work to produce a strong, quick-setting, water resistant cement has been shown to have produced a material that was known and periodically used by European builders and artisans, his work formalised and disseminated the knowledge. Cement is also central in the production of **concrete,** the most widespread building material in the world, as well as **mortar**. Cement is eminently recyclable and uses some of the most common and easily accessible ingredients on earth but the industry also creates huge amounts of carbon dioxide (CO_2), around 5% of worldwide emissions of the gas. **See John Smeaton**, **Joseph Aspdin** and **Concrete**

Cento Productions is a Leeds based professional theatre company, founded in 2006, which seems to help new writers develop scripts for The Script Night at **The Carriageworks** in which five to ten minute plays are performed by professional local actors, script-in-hand, fully staged. The performances are regular so keep an eye for it and, if you fancy it, support some local writers and actors.

Central heating. By incorporating **Steam Hall** into the **Round Foundry** complex and heating each room by piped steam **Matthew Murray** created the first building in the world to be heated by steam and a very early example of modern, domestic central heating.

Ceres Division Royal Naval Reserve Leeds is a unit of the Royal Naval Reserve (RNR) based in Leeds. Serving West Yorkshire and the North East of England, Ceres trains up to 100 reservists sharing barracks with RMR Tyne in Leeds. The Divisional Headquarters was opened in 2005 by Rear Admiral Kenneth Borley after having been fully refurbished.

Leeds United fan **Paul Chambers** became the first person in Britain to be convicted of sending a public electronic message that was grossly offensive or of an indecent, obscene or menacing nature, contrary to the Communications Act 2003. In January 2010 Paul was worried about the snow leading to the cancelation of his flight and tweeted, 'Crap! Robin Hood Airport is closed. You've got a week and a bit to get your shit together, otherwise I'm blowing the airport sky high!' Even though the airport's security staff had graded his message's threat level as 'non credible' he ended paying a total of £1,000. Sending his message from his iPhone he thought it would just be seen by his 600 followers but it appeared on an open part of the site. **Stephen Fry** paid his fine, some twitter users repeated the 'threat' and one of his followers posted that he was 'going to blow up the CPS offices (i.e. enlarge a photo of them and burn it on my own property).'

A baby was born in Leeds 1961, the medical people said it would be blind, deaf, unable to communicate and would have no noticeable mental function. 'Forget it. That life is worth nothing.' 40 years later the baby was made a peer of the realm. **Baroness Nicola Chapman** (1961–2009) was a disability rights activist and the first person with a serious congenital disability to be elevated to the Lords – something that flabbergasted her as she thought of herself as 'not the acceptable face of disability'. She was born with brittle bone disease and suffered over 600 fractures throughout her life. After being taught at home and then by a tutor for a couple of hours a week, she attended John Jamieson School for the physically disabled, which for its time was well-regarded but Nicky thought it restrictive. She joined mainstream education when she went to Park Lane College and then Trinity and All Saints in Horsforth. After graduating she found it hard to find work until finally she taught computing to young offenders and eventually headed the computer department of East Leeds Women's Workshops, before chairing the Leeds Centre for Integrated Living.

She wasn't averse to 'kicking off' either, *The Guardian* reported (in her obituary) the huge scene she caused at the taxi rank outside the House of Lords, when a taxi driver said he couldn't take her. It ended with a load of old peers gathering around the taxi in support. During her first year visiting London she made 17 complaints to the Public Carriage Office and one finally led to court action which triggered the proper enforcing of section 36 of the Disability Discrimination Act, which had largely been ignored since 1995. Nicola pointed out that 'this benefited an estimated 1.2 million wheelchair users, not just a 3ft-tall peeress from Leeds.' That's roughly 1 in every 50 people living in the UK.

Lady Chapman had an absolute passion for Leeds United and was a regular at Elland Road. She was the chair of the **Leeds United Disabled Supporters Organisation** (Ludo) and helped make the ground 'one of the best, if not THE best, football ground in the country for disabled supporters.' For the home game after her death in 2009 (Stockport County) the players wore black armbands and a book of condolence was opened at Elland Road. In 2010 Leeds United renamed the banqueting suite at Elland Road the 'Nicky Chapman Suite'. Lastly, an interview with the Telegraph (06 Feb 2005) described her as 'bold, assertive, (and) brimming with humour'

Chemical Compounds occur when two or more elements come together to form a pure chemical substance that itself can be broken down/separated by the introduction of external forces, for example heat. Original work carried out on solid sodium chloride ($NaCl$) by Sir **William Henry Bragg** (Cavendish chair of physics, University of Leeds) and his son **William Lawrence Bragg** in 1912/13 found that elements did not 'mix', there were no $NaCl$ molecules linked by covalent bonds as chemists had thought but separately connected Na and Cl ions held together by ionic bonds. They showed that in solid sodium chloride these oppositely charged sodium and chloride ions are regularly arranged in alternate positions in a 3-dimensional chequer-board pattern and there are no individual sodium chloride molecules. Prior to this discovery (and after) many chemists refused to accept the fact that $NaCl$ doesn't contain any $NaCl$ molecules - crystals contain just an alternating array of Na and Cl ions.

Now I'm sure that there's something fairly fundamental (maybe general) first noted here – perhaps with a few provisos – but every time I try to put it into words my extremely knowledgeable science advisors say 'nah, you can't say that' apparently 'chemical compounds are too complex'. So if you also have a doctorate in this field can you do it for me? Ta.

Thomas Chippendale (1718–1779). I shouldn't say stuff like this but he's Britain's best known cabinet maker, in fact I'm probably not stretching it too far by saying, **the world's best known cabinet maker**....the 'Shakespeare of English furniture'. I've watched loads of *Antiques Roadshow*, I should know. As he came from a 'modest' family (son of a joiner) his place and date of birth is not certain but the location is thought to be **Farnley** (LS21) but what is known is that he received a basic education at **Prince Henry's Grammar School** in Otley.

His master stroke, coupled with being technically brilliant, was that in 1754, he became the first cabinet-maker to publish a book of his designs, entitled *The Gentleman and Cabinet Maker's Director* which defined the furniture fashions of the day and went to a definitive third edition. Editions were owned by many of Europe's royalty and aristocracy and highly fashionable 'Chippendale' furniture (copies) was produced for the elites of the world. Thomas didn't just design furniture, he was also a bit of a Laurence Llewelyn-Bowen, taking large interior design commissions (26 known), for the stately homes of aristocrats. If you fancy perusing a bit of Chippendale get yourself over to Temple Newsam House or Harewood House. Ooh, and the **Leeds Art Collections Fund** bought some so there's some Leeds 'civic' Chippendale, although I don't know where it is. If you've got spare £2.5 to £4 million you may even be able to pick up a top quality bit of Chippendale yourself.

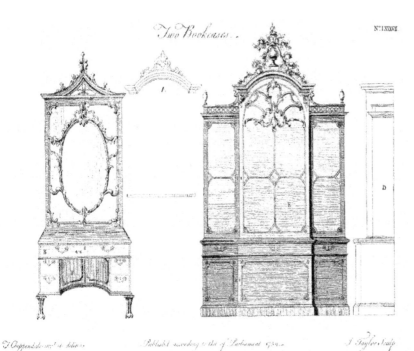

Two book cases,
fac-simile of page from
Chippendale's Directory.

FAC-SIMILE OF A PAGE IN CHIPPENDALE'S "DIRECTOR."   (The original is folio size.)

Jesus Christ (0000 – 0031). There is absolutely no evidence at all to suggest that Jesus was in any way associated with the city of Leeds. He will now, obviously, be fully aware of the city and everything that happens here but during his lifetime he had no knowledge of the city whatsoever. It has been proved however that **John the Baptist** was born in Holbeck and attended **Matthew Murray High School.** He was expelled aged 15 for shoving kid's heads down the toilet bowl. *
* This is not true

Chumbawamba. One-hit wonders Chumbawumba have had five top 60 UK singles, three of them being top 30 and two of them top ten. Best known for the singles *Amnesia* and *Top of the World (Ole, Ole, Ole)* they were formed in Burnley but moved to Leeds in 1982 in search of fame and anarchy, becoming Armley's most notorious squatters. The hard core anarchists were in uproar when they signed to a major record label (EMI) but the band could justify it to themselves and any questions of sticking to beliefs was answered when they turned down £1 million plus royalties for use one of their lesser known hits (*Tubthumping* with its seldom heard refrain about getting knocked down and getting up again) on Nike's World Cup 1998 ads. I have to say they considered the offer carefully taking a whole 30 seconds to decide. Nike offered to take them on a sightseeing tour of their factories in the Far East but the band declined, suspecting a whitewash. They allowed the use of the song for an EA Sports football computer game, the only stipulation being that they got eight tickets and transport to see England play in the World Cup France '98.

One thing you can say for sure is that they stuck at it, around 15 years until their 'big breakthrough' and 15 years later they're still going, playing folk influenced material that was hinted at in their 1988 acappella album ***English Rebel Songs 1381–1984***. I've got ***Get on With It: Live*** from 2007 and although I'm not particularly into folk music, it's a fine album. They still gig all over the place and are particularly successful in Germany where people are fascinated by the bands take on 'traditional' English music. Their stuff is used throughout popular culture (and no, not just *that* song) from *The Simpsons* to films and multimedia games. See **Alice Nutter** and **Boff Whalley.**

Cinema, see **The Western Cinema** where there's a list of some old Leeds cinemas and a bit of reminiscing.

City Square. Completed in 1903 it's in the middle of Leeds, near the Railway station, you can't miss it, it's sort of square. As well as the more obvious stuff like the Black Prince, proposed and financed by **Colonel Thomas Walter Harding**, there are four pairs of figure lamps representing Morn and Eve. They were the work of Alfred Drury in 1903, who took his inspiration from the lamp standards around the Paris Opera House. Have a dig around on Leodis or numerous books for more info. See **Royal Exchange Chambers** and **Mill Hill Chapel.**

The **Leeds City Varieties**, off Briggate, was built in 1865 as an adjunct to the White Swan Inn and fortunately for us the original interior is virtually unchanged since the late 19th Century. The Grade II* listed music hall is known as the longest continuous running music hall in Great Britain but I'm not sure if that's affected by the £9.2m refurbishment, planned to be finished by summer 2011. It's famous as the venue that hosted ***The Good Old Days*** which, after TV had gone, still recreated it seven weekends a year. See ***The Good Old Days.***

Anthony Clavane is a journalist and author. He's a former regional journalist of the year, currently the chief sports writer of the ***Sunday Mirror*** covering all sorts of sports, has co-written a play *Still Waiting For Everything* – which played at the Halifax Square Chapel Centre and the Camden People's Theatre (London) – and had his first book ***Promised Land: The Reinvention of Leeds United*** published in September 2010.

The problem is that although he was born at St James' Hospital in 1960, went to Roundhay School, spent his formative years (into his 20s) in Leeds and has supported Leeds United all his life with the same passion as any other Leeds fan he was too posh to actually come from Leeds. So, even though all but one of his ancestors are buried overlooking Eland Rd. (the other dying in Wortld War 1) and his forebears worked their way out of the Leylands (squalid central Leeds back to back housing) he's still not proper Leeds…too posh. Or so he's been told/made to feel on numerous occasions, he was even chinned by a drunken fan in the Kop after the bloke's mates thought he was an interloper. He moved to Brighton during the eighties and then Essex, working as a history teacher, then became a news reporter and finally chief sports writer of the *Sunday Mirror*. **Promised Land**, his first book, tells the story of Leeds' reinvention through its writers, artists - and football club. 'Promised Land is part memoir, part social and cultural history. It explores industrial and post-industrial Leeds, the role of the Jewish community in the making of the city and the football club, and the rise of working class Leeds writers such as Alan Bennett and Keith Waterhouse.'

Cloth Cat Studios describes itself as 'a not for profit social enterprise based in inner city Leeds which 'aims to provide:-

a) FREE/low cost music courses and other music-based training for local people.

b) facilities to promote people who want to be involved in music, particularly those on low incomes.

We use music training to help local people improve the quality of their lives. Through empowerment, confidence building, making music contacts, learning musical and other skills, we help our users to gain control over their lives and find avenues into employment. We operate on a not for profit basis, so any money we do make goes towards our current activities and expanding our programme of music projects.'

In the early 1990s some the founders of Cloth Cat got on to the Arts Programme, a government run scheme for artists and musicians who were signing on, run at what is now The Burley Lodge Centre. A supervisor there (Andy Philpot) had a show on **Radio Aire** showcasing local bands and promoted a Wakefield venue (Post Haste), a hive of activity for local bands and artists with a supportive DIY ethic. The scheme was dropped but a few on the programme were so fired up that they tried to emulate it and formed Blue Heaven Studios, an arts collective, which went on to run **Oblong** at Carr Mills on the corner of Meanwood Road and Buslingthorpe Lane. On the top floor of a rundown mill building they ran artist studios and exhibitions, a rehearsal room and developed a resource centre for people to promote their art/music and set up new projects. Around 2000 the building was redeveloped as student flats so Oblong moved to Westfield Road in Burley which wasn't able to accommodate the music and arts side of the project and a couple of people decided to set up Cloth Cat.

They were looking to set up some community based recording studios but weren't able to quickly find the funding. Instead they obtained smaller grants, bought some iMacs and music software and ran free courses at the local community centres which were very popular – I've worked with people who trained there. Based at Charing Cross in Woodhouse they brought in volunteers, ran events including an open mic at The Primrose, and developed some of their courses. Through the Woodhouse Festival in 2001 they met the WEA (Workers Educational Association) and together they set up a whole programme of free community music courses from music tech, performance, journalism, to singing and song writing. They gained help from local people in the music industry such as Si Denbigh, Stewart Coxhead, Paula Temple and Jenny Kosmowsky.

They aim to open up new avenues for people who live in disadvantaged circumstances around the city, trying to get people motivated, into jobs (doing something they enjoy) or education. They've built relationships with WEA, Leeds Met, Leeds City College, Mental Health Services and with homeless shelters across the city. They survive on very little money but, with the help of volunteers, organise exciting projects and have been lucky to involve inspirational people. Some of the more 'known' of these include Jez Willis (Utah Saints), Steve Parker (producer for The Rolling Stones, Aretha Franklin, James, The Fall etc), Joolz Denby and Al Overdrive.

They moved to Old Chapel Studios in Holbeck in 2010 which, although they will still be working in north Leeds, will enable them to include people south of the river to extend and expand the scheme. Both organisations have already delivered Youth Music Mentoring schemes through Leeds City Council. **Cloth Cat Open Mics** are at The Chemic, Woodhouse Street on Thursday nights, (except the first of the month) so go down and support them and maybe get entertained as well.

Cluedo is the classic how, where and 'whodunit' board game, a deduction game developed and published in 1949 by **Waddingtons** in Leeds. It was devised by a solicitor's clerk from Birmingham called Anthony E. Pratt who described himself as "an introvert full of ruminations, speculations and imaginative notions" and I'd bet good money on the fact that he read a lot of **Agatha Christie.** Pratt's original design called for eleven rooms and ten characters, one of whom was to be designated the victim as well as few other small differences from the game as released, such as hiding the cards around the room for the players to find in order to start the game. The original nine weapons were: axe, bomb, rope, dagger, pistol, hypodermic syringe, poison, poker and a shillelagh (a traditional wooden Irish folklore weapon/walking stick, typically made from a stout knotty stick with a large knob on the end). Even with fewer people, rooms and weapons the game today still has hundreds of possible outcomes.

The original patent was granted in 1947 but due to shortages caused by the war it wasn't published in the UK and USA until 1949. Just as Waddingtons had taken **Monopoly** from **Parker Brothers**, they took Cluedo and changed its name for the American market to **Clue** as the Americans did not know the game **Ludo** and would therefore not understand the pun contained in the title.

The number of different editions, spin-off games (at least 24), feature films, television series, musicals/plays, puzzles, books is surprising, as is the way the game tracked the development of video games from the **Commodore 64** through to the Apple **iPhone/iPod Touch**. In addition to all this the Cluedo/Clue brand name can be seen on everything from umbrellas, mouse mats and badges to miniature collectable cars. The brand and themes have been successfully licensed to, amongst others, cologne makers, clothing manufacturers and food distributors.

Coal and mining, like wool and the mills, were central to the development of Leeds into the place it is today. There's plenty of material available online and in books so I'll keep this briefer than its importance deserves but it'll provide some pointers. The industry stretches back as least as far as the Romans who worked coal in Garforth, for example. Coal helped shape the city, supplying industries such as mills, brickworks, potteries, glassworks, limeworks, iron and steel making, iron founding, engineering as well as taking in goods to make the mines function. Like all these industries, coal needed workers and workers needed accommodation, whether it be a small cottage on an estate or integral to the development of somewhere like **Middleton** or **Morley**. Obviously this happened over a period of time. Depending on what source you believe, the working of coal in Middleton goes back to the 13th/14th Century (you can see the mounds and dips in Middleton Park) and mining was extensive across the area, now Leeds, although not intensive. The start of the more industrial scale mining was in the 18th century and was influenced greatly by the development of inland waterways and canals such as the **Aire and Calder Navigation** and the need to feed the different types of fuel that the coalfields produced into the mouth of the industrial revolution. The industry was also responsible for shaping its environment with housing, infrastructure and innovations, such as happened at **The Middleton Railway** or later, for example, its contribution to the development of trams. As Leeds expanded, filled with industrial buildings and workers houses, the larger pits were developed in more outlying areas, usually near a waterway, railway or a single large customer. The expansion of the city also started to suck in some of the old outlying townships and villages such as Armley, Wortley, Woodhouse and Meanwood. The coal industry expanded in conjunction with improved transport systems that eventually gave access to the North and Irish Seas, as well as the rest of the country and world.

Coal mining in the **West Yorkshire Coalfield** was one of the biggest powerhouses of the industrial revolution and here's a list of some of the larger collieries which were based in and around Leeds. **Garforth Colliery**'s Sisters' Pit and Isabella Pit; **Victoria Colliery** (Bruntcliffe) **Morley Main Colliery** and **Howley Park Colliery** all in Morley; **Rothwell Haigh Colliery**'s Rose Pit (known locally as Rodill Pit), Fanny Pit and later Beeston Pit; **East Ardsley Colliery**; **Foxholes Colliery** (pits 1 & 2), **Methley Junction** pit, **Savile Colliery** and **Newmarket** pit all in Methley; **Broom Colliery** Middleton as well as smaller ones such as **Halton Colliery.**

Mining was a hard, dirty and dangerous job and many miners lost their lives. During the 20 year period from 1881 to 1900 there were 13 fatalities at **Foxholes,** three of which were workers aged 15 and under. The explosion at **Morley Main Colliery** took place on Monday the 7th of October 1872. 34 miners lost their lives and 58 children were left without a father as well as the six children, 16 or under that died during this disaster which made front page news on national weekly newspapers like the *Illustrated London News.* For more recent information on the coal industry around Leeds have a dig around, you'll find plenty of nuggets.

Cock Beck is a stream in the outlying areas of east Leeds, which runs from its source due to a run off north-west of Whinmoor, skirting east of Swarcliffe (where there's the 'The Cock Beck' pub) and Manston, past Penda's Fields, Scholes, Barwick-in-Elmet, Aberford, Towton, Stutton and Tadcaster, where it flows into the River Wharfe.

In the past the beck was known as the **River Cock** or **Cock River**, even though it was only a tributary of the River Wharfe. In places the beck was relatively narrow, but too deep to cross unaided; a feature which can still be seen today at many points. Historically, the major crossing for the Cock was sited along the Tadcaster-Ferrybridge road.

In the aftermath of the 1461 Battle of Towton remnants of the Lancastrian forces fleeing the victorious Yorkists were forced to cross the Cock Beck. According to observers, the bridge at Tadcaster collapsed under the weight of those crossing, plunging many into the icy waters where they drowned, and trapping many on the wrong bank leaving them to face the enemy - having already disposed of most of their weapons. The massacre is said to have been so brutal that the beck ran crimson with blood for several days, which could be a confusion with the **Battle of Seacroft Moor** in 1643, which reports say certainly made the beck do so.

Coel Hen was a noted leader of the Hen Ogledd (the Old North, including Elmet) in post-Roman Britain perhaps between AD 350 and 450, some trace him back as far as 320. He figures prominently in the genealogies of the period and continued to be known in legend and into the modern era. Later writers such as Henry of Huntingdon and Geoffrey of Monmouth claim him as the father of Saint Helena of Constantinople, mother of Roman Emperor Constantine the Great. The traditional 'King Coel' is likely to be the historical basis for the nursery rhyme *Old King Cole* but, being so long ago, it's all a bit hazy and the name may have been associated with many people. His line, collectively called the Coeling, included Gwallog ap Llaennog, probable king of Elmet. See **Elmet** and **Gwallog ap Llaennog**.

Cog railways use a toothed-rack rail, usually positioned between the rails, to connect with one or more cog wheels (or pinions) on the train. The engagement of the two creates extra friction/bite allowing the trains to operate on steep inclines or haul heavier weight. Most rack railways are used on mountain railways, although a few are used on transit railways or tramways built to climb steep gradients in cities and towns. Cog railways – also known as pens and rails railway, rack-and-pinion railway or rack railway – were first designed and patented in 1811 by **John Blenkinsop** who used the system on the world's first cog railway, the Middleton Railway between Middleton and Leeds where the first commercial steam locomotive, *Salamanca* (or possibly the less well known *Prince Regent* by the same company, on the same line), ran in 1812. See **John Blenkinsop, Middleton Railway**.

Leonora Cohen (1873–1978 born Thorp) came relatively late to the suffrage cause but gained huge notoriety when she smashed the case of the Crown Jewels (the Regalia of the Order of Merit) in the Tower of London with an iron bar that she'd hidden under her coat. She was part of a group of women who met with cabinet ministers of **Herbert Henry Asquith's** Liberal Government whom she thought had already betrayed a commitment to votes for women a couple of years earlier. At this meeting they received assurances on the vote for women which were withdrawn a few days later; this incensed Leonora, leading her to the Tower of London. She got away with the act as she convinced enough of the jury that the glass was worth less than £5 and she could only be convicted if the cost was £5 or more. The case attracted lots of press interest and headlines such as 'Leeds Suffragette Acquittal follows Smashing of Tower Show Case'.

She lived at 2 Claremont Villas, Clarendon Road where there's a blue plaque commemorating her life. She was also pictured on the front cover of the *Radio Times* (30 March 1974) and did interviews and ads to publicise the BBC TV feminist series, *Shoulder to Shoulder*. There's plenty more to say about this woman including marrying a Jew when, socially, it was extremely difficult for both parties, many sorties of window smashing (especially around Leeds), imprisonment in Holloway and Armley prisons, hunger and thirst strikes, gaining an OBE, helping **Lilian Ida Lenton** escape, being a magistrate in Leeds for over 30 years and living until she was 105 but there's lots online so I'll let you go and get it. See **Lilian Ida Lenton, Herbert Henry Asquith, Suffragettes**

Barney Colehan was born Bernard Colehan in Calverley (1914) and went on to have a major influence on popular culture. Barney was a pioneer of TV and radio and produced the first programme when television production arrived in the north of England in 1951. His first breakthrough was in the development and as the producer of the hugely successful radio show *Have A Go* which ran from 1946 to 1967 and at its peak attracted audiences of around twenty million. The show, a celebration of ordinary folk, featured Halifax born **Wilfred Pickles** and his wife Mable visiting church halls or places of work where people would tell up-lifting stories from their lives and then answer quiz questions for money prizes – hence the catchphrase, 'Give 'em the money, Barney.' One of the reasons why the show was 'cutting edge' was that it was the only place you would regularly hear regional accents or 'ordinary' people from around the country speak – see rant attached to Chris Moyles. Wilfred is interesting on this issue as he had previously caused a furore as the first newsreader to speak in a regional accent. He regularly annoyed the 'establishment' by signing off with 'and to all in the North, good neet'. Anyway the 21 years of *Have A Go* launched such catchphrases as 'How do, how are y'?', 'Are y' courting?' and, I would argue, helped normalise the regional accent.

The catchphrase from the show 'give 'em the money, Barney' brings me back to our main subject. Barney usually devised and produced his own shows and brought Britain its first TV talent competition with the early 1950s variety show *Top Town*, a show pitting contestants from neighbouring towns against each other. He also brought us *I'll Give It Five* – a panel show judging contemporary 'acts' which brought us early TV performances by The Beatles, for example. He's probably best known for developing ***Top Of The Pops***, ***The Good Old Days*** and ***It's a Knockout***. I've covered the first two elsewhere so I'll have a quick few words on the latter. Barney brought *It's a Knockout* to our screens in 1966 and it ran (on the BBC) for 22 years until 1988 with Barney responsible for its first 16 years. My enduring memories of the show are Stuart Hall and Dewsbury's Eddie Waring, who was already a Rugby League commentary but it was this show (and Mike Yarwood) that brought him national fame.

As there's only sparse info on Barney out there I relied on the help of his daughter Eileen to fill in some of the gaps. She told me that Barney had written a book which would be a goldmine of information if it was ever published. Eileen also spoke about how Barney used to go out talent spotting and credits him with bringing us people such as Jimmy Saville, Frankie Vaughan, Rod Hudd and Ken Dodd – that was just off the top of her head so I'll add Jake Thackray. Barney died in Rawdon during 1991 and I'd like to thank him for bringing some fantastic TV and radio to the nation but more so for bringing it the regional accent. See *Top Of The Pops*, **Jake Thackray** and *The Good Old Days*.

Coliseum Building, Cookridge Street, was opened in 1885 by the Prince and Princess of Wales (became King Edward VII and Queen Alexandra in 1901) as a concert hall, debating hall and indoor circus. It was converted into a theatre in 1895 and the Coliseum Cinema in 1905, becoming **The Gaumont** cinema in 1938. After over 55 years it switched to the dreaded bingo. Bingo lasted until 1969 and it was bought by Leeds City Council who, until it became a listed building, had it down for demolition. A television production company purchased the building with grand ideas which didn't come to fruition and by this time the building had been stripped of its once fabulous interior and lay dormant for years. It had, however, been spotted by Brendan Croker who showed it to his close friend Ollie Smith (director of the Town and Country Club in London) and, after a major refurb, the Leeds **Town and Country Club** opened in October 1992. Not only has David Bowie played there but also lesser acts such as INXS, Mark Knopfler, Blur, Jack Dee and The Stone Roses. The Town and Country Club closed at the end of the 20th Century and re-opened as the **O2 Academy**, once again hosting loads of ace bands.

Concrete was originally developed by the Romans but its use disappeared for around 13 centuries until Leeds engineer **John Smeaton** pioneered the use of hydraulic lime in concrete, combining it with pebbles and powdered brick as aggregate. You'll often hear this presented as fact but it's a bit more complicated than that, it has been contested by **Chandra Mukerji** (University of California) who states that the **Canal du Midi** in France was constructed using concrete around 90 years earlier.

You may be surprised to hear that I'm not a civil engineer or a bricks and mortar builder but I think a few things need clearing up here as I can see confusions. We need to get a few terms straight and these are cement, mortar and concrete, closely connected building materials with specific definitions. Each can be adapted by other additives and mixes but here are some basic definitions:

Cement is a binder, a substance which sets and hardens independently and can bind other materials together, technically, it's cement in its dry form when it's fine and powdery. Can be used as a render.

Mortar is used to bind blocks/bricks together and is usually sand with cement or lime and water.

Concrete in its basic form contains cement plus sand, gravel (aggregate) and water, the aggregate being both course (lumps of broken rock/stone) and fine (sand). It can have other additives such as fly ash, slag cement or chemical admixtures, but cement is usually only around 10% - 15% of the total mass of concrete.

Smeaton's supposed breakthrough was two-fold and connected to the building of **Eddystone Lighthouse** (1755-59). He pioneered and carried out extensive research into the use of 'hydraulic lime', a form of **mortar/cement** which sets quickly, under water, measuring the speed at which it sets and its resistance to water, starting work that led to the development of **Portland cement**. He also added mixed aggregate producing **concrete**. Both of these are claimed as breakthroughs in the modern world and the rediscovery of concrete and specialised cement.

I've read Chandra Mukerji's paper *Tacit Knowledge and Classical Technique in Seventeenth-Century France: Hydraulic Cement as Living Practice among Masons and Military Engineers* (Technology and Culture, 2006 47:213-233) a few times. The title of the paper includes the phrase **hydraulic cement** and in this matter she is clearly correct. Chandra shows that John Smeaton did not develop the first waterproof, quick drying cement since the Romans, the technology had not disappeared. Although Smeaton researched it independently, earlier studying Dutch canals, and clearly documented his 'discovery' through experiment, Chandra's article is fascinating and clear in showing how the technology has lived on since 'the Romans'. I enjoyed the way she explored the information being passed on through the 'collective memory' of French and Italian builders, engineers and artisans, not appearing to be formally documented until the building of the **Canal du Midi** and I find her argument both compelling and interesting. The idea of an earnest British engineer, travelling around looking at structures, doing repeated detailed and complex experiments, struggling valiantly with a huge problem until he finally had his 'eureka' moment, when all he had to do was just pop over to France or Italy and have a chat with a couple of builders made me chuckle and I can hear his wife tutting. And Smeaton's key ingredient appears to have been a pozzolanic material (volcanic ash) exactly the same as the French, Italians and no doubt other European builders, stretching back to the Romans. Here, there is no doubt that Chandra is correct; they used the cement under water and everything.

Although this is constantly confused, **hydraulic cement is not concrete**. It can be a constituent of concrete but concrete needs aggregate, it's part of what makes it concrete, around 80 to 90% of the dry material of concrete is likely to be aggregate, it's fairly crucial. On this second issue, of **concrete,** I have to qualify it with the fact that, although I have worked extensively with and around builders, I didn't listen to them when they got all technical and I'm not an expert on building materials but neither is Chandra, she is a sociologist. I find the use of the terms cement and concrete very confusing throughout the paper. They appear to be interchangeable, as if they are the same, and at no point does she make clear the distinction between concrete and cement. My feeling is that if she understood the distinction she would have made it more transparent and there would have been little confusion. The use of the terms cement and concrete are all over the place, she hasn't nailed the definitions or kept them distinct. Here's the only detailed description of the making of concrete in her paper:

'a formula and method for making for good concrete: The best cement of lime, sand, and pozzolane or pulverized brick is passed through a baker's basket, making sure to to regulate the proportions according to the formula: two fifths of lime with three fifths of sand, and all of it sifted through a sieve to remove little pebbles, and for a cement for better cement, the same amount of lime with two of pozzolane well pulverized and passed through a baker's basket, and for a long time ground together.'

Yes I know there's a couple of 'typos'. What can I do? I'm not her proof reader. So, ok, she's a respected academic, I accept that, but the material she describes is not concrete but mortar. Had they left the small pebbles in it would have been open to debate. That is not to say that there was no concrete involved in the canal, it's still possible, and there are phrases in the paper that hint at it but still leave me with suspicions or needing clarification. So, for me, Chandra came nowhere near proving an existing modern use of concrete pre-Smeaton but perhaps I've simply got it all wrong.

What Smeaton did was mix his 'new' cement with aggregate (pebbles and powdered brick) creating **concrete**. Again, this is slightly confused as not all accounts of Smeaton's achievements make clear this distinction between cement and concrete or include the use of aggregate but there's enough that do to make me confident that he did. There is also no doubt that, although the technology had not died with the Romans, he developed the special, quick drying, water resistant cement independently and through scientific endeavour. When John Smeaton was building Eddystone Lighthouse in the 1750s, there's an important historical factor that I need to make quite clear as it's crucial to the whole debate. I wasn't there, I didn't see the concrete mix, I was visiting some writer friends in Haworth. That's a joke, the Brontë sisters weren't alive at the same time as me....I was visiting **David Hartley** and explaining some modern philosophical theories.

Leeds has three important contributions to the development of concrete, John Smeaton and later **Joseph Aspdin** who invented Portland cement and Joseph's son **William** who went on to hugely improve his father's mix. Strangely, reports suggest that Smeaton did not see the bigger potential of his 'new' cement or concrete and I have to say that I've heard rumours of concrete used in Finland during the 1500s but I looked and found no evidence. **See Joseph Aspdin, Cement**.

Some concrete facts:
Concrete is the most frequently used construction material on earth.
About 6 billion tons of concrete are produced annually.
Around one ton of concrete for each person on the planet is produced every year.
It is estimated that one-half to two-thirds of our infrastructure is made of concrete.
Concrete has an extendable life of 50,000 years
The actual material concrete is as green as a badger, easily recycled, long lasting, no by-products and the ingredients are amongst the most abundant on earth.
The production of concrete and the transportation of the ingredients cause absolutely huge carbon dioxide emissions. **See cement**.
(Mukerji, Chandra. *The Politics of Rediscovery in the History of Science: Tacit Knowledge of Concrete before its Discovery.* Paper presented at the annual meeting of the American Sociological Association, Marriott Hotel, Loews Philadelphia Hotel, Philadelphia, PA, Aug 12, 2005)

Sean Kieran Conlon was born in Leeds (1981) and is a former member of the boy band **Five**. Of Irish descent, Sean had his first recording session at eleven and by the age of 13 performed for Elton John, Andrew Lloyd Webber and Phil Collins after winning **Yamaha's Young Composer Competition**. Shortly after, Conlon enrolled in a performing arts school and, encouraged by his mother, auditioned for Five after seeing the advertisement in national newspaper, The Stage. As a child his interests lay in becoming a record producer of soul music or a rugby league player. Conlon was the youngest member of Five at 15, officially too young for the auditions. Since Five disbanded in late 2001, Conlon has been pursuing a solo career as an R&B/jazz/soul pianist/singer in the cafes of London,

Christian Cooke (born 1987) was born and went to school in Menston, which is part of Bradford but has a Leeds postcode and the school he attended, St Mary's, is part of the LEA and the Evening Post describe him as 'Leeds actor' so I'm having him. He's been in shed-loads of

TV such as *Where the Heart Is, Demons, Trinity, Doctor Who* and Ricky Gervais and Stephen Merchant's film *Cemetery Junction*.

Harry Corbett (1918–1989), father of **Sooty and Sweep**, was apparently born in Bradford but certainly spent his adolescence living in his parent's fish'n'chip shop in Guiseley called Springfield's (opposite Morrison's) which last time I passed was still open. The shop, above' which Harry used to practice the piano, was featured in *The Comedy Map of Britain*, broadcast on May 10th, 2010 on BBC 2. Before I move on, Harry's mum was **Harry Ramsden**'s sister and Harry used to play piano in his uncle's Guiseley restaurant.

When Harry was offered his first BBC shows he had 'a very nice job, security n'pension n'all the sort of thing,' as a surveyor at an engineering firm, and the company refused him the six Saturdays off, 'y'can't mix television n'engineering.' So he made the break and completed the first six shows of 'Sooty and his subversive bursts of anarchy' in 1952. Back then the airways were packed full of 'Received Pronunciation' and Harry brought a Leeds/Bradford accent to the nation's children, Harry didn't do 'Queens English'. But the timing of the Queen's Coronation was very good for Harry, massively increasing the amount of television sets in Britain. In 1947 there were only 17,000 tellies in Britain yet in 1952 over 20 million people watched the coronation, obviously some visited friends but by 1953 21% of households had a set.

He was awarded an OBE in 1976, but even that had a bit of the Sooty and Sweep about it. It seems that Prime Minister Harold Wilson had *Steptoe and Son* actor Harry H. Corbett in mind but the middle initial "H" was lost in the bureaucratic process, and Harry Corbett got it instead. After 23 years he stopped doing the TV work (see below) but carried on gigging and died in his sleep on the 17th of August 1989 after playing to a capacity audience at Weymouth Pavilion. See **Sooty and Sweep.**

Matthew Corbett was born in Guiseley (1948) **Peter Graham Corbett** but had to change his name for showbiz as there was another Peter Corbett already registered. Son of the legendary Harry Corbett, Matthew is best known for **The Sooty Show** and **Sooty and Co**. He took over Sooty from his dad in 1976, apparently buying him out for £35,000. Matthew already had plenty of TV experience and had been appearing on *Rainbow* since 1974 singing, performing and writing with Rod Burton and Jane Tucker as Rod, Matt and Jane which later became Rod, Jane and Freddy. Matthew retired in 1998 but still does occasional TV.

The **Cotton Club** was a night club in New York City that operated during Prohibition and was set up by Leeds lad, **Owney Madden** who moved to New York aged 11/12 and became a top gangster. The famous club, based in Harlem during the 1920s and 30s, was a Mecca for the famous and glamorous of the time, Jimmy Durante, George Gershwin, Al Jolson, Mae West, Irving Berlin etc and I'd suggest that it's the most famous club ever, but that's opinion so I won't mention it. The club was a hot-bed of jazz and the artists performing there are a who's who of black American music; Fletcher Henderson, Duke Ellington, Count Basie, Bessie Smith, Cab Calloway, Ella Fitzgerald, Fats Waller, Louis Armstrong, Dizzy Gillespie, Nat King Cole, Billie Holiday, Ethel Waters to name but a few. Looking back, it's staggering that, due to the racism of the day, these truly great and iconic artists were not allowed to enter the club through the front door or go into the main body of the club and mingle.

The club (originally called *Club Deluxe*) belonged to famed black prize-fighter **Jack Johnson** (the first black world heavyweight boxing champion, reigned for seven years), but Madden **forced** Johnson to sell him the club and it quickly became the hottest spot in New York. Wiki say that he took control of the club whilst still in prison (1923, the year he was released) but I don't think the dates agree with most other material I've seen. I've got my opinion of the sequence of events but it's a guess and staying in my head. The club instituted a strict "whites only" policy and all blacks, including employees or performers, were forbidden to enter by the front door and no blacks whatsoever were allowed into the club as patrons. Live radio broadcasts were transmitted across America (and the world) from the club and the artists gained national and international exposure. **Duke Ellington** ran the 'house band' from 1927 to 1931 and this residency allowed him the freedom (not experienced by touring bands) to experiment, develop and play with arrangements. Eventually, after a request by Ellington, the club slightly relaxed its policy of excluding black customers.

A Chicago branch of the Cotton Club was run by **Al Capone**'s older brother Ralph Capone (I suspect a favour to Maddens friend Al – and don't mention Fredo Corleone from *The Godfather*) and there was a West Coast branch of the Cotton Club in California. A fictionalized history of the club blending the race relations of the 1930s and the battles between Madden and rival mobsters was released as the film *The Cotton Club* (1984), directed by **Francis Ford Coppola** with the ever so Leeds Bob Hoskins playing Madden who was apparently renowned for slipping into his Leeds accent when trying to intimidate people.

Count Arthur Strong is a SONY Radio Award winning, fictional comedy character created by Leeds comedian **Steve Delaney**. The series was commissioned following a string of star guest appearances on BBC Radio 2's Mark Radcliffe Show by Count Arthur Strong. A Komedia Entertainment and Smooth Operations production, the shows are actually produced by Mark Radcliffe himself. There have now been five series recorded and aired on BBC Radio 4. The show charts a confused and muddled 'day in the life' of the one-time Variety Star, Count Arthur Strong. He is an elderly, forthright, pompous, mostly-out-of-work, deluded, thespian from Yorkshire, who 'says it how he sees it'. His delusions of grandeur are often a source for the comedy and an interesting take on celebrity culture. His 'celebrity' is never recognised no matter how often he says 'do you know who I am?' (For why I find this interesting, see **Steve Delaney**.) He's a bit fuddled and suffers from ADD, memory loss and is often too 'straight talking' and a bit rude to people, as he blames them for the confusion he has caused as he takes the conversation/monologue off in bizarre directions. He uses malapropisms out of confusion or in an attempt to sound educated. This mixing up of words is at the heart of the comedy. Although it can at first have the feel of an old music hall character/routine, it's very funny and certainly reminds me of people I know or have known. A pilot of **Count Arthur Strong's Entertainment Game** with **Delaney** will be filmed in front of a studio audience in July 2010; I have no idea when, or if, it will be screened but by the time you read this it could be a big 'hit'. The pilot is co-developed by **Jeremy Dyson** another successful Leeds lad who is a bit of a recluse. Delaney has also performed the character on stage.

John Craven OBE (born 16 August 1940) is a journalist and television presenter, best known for presenting the BBC's *John Craven's Newsround*. He presented/anchored the classic children's news show from 1972 until 1989 when, just before he left, the programme was renamed *Newsround*. He was also editor of the prog from 1986. It was one of the first children's news programmes in the world and John fronted more than 3,000 editions, reporting from more than 40 countries. For ten years he presented news items on other children's programmes, such as *Multi-Coloured Swap Shop* and *Saturday Superstore*.

Although it was a programme for children, *Newsround* was not patronising and often took on serious and difficult issues. For example, during the first National AIDS Week in the late 1980s it dedicated a whole episode to AIDS in order to dispel many of the myths and rumours that had built up around the topic in children's gossip. In 1989 he started presenting the countryside news programme ***Countryfile***, which he still presents; he sticks at his projects does ar'John.

Brendan Croker is a musician from Leeds who has recorded albums under his own name along with his sometime backing band The Five O'Clock Shadows. He was also a member of The Notting Hillbillies, and during the late 1980s, as an auxiliary member of The Mekons and a full-time member of Sally Timms and the Drifting Cowgirls. He has recorded with Eric Clapton, Tanita Tikaram, Mark Knopfler, Kevin Coyne, and Chet Atkins, to name but a few.

The Culture Vulture is a funky website and e-newsletter covering cultural issues and events primarily, but not exclusively, in Leeds.

Leeds art expert **Penelope Curtis** has become the first female director of **Tate Britain**, one of the most important roles in the industry. She joined Leeds Museums and Galleries in 1994 as head of the Henry Moore Centre for the study of sculpture and led its transformation into the **Henry Moore Institute** becoming curator in 1999.

The Cup and Ring Stone, according to the Ee Po is 'one of the oldest examples of prehistoric graffiti' and is thought to be up to 5,000 years old – between the Neolithic and Early Bronze Ages. It has circles with large dots in the middle carved on its surface in a style often found near burial mounds, so it could be a religious mark or it could be a boundary marker. It was discovered in **Horsforth** during the 1960s renovations of **Low Hall** and was at some point moved to Kirkstall Abbey and has recently been returned to Horsforth. There is a second ancient stone (the Horsforth Milestone) near 154 New Road Side in Horsforth.

Mark Curry (born 1961) is an English television presenter probably best known for his three years as a **Blue Peter** presenter. Although he was born in Stafford, Wiki lists him as having attended **Lawnswood High School**, although there is no citation and I can find no record of it online. Although I do remember him having a 'northern' twang so it could well be true.

D

Henry Drysdale Dakin (1880–1952) Chemist. Although he was born in London, he was the youngest of eight children of a family of steel merchants from Leeds. Whilst growing up in Leeds, and still at school, he did water analysis with the Leeds City Analyst, where he was an apprentice for four years. He studied chemistry at the University of Leeds and obtained his PhD from Leeds. In the early twentieth century and with a fellow chemist he developed the Carrel-Dakin method of wound treatments where the wound would be regularly irrigated with a weak antiseptic developed by Dakin. **Dakin's Solution** was modified in 1982. Also known for **The Dakin oxidation** used in the production of pesticides, perfumes, pharmaceuticals, developing photographs, the synthesis of indolequinones (anti-biotic, anti-fungal, and anti-tumour), and the **Dakin-West reaction.**

Liz Dawn MBE (born **Sylvia Butterfield** in 1939) played **Vera Duckworth** in *Coronation Street*. Liz was diagnosed with a terminal illness in 2004 and left the show after 34 years with her character, Vera, dying in her sleep on 18 January 2008. In 2000 she was made Lady Mayoress of her home city of Leeds and has been given an honorary doctorate by Leeds Metropolitan University for her voluntary work. Liz has obviously featured on *This is Your Life* (January 1990) and has written an autobiography called *Vera Duckworth – My Story*. Vera Duckworth is an iconic character of British TV.

Alan 'Dosher' Dawson is one of Leeds' best kept secrets and was one of the world's greatest (known) **bass player**s, I'd argue **the** best. Obviously that's opinion but it's my firmly held opinion and he's certainly the best musician I've ever seen and I've seen a few. He was the bass equivalent of Hendrix or John McLaughlin/Paco de Lucía and used to warm up by playing Stanley Clarke's most complicated stuff, faster and with bits added or by a note perfect rendition of Jaco Pastorius's (based on Johann Sebastian Bach's) *Chromatic Fantasy*. In the 1980s he turned down many decent offers and opportunities (because he was into what he was playing or wanted to play jazz) including an offer to join New Model Army, and invitations to audition for Simply Red and The Mission. He played in local bands Hang The Dance and Leitmotif and is also my best mate. This entry is genuine as I believe him to have been one of the world's virtuoso musicians but there is little record of his playing and little supporting material which makes it difficult – I feel like I shouldn't include an entry but that would mean excluding a modern, virtuoso musician.

What I need is quotes from people who saw him play. I contacted John Lake, who was writing for *Sounds* music paper during the 1980s and also played bass. He reflected, 'Mark King of Level 42 took slap bass to a mass audience but Dosh made his technique look sluggish. He could do stuff I don't think other bass players could.' Conrad Farlow made a living in the music industry for 26 years as a decent musician and sound engineer. Cutting his teeth with heavy dub and reggae in Brixton studios and going on to teach sound engineering at Barnsley College, Dewsbury College and Sheffield Red Tape studios, he said, 'I was, and indeed still am, something of a musical anorak and know who the great bass players were or are. Dosher was on fire when I worked with him and I would say the best way to describe his ability was world class.

If it was physically possible, Dosher could do it as well as if not better than anyone else on the planet.'

His latent musical talent meant that he developed an outstanding knowledge of music theory and became a Q-Base expert producing high quality backing tracks for club bands as well as note for note renditions of Charlie Parker's (his musical hero) most complex pieces. I feel it's a crime that he now works in an office and his expertise isn't being passed on to younger generations but isn't that life? I suppose the real question is 'Why is he unheard of?' Well, he has a mythical status amongst those who saw him play but that's a complex question. I put it down to primarily two things, class and his stubbornness or principles depending on how you wish to look at it. He turned down opportunities if his heart lay elsewhere. The class thing meant that he suffered some typically working class things for daft kids with too much energy and belief, borstal and expulsion from school but it also meant that he had no formal musical training. He did earn a living from music for over 15 years but damaged a tendon in his arm during a fight and after the operation and the subsequent loss of function gradually moved away from music. The video of the first single by Hang the Dance may at some point turn up on YouTube but although his ability is clear he is only playing at quarter complexity and speed. If you're interested I'd search YouTube for 'Dosher' as I hope that this entry may get people to dig stuff out, post it and allow us to celebrate an unknown, 'world class' Leeds musician.

DCI Banks: Aftermath is a 'gritty' ITV crime drama filmed, located on the streets of Leeds and based on **Peter Robinson's** novel of the same name. The two-part pilot episode was broadcast in September 2010 and if the British public has an appetite for more 'gritty' cop shows, they'll make more. *Aftermath* was made by Left Bank Pictures with the backing of Screen Yorkshire – a partnership that also brought us the Leeds based ***Married Single Other*** and ***The Damned United***. Unfortunately *DCI Banks: Aftermath* made the classic, shoddy mistake, often seen on Leeds/Yorkshire dramas (watch Emmerdale), of casting some Leeds folk who had Lancastrian accents....not to worry, no-one will notice and it doesn't matter, I've often met people, born and bred in Leeds that have Bristol or Glasgow accents. It happens all the time.

Death Valley Screamers. You might have read five or six years ago about a Leeds Market trader meeting and marrying the daughter of the Ukrainian Prime Minister, the fairytale romance of it all as featured on Michael Palin's BBC 1 show received a lot of press. Anyhow, Sean Carr was on a scuba diving holiday in Egypt when his eyes met across the Hard Rock Cafe bar with a young woman's. He thought little more about it until he received a text from her and the rest is history. They married and became the Posh and Becks of the Ukraine, Sean forming the Death Valley Screamers whilst out there and recruiting Mick Lake, his old guitarist mate from Leeds. The rock'n'roll band are big out there and other parts of Eastern Europe and played the Independence Day Celebration in Maidan Nezaleshnosti, Kyiv to a live audience of 250,000 people – televised to about 60 million. They play all over the place; a recent skeg at their itinerary included the Hard Rock Cafc's 10th anniversary celebration in Egypt, Tbilisi capital of Georgia and New York. The Ukraine doesn't have a singles chart, only the M1 Chart which is a national music TV channel chart calculated by people texting in and voting – they've topped that twice. They've released three albums, the most recent *Back In The Doghouse* was released in early 2010 and their sixth video filmed in Orange County, New York featured actor Armand Assante and Paul Teutal Senior of Orange County Choppers.

Decomplex is a word created by **David Hartley** that has disappeared – the etymology (history) of the word is interesting. The prefix de, now means a negative, a loss, (deflate, declutter, decompose, derail etc.) but in the 1730s/40s it meant a loss or a gain, an increase or a decrease. Obviously, this duality couldn't remain, it'd be too confusing for us simple folk, and reduction won. Before this linguistic survival of the fittest had run its course, Hartley created the word **decomplex** to mean a further level in the complex nature of a human action. To read and play a C note from a musical score is a complex action but to sight read and fluently play *Soul Love* is a decomplex action. To pick up a pencil and write a word is complex and to string words and grammar together to write a novel is decomplex. I suspect it also includes that **going off on one** thing that creatives do, completely losing yourself in something you're playing, painting, saying or writing and going to a beautiful place you've never been before. We own, know and use his word **automatic**. Can anyone tell me a common word that conveys the same meaning as **decomplex**? **Automatic** he created for the starting point of a process where the stages in the functional development of our actions get passed back and forth between the body and the brain in an increasingly intricate set of relationships between the two until it becomes **decomplex**. See **David Hartley, Automatic**

Steve Delaney grew up in Leeds. He's best known for his Radio 4 character **Count Arthur Strong** whom he created in the 1980s. The count first appeared when Steve was a drama student at Central School of Speech and Drama in London and performed as him at the end of term show, having drawn inspiration from characters he met during his childhood. However, he put him to one side for several years during which he worked as an actor, appearing in television dramas such as *Juliet Bravo*, *The Flying Lady*, *Casualty*, *The Bill*, *All Creatures Great and Small* and *Agatha Christie's Poirot*. Seems to keep his head down this lad, preferring to stay 'in character' for press stuff.' I find this interesting as **The Count** is obsessed by his 'celebrity' and seems to dump his northern background for his 'sophisticated' persona, although, obviously, he never quite can and to comic effect. In contrast Delaney, in real life, appears to display something that I've always thought to be a Leeds trait (**Leedsness**) of not 'blowing your own trumpet', 'getting ideas above your station' and 'keeping your feet on the ground'. Although, perhaps I've drunk too much coffee and forgotten to do that thing with the bed......that shut eyes and snore thing; it's got a name and everything, hang on, it'll come to me. It's something to do with floors and brushes.

Disco – or a **Dance** as it should be known. Although the *Whiskey à Go-Go* nightclub is widely considered to be the world's first discothèque, or disco when it opened in Paris, 1947, I dispute that, and credit it to **Jimmy Savile** in Leeds four years earlier, see below. The world's first ever disco was in Leeds, for me, that's a fact. The wiki definition is: 'A discothèque, is an entertainment venue or club with recorded music played by Disc jockeys through a PA system, rather than an on-stage band.' That is **exactly** what Jimmy did in 1943, when Leeds hosted the world's first ever disco, writing on the tickets 'Grand record dance' one shilling'. When he held his 'grand record dance' it wasn't even imagined that people could dance to records in public.

The world's second ever disco was in Otley, in a cafe above a cake shop. Jimmy got the room for free by saying all the people would buy cakes and tea during the interval....they didn't, they went and bought fish'n'chips instead and while they were out Jimmy did a runner back to Leeds on the last bus saving himself one pound five shillings (in 1943) on the taxi fare back to Leeds.

DJ (Disc Jockey) Due to one man, the concept as we have grown to know it, came from Leeds on two accounts. The term was in use from 1941 but in 1943 **Jimmy Savile** became the first person in the world to have a record/disc dominated dance, playing big bands/jazz/dance records upstairs at the Belle Vue branch of the Loyal Order of Ancient Shepherds, a friendly society, in **Leeds**. Not only that but Jimmy claimed to be **the first person to use two turntables and a microphone** for continuous play of music, which he did at the Grand Records Ball at the Guardbridge Hotel in 1947. This claim was made almost 40 years ago in his autobiography and other places. It doesn't appear to have been contradicted so the DJ, with two turntables and a mic, is Jimmy Savile's invention. According to djhistory.com he argued that DJs not musicians are pop music's true revolutionaries and, for these and other reasons, Jimmy created the new celebrity, the new power in music, the person who controlled the records, who has become more influential as the years have moved by. See **Jimmy Savile**

DNA: Back in the days when it was thought to be to be a fairly dull molecule of no great consequence **William Astbury's** pioneering **work** at the **University of Leeds** (with his student **Florence Bell)** took the first X-ray photographs/images of DNA. This break through brought forward its study and, as its importance emerged, allowed the structure of DNA to be later, fully identified. Through his work he proposed further details of the nature/structure of DNA that were in essence true but later scientists with more information tidied up his work and were duly rewarded and credited. Also double **Nobel Prize** winning chemist **Linus Pauling** cited Astbury's insufficient data and a lack of quality in his images for his basic mistake and losing the race to nail down the structure of DNA. This race was finally won by **Francis Crick** and **James D. Watson** in 1953 working under **William Lawrence Bragg** at Cambridge. Bragg, whose family home had been in Leeds, had won the 1915 Nobel Prize in Physics with his **University of Leeds** based father, **Sir William Henry Bragg**. As their boss and director of the lab Bragg backed Crick and Watson to the hilt and was the person who announced the earth-shattering discovery of the structure of DNA to the world, he had to do it twice, as the first time it was largely ignored by the press.

The basic path to the structure of DNA were Astbury's insights which led directly to the work of **Maurice Wilkins** and **Rosalind Franklin** and from there to the structure of DNA as devised by **Francis Crick** and **James D. Watson** in 1953. **See William Astbury, Sir William Henry Bragg and X-ray.**

Bonamy Dobrée (1891–1974) was an academic and Professor of English Literature at the **University of Leeds** from 1936 to 1955 and married artist **Valentine Dobrée** on November 21, 1913. Bonamy produced many full length published works, prefaces and introductions to other works, contributions to anthologies and encyclopaedias, literary articles, and book reviews. He also wrote a novel, a play, and poetry.

His work was mainly literary criticism and biographies, *Rudyard Kipling: Realist and Fabulist* (1966), *English Literature in the Early Eighteenth Century* (1959), *Milton to Ouida; a collection of essays* (1970), *English essayists* (Collins, 1946). Contributions include an article on George Meredith for **The Encyclopaedia Britannica**; an essay on Jonathan Swift entitled *"The Jocose Dean"*, essays on Robert Smith Surtees, Joseph Conrad, D.H. Lawrence and more published in his book *Imagined Worlds: Essays on Some English Novels and Novelists in Honour of John Butt*. Articles on various literary topics which include *T.S. Eliot: A Personal Reminiscence*; *English Literature 1866-1966*; Sir John Vanbrugh; Jonathan Swift; and William Shakespeare. The book reviews were written primarily for the **Yorkshire Post**, **The Times Literary Supplement**, and **The Times Educational Supplement**. The reviews are on a variety of subjects including the work of Rudyard Kipling, Ezra Pound, William Shakespeare, John Donne, and Jonathan Swift. I found over 40 titles by Dobrée online at McMaster University Libraries and more general information at The University of Texas at Austin, Harry Ransom Humanities Research Center.

"A man of this world, who liked good wine, good prose, and good verse, was faithful in friendship, and felt deeply about the life of men and women." *The Times* obituary, 4th Sept, 1974.

Georgina Dobrée (1930–2008, daughter of Valentine & Bonamy) was a clarinettist who championed the basset horn and rarer repertory, she was a very successful concert clarinettist and music historian, digging up some of the more obscure pieces of the 18th and 19th centuries and publishing some of them from 1968 onwards (Musica Rara, Oxford University Press, Schott, Chester and Nova). Later including work by Pleyel, Ries, Wanhal, Lefèvre, Wanhal and Krommer. She also edited an entire volume of French music (Mel Bay Pubns, April 2000).

She founded her own recording company, Chantry records, and her own publishing company, Chantry Publications. A professor of clarinet at the **Royal Academy** from 1967, she gave up regular teaching in 1987 due to touring and lecturing although she continued with individual lessons, master classes and workshops. Spookily, I can't find any references to **Georgina** living in Leeds but her parents came to Leeds when she was six and stayed here until she was 25 so I reckon she may have visited. I do know that at some point during World War II she was evacuated to the US of A.

Artist, poet and novelist **Valentine Dobrée** (Gladys May Mabel Brooke-Pechell) was born in Cannanore, India, 1894. From 1936 (until the1950s) she lived with her husband Bonamy in **Collingham**, Leeds. Her early figure paintings of the 1920s diversified into cubism, surrealism and collages. The University Gallery, Leeds, (it's free in, is the Stanley & Audrey Burton Gallery, Parkinson Building) owns a number of her works and exhibited them in 2000.

It seems to be in the field of visual art that she was best known, her Claridge Gallery show of 1931, where she exhibited 34 works (most of which are unaccounted for), was apparently pivotal. The art critic of *The Times* (9 Dec. 1931) said of her work, 'Her designs, mostly cut out of patterned wallpapers, are definitely and very intelligently "cubist". Indeed the first response to them is the feeling that here at last is the proper application of an artistic formula that is never quite satisfactory in painting.' She exhibited all over the place, during the 1920s at the *Salon des Indépendants* and in 1963 there was an exhibition of her collages at the Library of the ICA, London.

She led a 'Bohemian' life and was friends with some of the Bloomsbury Set and exhibited with 'the London Group'. She had two novels out, *Your Cuckoo Sings by Kind* (Knopf, 1927) & *The Emperor's Tigers* (Faber & Faber, 1929). A book of poetry called *This Green Tide*, (Faber and Faber, 1965) and another title, that I can't find proper reference to, called *To Blush Unseen* (The Crescent Press, London, 1935). Her and her husband were friends of, hung around and exchanged letters with **D. H. Lawrence** and her writing was admired by **T. S. Eliot** and **Graham Greene**.

Wordsworth Donisthorpe (1847–1914). Although we as a city, quite rightly, celebrate Louis Le Prince we had another, less well known, film-making pioneer. Wordsworth Donisthorpe produced his moving images before the internationally celebrated Thomas **Edison** and the **Lumiere** brothers but couldn't find funding to develop his invention. A panel of experts (think *Dragon's Den*) in London rejected the concept of moving pictures as 'wild, visionary and ridiculous'. There's a very brief film that Wordsworth took of Trafalgar Square in 1890. Wordsworth, an interesting first name, guess where it came from? It was given by his mother as they were related to poet William Wordsworth.

Anyway, moving on from the tittle-tattle, Wordsworth, with his cousin **William Carr Crofts** (1846-1894), was way ahead of the game and in 1876 filed a patent for his kinesigraph – a film camera – which was designed to, 'facilitate the taking of a succession of photographic pictures at equal intervals of time, in order to record the changes taking place in or the movement of the object being photographed, and also by means of a succession of pictures so taken of any moving object to give to the eye a presentation of the object in continuous movement as it appeared when being photographed.' A series of photographic plates were exposed in rapid succession and the resulting images printed onto a sensitive paper strip which, according to discoveringyorkshire.net, was 'one of the first inventions which used sensitive paper to capture the image....before Eastman Kodak's transparent celluloid film was first produced in 1889.' To me Wordsworth is a bit of a misunderstood visionary and other than his 1878 letter 'Talking Photographs' (no doubt seen as a symptom of insanity) which appeared in *Nature* he appears to have dropped his invention until he later heard of Le Princes' work in his home city. In his 1878 letter Wordsworth suggested that the invention be used in conjunction with Edison's newly invented phonograph as a means of recording and reproducing dramas and, more specifically, of making a talking picture of William Gladstone, the Prime Minister. Even though *Nature* is aimed at research scientists, one of the world's most prestigious and **the** most often cited interdisciplinary science journal and that the letter was about the phonograph, I'm not going to speculate about whether the letter was seen by Edison (or drawn to his attention) and sparked an

Wordsworth Donisthorpe pictured in *Chess Monthly* December 1890.

idea for moving pictures.

One thing that tickles me about this tale is that Wordsworth was influenced by his inventor father who had a number of patents to his name and designed a successful wool-combing machine (still used in the 1970s) and it was the technology of the textile industry that provided much of the inspiration for Wordsworth's cameras. It seems that he replaced the falling combs of his father's square motion wool-combing machine with falling photographic plates and employed shuttles (used in mills) to carry and rotate the film. He also deployed a treadle, fly wheel, pulley system and automatic braking on the film. A problem Wordsworth encountered was how to project his images and his idea was to place electric sparks behind the 'film' and project onto a magic lantern screen. I'm obviously speculating but with funding and encouragement I'm sure he would have solved this problem and brought the first moving pictures to the world. Isn't it interesting how power and influence can write history and shape the world and the lack of it stop gifted people from fulfilling their potential?

Wordsworth attended Leeds school, invented a new language (Uropa), was a political activist, an individualist anarchist and, with others, set up the Liberty and Property Defence League to promote Individualist/Libertarian ideas. He loved chess and in 1885 co-founded the British Chess Association, and the British Chess Club. There's a small book on him by Stephen Herbert called *Industry, Liberty and a Vision: Wordsworth Donisthorpe's Kinesigraph* (The Projection Box, 1998)

Returning to the 'Dragons Den'-type panel, who thought he was a nutter, I'd agree with them in describing him as a 'visionary' and will leave you with one of his dreams; 'Being unable to retrace our steps in Time, we decided to move forward in Space. Shall we never be able to glide back up the stream of Time, and peep into the old home, and gaze on the old faces? Perhaps when the phonograph and the kinesigraph are perfected, and some future worker has solved the problem of colour photography, our descendants will be able to deceive themselves with something very like it: but it will be but a barren husk: a soulless phantasm and nothing more. "Oh for the touch of a vanished hand, and the sound of a voice that is still!"'

Ian Duhig is a writer best known as an extremely successful poet. He's not from Leeds but studied at the Uni and has lived in the city a long, long time, has a good knowledge of local history and has written widely about Leeds. He's won a Sicilian octave load of awards and has been shortlisted for many more.

Ian has a new collection of poetry out called *Pandorama* (Picador, Nov 2010) – unless you're reading this in 2015 and in that case, it's old – which will be his sixth collection. The main thing you need to know is I've heard him read twice and really rate him. This lad can write.

After a reading I once asked him if he knew how many Irish Navvies had dies building the infrastructure of Britain, the canals, railways, tunnels, roads etc as I suspect that it's a largely ignored, huge number. Anyway here's a poem from *Pandoram*:

Roisin Ban
The M1 laid, they laid us off;
We stayed where it ended in Leeds,
a white rose town in love with roads,
its Guinness smooth, its locals rough.

Some nights we'd drink in Chapletown,
a place not known for Gaeligores,
to bear O Cathain singsean-nos –
O Riada gave him the crown.

Though most were lost by'Roisin Dubh',
all knew his art was rich and strange
in the pub we drowned with our own black stuff
when we laid the Sheepscar Interchange.

Pulped books help asphalt stick to roads
And cuts down traffic-sound as well;
between the lines a navvy reads
black seas of words that did not sell.

The **Dunkirk Veterans Association** was founded in 1953 in Leeds. If you haven't heard about Dunkirk, early in World War II almost all the British Army (Expeditionary Force) was trapped at the French port and surrounded by the German Army. They'd left most of their heavy gear behind in the retreat and were sitting ducks for the *Luftwaffe* and heavy artillery. As the British appeared to have nowhere to go the Germans made the decision to bomb them into submission to save losses to its army. Prime Minister Winston Churchill ordered any available ship or boat, large or small, to pick up the stranded soldiers and in around a week 338,226 men were evacuated.The community-based *East Leeds Magazine* interviewed James H Else who was the 18th member to join the Dunkirk Veterans Association. James became the National Treasurer the following year and has organised many remembrance trips to France and Belgium and in 1998 became the National Chairman. Due to diminishing numbers the veterans disbanded in 2000. Their international standard is on display in the Royal Armouries.

E

The Eagle Has Landed....it flew out of Leeds. See **Jack Higgins.**

Elmet was the Celtic kingdom roughly similar to the old West Riding of Yorkshire, much bigger than the current West Yorkshire, it took in much of South Yorkshire, North Yorkshire and as far across as bits of what is now Manchester. It was established during the early Middle Ages, between approximately the 5th century and early 7th century. It is unclear how Elmet came to be established, though it has been suggested that it may have been created from a larger kingdom ruled by the semi-legendary **Coel Hen (King Cole).** The inhabitants of Elmet are believed to have called themselves the Loides, a name which is still reflected in place names: notably Ledston, Ledsham, Leathley and obviously Leeds which Derek Fraser in his *A History of modern Leeds* thinks may have been the last independent capital of Elmet. See **Barwick-in-Elmet, Coel Hen** and **Gwallog ap Llaennog.**

Emmerdale, Britain's second most popular soap (by audience share) – and in my opinion the one with the best production values – is thought of as soaps poor relation. Its 7pm slot makes it difficult to directly compare to the busier 8pm slot but *Emmerdale* often gets bigger audiences than *EastEnders* even with the slot disadvantage.

Soaps exist in an industry dominated by London and Manchester and in which the *EastEnders* and *Coronation Street* closed shop of tit for tat, self hype and over bloated, 'iconic' self esteem ignores the real world. Witness how the BAFTA for 'Continuing Drama' – or 'Soap' as it used to be called – lives on a loop passing between *Corrie, Casualty* and *EastEnders* (seven years out of the last nine) interspersed by *The Bill* and *Holby City. EastEnders* has 'gone up against' *Emmerdale* on a number of occasions in the TV schedule, sometimes looking like a targeted move. The naive BBC decision makers no doubt expected to put the poor, parochial competitor in its place only to end up losing viewers. The public aren't influenced by the largely southern media's ignorant high regard for *EastEnders.* They don't believe the hype and watch what they see as the most entertaining programme and those viewing figures regularly show that to be *Emmerdale.* The flagship BBC soap had to ditch its original 7pm slot due to *Emmerdale's* audience and when the two programmes have gone head to head EastEnders has suffered some of its lowest ever viewing figures, dropping to below six million. Wiki notes that when an hour-long episode of *Emmerdale* cut into the *EastEnders* slot *Emmerdale* was watched by 8.1 million and *EastEnders* by 6.2. Then there's *Emmerdale's* 4,000th episode which went 8.8 million to Leeds and 6.2 to London – looks like 25% less popular to me does that.

I contacted ITV to try to get more figures: 'The soap is one of the most watched programmes on television. Emmerdale has averaged an audience of 7.3 million with a 34% share of viewing (2010 ratings). The soap is currently outperforming its ratings in 2009; an improvement of an additional 0.6 million viewers (1 share point) watching an average episode....Back in January, an episode of the soap drew in 10.0 million viewers, which was the most watched episode of the soap since 2005.

When I've seen snippets of *EastEnders*, it's like Groundhog Day, with the rehashing of old, predictable storylines such as Pat Butcher knocking someone over in the Square being lovingly recreated decades later, with different characters, frame by frame. Just because it's the BBC's 'flagship' soap does not guarantee the quality we expect from the Corporation, I think that the production values on *EastEnders* are shockingly poor and some of the worst script writing I've ever come across has been on this 'special' show. Compare the two whenever you like, look out for over used, shoddy sets, poor continuity, repetitive and limited camera work, largely amateurish acting, endless clichés and you'll find victories *EastEnders* can claim over *Emmerdale* every time.

Emmerdale has urban locations, more varied external scenes and expansive shots of the Yorkshire countryside. The *Emmerdale* studio is the biggest such space in Europe and this provides the show with more varied interior locations and more interesting camera techniques, angles and crane work. If the outstanding Danny Miller doesn't win the 2010 BAFTA for Leading Actor for his portrayal of Aaron Livesy coming to terms with his sexuality there is no justice, but we know that.

Emmerdale received three awards in the 2010 publically voted *TV Choice* Awards and is one of ITV's few 'cash cows' that funds the organisation in an increasingly competitive environment, *Emmerdale*'s viewing figures have gone up by a staggering 10%. Guess in which direction *EastEnders* figures have gone? Should you require proper information regarding *Emmerdale* please feel free to surf the thousands of internet pages or consult your nearest newsagent. What is the role of a 'soap opera'? I'd say it's to allow people to immerse themselves in the lives of others and escape reality for half an hour. How do you judge which one best fulfils this role? I'd say by viewing figures – not the political BAFTAs.

Encyclopaedia Leeds I claim as the first encyclopaedia of a British city, maybe European – not world I've just found one for New York. Yes there are travel guides or books on cities and dictionaries of local history but they do not usually contain contemporary writers or modern musicians for example and I claim it due to the breadth of topics covered and the fact that the entries are not 'dry' listings. I searched extensively for encyclopaedia in conjunction with major British and European cities and came up with one, *The London Encyclopaedia* but it is not an encyclopaedia of London but of the built environment of London; streets, buildings, museums, breweries, old established shops, markets etc. So Solid Crew are not in, neither is Ken Livingstone or Charles Dickens, unless of course they're featured in a museum; it is not an encyclopaedia of London. So there y'go, I reckon you're holding the first encyclopaedia of a British/European city in your hands, I could be wrong and if you know differently let me know via email. And yes I know it's not comprehensive but encyclopaedias never are....but if you know of interesting stuff I've left out email me for the second time in a day, with supporting evidence obviously.

Robert Endeacott (Born 1965) is a Beeston lad best known for his mural on the stairwell inside Elland Rd. Just kidding, he isn't, he's best known as an author. His books started with the coming of age and following LUFC tale of *One Northern Soul* (under J R Endeacott, Route, 2002) followed by *No More Heroes* (Relish Books, 2005), he also co-edited *Fanthology* with Graeme Garvey (Relish Books, 2005), *Dirty Leeds* (Tonto Books, 2009) an finally *Disrepute:*

Revie's England (Tonto Books, 2010). They're very popular football based books that sell well, ooh, and he really did paint the mural in the East Stand, stairwell nearest the Kop, about four flights of steps up. Mindst you it's the East Stand Upper so it's a lost treasure, although hopefully by the time you read this it'll be seen on a regular basis.

Friedrich Engels (1820–1895) provided some telling insights into the living and working conditions of the poor people of Leeds in his book ***The Condition of the Working Class in England in 1844*** in which he considers the nature of work in the great industrial cities of England. He describes the countryside of West Yorkshire as 'a charming region, a beautiful green hill country' and contrasts it to the horrors of the poor, working people living on the banks of the Aire (The Bank). He notes how the death rates have risen amongst the people working in industry compared to the countryside, the workers in the city are four times as likely to die from smallpox, measles, scarlet fever and whooping cough and ten times as likely to die from convulsions. Engels uses the following quote from the *Artisan* – I'm going to use most of it as it's so telling – and adds that 'it must be borne in mind that these cellars are not mere storing-rooms for rubbish, but dwellings of human beings.' :-

"on a slope running down towards the river Aire, which meanders about a-mile-and-a-half through the town, and is liable to overflows during thaws or after heavy rains. The higher or western districts are clean for so large a town, but the lower parts contiguous to the river and its becks or rivulets are dirty, confined, and, in themselves, sufficient to shorten life, especially infant life; add to this the disgusting state of the lower parts of the town about Kirk-gate. March-lane, Cross-street and Richmond-road, principally owing to a general want of paving and draining, irregularity of building, the abundance of courts and blind alleys, as well as the almost total absence of the commonest means for promoting cleanliness, and we have then quite sufficient data to account for the surplus mortality in these unhappy regions of filth and misery.... In consequence of the floods from the Aire" (which, it must be added, like all other rivers in the service of manufacture, flows into the city at one end clear and transparent, and flows out at the other end thick, black, and foul, smelling of all possible refuse), "the dwelling-houses and cellars are not

Engels in 1856

infrequently so inundated that the water has to be pumped out by hand-pumps, on to the surface of the streets; and at such times, even where there are sewers, the water rises through them into the cellars, creating miasmatic exhalations, strongly charged with sulphuretted hydrogen, and leaving offensive refuse, exceedingly prejudicial to human health. Indeed, during a season of inundation in the spring of 1859, so fatal were the effects of such an engorgement of the sewers, that the registrar of the North district made a report, that during that quarter there were, in that neighbourhood, two births to three deaths, whilst in all the other districts there were three to two deaths. Other populous districts are wholly without sewers, or so inadequately provided as to derive no advantage therefrom. In some rows of houses, the cellar dwellings are seldom dry; in certain districts there are several streets covered with soft mud a foot deep. The inhabitants have from time to time vainly attempted to repair these streets with shovelfuls of ashes; and soil, refuse-water, etc., stand in every hole, there to remain until absorbed by wind or sun.... An ordinary cottage, in Leeds, extends over no more than about five yards square, and consists usually of a cellar, a sitting-room, and a sleeping chamber. This small size of the houses crammed with human beings both day and night, is another point dangerous alike to the morals and the health of the inhabitants." – The quotation marks in this version were wrong so, consulting other editions, I've made my best guess as to where they went wrong.

Engels also contributed articles to the chartist newspaper **The Northern Star and Leeds General Advertiser** and **I'm guessing** that he'll have consulted the seminal work by **Charles Turner Thackrah** on the subject of working conditions, the exploitation of workers and the effects on their health, published over a decade earlier which was influential in changing the employment laws. Anyway, just three years later he wrote *The Communist Manifesto* with **Karl Marx** and completely changed the world.

The **Theory of Evolution** has roots in Armley, Leeds. Yes I know, it sounds crazy but **Erasmus Darwin**, Charles Darwin's granddad, wrote a statement of **evolution** and the relatedness of all forms of life before his grandson was even born. He did this in his most important scientific work *Zoönomia* (1794–1796), which anticipated the modern theory of evolution and the modern evolutionary synthesis. Darwin senior based his theories on **David Hartley**'s developmental and psychological theory of Associationism. (Allen, Richard C. 1999. *David Hartley on human nature*. Albany, N.Y.: SUNY Press.)

Now I am not claiming that Hartley 'discovered' evolution and I am not trying to undermine Darwin the younger's great achievements in developing and 'proving' the theory of evolution. What I am saying is that when you see a documentary (or read an article) that uses professors and experts – I saw one recently that included quotes from many eminent scientists, including Stephen Hawking – that treats the concept as if it was brand new thought by **Charles Darwin** and **Alfred Russel Wallace** be sceptical, you are having science 'sexed up' for you. These serious scientific presentations usually have 'ding moments' where the basic theory takes shape and they are feeding you a line, the idea developed over time. Below is a quote straight off Wiki and out of *Zoönomia* by **Erasmus Darwin** which was based on the theories of **David Hartley**. Now, it is always possible that Charles Darwin was in no way aware of his Granddad's most famous work but the following was written by **Erasmus** before Charles was born and describes something.

'Would it be too bold to imagine that, in the great length of time since the earth began to exist, perhaps millions of ages before the commencement of the history of mankind would it be too bold to imagine that all warm-blooded animals have arisen from one living filament, which the great First Cause endued with animality, with the power of acquiring new parts, attended with new propensities, directed by irritations, sensations, volitions and associations, and thus possessing the faculty of continuing to improve by its own inherent activity, and of delivering down these improvements by generation to its posterity, world without end!'

Public Execution in Leeds: with particular reference to the *Leeds Mercury*.

The only modern era **public executions** to take place in Leeds were those of **Joseph Myers** and **James Sargisson** at Armley Gaol on Saturday, 10th September, 1864. They emerged through a gate (still there but bricked up) in the prison wall to be greeted by crowds of between 80,000 and 100,000. These spectators, who had turned out to witness the hangings, were described by the *Leeds Mercury* as 'a sad and horrible picture of humanity.'

After murdering his wife, Myers had tried to commit suicide several times. His final attempt was by slitting his throat but the Surgeon to the Gaol (Mr W.N.Price), to avoid Myers escaping justice, stitched it up and applied plaster to the wound to try to prevent his throat from opening up during the hanging.

Snippets from the *Leeds Mercury* newspaper:

'....the crowd, even on the previous night, began to occupy the field in front of the gaol and the road which leads up to its gate....' Of the scaffold: '....its limbs were screened by the black cloth, which to some extent was also to hide the wretched men when they stood upon the drop, from the crowd beneath.....As the hour of the execution approached, the spectators continued to pour in large numbers until the wide open space in front of the gaol and every available spot around were occupied. The roof of every house and mill, walls and even the lamp-posts were thronged with those anxious to witness the execution and there could not have been less than 80,000 to 100,000 people present....'

'There were also some hundreds of spectators on the Burley Road and near Woodhouse Moor, but they would be unable, except with the aid of glasses, to witness the execution. They were, speaking of the mass, of the class usually collected together on such occasions men employed in mills, factories, workshops, etc. with a not inconsiderable sprinkling drawn from a lower and more degraded Stratum of Society, but embracing a few of what were called 'the respectable class'. Here and there, until the fatal hour had nearly arrived, the more thoughtless of the mass indulged in jests, and others even so far forgot the solemnity of the event as to engage in games of 'thimblerig' and 'fly the garter'....'

'Amongst the crowd were a large number of women, many of them with children in their arms, and their anxiety, if possible, exceeded that of the men to obtain 'good views'.'

'During the process of pinioning Sargisson turned to Myers and said - 'Are you happy". 'Yes, I am', the latter replied. At five minutes to nine, the bell of the gaol, which announced the arrival of the fatal hour, began to toll. There was then a cry from the dense multitude in front of "Hats

Off", and almost immediately, the Under Sheriff Mr. Keene passed from the door to the scaffold, followed by the Chaplain in his canonical robes, repeating the funeral service. Immediately behind him, supported on each side by warders, were the two prisoners, pale and anxious-looking. They knelt upon the drop whilst Mr. Tuckwell most impressively continued to read the Service. Both of them uttered the responses and frequently ejaculated 'Lord have mercy upon me", and "Lord Save my soul". Mr. Tuckwell, having pronounced the absolution, the executioner at once stepped forward, placed a white cap over the head of Sargisson and next over that of Myers. He then adjusted the rope upon Myers and after that upon Sargisson. Myers appeared quiet, but Sargisson shook his head and breathed heavily. Both of the men continued to call out ' Lord. save me", and the last words uttered by Sargisson were to his brother murderer. He called out 'Art thou happy lad?' to which Myers responded 'Indeed I am".'

'The crowd, immediately after the drop, rapidly dispersed, though a number remained to witness the cutting down of the bodies at ten o'clock....'

'Also that the fears entertained regarding the wound in Myers' throat were not without foundation. The results of the sudden drop had been to tear open the wound, producing in the throat an orifice sufficiently large to admit the insertion of a pocket-handkerchief and we are informed that blood flowed from the wound some minutes after the drop fall. In accordance with the sentence, the bodies were buried within the precincts of the gaol.'

James Sargisson may not have hanged if he'd kept his gob shut, but he blabbed like a school kid, being held captive by a teacher in search of the truth, just wanting to go home. Mindst you, there was a promise of a reward and a pardon for anyone who didn't actually crack open the head but knew what happened. Now this is Sargisson's version of the events that happened at Laughton, near Rotherham, 'it won't me guv, he did it.' In the olden days, before mobile phones and them there *A-pods* (or whatever they're called), people used to ask each other the time. He reckoned that he heard another drinker ask the landlord the time and gardener, John Cooper, showed the fella the time and he left the pub. Outside he met his mate George Denton and told him about the young stranger, who'd just left the pub, and after a chat Denton said, "I'm going to kill yon man. Don't thee split a word. I'll give thee half of what he's got." So they followed John Cooper, Denton put on a fake beard and battered him to death with a stake from a hedge. Denton went through the man's pockets, took seven shillings and sixpence for himself and gave the silver watch and keys to Sargisson. "'Now,' he says, 'Jim, whatever thou does, don't split a word to nobody. No one's seen us do it and they'll never find us out. Thee go tomorrow and look at the place where it was done with other people,' which I did do...'"

Sargisson became the prime suspect. He'd been seen with the victim and witnesses said he'd left the pub within minutes of Cooper and a young lad saw someone who looked very like him follow Cooper down the track. So the police questioned him. Here was Sargisson's mistake. Knowing that there was a pardon for anyone who didn't actually strike the blows and hearing of the reward of £100, he offered to make a statement. He included Denton as the murderer. There were two problems. The first was that he claimed to have had a conversation with a woman who said there was no conversation and Denton denied everything. Even though Sargisson could have been telling the truth, there was absolutely no evidence against Denton.

Had Sargisson kept his gob shut, he may have lived but he even told the police where he'd hidden the watch and keys. Also, the discovery of bloody trousers (the blood being that of any mammal) added to the case against him. He was found guilty and hanged. To add a bit of spice to the situation, it came out in evidence that Sargisson was of 'good character', while, not long before, Denton had been confined in York Castle on a charge of perjury and the prosecution had 'not dared' to put Denton on the stand. Unlike Myers, Sargisson died hard, struggling for two or three minutes on the end of the rope.

The story of Joseph Myers was that of the alcoholic and wife beater, with all the age old attributes and cycles. He was already in prison for beating his wife and she was playing the role so often adopted by the person suffering domestic violence by lobbying for his early release. She was successful and he was released early to continue his habitual behaviour. A few days after his release, he went out, got pissed and took a pair of scissors to his wife, stabbing her in the face, breast, shoulder, and neck.

She died and he tried to slit his throat with a table knife. He pleaded guilty to murder and was sentenced to death. Apparently, he was a lovely man when he was sober and his kids visited him the day before the hanging when he asked for their forgiveness and they cuddled and cried a lot. For further Leeds based excitement of a public hanging nature see **Farnley Wood Plot**.

Exhibit A (2007) is a film which was supported by *Screen Yorkshire* and mainly shot in Bramhope over 18 days – that's quick. It was Best UK Feature winner at the Raindance Film Festival and nominated three times at the British Independent Film Awards and the last film of stunt supremo **Roy Alon**.

EX magazine. There was only one issue of **EX** magazine (see back cover, produced in September 1991. It was **the first Lads' Mag**, featuring the staple of football, semi naked women and men's 'issues' dealt with in a playful, tongue in cheek manner. The mag was the brain child of visionary entrepreneur **Dave Benson,** who died of cancer in the late 1990s (98/99). It only managed one issue due to financing, marketing and distribution problems coupled with Dave's ill health. Having said that, the first issue was always planned as a 'proof of concept' for possible advertisers and contributors, although it was distributed nationwide through W.H. Smiths. I have a memory of seeing/hearing **James Brown** in the media citing **EX Magazine** as an 'influence' around the time of the launch of *Loaded* although it's a long time ago and my memory isn't all that.

F

Fad Gadget (1956–2002), was in the vanguard of late '70s/early '80s electronic/industrial music and club scene (also including bands like Cabaret Voltaire, The Normal, The Human League etc) which spawned the **New Romantics** and also influenced techno/dance bands of the '90s. He was the first act signed by Daniel Miller (The Normal/ Silicon Teens) of Mute Records and in 1980 was supported by Depeche Mode. As a youth he was obsessed by Bolan, Bowie, Lou Reed and Iggy Pop.

He exemplifies something I was trying to explain in *Coming Out as A Bowie Fan* about how the immediate roots/precursor to the fluffy New Romantics were much darker than the re-packaged London version. His lyrics were dark, detached but humorous and concentrated on the seedier and sinister aspect of life. I thought they were interesting and expansive. His live gigs were dynamic, chaotic affairs, he'd be confrontational with and try to goad the audience, regularly diving off the stage into them and being carried overhead. He'd cover himself in tar and feathers and was infamous for plastering his naked body in shaving cream. He'd incorporate electric drills, electric razors, bottles etc. into his recordings and well as 'using' them at gigs.

'At one concert, I swung the mike around my neck and it came round and smashed me in the face. It cut my nose open and blackened both my eyes. I have lacerated my back with glass and every joint in my knuckles and toes have been grazed so when I came home with both my legs in plaster, I started to sort out why I was doing it. The trouble is I get so involved on stage, there's so much adrenaline flowing, that I don't feel pain. I think in the end, it all comes down to entertainment. Whether you have something to say or not, people want to be impressed and excited.'

Wiki lists his 'origin' as Leeds. The official and fan sites make no reference to his birthplace or where he grew up. Other (London) media say that he was born in the East End but he certainly studied for a degree in Fine Arts at **Leeds Polytechnic**, becoming interested in performance art and 'fiddling around with tape recorders'. He left for London in 1978/9 and ***Back to Nature*** was certainly played at **The Adelphi** Bowie /Roxy night in '79 - I seem to remember it being played before it was released but I could be wrong. Frank Tovey died on the 3rd of April, 2002 and I'd like to thank him for making life a bit more colourful.

Sir Peter Fairbairn (1799–1861) was an engineer who improved the woollen and flax spinning machinery. He is commemorated in a statue on Woodhouse Square, near the University and was Mayor of Leeds in 1857 and 1858. The bronze statue, costing £1,000, was erected in 1868. Queen Victoria stayed at his house (Woodsley House, later Fairbairn House, in Clarendon Road) when she came to open Leeds Town Hall in September 1858 and knighted Peter there. He is buried at **Adel Church**.

Pablo Fanque (1796–1871) was born **William Darby** in Norwich and was the first black circus proprietor in Britain. A famous showman, he's remembered today through the lyrics of the Beatles song *Being for the Benefit of Mr. Kite*! John Lennon was inspired by an antique circus poster that he'd bought, in which the Henderson family is described as 'late of Pablo Fanque's fair.' William (Pablo Fanque) is buried in Woodhouse Cemetery, Leeds, next to his first wife

Pablo Fanque

Susannah Darby who died in 1848 when a gallery collapsed at the circus in Lands Lane, Leeds, after 6,000 people had turned up to see the show.

Premier Farnell plc is a global electronics multinational which was founded in Leeds by **Alan Farnell** and **Arthur Woffenden** in 1939 under the name of *A.C. Farnell Limited* and I usually drive past their site in Armley twice a day. It used to be a significant manufacturer of electronic lab and bench equipment.

Farnley Hall. See **J. M. W. Turner**.

The Farnley Wood Plot was a 1663 plot to re-take Leeds from the Royalists soon after the end of the English Civil War and the English Restoration and was hatched by people from Farnley, Gildersome, Morley and Leeds. The plot was never followed through as not enough turned up and many didn't want the battle, so they disbanded and returned home. At least they hadn't followed through with it, at least it was still their little secret. Oops, one of the central figures of the plot had been overruled by another and turned into the King's spy, reporting their activities over a period of time. 26 were arrested and taken to York assizes and held in Clifford's Tower. But the Tower wasn't strong enough for Leeds lads fighting for their rights and three valiantly escaped and battled their way back to Leeds. To Leeds? Where they had hatched their plot and had been arrested? Der-er-er, go the other way, you fools! Amazingly they were re-arrested, taken to Chapeltown Moor, hanged, drawn and quartered (by a local joiner called Peter Mason) in front of one of the largest crowds ever seen in the city. Their heads were rammed onto the railing of **Moot Hall** and stayed there for 13 years until they were blown off in a gale.

Helen Fielding was born (1958) and raised in Morley in and is best known for the creation of **Bridget Jones** a character which spawned a couple of moderately successful films – although the first one only grossed $281,929,795 worldwide, a profit of a mere $256, 929,795....so, not all that, not to worry, if she keeps going she may have a breakthrough. Her two Jones based novels *Bridget Jones's Diary* and *Bridget Jones: The Edge of Reason*, have sold over 15 million copies in 40 countries. The novels came about as an anonymous column in *The Independent* during 1995 hit a chord with the public and *Bridget Jones's Diary* was the first 'Chick Lit' hit in the world opening up a rather large genre.

   She was part of the Oxford revue (1978 Edinburgh Festival) and is mates with a group of comic performers and writers including Richard Curtis and Rowan Atkinson, with Richard working with her on the screenplays for both the Bridget films. She first worked as a researcher and then Production Manager for the BBC and in 1985 produced the live satellite broadcast from a refugee camp in Eastern Sudan which was part of the launch of **Comic Relief**. The first Jones novel won the 1998 British Book of the Year and she was nominated in 2002 by BAFTA and the Writers Guild of America for Best Screenplay, winning the same Evening Standard award.

The Leeds Fight happened in 1753 and its cause was tolls charged to use the roads. The roads were pretty much impassable by anything more than a horse so central government appointed local turnpike trusts to construct and maintain specific lengths of road, a costly process carried out through local taxes and payments at turnpikes. These charges led to wide scale rioting with armed gangs intent on burning down toll-houses and smashing the gates. The flashpoint occurred at Harewood Bridge with Lord Harewood raising 300 men who battled it out with rioters trying to wreck the new turnpike. The tension continued as a man was arrested for refusing to pay a toll in Beeston, more riots followed with three men held at the King's Arms inn where the authorities met and hung out, protected by troops. Another angry gang went on the rampage, attacking the King's Arms with the intention of freeing the men. The soldiers couldn't hold them and finally opened fire on the men, women and children, killing three and wounding 22.

Fish'n'chips originated at **The Oldest Fish and Chip in the World** in Yeadon although, obviously, they didn't. I've read a bit about it and I don't think anyone can say with any authority where fish and chips originated or where the first shop was, although wiki say that in '1860, the first fish and chip shop was opened in London by Jewish proprietor Joseph Malin' and I like the fact that the battered fish are 'fish fried in the Jewish fashion.' There are claims from a shop opened in Mossley near Oldham in 1863 but I'm not sure I trust the info, it looks like they started selling fish and chips in the market in 1863 and opened the shop later with a sign in the window saying 'Chip Potato Restaurant. Oldest Established in the World' and that's interesting as the two things, shops selling fish (deep fried) and those selling chips developed separately. Anyway the National Federation of Fish Friers Limited, based on Greenwood Mount in Leeds, spent three years researching it and in 1968 gave the first fish and chip shop mantle to Marlin's of Bow, sometime between 1860 and 1865. The shop on The Steep in Yeadon, dating back to the 1870s, doesn't claim to be the first but the *oldest* chippy in the world and that may be true. It looks like the one in Mossley is no longer open and almost certainly not on its original site and during the 1960s Marlin's of Bow was bought by Arthur Treacher's Inc and I can't find a record of the business still running......although it may still be trading but if it is, is it still on the original site? Do we need to ask what we mean by a fish and chips shop? Does the size/cut of chip matter, or would sliced potatoes qualify? Does the fish have to battered or simply fried? Have you lost the will to live? Have I mentioned that I've got roots in a chip shop?

Anyway Leeds certainly has the best chippys in the world, no doubt. Obviously that's simply a very ignorant opinion and based on nothing at all, not a thing, but we traditionally use beef dripping as opposed to the effeminate veggie oil preferred in Lancashire and in Leeds you get none of that nasty, slimy looking skin that's simply not right, we're way too sophisticated for that, and haddock is the preferred fish. Anyway in a 2009 survey 93% of northerners said the food at their local chippy was tastier than anything they had sampled down south and one in three southerners agreed – that'll be all the southerners who've tasted them then. Nationwide, six out of ten respondents said they thought chips in the north superior.

The rise of fish'n'chips happened during the **Second Industrial Revolution**/the **Technological Revolution** and coincided with the introduction of steam trawlers (1870s & 80s) and icing equipment greatly increasing range and yield while reducing costs. British industry was in part fuelled by fish'n'chips. During the early part of the 20th Century food was expensive, the average wage was such that a portion of fish and chips with mushy peas at around 5/6d was affordable for the working class, who in 1914 would spend around 60% of their income on food. It would also add vital proteins and vitamins to the regular diet built around potatoes, sometimes bacon, bread, dripping, tea and condensed milk (my Dad used to try to get me to eat bread and dripping) yet at the time (early C20[th]) there were official pieces of literature falsely claiming and informing people that the meal was unhealthy. If you're interested dig out John Walton's *Fish and Chips and the British Working Classes 1870-1940* (Leicester University Press, 1994).

I also remember in the 1990s people started wittering about how unhealthy fish'n'chips were but they had to bow to reality and drop their prejudice. The frying is done at such high temperatures that it seals the food quickly and doesn't absorb a lot of fat, also the chips are quite chunky, reducing the surface area per weight, so although the fat content is very high in the thin fast-food, American chips, it's not in our chippy chips. A portion of chip shop chips contains less fat than a prawn mayonnaise sandwich (I'm proud of myself for resisting saying, 'so popular at Old Trafford') and can provide you with a third of your daily recommended Vitamin C. An average portion of fish'n'chips represents just 30% of a female's recommended calorie intake and 23% of a male's, as with everything it's about doing it in moderation. See **Harry Ramsden's**.

Here are some fish'n'chips facts:

Fish'n'chips was the only take-away food not rationed during WWII, they even had mobile frying vans taking portions out to evacuees.

A portion of fish'n'chips has substantially less fat and calories than take-away pizza, an average Chinese (although it depends what you have), burger and medium 'fries' and almost half that of a Doner Kebab.

There are currently around 10,000 fish and chip shops across Britain; fourteen for every McDonalds. (National Institute of Fish Fryers) The peak number was in 1927 at around 35,000 chippys.

On a Friday in the UK, 20% of meals purchased outside the home are from a fish and chip shop (www.seafish.org). The historical background to the Friday night rush is linked to Catholics eating fish instead of meat on Fridays which seems to have also been widely adopted by non-Catholics.

Leeds has the best fish'n'chips in the world. Actually, that's an opinion not a fact and I bet people from Grimsby or Hull or Cas might not agree but what is true is that, per head, Yorkshire folk eat more fish'n'chips than people from any other part of the country.

Last year around 255 million fish and chip shop meals (featuring fish) were sold throughout Britain, making them the nation's favourite hot take-away and beating curries by well over 2 to 1. (www.seafish.org & www.woodys-chippies.co.uk)

Nationally, fish and chip shops' takings are around £1.2 billion a year and chippys sell roughly 25% of all the white fish consumed in the United Kingdom, and 10% of all potatoes.

Fish and chips are apparently popular at celebrity weddings with Steven Gerrard, John Terry, Wayne Rooney (might explain the 2010 World Cup performances) and Myleene Klass being amongst those rumoured to have served them on their big day.

50% of us eat fish and chips once a month, more than one in six of us can't resist going to the fish and chip shop at least once a week and nearly 70% eat our fish and chips at home.

Flat Caps, that clichéd but fair symbol of northerness, were last mass produced in Britain by **JW Myers** of Holbeck but the world's biggest cap maker's factory was closed in 2000 by the parent company Kangol and production switched to the city of Panyu in China. The company's heyday was in the 1920s and they exported to 22 countries but despite them growing in popularity since the 1980s with their adoption by DJs, rappers and sports people, the factory closed after 111 years of production. A daft flat cap fact is that a 1571 Act of Parliament ordered that on Sundays and holidays, all males over six years of age, except for 'the nobility and persons of degree' obviously, were to wear caps or face a fine of 3/4d per day and the Bill was not repealed until 1597. And did you know that Featherstone Rovers (RL team) supporters are known as 'The Flat Cappers', due to the fact that every supporter in years gone by used to attend matches in a flat cap? Oh, you did, I'd best shut up then.

Jan Fletcher OBE is a high-roller, mover, shaker Leeds business woman. She was central in setting up Marketing Leeds, of which she later became Chairman with its 'Leeds. Live it. Love it' tag. She's built up and sold on various businesses and her current vehicle, Montpellier Estates has submitted regeneration plans for a near 10 acre development of a site at the southern entrance to Leeds City Centre called City One.

The lack of **folic acid** and its link to **spina bifida** and other serious conditions in babies was noted by **Richard W Smithells.**

Isabella Ford

Isabella Ford (1855–1924). A'swear down, no lie, I'm in tears here. Sad that this will be brief, you could write a book on this woman. No worries, June Hannam's interest in 'the relationship between feminist and socialist politics' meant that she did and snappily called it *Isabella Ford, 1855-1924* (Blackwell, 1989), so it'd probably be a bit of a waste for me to do so and it's possible that June may have done a better job of it. Isabella's family were absolutely minted and her parents were involved in radical, liberal politics although later in life Isabella switched to the Labour Party but we're getting ahead of ourselves. Isabella was born in Headingley but spent most of her life living at Adel Grange and grew up in this atmosphere of radical liberal politics, women's rights, prison reform and humanitarian causes. At the age of 12, after getting to know girls working in the mills, she took an oath with her friend that they would, 'improve the state of the world.'

Here's a list of **some** of the ways she tried to do that, which was often campaigning to improve the pay and conditions of working women, initially in Leeds' textile industry. In 1883 (the year of its formation) she joined the Fabian Society which aimed to 'reconstruct society in accordance with the highest moral possibilities through political means'; in 1885 she helped to form a Machinists' Society for tailoresses in Leeds; in 1889 she founded the Leeds Tailoresses' Union and became its president, in 1890 she helped form the Leeds Women's Suffrage Society and was involved in establishing a Leeds branch of the Independent Labour Party during 1893 – the Leeds Independent Labour Party formed the year before the national party. She was later elected to the national executive committee of the ILP and the National Union of Suffrage Societies. She also became a delegate at the conference of the Labour Representation Committee (which became the Labour Party) and in 1903 she became the first woman to deliver a speech at such a conference. She worked tirelessly to convince men that women's rights were linked to theirs.

Her giving the first ever speech by a woman at the Labour Party conference did not happen by chance, she was brought up to think about and debate socio-political issues from an early age – the children were even encouraged to treat the servants with 'esteem, equality and friendship'. Her radical parents ensured that her education mirrored that of her brother's, including the unladylike subjects of science and history. She was a nationally renowned campaigner for labour rights and women's suffrage and forged international links; she would march, stand side by side with the workers and encourage them to get political and active and was a member of the Leeds Juvenile Advisory Committee. She organised and played at a series of free classical concerts for workers, was on the committee of the **Leeds Art Club**, wrote articles for the press, novels steeped in social realism – *Miss Blake of Monkshalton* (1890), *On the Threshold* (1895), *Mr Elliott* (1901) – as well as socio-political books and booklets including *Industrial Women* (1900), *Women's Wages* (1893), *Women and Socialism* (1904) and was mates with writers such as George Bernard Shaw, WB Yeats, Edward Carpenter and Walt Whitman.

In March 1918, women over the age of 30 were granted the vote and Isabella commented, 'It is indeed wonderful when one wakes up in the morning to remember that now, at last, one is considered to be a real, complete human being! After thirty years of endeavour to make men understand they were only half the world…' Anyway never mind all that political struggle and equality stuff, she was apparently top totty as well.

As a slight aside, over 100 years after Isabella's fire for the rights of female mill workers was ignited a *Play for Today* was broadcast on BBC1 entitled **Leeds United** (1974, Season 5, Episode 1) following the true story of a strike in 1970 by female textile factory workers in Leeds who wanted to be paid the same as their male colleagues.

John Fowler (1826–1864) was an inventor and pioneer in the mechanisation of agriculture. Based in Leeds he is credited with the invention of steam-driven ploughing engines and drainage ploughs and (with other people) filed 32 patents for ploughs and ploughing apparatus, reaping machines, seed drills, slide valves, traction engines, the laying of electric telegraph cables, and the making of bricks and tiles. John had been in Ireland during the potato famine which killed approximately one million people and had a huge affect on him. Much of the Irish land was unusable due to poor drainage (which also encouraged the potato blight) and he returned to England to invent the steam-driven drainage plough. He applied this technology to normal ploughing and by 1858 40 sets of the plough were in use and by 1861 this figure had risen to 100. They were sold all over the world and helped bring uncultivated land back into production.

He was involved with various companies most notably **John Fowler and Company** in Hunslet who went on to produce traction engines, steam rollers, railway equipment, concrete mixers and equipment for the construction industry and by 1887 were producing electric generating equipment. The company went from strength to strength and during World War II produced tanks, armoured fighting vehicles, diesel locomotives, generating sets and petrol engines. I think it's sometimes easy to overlook the work of people like John. It's not 'sexy', but he revolutionised agriculture and helped feed the people of the second Industrial Revolution and his method of ploughing continued to be used well into the twentieth century.

Leigh Francis (aka Avid Merrion and Keith Lemon) is a comic genius. My kids used to tell me to watch the smash hit *Bo' Selecta!* (three series between 2002 and 2004) as it was 'the funniest thing on telly'. Unfortunately I didn't, there must have been something on the other side. I've since watched quite a lot, on YouTube and they were right. He's the master of awkward and 'inappropriate' comedy and is extremely 'Leeds'. There's been spin-off series such as *A Bear's Tail, Bo! In The USA, Keith Lemon's Very Brilliant World Tour* and *Celebrity Juice* and the one off 'tribute' *Cha'mone Mo Fo Selecta - Michael Jackson Special 2009*. He was born and raised in Farnley and studied at Leeds College of Art. His career is well documented but if you don't know his stuff, get onto YouTube and give yourself a treat.

Frankenstein. The nature of Mary's tragic 'beast' was based on......see **David Hartley**

Freight (2010) A film in which a Russian gang operating in Leeds with no respect for the laws of England, traffic Eastern Europeans in containers then enslave them; the women to sex, the men to illegal fights. They cross local businessman Gabe Taylor and a war escalates, but when his daughter is taken to be sold into the sex trade, Gabe fights back. Written and directed by **Stuart St. Paul** who for a number of years has been stuntman and stunt co-ordinator on **Emmerdale**.

FU is the prefix attached to all Leeds planning applications and which has had almost humorous consequences. The first was a planned signal raised in naval flags (semaphore) at the end of the life of the much pilloried **Quarry Hill Flats**; a phrase derived from the planning application code being narrowly beaten by the banal 'goodbye world' – sometimes you have to have the courage of your convictions and bu...fu....bugg....forget the consequences. The second was an informal group formed to promote Leeds almost going under the banner of the FU club. They decided against it which may have been sensible considering their aims.

Although I can't find a start date for **CE Fulford's** they were manufacturing patent medicines from Greek Street from around 1900. They started developing their own products soon after and first made **Pep Pastilles** (I'd guess at some kind of cocaine or caffeine based pick-me-up), they also made **Vitapoint** hair conditioner which is still produced today, **Zam-Buk** herbal balm and **Bile Beans**, mmm, sounds lovely. Zam-Buk, which C.E. Fulford and his business partner developed, was advertised in 1907 as 'The English Remedy' or 'The Great British Cure'. Zam-Buk, 'Of all Chemists and Drug Stores or the Zam-Buk Laboratories, Leeds' was for the treatment of minor wounds, burns, scalds, chapped hands, insect bites, itching, muscular pains, chilblains and bruising. It was a big seller and 'available on four continents' and according to online reports (where people swear by it) Fulford's set up 'labs' for its production in several countries, including Australia. In South Africa it has apparently remained popular for over a century and has become a part of the South African way of life. Zam-Buk was used by ambulance-men and first aiders at rugby league matches on injured players from the 1900s. In Australia and New Zealand the term was soon being used to refer to the ambulance-men and first aiders themselves.

Around 1958 Fulford's relocated to Blyth in Northumbria and it looks like the production of Zam-Buk ceased at some point but here's an interesting twist. A mother and daughter combo bought an 'old druggists shop in Yorkshire' (Howarth) renovated it to its original state and decided to set up **Rose & Co**. They stocked the shop with 'preparations based on traditional recipes using natural, old-apothecary ingredients', including a **Zam-Buk** range using the original formula and packaging. They also have another shop in the Victoria Quarter and supply 'Harvey Nichols, Harvey Nichols Hong Kong, John Lewis and selected fine stores.' In't that lovely? So why not pop into the Rose & Co shop and get yourself a genuine, old Leeds cure.

Early **Fulling Mills** used heavy wooden hammers to carry out fulling, cleansing cloth (particularly wool) to remove lanolin (natural oil), dirt, skin and impurities, and make it thicker. It's claimed (*The Knights Templar in Yorkshire*) that the first one was at **Temple Newsam**, which was noted in the Knights Templar's paper work and had been there for some time before it was catalogued (1185). Although other sources point to the 9th/10th century Islamic world.

Fulneck School/Moravian settlement, in Pudsey, was established in 1744 and named after the Moravian town of Fulnek. As the architecture attests, the settlers had travelled from the European state that borders Poland, Austria and Slovakia and which is in the north east of the current Czech Republic. Many of the buildings in the village are listed with the chapel building being Grade I. The school was established in 1753 and ex-pupils include hymn writer, poet, editor and humanitarian James Montgomery, Diana Rigg and Herbert Henry Asquith. Cricketer Len Hutton, architect Benjamin Latrobe, who helped design the United States Capitol and White House, and his musician/composer brother Christian were born in the village.

The Futurama Festivals were music festivals held at Leeds **Queens Hall** organized by **John Keean**. In 1981 I'm totally guessing that some skullduggerry was afoot when the copycat Daze of Future Past was staged at the venue without John's involvement and John moved Futurama to Stafford Bingley Hall and then Deeside Leisure centre the following year. John returned to the Queens Hall with Futurama 5 in 1983 when there also seems to have been a 'shadow' festival at Deinze in Belgium. Here's what Leeds' Dave Simpson, currently a music critic at The Guardian, said about the first, 'I went to Futurama liking Sham 69. I came out rejecting everything I knew, having realised that music could be about power, passion, psychology, even the genuinely futuristic, and be far more than "entertainment". That principle colours my thoughts on music to this day. If I hadn't gone, it's almost certain that I wouldn't now be writing about music for a living, never mind still experiencing the unique thrill of watching bands.'

None of the following line-ups are complete and it's possible the occasional band may have pulled out at the last minute.

Futurama One Festival, 'The World's First Science Fiction Music Festival' 1979, Queen's Hall.

Saturday 8th September: Public Image Ltd/Punishment of Luxury, Joy Division, Cabaret Voltaire, The Invaders, Orchestral Manoeuvres in the Dark, PragVEC, A Certain Ratio, Spizz Energi, The Edge, Expelaires, The Tunes, Stranger Than Fiction, The Void, Vincent Units, Paraad, Sonny Hayes Magic Fantasy, Tymon Dogg

Sunday 9th September: Hawkwind, The Only Ones, The Fall, Scritti Politti, The Monochrome Set, The Teardrop Explodes, Echo & the Bunnymen, Teenage Werewolves, Manicured Noise, Agony Column, Twist, E2R, Nightmares In Wax, Screens, Revelation Reggae, Robert Calvert, Nik Turner's Inner City Unit, Roger Ruskin Spear and his Kinetic Wardrobe

Futurama Two Festival 13th & 14th September 1980. Futurama Two was filmed in its entirety by the BBC, but they didn't air the whole show. They aired four shows with excerpts from the two days.

Saturday 13th September Blah Blah Blah, Wasted Youth, U2, Echo & the Bunnymen, Siouxsie & the Banshees

Sunday 14th September: Household Name, Naked Lunch, Artery, Boots for Dancing, Vice Versa, Flowers, Frantic Elevators, Not Sensibles, Brian Brain, Classix Nouveaux, Blurt, Gary Glitter

Also playing over the two days were: Acrobats Of Desire, Robert Fripp and the League Of Gentlemen, Young Marble Giants, ABC (Vice-Versa), Hazel O'Connor's Megahype, The Flowers, Boots For Dancing, Music For Pleasure, The Mirror Boys, Guy Jackson, Athletico Spizz 80, Eaten Alive By Insects, Soft Boys, Altered Images, Tribesman, Blurt, The Danse Society, Clock DVA, 4 be 2's

Daze of Future Past, 1981, Queen's Hall.

Saturday 26th Sept: Echo & the Bunnymen, The Cramps, Bauhaus, The Thompson Twins, Theatre Of Hate, Wall of Voodoo, X, Altered Images, The Weathermen

Sunday 27th of Sept: Japan, Killing Joke, Tom Verlaine, The Professionals, The Meteors, Funkapolitan, O.K. Jive, Miles Over Matter, Alternative T.V.

Futurama Five Festival, 1983, Queen's Hall.

Saturday 17th Sept: Bay City Rollers, Howard Devoto, Comsat Angels, John Cooper Clarke, The Smiths, Clock DVA, Gina X, Silent Running, The Chameleons, Danielle Dax, The Chevalier Bros, Red Lorry Yellow Lorry, A Popular History of Signs, Red Guitars, Sex Beat, Edward's Voice, Masque of Bizarro, Real Foo Foo, MRA, Colenso Parade, The Lost Boys, Curia Veritas

Sunday 18th of Sept: Killing Joke, Death Cult, The Armoury Show, Billy Bragg, New Model Army, The Mekons, Beast, The 3 Johns, Flesh For Lulu, Play Dead, Poison Girls, Ground Zero, Box, Action Pact, Joolz, Bone Orchard, Jayne County, Under Two Flags, Holy Toy, Lavolta Lakota, Pleasure and the Beast, Pink Peg Slax, Janine Andrews, Ekome African Drummers, Ligotage, Zero Slingsby, Mark Miwurdz

*Thanks to Dave Simpson for helping me fathom this out.

G

William Gascoigne (1612–1644) was one of the founding fathers of British research astronomy and intellectual heir of Galileo and Kepler whose work he improved upon. It appears that he died in his early thirties (although earlier accounts make his life much shorter) or who knows what else he would have achieved. His formal education was limited but he was an astronomer, inventor, mathematician and designer/maker of scientific instruments from **Middleton** who invented **the micrometer** (1641), **telescopic sextant**, and the **telescopic sight.**

The relatively newly invented telescope was hugely improved and astronomy leaped forward with Gascoigne's **micrometer** which allowed angular distances to be accurately measured and was central to astronomical measurement up until the twentieth century. His adding of this to a sextant allowed the measurement of the distance between astronomical bodies. His introduction of **crosshairs** allowed the telescope to be pointed even more accurately and the fact that they were moveable across the lens gave unprecedented accuracy to the measurement of the size of astronomical bodies – using the pitch of the screw and the focal length of the lens. He was the first man to be able to accurately calculate the size of planets and the distance between them.

His invention of the **crosshairs (telescopic sight)** happened by pure chance. He was recreating one of Kepler's optical set-ups when a thread of spider's web became caught between the two lenses. By chance, it fell precisely at the combined optical focal points of the two lenses and Gascoigne,

Gascoigne's Micrometer as drawn by Robert Hooke for the Royal Society, 1667.

seeing the web sharp and clear through the lenses (as well as the object being looked at) realised that the accuracy of the telescope was greatly increased by the use of the web as a guide. He increased the accuracy even further by introducing the other line of the cross meaning that the focal point could be centred on an object thus creating the **telescopic sight**.

He was one of "nos Keplari" a group of astronomers in the north of England who followed the astronomy of Johannes Kepler which included Jeremiah Horrocks and William Crabtree. Crabtree and Horrocks were amazed by and giddy with anticipation at Gascoigne's inventions. Unfortunately Horrocks never got to use them. This hugely influential and impressive trio compiled, for themselves and probably intended for future publication, a series of ground breaking papers which they entitled *De re Astronomica*, which were passed onto the Townleys family, who chronicled much of their work and then to William Derham who produced the earliest, reasonably accurate, estimate of the speed of sound.

Many of Gascoigne's papers and correspondence were lost during the English Civil War and then the Great Fire of London, but most of what is known to remain is kept in the Bodleian Library at the University of Oxford. John Flamsteed (the first **Astronomer Royal**) saw Horrocks, Crabtree and Gascoigne as the founding fathers of British research astronomy.

Gascoigne fought for King Charles I (see **Red Hall**) against the Parliamentarians and died in the Battle of Marston Moor. At the time of his death he had at his father's residence, New Hall, Middleton, 'a whole barn full of instruments,' constructed by him, to carry out ideas which, unfortunately, died with him. Accepting the mid-nineteenth century correction to Gascoigne's age at the time of his death, (raising it from early 20s to around 31/2 years old – unlike Galileo and Kepler, who lived until around 60 and 77 respectively) this still early death leaves me wondering what the barn full of instruments were designed for, what else he would have discovered and invented and how else he would have changed our knowledge of the world and universe and our interaction with it.

Paul Gately, PhD, is Carnegie Professor of Exercise and Obesity and Technical Director of Carnegie Weight Management at Leeds Metropolitan University. He's been in Leeds since 1992 and graduated from Leeds Metropolitan University with a Bachelors degree in sports science. He runs the Carnegie International Camp to help obese children (featured in a TV documentary) and community-based weight loss club programmes throughout Britain. Amongst his other TV work was the ITV documentary *Too Fat to Toddle* (TV 2008), *The Duchess in Hull* featuring Sarah Ferguson (Duchess of York) and he is a regular contributor on national and local radio.

His main research interest is childhood obesity treatment strategies and the course that he runs at Leeds Metropolitan University is adapted from an American residential weight loss model and its treatment of overweight and obese children. He's co-authored three books, has over 100 scientific publications and speaks at international conferences on a regular basis. Paul is a consultant to government agencies, health organisations and corporations throughout the UK and internationally and has contributed to the International Obesity Task Force/World Health Organisation's report on childhood obesity.

Mary Gawthorpe (1881–1973) was a right'un, a courageous, proud, determined, feisty suffragette, socialist, trade unionist and editor, described by Rebecca West (top author) as 'a merry militant saint'. She was born in Leeds into a poor family but her mother was determined that she should finish her education. Being poor they could not afford for Mary to go to college so she worked during the day, studied at night (see **Night-school**) and weekends and qualified as a schoolteacher.

After attending meetings of the Independent Labour Party (becoming the vice-president of the Leeds branch in 1906) and converting to socialism, she became active in the **Women's Labour League** earning a reputation as a powerful public speaker. Her first public speach occured at the Leeds Art Club, I'm guessing encouraged by Isabella Ford, and Leeds Suffragette events often attracted crowds of 100,000. She also became a leading light in the Leeds branch of the **National Union of Teachers**. Along with Isabella Ford, and Ethel Annakin she formed a Leeds branch of the **National Union of Women's Suffrage Societies** and was nominated by Isabella to the executive committee. She organised all sorts of political organisation and movements which all sounds very nice doesn't it? The reality was that it was a brutal world for active suffragettes. Her convictions and courage led her into dangerous situations and she was badly beaten, receiving serious internal injuries for heckling Winston Churchill in 1909. Mary was also violently assaulted whilst demonstrating at the polling booths – obviously the men didn't get charged. She travelled Britain and Ireland speaking for women's rights and was apparently 'a splendid speaker, full of humour, brilliant and lucid' with a 'big fog-and-frost' voice. She was also imprisoned several times, went on hunger strikes and suffered force-feeding (see **Lilian Ida Lenton**) which, in conjunction with all the beatings, badly damaged her health and in 1912 she retired from the more militant activities. The same year she also gave up her role as co-editor of the radical periodical *The Freewoman: A Weekly Feminist Review* which contained frank discussions of sexuality, morality, and marriage and, amongst other things, defended homosexuality, advocated free love and encouraged women to remain unmarried. She emigrated to the US in 1916 and carried on her work to change the world.

Although she helped promote it in the US, she was apparently concerned that Sylvia Pankhurst's book *The Suffragette Movement: An Intimate Account of Persons and Ideals* down played her own role. In 1962 she published a memoir of her active years called *Up Hill to Holloway* (Traversity Press, 1962)

Shockingly, she doesn't seem to be in A Historical Dictionary of British Women (Routledge, London, 2003) but Elizabeth Crawford's *The women's suffrage movement: a reference guide, 1866*-1928 (Routledge, London, 2001) has a good section on her and the Spartacus Educational website is an excellent resource for the suffragettes and related issues. See **Suffragettes**, **Isabella Ford**, and **Lilian Ida Lenton**.

Glassflake Ltd, (based at Stafford Street, LS10) is Europe's largest producer of microscopic flaked glass particles, which are used for a variety of applications from paints and plastics/polymers to anti-corrosion coatings and power stations. Their technological edge originated in a 1981 R&D project, resulting in them developing thinner flakes with improved performance. This is the sort of techy stuff that although you can get your head around it is difficult to paraphrase so I'll just say that their product is very hard to pirate and they are expanding into the Chinese market and then leave you with a quote from their website. 'Glassflake Limited is responsible for the development of a patented process for manufacturing high specification glass flakes. This process facilitates the production of high quality product with a very low deviation on flake thickness. In comparison with other glass flake products on the market having a large deviation in thickness not suitable for certain applications, this consistency results in further significant improvements in applications.'

I've read that the longest running TV music show is *The Good Old Days* which was transmitted from **Leeds City Varieties** from 1953 to 1983. Now I'd like it to be true but feel that the **Eurovision Song Contest** may be a music show and that it's possible that1959 to present is more than 30 years. Anyway, *The Good Old Days* was developed and produced by Leeds lad Barney Colehan and was a show which recreated the look and atmosphere of the Victorian–Edwardian music hall – Leeds had seven music halls in the Victorian era. The entire audience dressed up in old fashions to watch songs and sketches from that era performed in the style of the original artistes. In order to recreate an authentic Victorian–Edwardian music hall feel audience participation was very important. This audience participation followed a set format and was not as 'spontaneous' as it would have been back in the day. It was led by **Leonard Sachs** as compere and the Chairman of Leeds City Varieties using as much alliteration and as many unusual, big words as he could. The audience would respond with amazed 'Oohs' and 'Ahhs' at his mastery of the English language. See **Barney Colehan**.

Goth is the only youth culture and musical genre that I know of as attributed to Leeds – although Wiki doesn't appear to agree. From, at least, the early 1980s the London music press constantly associated the movement with Leeds, usually with a bit of a sneer, and often citing the Phono (Le Phonographique) as its spiritual home. This fact seems to have disappeared from much of the known world, although if you trawl the sites of old blokes who were there in the first place you'll find quotes like 'the legendary **Phono** in **Leeds**, reputed to be the country's oldest goth club'. I don't know when the term was first used but Wiki has The Batcave club in London as 'the birthplace' of Goth in 1982, which I think is utter nonsense but how **do** you pin down a youth culture that evolved over a period of time? Goth emerged out of punk and the early established bands associated with it include The Damned, Siouxsie and the Banshees, The Cure, Bauhaus and The Cramps. I think Bauhaus were the ultimate, pure goth band and in 1979 you could certainly see young folk with massive spiky hair, dark eye make-up, 'punky' leather clothing and metal work swaggering around the dance floor to *Bela Lugosi's Dead* at Leeds' venues like The Precinct. I'd argue that its roots were in a coming together of punks and Bowie fans (people were often both) but that's just opinion based on being there. I'd also argue that it was more of a West Yorkshire movement than simply a Leeds movement and it was one of the few times when the region was extremely productive in terms of musical success. West Yorkshire bands associated with the movement is a difficult one but I'd go for Sisters Of Mercy, The Southern Death Cult (The Cult), Red Lorry Yellow Lorry, Ghost Dance, The Rose of Avalanche, Salvation, The Mission, The March Violets, New Model Army and The Skeletal Family.

During one of his live televised theatre shows Vic Reeves in a joke said something akin to, 'one of those Leeds goth bands like The Mission or Hang the Dance', proof enough for me that Goth was a Leeds youth movement....Vic knew y'know.

Here's a poem by Leeds poet **Ian Duhig** from *Pandorama* (Picador, Nov 2010) about the modern day goths...entitled *goths*:

I love them. They bring a little antilife and uncolour
To the Corn Exchange on city centre shopping days,
as if they had all just crawled out of that Ringu well,
so many Sadokas dripping tarnished silver jewellery
onto the undead fashions they dig up at flea markets.
They are the black that is always the new black.
Their perfume lingers, freshly-turned-grave sweet

Black sheep, they pilgrage twive a year to Whitby,
Through our landscape of dissolved monastery and pit,
Toasting themselves in cider'n'blackcurrant, vegan blood.

They dance macabre at gigs like Dracula Spectacula.
The next morning, lovebitten and wincing in the sunlight,
They take photos of each other, hoping they won't develop.

Benjamin Gott (1762–1840) became a Leeds textile giant and by the time of his death was a millionaire, which in 1840 was serious cash. In 1792 he established the Park Mills on a 16 acre site at Bean Ing (where the current Ee Po building is) which Gilleghan claims as 'the first woollen mill in the world' – it was demolished during the 1960s. He rebuilt Armley Mills, had a mill in Burley and across the three sites was running 133 looms becoming one of Europe's largest employers and changing the means of manufacturing by introducing steam power and power looms into his mills.

He became Mayor of Leeds in 1799, collected fine art (some of which is held at Leeds Art Gallery and the central library's) and played a big part in the founding of the Leeds Philosophical & Literary Society in 1819. He bought Gott's Park, including Armley House (built in 1781 for Thomas Woorick) which he redeveloped in 1816 – employing Humphrey Rempton – as Armley or Gott's Mansion, now known as Gott's Park Mansion and used as the club house for the golf course. The estate also included Gott's/Armley Park and the area of the golf course which LCC later acquired in 1928. Benjamin also established almshouses in Armley and is buried at St Bartholomew's, Armley Parish Church where there is a statue of him from 1841 by Joseph Gott, a Rome-based sculptor from Calverley who enjoyed Benjamin's patronage. See **Armley Mills.**

Dom Grace (Born 1965) is a writer, obsessed with the Battle of Stalingrad and Mark E Smith, currently doing theatre stuff, usually with Boff Whalley. A friend once pointed out to Dom that in north Leeds they have a different, better, bone structure than south of the river so, 'I feel uncomfortable when I cross the river Aire into north Leeds and don't relax again until I've crossed the river north to south.'

He's currently writing two plays, a love story about a boxer and a barmaid and another about an Irish singer called Darach O'Cathain. He's written the following with Boff:

It's A Lovely Day Tomorrow – a wartime play about two brothers with a cricket obsession going to Hull to get their mother an orange. I loved it. (The West Yorkshire Playhouse.)

Play Up, Play Up – based in Leeds Prison, 1961, and around the inmates producing *Wuthering Heights*. (For the I Love West Leeds Festival.)

Riot, Rebellion & Bloody Insurrection – an adult pantomime tracing the story of a Luddite rebel which toured the north of England. (For Red ladder Theatre Company.)

John Atkinson Grimshaw second half of the 19th century

John Atkinson Grimshaw (1836–1893) was a self taught Victorian-era artist, and according to expert Christopher Wood (*Victorian Painting*, Weidenfeld & Nicolson, 1999) a 'remarkable and imaginative painter.' He was known for his nocturnal city scenes and landscapes and his Pre-Raphaelite style, capturing of detail and light was unique. He was an extremely prolific painter and there's a very untypical example of his work (*Snowbound*) on the back cover which is a close up of a woman's face with what looks like a halo around her and in the top left corner is a detail from his stunning painting *Under the Leafless Trees.*

There's little known of Grimshaw as, unlike many other artists, he left behind no letters, journals, or papers so people (that'd be academics and critics) struggle to get a handle on where he was coming from. All I know is that he was an extremely gifted artist who captured water, light, puddles, mist, clouds and reflections brilliantly. When I first saw his work I thought it was a bit 'Athena' but that's the problem with an untrained eye judging the aesthetics of someone who worked 120 to 150 years ago. The world of art has changed and I was born into that completely changed world. The more I looked at his stuff the more I marveled at his technique but the main thing that struck me was atmosphere, they are dripping with the stuff. There was a revival of interest in his work in the second half of the 20th Century. Some of the places he lived in Leeds were Wallace Street (off Wellington Road), Cliff Road (Hyde Park) and later Knostrop Hall (demolished in 1960). He's buried in Woodhouse cemetery and there are a couple of examples of his work at Leeds City Art Gallery. Just in case you fancy one, some of his average paintings are going for around £300,000.

The Grand Pygmalion was Leeds's first Department store, opened by Alexander Monteith in 1888, *Yorkshire's Great Stores and Drapery Emporium, where every section of the stores was claimed to be alive and interesting, while offering the best of everything and at economical popular prices.* (From The Press (York) archive.) Situated on Boar Lane where **C & A** used to be, on a site being redeveloped as part of 'Trinity Leeds'. 'The most complete general drapers & house furnishers in Yorkshire,' it was a very large store employing 200 people who lived above the store on the 4th floor, it closed in 1927.

Peter Grant (born 1987) is a Guiseley born singer of easy listening/jazz music whose first album *New Vintage* reached number eight in the album chart, going gold. His cover of The Turtles song *Happy Together* has been used on the Twix TV ad since 2007 and he is remembered, by some, for having won through the auditions and selection on ***The X-Factor*** and then declining to go on to the programme. He only did it for a laugh saying 'I wanted to make a career properly, by gigging and getting a name for myself that way.' His first ever 'gig' was at the Guiseley Factory Worker's Club, aged nine.

I grew up with **Harry Gration** on the telly and have always thought he was well under-rated, with his friendly ease on camera. We know him best for *Look North* but I remember him for a short time as the main presenter on *Grandstand, Sportsnight* and *Final Score* and he even had a time on *Match of the Day*. I was dead chuffed for him and later amazed that he didn't get a full time, major gig on these shows or other national telly, I think he's an absolute natural.....ah well, our loss. Although he still did reports for *Grandstand* and *Final Score* as well as being a regular reporter and commentator for the BBC's Olympic and Commonwealth Games coverage.

He started out doing sports commentaries for *Radio Leeds* (1972) whilst still a history teacher at the Rodillian High School in Rothwell, and became the sports editor in 1978. Harry worked on *Look North* from 1982 – becoming a *Grandstand* regular in 1986 – until in 94 he took a break from TV work to become Rugby League's Director of Publicity. He returned to TV on *South Today* in 1995 returning home to anchor *Look North* in 1999. He's also done BBC Radio 4's

Today programme and won two Royal Television Society Awards for his sports documentaries: White Rose in Africa (1992) and Dickie Bird - A Rare Species (1997). He still co-presents the *Super League Show* with the fantastic **Tanya Arnold,** the BBC's first woman sports reporter in Yorkshire and I bet, close to the first in the country. The *Super League Show* won the Royal Television Society Sports Award for best Nations and Regions Sports Actuality Programme in 2007 and the Best Sports Programme at the Royal Television Society North West awards the same year.

The **greenfly plague of 2010.** On the 17th and 18th of May 2010 'clouds' of green fly were reported around Leeds, the bottom end of Burley Road, South Leeds, Morley, Horsforth, Yeadon were blighted. In Horsforth a young lad fell off his bike and into a hedge as he tried to waft them away.

Greenhouses have been around since the 13th century and the Romans used glassless versions with oiled cloth or mica. Now I'm not going to tell you that Leeds had anything to do with the origins of greenhouses but experiments by **Joseph Priestley** explained the mechanics of greenhouses and how 'luxury air', light and heat increase the growth and health of plants. This was the century before the 19th Century French botanist and nephew of Emperor Napoleon, Charles Lucien Bonaparte, built the first practical modern greenhouse in Holland.

Green Shield Stamps will be a mystery to you if you're a certain age but all the old folk reading this will have just gone, 'Oh, God yeh, I'd forgotten all about them.' A British institution (although the idea is American – 1896) they were all over Britain in the '60s and '70s. I remember my parents collecting them and avidly sticking them in a book of an evening; it was so exciting – kids love collecting things. Although we didn't have magnetic strips or barcodes in them days, they were similar to a loyalty card and if you bought your groceries or petrol at outlets in the scheme the retailer gave you stamps to stick in a book. Once you had collected enough you exchanged the books for gifts chosen out of a catalogue and WOW! What a catalogue. I don't think you're quite getting the excitement, it was well stirring, the catalogue had all sorts of thrilling gadgets in it, all the way up to motor boats (outboard motor not included! - 170 books) and cars. The best things in life, at last, were free, although you'd struggle getting enough stamps for a Kenwood Chef. Who paid? The retailer paid the stamp company for the stamps and bought our loyalty. 1970s inflation and the dropping value of the stamps pretty much turned you into a 1920s German with a wheelbarrow and the stamps lost their appeal. Anyhow, Green Shield Stamps were printed in Leeds by **Waddingtons**.

Greenwood & Batley (Thomas and John) is one of those companies that powered Leeds into the city it now is and moved and diversified in an impressive manner. Amongst the many things they did was to produce the band knife for John Barran's that made mass clothing production feasible. At the Albion Works on Armley Road they made all sorts of stuff and installed their own electricity generating station in the factory – allowing machine tools to be electrically driven rather than steam – and started flogging them to other people. There's a list of what they made under **Industry**, it's quite long. See **John Barran**

Angela Griffin (born July 1976) is a television actress and presenter best known for her roles in *Emmerdale*, *Coronation Street*, *Cutting It* and *Waterloo Road*. She is also the voice of Amy the Vet in *Postman Pat*. She now fronts Sky 1's 'flagship' daily show ***Angela and Friends***. She attended Intake High School in Farsley, where she was friends with Spice Girl **Melanie Brown**.

The Guardian. I'd struggle listing all the journos who have come from or have strong links with Leeds so I've picked *The Guardian* and have tried to root out a few Leeds connections with its production – yes I know it's a bit random but I've got a deadline y'know, can't spend the next 40 years on this. Although it was originally the *Manchester Guardian*, Jeremiah Garnett from Otley was the paper's first reporter. Its current northern editor, Martin Wainwright, is Leeds born n'bred and lives here now. When the paper decided to set up 'new city bloggers' the first was John Baron, appointed in and writing about Leeds. John Baron started his career as a trainee reporter at the *Leeds Weekly News* and his blog is well worth dropping in on, just go to their website and search John Baron. Columnist Martin Kettle (probably Leeds born and certainly attended Leeds Modern School) is the assistant/associate editor of *The Guardian*. Leeds born Andrew Rawnsley worked at *The Guardian* from 1985 from until 1993 spending six years as the newspaper's parliamentary sketch writer and since 1993 has been Chief Political Commentator and Associate Editor of *The Guardian*'s sister paper *The Observer*. Leeds born Dave Simpson is currently a music critic at *The Guardian* – see Futurama. Educated at Leeds Uni are: Polly Curtis, the Guardian's Whitehall correspondent and formerly education editor, Dr David Adam formerly science and now Environment Correspondent, Simon Hattenstone, a features writer who also has a weekly sports column. After over 1,200 articles it looks like Anthea Lipsett stopped being an education reporter in 2009. Michael Howard, who has been reporting from Iraq for *The Guardian* since 2002, did his degree at TASC in Horsforth, has a love of Leeds and has been a Leeds United fan since the early 1970s when the young Michael noticed this fantastic football team being constantly savaged in the media. He's a world expert on the Kurdish situation in Iraq, has given various talks at the House Of Commons and in 2007 won the 'coveted' The International Marco Luchetta Prize for journalism concerning children for his article '*Children of War: the Generations Traumatized by Violence in Iraq.*' Oops, I've gone off on him slightly haven't I? Anyway there y'go, some of the contemporary, Leeds related *Guardian* folk.

Guinea Graves seem to be peculiar to Leeds, starting at **Beckett Street Cemetery**, but I'd be interested to know if they spread into other parts of Yorkshire. The guinea graves, officially called inscription graves, were a halfway house between the common/paupers/open/lock-up grave and the private grave.

The set-up was very similar to the common graves above except there was a headstone and an inscription of up to 35 characters for each person in the grave. Your relative may be in a shared grave and part of the list of people on the headstone but it avoided the 'shame' of an unmarked grave. Both sides of the headstone were used for burial and inscriptions. It's not known whether this type of grave was a lock-up grave where a deep hole was dug, a wooden frame and door built across the top which was opened each time a body was placed in and only filled when the grave was full or a public grave which was filled after each burial. The lock-up grave was the cheapest common grave with different prices for stillborn babies, children under and over seven

(5 shilling during the C19) whilst the public grave was almost three times this price at 14 shillings. Due to this pricing and the extra cost of the headstone and inscription, it is suspected that the guinea graves will have taken the form of the lock-up grave as, unsurprisingly, they cost a guinea (one pound and one shilling – 21s/-) with children half price.

I have found graves described as guinea graves in Bristol but they are a completely different thing and not multiple inscription graves but Holbeck cemetery, opened in 1857, also has guinea graves with bodies buried both sides of the headstone and multiple inscriptions.

Guy's Fireworks Ferncliffe works, in Calverley woods, was the site of an explosion on June the 19th, 1957, in which three people died and others were injured, the foundations of the buildings can still be seen in the woods. Over a decade earlier there had been a temporary military camp constructed in the woods to train soldiers for the D-Day landings. During the 50s some of the wood's redundant buildings were converted for use as a fireworks factory, which employed as many as 80 people. I found two different 'reports' that vary slightly; the number of deaths is the same in both, but one reports four injured and the other just two. As to the cause of the explosion, both could be right – a spark igniting gunpowder stored in the hut and/or rockets being produced and stored in the same room. A HMSO Report led to the factory being closed, unsurprising as the explosition was caused by a sparking metal bit being used to drill into rockets in order to test them..........d'y fancy that job? Or perhaps the job of feeding the lions whilst having a raw steak hanging out the top of y'pants?

Gwallog ap Llaennog was a Welsh name for the probable 6th Century king of **Elmet** – they had a few other names for him as well – who is thought to be a descendent of **Coel Hen** (King Cole or Coel). Elmet appears to have been a larger area that incorporated much of what is now Leeds. He formed a confederation of British Kings in mainly the north of England to resist the Angles of Northumbria and lower Scotland. His son, King Ceretic/Certic (Ceredig ap Gwallog), was the last 'King of Elmet' as them dirty Northumbrians came down and chinned him and his army during the autumn of 616 or 626......better not try it again, we'll be ready for them this time. Search Elmet online, there's loads of stuff. See **Coel Hen** and **Elmet**.

Top Armley Philosopher Gets Lost Somewhere in the Eighteenth Century Shocker.

David Hartley, M.A., (1705–1757) This bloke's amazing and has pretty much disappeared, a free thinker who changed radical thought of the 18th/19th Centuries, helped shape the world as we know it, and it's sad that I can't do him justice here. Largely forgotten by history, Hartley was a hugely influential philosopher, inspiration for the **Associationist School** of psychology (precursor to elements of the **Behaviourist School**), an eminent physician, vegetarian, mystic, metaphysician, proposer of neuroscience, influence upon the theory of evolution and on 'great' writers. Online, Hartley expert Richard C. Allen says, 'In Britain, America, and Europe, other scientists, social reformers, and religious radicals also looked to Hartley's ***Observations on Man*** as the paradigm of the "new science" of human nature.' This 'new science' dealt with how the mind and body interact so that we learn, function and act, experience the world, respond to it and, crucially, how we interact with each other.

There is some confusion about Hartley's birth place – no one actually knows the exact location. Although it appeared that he was Armley born, he was not; he moved there at the age of 11 and was born near Halifax. *The Biographia Leodiensis* (1865) states that he was born in Armley, referring to a book on the history of Halifax, and this confusion was fuelled by Hartley's son writing that Hartley "was the son of a very respectable and worthy clergyman at Armley, in the county of York." I contacted Richard C. Allen who wrote the Hartley entry for *The Stanford Encyclopedia of Philosophy* and the book ***David Hartley on Human Nature (Philosophy of psychology)***, State University of New York Press, Sept 1999. Richard's research was absolutely solid and showed that Hartley was born in Luddenden or Illingworth, both near Halifax, and that the family moved to Armley when Hartley was eleven.

Many 'fictional' writers were influenced by Hartley and he is connected to two of my favourite mad poets. **Samuel Taylor Coleridge** had a portrait of himself holding *Observations* and named his first son (David Hartley Coleridge) after him and **William Blake** did the etching for the front cover of radical publisher Joseph Johnson's 1791 "deluxe" edition of Hartley's *Observations*. **Shelley** (Percy Bysshe) in preparation for his first major poem, ***Queen Mab***, was re-educating himself and studying, amongst other things, Hartley's *Observations* and I'd guess, it's no coincidence that he became a vegetarian the same year. Shelley's second

David Hartley

wife, **Mary**, was creator of **Frankenstein**, daughter of political philosopher **William Godwin** and philosopher/feminist **Mary Wollstonecraft**. Kim A. Woodbridge, academic (MS Drexel Uni) and expert on Frankenstein/Mary Shelley says of Frankenstein, 'Mary's account of the creature's mental and moral development follow the theories of David Hartley and John Locke.'

Hartley was a committed **vegetarian** and *Observations* (published in 1749, the British **Vegetarian Society** being formed almost one hundred years later in 1847) contains this philosophy and, as the book was required reading for radicals, I think it likely that the book was influential on this movement. In *Observations* he argues, against the contemporary thinking, that animals are conscious beings and, in more complex creatures, have intelligence; humans are simply wired differently.

Although he will be remembered primarily as a philosopher, he also engaged in mathematical research and wrote on medicine, with extensive writings on the 'the stone, a disease' (**Stone Disease** - Urinary calculi, solid particles in the kidneys, bladder, or ureter), a condition he suffered from and which eventually killed him at the age of 52. He also wrote in defence of **inoculation/vaccination** for the small-pox, against objections from peers. The effectiveness of cowpox to protect humans from smallpox was not demonstrated until 1796, 40 years after his death, but it has to be said, Hartley was considering variola inoculation (inoculation with the smallpox virus) – infecting the person with a mild form of the disease.

His major work was ***Observations on Man, his Frame, his Duty, and his Expectations*** (1749) — 'a wide-ranging synthesis of neurology, moral psychology, and spirituality.......... In the 18th and 19th centuries, Hartley's *Observations* was valued very highly by people within the realm of **religious dissent, scientific progress, and social reform**........Priestley and his fellow **Unitarians** gave the *Observations* a central place in the curriculum in the dissenting academies. From one report, we learn that students in one academy studied it for two hours every morning. In addition, in the late 1700s student radicals at Cambridge and Oxford also had their copies.' (1) Unitarians believed in 'the one God' against the tradition of 'the Trinity' of God as three people. Dissenting academies had to be set up as Oxford and Cambridge Universities would not accept people with beliefs against the doctrine of the Church of England – dissenters.

Joseph Priestley wrote that the book that influenced him the most, save the Bible, was **Hartley's *Observations on Man***. Hartley's psychological, philosophical, and theological theory suggested a material **theory of the mind**. Hartley aimed to construct a Christian philosophy in which both religious and moral "facts" could be scientifically proven, a goal that would occupy Priestley for his entire life. In 1775 Priestley published Hartley's *Theory of the Human Mind on the Principle of the Association of Ideas, with Essays on the subject of it*. A wide variety of philosophers, scientists, and poets became **Associationist** as a result of Priestley's redaction of Hartley's *Observations on Man*, including

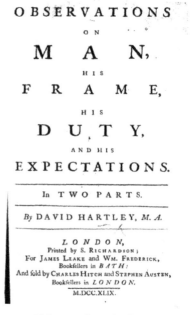

OBSERVATIONS
ON
M A N,
HIS
F R A M E,
HIS
D U T Y,
AND HIS
EXPECTATIONS.

In TWO PARTS.

By DAVID HARTLEY, M. A.

LONDON,
Printed by S. RICHARDSON;
For JAMES LEAKE and WM. FREDERICK,
Bookfellers in BATH:
And fold by CHARLES HITCH and STEPHEN AUSTEN,
Bookfellers in LONDON.
M.DCC.XLIX.

Title page from the first edition of
Observations

94

Erasmus Darwin – Charles Darwin's granddad who wrote a statement on **evolution** and the relatedness of all forms of life before his grandson was born. Although Hartley remained C of E, he radically wrote against the accepted idea of eternal punishment, preferring instead the idea of God's "infinite benevolence" and universal salvation which was the starting point from which his work developed.

He appears to be a founding father of branches of psychology; you could argue that he got to psychology 50 to 100 years before the subject, as we know it today, was putting down its roots. Some of the ideas of the **Associationist School**, which he inspired, anticipated **behaviourist psychology**, especially the idea of conditioning. Having all studied *Observations* in dissenting academies, **James Mill**, **John Stuart Mill**, and **William B. Carpenter** (with **Alexander Bain**) credited Hartley with being the forerunner of their 'new' science when they founded the school of thought known as "association psychology." **Associationism** in psychology/philosophy refers to the idea that mental processes operate by the association of one state with its successor states, but this ignored one of the central aspects of *Observations* and led to Hartley's 'new science' being misrepresented, attacked and dismissed as simplistic. The detractors ran off laughing into a study of how the mind perceives, in isolation from the body, almost ignoring the fact that Hartley wasn't concerned with that but rather with how we learn to perform all the tasks we carry out in everyday life.

There were also cynical socio-political reasons for misrepresenting, dismissing and ignoring Hartley's thesis. At the time society depended on a separation of the mind from the body and Hartley's theories moved beyond this simple dichotomy, (almost binary opposition, if you will – light and dark, big and small, body and mind) to propose an interdependency, a fundamental interplay between the two. Even at its simplest level, **automatic**, Hartley's theory makes that clear; although at times the heart beats with regularity, it is also responsive – if **Leeds United** are about to score it speeds up, they miss, it starts to slow down. The religious doctrines were of a partition of the sacred, immortal soul and the body whilst the morally dominant social construct was of mind over body, the mind the decision maker, directing the body and in complete control. The spiritual and intellectual were active whilst the body and its relationship with the material world were passive. Hartley's 'new science' of the relationship between the body and mind being, in Priestley's words, 'one uniform composition', led the majority of the religious and moral gatekeepers to extrapolate it as an attack on religious beliefs, morality, 'free will' and a step on the road to losing responsibility for actions.

When Priestley wrote in praise of Hartley's theories he commented that 'the outcry.... can hardly be imagined. In all the newspapers, and most of the periodical publications, I was represented as an unbeliever in revelation, and no better than an Atheist' – Priestley's house was later burned down due to his beliefs. Priestley and Erasmus Darwin (see evolution) were a huge minority in defending *Observations*, and it was later largely squashed and forgotten, but this was achieved by offering a reductive version of the work, taken out of context, as presenting thought, experience and sensation as chiefly mechanical. Ironically, the detractors, along with the philosophy of the time, would then skip the central discussion of *Observations* and produce a study of the mind, of thought, separate from the body and actions which would be relegated to a metaphorical footnote.

We may have lost the word **decomplex** that Hartley created over 260 years ago. His theories may have been derailed by history, but we have not lost the essence of the theory. Someone, somewhere will be working on it in a real way, right now: the 'new science' is still new. I also absolutely guarantee that people will still be working on it in a hundred year's time because it connects how we are, what we are, who we are and why. How the external shapes the internal and vice a versa. What it is to be human.

I love the fact that now, when people specialise to the extent that the rest of the world can become a blur, we're ready for a guy from over 260 years ago who wrote about so many diffuse areas, understood and drew from the most specialised theories of physics, chemistry, mathematics, philosophy, and medicine (western psychology not really being around) of the time to propose a theory so huge that we haven't even seen the foothills of it yet.

I know I've gone off on one here and given this way too much time and space, soz, it fired me up, an incredible, renegade philosopher born over 300 years ago, lived in Armley, misrepresented, ignored and binned, for often political reasons and his work is still relevant today. A free thinker who was not scared to go against dominant thought, at a time when that involved serious danger. **David Hume**, one of the 'winners' in the debate, Hartley's contemporary, and according to wiki, 'one of the most important figures in the history of **Western philosophy**' said 'it is needless to push our researches so far as to ask, why we have humanity or a fellow-feeling with others'. I can hear Hartley shouting 'Is it?'

Frustratingly, I have been unable to ascertain any connection between David Hartley and the inspirational author J.R Hartley or the real or fictional book *Fly Fishing*.

(1) Allen, Richard, "David Hartley", *The Stanford Encyclopedia of Philosophy (Summer 2009 Edition)*, Edward N. Zalta (ed.) <http://plato.stanford.edu/archives/sum2009/entries/hartley/>.

H

Hainsworth Textiles. Just after the publication of ***Nailed – Digital Stalking*** I was contacted by a woman who was producing an arty booklet about interesting creative stuff going on in west Leeds. During the interview she told me about a company in Pudsey who produce 'all the red fabric for the Army'; it was a brief conversation as she had questions to ask. Hainsworth Textiles do so much more, they supply ceremonial cloth for military uniforms all over the world and have done since before the Battle of Waterloo and that's not a tenth of it. They are an example of the rich history that Leeds firms often have, adapting and changing through time from a starting point in 1783. The thing that really struck me about the company is how much information they seem to have kept. When you discover that, according to their marketing department, a company as relatively new and huge as Asda doesn't have an archive or part-time historian and therefore even their recent history is a blur you realise just what a treasure the Hainsworth stash of info is. Take a look at their website it's packed full of the company's history with fascinating facts and Ruth Strong has written the book, *The Hainsworth Story: Seven Generations of Textile Manufacturing* (Jeremy Mills Publishing, 2006) which is even available on Google books.

I'll keep this brief as it's all there online but the firm is still family run, looks to be hugely successful and I'd guess at it being the oldest Leeds company still trading and they claim to be 'one of the oldest companies in the United Kingdom'- I've found Procter Bros. in Garforth go back to 1740. In 1783 Abimelech Hainsworth began his working life with half a crown, as a cloth merchant by collecting fabric from local cottages and selling it at Leeds market and went onto to create vast wealth and industry. The company today is at the cutting edge (he-he) of fabric production and innovation, carrying out every step of the manufacturing process in-house – even having an accredited research and testing lab – and export all over the world. They provide a vast range of services and products, from piano cloth for Steinway & Sons to the nylon wrapping tape used in the production of huge rubber hoses that transport oil from drilling platforms to shore. For over 100 years they have supplied fabric to protect fire fighters from the effect of heat and flame and are still at the forefront of that technology as well as specialist cloth to protect riot police. At Charles and Di's wedding his full dress uniform of a naval commander was tailored from Hainsworth cloth and you know the example of Elizabeth I's costume that is proudly displayed at The Tower of London? Guess what, Hainsworth cloth. Hainsworth cloth has been worn by soldiers from the reign of George III to the current day, including uniforms worn at the Battle of Waterloo or the scarlet and dark blue cloths worn by the Household Division for Trooping the Colour or over 50,000 members of the Danish Home Guard. They furnish Royal palaces and homes throughout Europe and the Middle East and supply the cloth for snooker, pool and billiard tables including the Queen Vic in *EastEnders*.

Ooh , that reminds me, they supply cloth to TV dramas like Casualty, in a Bollywood film their para-aramid wick was recently wound around a banister and lit to create the effect of a burning staircase and in theatre their historical knowledge led them to supply many major theatre productions. Production line conveyor belts for McVities biscuits, textiles the thickness of a piece of paper, the woolsack, the seat of the Lord Speaker in the House of Lords (the whole chamber is covered in Hainsworth cloth) head linings for Rolls Royce's. Hainsworth fabrics were pivotal in the construction of the first hot air balloon to successfully circumnavigate the globe in 1999 – **Breitling Orbiter 3**. They make fabric to protect fighter pilots in the UK, are developing fabrics for use in the latest **anti-gravity garments** and in 2009 launched a new environmental product that is going down a bomb in the UK, US and Europe **a woollen coffin**. I'm stopping now, my heads spinning and I need to go shopping, get online and check them out.

Hair from Leeds was used to help mop up the major BP, Gulf of Mexico US oil spill. **Architect** hairdresser's in Headingley collected the cut hair and sent it to the environmental charity **Matter of Trust.** The hair was then stuffed into nylon tights to make defensive booms against the oil. The oil sticks to the hair, collecting it and making it easier to deal with.

In 1994 **June Hancock** was diagnosed with mesothelioma. The only known cause of this incurable cancer of the chest is exposure to asbestos earlier in life. June grew up in the streets surrounding the **J W Roberts Ltd.** asbestos factory in Armley, which pumped asbestos dust into the Leeds air through its ventilation system. Their factory put so much asbestos dust into the heart of Armley that local children used it to make 'summer snowballs' to hurl at each other or mark out hopscotch squares in the thick dust that lay on the ground. The same cancer had already killed June's mother and June was not a woman to go quietly.

Already ill, she took **J W Roberts Ltd.** (the Turner & Newall (T&N) group) to trial in 1994, the court combining it with an existing case that had been running for three to four years. Despite being terminally ill, June attended court on all but one day of the hearing and the trial gained much national and international attention. The case had initially been driven by the Yorkshire Evening Post (Ee Po), YTV, and Leeds MP John Battle through the 1980s when the UK government were completely unsympathetic to the case. What emerged through the case (and the previous work of the Leeds journos and John Battle) made Erin Brockovich's nasty corporation look like pussycats. In April, 1996, the court judged in favour of Margereson & Hancock and June was awarded compensation of £65,000. The court victory was a landmark decision as it extended the duty of care beyond factory employees to those outside a factory's walls. It opened the door to claims from asbestos victims around the world and T & N had 263,000 claims for injury pending by the time it was bought out by the US multinational **Federal-Mogul** in 1998. Even after the judgement the case dragged out, June never received her £65,000 and by 1997 the cancer had killed her. In 2004 the lawyers representing 50 of the Armley residents finally got a payment, which due to corporate/legal shenanigans, had been reduced to 24% of the award after £10,000 had been sliced off the top. Later successful applicants receive as little as 17% of their claim. Not to worry, all 50 of the victims were already dead.

Pivotal in the trial was the fact that the risks of asbestos dust exposure had been known by the defendant since 1933.

A play of the case, **Dust**, was produced in 2009. Drawn from trial transcripts, interviews and letters it was performed by local people, in association with I love West Leeds Festival, at an industrial building in Ledgard Way, Armley before moving to the West Yorkshire Playhouse. Dust is the story of that trial and the story of Armley: the memories and the courage of the people whose fight for justice continues today.' A charity, the **June Hancock Mesothelioma Research Fund**, was established shortly after her death to support victims of mesothelioma and mesothelioma research projects. **See Armley asbestos disaster.**

Hang The Dance are the reigning champions of the Leeds five-a-side bands competition after they beat the pre-tournament favourites The Wedding Present 5 – 0 in the final of the last competition. Their toughest game was the semi-final when they edged passed the band management company DNA 3-2. DNA's band, The Mission, were touring at the time and, apparently, reckoned they'd have won it. There was an open invitation to a play-off which The Mission never accepted, possibly after being told how ruthless Hang The Dance were.

The band passed up the best album title ever *Big in Allerton Bywater* (see Castleford) and chose instead the ponsey, literary reference *Ghost Bloody Country*. I was in the band so I can share anecdotes with no guilt for ignoring more important Leeds groups like The Three Johns or The Sisters of Mercy – anyway what y'whinging about? Alan Bennett only got six lines. It's my life and my book; I'm bound to talk about stuff close to home. We had a few records out but never set the world alight and when Red Rhino went bust (nudge-nudge, wink-wink) I tried to buy our back catalogue from the official receiver but it'd all been bought up by some American company – we'd had a documentary shown on American cable – and I didn't even have a copy of the album.

Right, a true story, for which I have witnesses that I can call up to take the stand and everything. We were headlining Dingwalls in some town down south and quite a few had gone down from Leeds as well as some London folk who liked the band. Some of the younger lads were buzzing as Johnny Marr (The Smiths guitarist) was in attendance. Me? I'd wrongly dismissed The Smiths as a ponsey, sixth form band and wasn't even slightly interested. As the night progressed the promoter came and had a word, saying that bands had over-run, that they were under serious pressure not to run over and that we'd have to cut ten minutes from the set. No problem, we'd just stick to the set and forget the encore. So, we played out of our skin, went down a storm and left the stage to chants of *Hang The Dance, Hang The Dance, Hang The Dance* – to the tune of *Here we go, here we go, here we go*. The lights came up, and the DJ started playing a record whereupon the chant instantly turned to a quite angry *Hang The DJ, Hang The DJ, Hang The DJ*. I'd guess that Johnny Marr said to Morrissey, 'saw this Leeds band tonight, they were crap, but there was almost a riot and their crowd started chanting *Hang The DJ, Hang The DJ, Hang The DJ*....what a line.' The single *Panic* with its refrain *Hang The DJ, Hang The DJ, Hang The DJ was released* about three months later and as a one-off single,

I have to say Wiki talks of a different source for the song but that's a witnessed story and the song, about social unease, has the chorus:
On the Leeds side-streets that you slip down,
Provincial towns you jog 'round
Hang the DJ, Hang the DJ, Hang the DJ
Isn't it pathetic that after over ten years trying to develop a career in music the most I have is a dubious story about another band's song and being part of the punch line to a Vic Reeves joke on telly....but that's another story. Before you go looking, there's nothing on YouTube, (although you never know someone might have got their act together by now) other than a middle eight at 2.20mins in a *Book flogging interview* – but by'eck, we knew how to knock out a good middle eight.

Leeds born and educated **Professor Sir Edmund Happold** (1930–1996) was a structural/civil engineer and founder of **Buro Happold**. Buro Happold is into 'engineering consultancy, design, planning, project management and consulting services for all aspects of buildings, infrastructure and the environment.' Originally set up for work in the Middle East it now has 30 offices employing over 1,600 staff. Ted, as he is better known, was the son of Frank Happold, Professor of Biochemistry at Leeds University and he himself studied geology at Leeds Uni and in 1957 returned to Leeds University to get a BSc in Civil Engineering. After becoming head of Structures 3 at Ove Arup and Partners in 1967, he worked on such landmark buildings as the Sydney Opera House and the Pompidou Centre. He also collaborated in setting up a lab to study lightweight, tensile structures and became a leader in the field that allows all those curvy and strangely shaped buildings to remain standing. After Arup wouldn't give him more autonomy he left in 1976 to become professor of Architecture and Engineering Design at the University of Bath and it was around this time that he set up **Buro Happold**. They obviously had an office in Bath, opened an office in Riyadh in 1983 to be closer to their customers and the next office they opened was in Leeds. Ted and his company have won a sack full of awards, innovated the built environment and worked on many landmark projects around the world including , Sydney Opera House, the Pompidou Centre, Pink Floyd 'The Wall' concerts, Al-Masjid al-Nabawi (Mosque of the Prophet) in Medina, the Weald and Downland Gridshell, the Savill Building in Windsor Great Park, the Millennium Dome, The Sage Gateshead etc...

Colonel Thomas Harding (1843–1927). According to the Holbeck urban village website, his father (T.R. Harding) started out in business as a gill-pin maker in Great Wilson Street in Leeds in 1836. As the industrial revolution began to take off Colonel Thomas Harding opened the new Tower Works factory at Globe Road in 1864. The design of the new factory was heavily influenced by his love for Italian architecture and art. Harding's classification for pin sizes, the Harding Gauge, went on to become the international standard. The company made nails as well as pins for carding machines for the woollen industry and later gramophone needles. I should mention that I've seen other compelling sources say that T.R. Harding (his father) was responsible for the original 1864 buildings (by Thomas Shaw) and the lager towers came with works extension in 1899. I'd also guess that the Harding Gauge may have been connected to the father.

The most notable features of Tower Works are the three towers that give it its name and served as chimneys for the gill-pin factory. The largest and most ornate tower is based on the iconic Giotto campanile (bell tower) in Florence. The smaller ornate tower is based on the Lamberti Tower in Verona. A third plain tower, built as part of Harding's final phase of expansion in 1919, is thought to represent a Tuscan tower house. All three are listed structures, the two ornate towers being Grade II * and the plain tower Grade II. He built extensions to Tower Works in Holbeck in 1899 and the 1920s, and proposed and financed sculptures including the Black Prince when Leeds City Square was remodelled.

John Harrison (1693–1776) invented, amongst other things, the **marine chronometer**, solving the age old problem of being able to accurately position yourself at sea and winning a £20,000 prize – equivalent to around £3 million today – from the British Parliament as they thought the problem was nigh on impossible to solve. This inability to accurately position yourself at sea had led to significant loss of shipping, cargoes and lives. I'll keep this brief as I shouldn't really include him as he was from **Foulby**, near Wakefield (around eight miles outside Leeds) but as a forerunner, and directly connected to, the marine chronometer he made one of the most accurate timepieces of the era and **Leeds City Council** has the only publicly owned one (of three ever made) – precision pendulum-clock No. 2, which they plan to put on display in 2011 at **Leeds City Museum**. 'It's exact time keeping that, in part, fuels the Industrial Revolution.' (*A History of the World in 100 Objects*, Radio 4, 11 Oct 2010)

In clock-making, he also invented the **gridiron pendulum**, and the **grasshopper escapement**. His other inventions include the **bi-metallic spring/strips**, still commonly used in thermometers, thermostats and miniature **circuit breakers** in electrical devices, and **caged roller bearings** still used today in everything from **cars** to the **Space Shuttle**. This is technology he invented over 250 years ago which is still crucial today in all sorts of machines. He came 39th in the BBC's 2002 public poll of the **100 Greatest Britons.** Harrison saved his best until last, his greatest achievement, nay, his lifetime achievement, was undoubtedly saving **Del Boy** and **Rodney** from a lifetime of continued ducking and diving in *Only Fools And Horses* as it was one of Harrison's marine time pieces (the mythical H6) that fetched them £6.2 million in the auction at Sotheby's, causing Del Boy to faint.

Robert Harrison, who works as an IT director in Leeds, made national and international news and was called by an amazed NASA asking how he took pictures of Earth from the edge of space – 21.74 miles up – that would cost them millions of dollars. Spending £500, he put a digital camera in a padded box, with a GPS tracking device linked to a radio transmitter and attached it to a weather balloon. He then tracked it on his laptop and when the balloon eventually burst, a small parachute and loft insulation attached by duct tape protected the camera. He did much of his research online and downloaded software to make the camera take eight photos and video every five minutes. He plans to develop the idea for his next launch by deploying a rotating and fixed camera as well as sensors for pressure, temperature and humidity.

Tony Harrison. *As he's better qualified, I asked* **Ian Duhig** *to do Tony for me and here's what he thinks:* From Anthony Thwaite to Andrew Duncan, contemporary poets from Leeds have been at the forefront of their art in this country, showing a great range of styles and approaches; but unquestionably, the most famous of them all is **Tony Harrison**. A radical classicist, he uses traditional forms such as the sonnet to re-enact political struggle in a language itself a battlefield between dialect and RP: Tom Maguire would have saluted Harrison's craft and politics as do now his international audiences. Multi-linguistic, he is also multi-talented, writing, directing and translating plays and films while also being involved in ground-breaking television projects. Harrison maintains that all these activities fall within the larger heading of his work as a poet, and he continues to be one of the most important poets in Britain today. The Poetry Archive selection includes some of his best work, giving you the opportunity to hear his unique voice first hand.

Joanne Harris, author of (amongst other things) *Chocolat* taught at Leeds Grammar School for 12 years.

Hartley Greens & Co (Leeds Pottery) was set up in Hunslet around 1770, by Richard Humble and John and Joshua Green as Humble, Green & Co before becoming Hartley, Green & Co in 1781 when a money man called Hartley joined and presumably Mr Humble left. By 1790 the company employed 150 people and exported throughout Europe and America. They made all sorts of pottery, such as their Block Egyptian Ware, (black glazed, red earthenware) but it was **Creamware** that gained the company's reputation. This new type of earthenware was fire-glazed pottery with intricate pierced patterning and decorative detail made from white Cornish clay combined with a translucent glaze to produce its characteristic pale cream colour. This highly decorative Creamware was very popular in the Georgian period and the success and quality of Hartley, Green & Co's products meant that, in some quarters, all Creamware became known as **Leedsware.**

After various name changes (Wainwright & Co, Stephen & James Chappell, Warburton & Britton, Richard Britton & Sons) the company closed in 1881 and the buildings were demolished. In 1888 an ex-employee (James Wraith) used old designs to make 'Leeds Pottery' and his business was carried on by his family until 1957. In 1983 Leeds City Council started making reproductions of its museum pieces in a workshop set up for the disabled. When funding stopped, it was sold into the private sector and production was moved to Stoke-on-Trent. In 1992, when the company passed into its present ownership, they adopted the most famous company name of Hartley Greens & Co.

The **Harvey Nichols** store on Briggate was the second branch in the world of the famous, posh store and, obviously, the first outside London.

Heart Monitor. Quantum physics carried out primarily by **Ben Varcoe** and **Melody Blackburn** at the **Leeds Quantum Information Group** (School of Physics and Astronomy, Leeds Uni) has helped create a portable magnetic monitor (see **magnetometer**), a major advancement in the diagnosis of heart problems. It just happened that Ben developed a minor heart condition and, on visiting hospital, the cardiologist commented that Ben was the first person he'd seen that day who actually had a heart condition as they were so hard to diagnose without expertise and testing. The consultant commented that there had been a long standing problem with diagnostics and that medics had been searching for an effective diagnostic tool for years. Around the time Ben happened to be attending a conference in Australia about applying quantum physics to industrial problems and learnt that a device sensitive to magnetic fields was useful to heart research and diagnostics. Magnetometers are in two parts. The actual probe and the apparatus to interpret and run the probe and everything about the two parts is about shielding them from the Earth's magnetic field and other sources of electromagnetic interference, this shielding providing the bulk. PHD student **Melody Blackburn** had a medical physics background and brought her knowledge to atomic physics to assert that previous thinking was wrong, the sensor in contact with the patient didn't need the same shielding and she developed a compact device that worked. Her boss, **Ben Varcoe**, has been incredibly straight in giving her the due credit. By 2012/13 there could be a diagnostic device at work in a hospital saving much time and effort and freeing up and targeting the time of cardiologists.

Although there are a number of heart conditions that this breakthrough could be applied to, it is particularly useful in **arrhythmia** where the arrhythmic node has been extremely difficult to locate until now and I bet over time many other applications will appear. *Material World*, (Thursday, 11th of Feb 2010, 16:30, BBC Radio 4.) See **Magnetometer**.

John Deakin Heaton is primarily known for his role in the foundation of the Yorkshire College, the precursor of the present University. Educated at Leeds Grammar School he entered Leeds Medical School in 1835, followed by clinical work and qualification in Medicine at University College Hospital. A physician and lecturer at the School he became President of the School in 1850-1 and in 1858-9.

Barbara Hepworth (1903–1975). Although she was born in Wakefield she won a scholarship to and studied at the Leeds School of Art from 1920, where she met **Henry Moore**. Widely considered one of the most significant artists of the 20th century, she lived and worked in Cornwall (where her Museum and Sculpture Garden is situated) from 1949 until her death in 1975. One of her major works *Hieroglyph,* can be seen at Leeds Art Gallery.

HESCO Bastion is both the product and the company and the brain-child of Jimi Heselden (1948–2010). I was just pasting this entry into 'tranche 12' to send off for proofing when I heard of the tragic accident that killed Jimi. He is one son of Leeds of whom the city can be very proud and not just because of the £23m he gave to good causes in Leeds but also because of the way, after being laid-off from his job as a miner, he picked himself up and invested his redundancy money in creating a business that now employs more than 350 people at four sites in Leeds. The other reason Leeds should be proud of Jimi is that he was proud of the city (particularly east Leeds), refusing to relocate and investing in the city. Have a look at 'About Us' on the Hesco website with its pulsing dot on Leeds, in the very centre of Britain, that slowly homes in on the city and right under their logo, *HESCO Bastion Ltd. Based in Leeds, Yorkshire, UK.* Ok, the east Leeds expression is more often *Leeds, Yorkshire, England* but we'll forgive them that.

I've a slight confession to make, the product is strictly called and patented as the Concertainer but it is known as the Hesco Bastion or just the Hesco. Jimi founded the company in 1989, after setting up working in sandblasting, to manufacture his invention of a collapsible wire mesh container and heavy duty fabric liner which is used as a temporary or semi-permanent barrier. The Hesco was originally developed to hold back sea erosion threatening East Coast homes but was adapted for other defence uses as it's ten times quicker than sandbags. The containers can be simply folded out and then filled with sand, dirt or rubble by a front end

Barbara Hepworth in 1966 by Erling Mandelmann

loader (digger) to make a strong wall. They are sold in huge quantities and used in flood defence around the world (around New Orleans in the few days between Hurricanes Katrina and Rita) but have also been adopted by armies as barriers, blast-protection systems and to provide a protective wall for army bases. The Hesco website says, 'Concertainer units are one of the UK's most successful defence exports, with units used by military organisations including the US Army, USMC, USAF, NATO and the UN in every major conflict area since the first Gulf war.' I'm also wondering whether Camp Bastion, the main UK base in Afghanistan, was named after the product.

The Concertainer is used across a wide variety of civil engineering applications, including land reinforcement, retaining walls and river and canal bank stabilisation. The basic idea has been adapted by the company into a new product called R-Houses which use tall Concertainers with coverings to provide relief shelters in disaster situations and were used in Haiti after the earthquake. In 2010 Jimi headed a buyout of Segway Inc. which makes the motorised two-wheelers.

Anyway, from a council house on Halton Moor Jimi had made his way onto the *Sunday Times Rich List* and with his business going from strength to strength he was moving up it. The word on the east Leeds streets was that he was a lovely, unassuming and very approachable fella. He didn't like giving interviews, so there's little material from him. In the weeks before his death he was persuaded (by the post recession fall in charitable donations) to make a statement after handing over a £10m cheque to the Leeds Community Foundation, (the largest single donation ever received by any of the 57 foundations across the country) 'There are people out there who are making money and when times are good I honestly believe people have a moral obligation to use their wealth to help others.' (Yorkshire Post, 18th September, 2010).

Jack Higgins (born 1929) is the principal pseudonym of UK novelist **Harry Patterson**; other pseudonyms are Hugh Marlowe, Martin Fallon and James Graham (after a Leeds college, see below.) Patterson is the author of more than 70 novels including ***The Eagle Has Landed***. Born in Newcastle upon Tyne, he grew up in Belfast (many of his books include 'the troubles') and Leeds, attending Roundhay Grammar School (now Roundhay School), and later went to Beckett Park College for Teachers, (now part of Leeds Metropolitan University). He later returned to Leeds and taught Liberal Studies at Leeds Poly and later Education at James Graham College (Harry used this as an alias, became part of Leeds Polytechnic in 1976) and he also taught at Allerton Grange School.

The Eagle Has Landed was his breakthrough novel (his thirty sixth book, thought to have sold tens of millions and still in print) and almost all since have been best sellers. *The Eagle Has Landed* was made into an iconic war film released in December 1976. My favourite quote comes from the character Liam Devlin, the Irish gunman, poet, and philosopher:

Colonel Steiner: Mr. Devlin, you are an extraordinary man.

Liam Devlin: Col. Steiner, you're an extraordinary judge of character.

Other films based on Harry's novels were *The Violent Enemy* (1967, from the novel *A Candle for the Dead*), *The Wrath of God* (1972, Rita Hayworth's last movie also starred Robert Mitchum), *To Catch a King* (1984, TV), *A Prayer for the Dying* (1987) a thriller directed by Mike Hodges, and starring Mickey Rourke, Liam Neeson, Bob Hoskins, and Alan Bates, *Confessional* (1989, TV), *Night of the Fox* (1990, TV) *Midnight Man* (1995, TV - based on *Eye of the Storm*), *Windsor Protocol* (1996, TV) or "*Jack Higgins' Windsor Protocol*" (complete US title), *On Dangerous Ground* (1996, TV), *Thunder Point* (1998, TV) or "*Jack Higgins' Thunder Point*" (complete US title).

Prior to *The Eagle Has Landed* Patterson knocked out thirty-five thrillers in 15 years – three or four a year during the early to mid 1960s and early 70s. The growing success of his early work allowed him to take time off from his teaching in Leeds and eventually become a full-time novelist.

Ronnie Hilton (Adrian Hill, 1926–2001) was a singer and radio presenter, with a close affinity with **Leeds United**. In 1964 he wrote and recorded 'Leeds United Calypso', his first Leeds song, to celebrate our promotion to the First Division. It was the first Leeds United-based record and was strange at the time, featuring calypso/West Indian rhythms and had '**Elland Road Baht'at**' (as in *Ilkey Moor Baht'at*) on the B-side. His best known Leeds song is probably '**Glory Glory Leeds United**' which he released in 1968, it was copied by Man U in 1983 and is still often used as their 'anthem' before each half. He also recorded '**We Shall Not Be Moved**', '**The Tale of Johnny Giles**', '**The Lads Of Leeds**' and '**The Ballad of Billy Bremner**'.

In 1954 he left his safe job in a Leeds engineering factory to sing professionally and had nine Top 20 hits between 1954 and 1957 including a number one and, until rock'n'roll exploded, was one of Britain's most popular 1950s singers. For several years he presented Radio 2's *Sounds of the 50's* show.

Carl Hindmarch and **Eliza Hindmarch** are a brother and sister combo (who don't work together) that I've chosen fairly randomly as an example of Leeds people working behind the camera – I could produce a very long list of them. Carl has directed 17 (that I can find) documentaries including multiple episodes – four early episodes of the *Lonely Planet* TV series which has run to over 60 episodes. He directed two programmes of Simon Schama's *Power of Art* series on Caravaggio and Rothko. I was shocked by the critical, sniffy response to these, they intermingled excellent dramatic scenes with the usual blurb. Me and Mrs Mick loved them and we're intelligent, educated people – she's been working in TV and theatre for over 25 years and I'm a renowned cultural shaper. We had no idea who had directed them but thought they were stunning and the fresh treatment of this kind of subject matter brought them out of the staid, dry presentation so often witnessed in history and the arts on telly. He does all sorts of different kinds of stuff from *Holby City* to his, *Bloody Foreigners – The real Battle of Britain* (2010) which explored 'the part immigrant communities played in key events of British history. These included Polish fighter pilots' in the Battle of Britain, black sailors involved in the Battle of Trafalgar.' I've not included here an entry on the absolutely crucial role that immigrants have made to the making of Leeds as it was a bit tenuous. **Eliza Hindmarch** produced *The September Issue*, an extremely successful documentary film about the behind the scenes drama that follows editor-in-chief of *Vogue Magazine,* Anna Wintour. She's done reels of stuff, her most recent (at time of writing) being *Waiting for Superman*, a 2010 documentary which follows promising children through the American academic process, examining how it restricts their potential. Soz this has been brief but I've got to go and design a book cover.

Hip hop/Rap music and everything it has developed into owes a debt to **Jimmy Savile** who, in 1943, was the first person in the world to use two turntables and a mic. I'd also point at flash Jim's mid-70s TV uniform of shell/track suits and leisure wear with training shoes and lots of big, flashy jewellery/bling and wonder, if he was black, whether comments/connections may have been made? Yes, I know, Hip-hop came out of the South Bronx (New York) and the first record is credited as 1979, but don't people travel? Is any movement purely 'street'? Jimmy was, at the time, one of the biggest things on British TV. Or perhaps, conversely, Jimmy travelled to New York in the early 70s and witnessed some of the roots of the movement. Or, obviously, it could be pure chance. Whatever, he's still the first person in the world to use two turntables and a mic and also the inventor of the modern **disco**/club.

The '**Armley Hippo**' is believed to be about 130,000 years old and was discovered in 1851 when workmen digging clay in Longley's brick field in Wortley/Armley discovered many huge bones, bones so massive that 'they could not be Christians' bones.' The site where the bones were found is where the Armley Gyratory is today, although some on Leodis suspect it may actually be a field just to the west of the gyratory. Henry Denny, then curator of the Leeds Philosophical and Literary Society Museum, identified them as the bones of the Great Northern Hippopotamus. It seems that a great many of the smaller bones will have been lost over the years of digging on the site but the first of interest found was a humungous thigh bone. While investigating the find Denny visited the site daily and gathered large amounts of bones and teeth which enabled him to identify the animals and samples from a molar tooth were later used to date the animal from between 117,000 to 130,000 years old.

Do you know how long ago 130,000 years is? I don't, I've no idea, it's just a number – a daft, abstract concept that means nothing. But if we think back to the birth of that Jesus Christ fella, that's yonks ago, like thousands of years and that, maybe even over two thousand years. And think of everything that's happened since then, Leeds has had a 'little ice age' or close to Mediterranean climate, wars, famines and diseases, Kings, Queens and assorted nutters ruling over folk, revolutions social, agricultural, industrial and technological, new religions and the continued evolution of music, endless drops of rain and the death of species, men on boats 'discovering' the far flung corners of the Earth, flying to the moon and measuring stuff, it's a fair few births, deaths and marriages. It's probably around 40 life times' or 111.66666666666666666666666666667 generations ago......actually it's not that long ago really is it?

But the 2000 years since Christ is only a 65th of 130,000 years. Now if we think about 65, again it's just an abstract number but it's way bigger than 50, 15 bigger than 50 to be precise and that is precise. I've just stacked up 65 Ritz Crackers and they reached the door handle, that's high for a Ritz Cracker. I bet if you got 65 chips and put them in a line, end to end, from where you are now it'd reach to your front door, maybe even start going down the path, don't think it'd stretch to Cleckheaton though. Well not unless you're in Cleckheaton but that's cheating because the line of chips started in Cleckheaton. So I don't expect any letters from Cleckheaton saying, 'Well the line of 65 chips actually did stretch to Cleckheaton, actually.' I don't expect any of that infamous Cleckheaton, chip-based cheating and you see, all you who used to say my old Dad was being racist when he used to say 'never trust a Cleckheatonite carrying chips' he wasn't was he? He was being visionary. Anyway stop distracting me, 65 times the length of time from the birth of Christ to now is a long time, not in geological terms but in human terms. To get it into a full, clear, unambiguous perspective the **Neolithic Revolution**, when people first moved from hunting and gathering to planting and settling was about 12,000 years ago, our hippo is 10.833 times as old as that. If you put 130,000 Neolithic goats one on top of the other I bet they'd reach the moon or maybe some clouds, it'd certainly be higher than a tree.

Anyway, it wasn't just one hippopotamus it was hippopotami. They found bones from an old individual and two adults as well as bones from an ancient elephant and an auroch – an extinct wild ox. Research later identified the animals as Hippopotamus amphibius, Elephas primigenius and Bos primigenius. The bones of the hippos are now kept at the Leeds Museum Resource Centre. The I Love West Leeds Festival 2010 adopted the **Armley Hippo** (which surely should be called the Armley-Wortley Hippo) by producing 500 clay hippos, decorated and spread them around Armley in shop windows and the like and had hippo-based displays on Armley Town Street. There was also the idea of building a model of a Hippoduct under the viaduct (Burley) on Kirkstall road, a huge hollow open-mouthed hippo that you drive through. I like the idea, it's ace, although surely using the space on the Armley Gyratory roundabout for some hippo memorial might be more apt. On a related note, **I've** decided that Armley Gyratory is a rubbish name for a roundabout and we should rename it the Armley Hippo. This was all my idea and not sent to me by **Rick Duniec**, absolutely not, I swear. Rick had no input in this whatsoever....none...other than the idea in its most basic form.

Hip replacement. Lancastrian Sir John Charnley, a pioneer of the hip replacement operation (his basic designs are still used today), wrote in his 1979 publication *Low Friction Arthroplasty of the Hip: Theory and Practice.* (Berlin, Springer, 1979) that, 'in Britain it is not considered good form to acknowledge commercial undertakings in too glowing terms, even though the work would not have been possible without their collaboration.' He was referring to Leeds company **Chas F. Thackray Limited** who, from 1947, invested time, expertise and money in making Sir John's pioneering work a success and developing an industry worth $17 billion a year in the US alone – 2004.

Damien Hirst was born in Bristol in 1965. He grew up in Leeds and took a foundation course at Leeds School of Art. He's a bit of a 'punk artist' and has done loads of controversial stuff, sold gallery loads and promoted his own work, yarda, yarda yah. Go look him up, he's probably the most famous living artist, it's certainly said that he's the richest artist in the world.

Ey, look what John Poulter who teaches Cultural Analysis at Leeds Trinity University College has just sent me: **Richard Hoggart** changed the way that culture was thought about and studied in Britain and further afield. Along with Raymond Williams and E.P. Thompson he is seen as having initiated the serious study of what Williams called 'ordinary' culture. Hoggart did this initially in his book *The Uses of Literacy* (1957) in which he contrasted the more commercialised and Americanised culture of the 1950s compared to what he saw as the more self-produced, 'authentic' culture of the 1930s in the streets of Hunslet where he was born (1918) and brought up.

This book, together with Williams' *Culture and Society and The Long Revolution* and Thompson's *The Making of the English Working Class* are often cited as the works that shook up the study of culture and laid the foundations for the multi-disciplinary field of Cultural Studies. This project has, in turn, had a huge influence on the wide range of academic disciplines it happily strode into including literary studies, sociology, philosophy, politics, history, geography and psychology. It also gave birth to new disciplines dealing with the study of gender, race, ethnicity, and sexuality. In all of these areas and more it validated and encouraged the serious study of such popular cultural phenomena as popular music, fashion, comics, television, gaming, social media etc. Anyone reading Hoggart's most famous book and feeling his dislike for much of what he saw as mass culture would find this aspect of his legacy somewhat ironic!

Next time you read someone deriding 'Media Studies!?' you know who to, partially, blame. But then before media studies was the scapegoat people rubbished sociology. Before that it was English Literature. Some people will only be happy when we're all learning Latin! What Hoggart and his peers recognised was that there was a complex and hugely influential world of popular culture outside the confines of the museum and art gallery that merited serious study.

You could also blame him, partially, for us being exposed to all the 'rude bits' in novels after his contribution to the successful defence as an expert witness in the Lady Chatterley's Lover trial in 1960. Writers and publishers, not to mention readers, have people like him to thank for the greater openness about sexual matters in much of today's world.

Hoggart set up the hugely influential Centre for Contemporary Cultural Studies at Birmingham University and was Assistant Director of UNESCO (United Nations Educational, Scientific and Cultural Organisation) before becoming Warden of Goldsmith's College in London. The main building at the college was recently renamed the **Richard Hoggart Building**. He has continued to write and publish books into the 21st Century.

Serial bigamist **Emily Horne** got married five times but never got divorced. She studied physics and electronics at **Leeds Metropolitan University** and married twice in a row at **Leeds Register Office**. She was cautioned when husband number three dobbed her in, went to prison for six months after marrying husband number four and was given a ten-month jail sentence (suspended for two years) as the court doubted her state of mind. She was the subject of a Channel 4, **Cutting Edge** documentary that investigated 'a darker tale of mental illness, addiction and neglect.'

Hot Springs, city in the U.S. state of Arkansas which became a national gambling Mecca in the 1930s, led by Leeds lad and gangster **Owney Madden** and his Hotel Arkansas casino.

The Humanist Community of Leeds meets once a month at the Cosmopolitan Hotel in Leeds city centre.

The **Hunslet Cricket, Football and Athletic Club** was the first club to win **All Four Cups** in the 1907-08 season. Between 1905 and 1970 there were four trophies available to any British rugby league side:

The Challenge Cup, the Rugby Football League Championship, the County league (Lancashire League or Yorkshire League) and the County Cup (Lancashire Cup or Yorkshire Cup). This was regarded as the Holy Grail for any Rugby League side and was only achieved on three occasions.

The pack of the Hunslet side – Tom Walsh, Harry Wilson, Jack Randall, Bill "Tubby" Brookes, Bill Jukes and John Willie Higson – was dubbed the "Terrible Six" by Lancashire sides.

The club has its roots in the 1850s. In order to protect the cricket pitch from a landlord who planned to rent it for winter rugby, the Hunslet Cricket Club formed their own rugby club and in 1883 the Hunslet Cricket and Football Club was formed.

When, in August 1895, northern rugby union teams split from the English Rugby Union to form the Northern Union (which led to Rugby League) Hunslet were founder members. Central to this split was the success of working class, northern teams and northern players (coal miners, mill workers etc.) being denied "broken time payments" when they had to take time off work to play, which they could not afford to do. They also refused permission for northern sides to charge entrance to spectators in order to fund the clubs. Southern clubs had 'other' sources of income.

In 1924, the club's record home attendance was set at 24,700 for a Challenge Cup tie. In 1938 Elland Road hosted an English Rugby League record crowd of over 54,000, who saw Hunslet win the RL Championship Final beating Leeds RL in the only all-Leeds final.

Paul Alan Hunter (1978–2006) was known as 'the Beckham of the Baize' due to his good looks and flamboyant nature. He went St Andrews Primary School and my old school (kinda) Cardinal Heenan High School and, a bit of a young whiz-kid, made his professional debut in 1995 at the age of 16. He was the Masters champion three times on the trot – 2001 to 2003. In 2005 he announced that he had malignant neuroendocrine tumors which took his life the following year at the age of 28 and the funeral took place at Leeds Parish Church on the 19th October. In his 11 years as a professional Paul cemented a place as one of the all-time greats of snooker. After his death the Paul Hunter Foundation was set up to give disadvantaged kids places to play sport and socialise.

Industry: Leeds, the City that Made Everything.

I can't do a proper job here, only a quick, selective overview but if you want more, go and get a copy of any number of books on Leeds' industrial heritage or have a look at the Thoresby Society website under Publications in Print. The breadth of industries in Leeds across time is so vast that a simple list of companies would go on for half a book – as far back as 1781 there were around 75 cloth merchants or 33 common breweries in 1886. The range of production and services is astounding, from industries to one person businesses. Although there are entries on companies and individuals throughout the book I can't do justice to them here; each would require at least a large pamphlet and most a book such as the one on **Hainsworth Textiles**.

It depends how far you want to go back, should we start at the prehistoric earthworks in Killingbeck and try to work out their function or the Mesolithic/Middle Stone Age people of Thorpe Stapleton in East Leeds (Knostrop/Whitkirk)? Perhaps we shouldn't be too ambitious and just do the three to five thousand years since the Bronze Age artefacts found at Roundhay, Hunslet and Tinshill? The point being there's been people in and around what we now think of as Leeds for a heck of a long time and we, including all the greatest experts in the world can only guess at much of what they were up to. Did they swap berries or mushrooms? Maybe help each other construct shelters or catch and kill things to eat? Maybe I'll kick off at the first written reference to Leeds (Leodis) by the Venerable Bede in his *History of the English Church and People* around AD 730 or the oldest pub in Britain traced to 953 in Bardsey. What about starting with the 12th Century Knights Templar, up at Tempsie, exporting wool to France, Belgium and Holland and renting out land, or the creation of Briggate (Bridge Street) by Maurice De Gant in the early 13th Century with the following charter (1207) granting fixed rents, a court, and the ability to practice crafts and commerce? The market, held on the bridge over the river Aire, was a help and there had been a stone bridge there since around 1376. Prior to 1258 a Monday market, probably on Briggate, had been established and flourished. Let's skip King Charles I's charter in 1626 creating a borough or town and move to the 1660s by which time Leeds had become the main Yorkshire centre for the textile industry. The processing and trade of cloth in and around Leeds was central to its growth and by 1700 £10 to £20,000 would be exchanged in around an hour - don't forget that's in old money when that amount of cash was enough to build three or four large churches for example - Derek Fraser's example that I wantonly stole.

It wasn't just cloth sold, the Tuesday and Saturday market dominated the streets of Leeds, selling fruit, veg and corn, livestock of all smells, fish from the sea (or more often locally farmed/caught), pots, pans and general utensils, meat, leather goods and dairy products, most of it locally produced and feeding (with Halifax) the greatest general market in the north of England. Back to textiles, (I shouldn't really, there are plenty of books on it) the output of broadcloth rose from 30,000 pieces to 60,000 between 1720 and 1740 – in 1724 the twice weekly cloth market was described by Daniel Defoe as 'a prodigy of its kind unequalled in the world' – and by 1770 Leeds alone was handling one sixth of England's export trade. Throughout the 18th Century the industry grew and five cloth halls were built, with one, on The Calls, big enough to hold 1,210 stalls. This growth needed people and obviously with any growth in population there is an associated growth in industry and trade, people need housing (6,000 houses being built in the last three decades of the 18th Century), bricks, clay and tiles, bread, food, abattoirs, blacksmiths, clothes, shoes, boots, books, newspapers, barbers, soap, churches, beer etc.

The brewing industry in Leeds shouldn't be under played, during the 1600s it's said to be famous for its nut brown ale and towards the end of the 1700s inns and beer houses were increasing until the 'deregulation' of the 1830 Beer Act, allowing people to sell beer from their home, resulted in over 450 beer shops. Goods and people need transporting, visitors needs a meal, beer, entertainment and a bed, or maybe something to read. *The Leeds Mercury* was first printed in the city during 1718 and Leeds became the largest centre for printing outside London by the 1800s. The entertainment could have involved watching some bear or bull baiting (Quarry Hill, Harewood or the Bull Ring in Wortley which still carries the name), a horse race on Chapletown Moor, cock or dog fighting or a visit to the Theatre Royal on Hunslet Lane built in 1771. By the early 1800s forty stage coaches a day ran to or from Leeds and within 15 years it was twice that amount. Much of the process of growth needs coal and this whole interplay

Magazine advert circa 1906.

generates money and trade which leads to further diversity and innovation as spare money searches out increased industry and more varied goods/services. For example, by 1814 there were 14 booksellers and stationers which grew to 54 in less than 50 years, by which point there were also 18 music sellers, 37 music teachers, 14 artists and 26 libraries.

Leeds was one of the Northern English cities that powered and took forward the Industrial Revolution. Obviously, these industries are often interlinked with one spawning another in support or as an unexpected consequence/bi-product. For example, the Leeds coal industry led the Middleton Colliery to build a horse-drawn railroad, which David Goodman (*The Making of Leeds*) reckons was the first in the world, an innovation which eventually led to Leeds becoming the largest producer of locomotives in Britain and, after a detailed search of the manufacturers of Europe and America, probably the world. The wool industry needed merchants, transport, the building and maintenance of mills and equipment but the abundance of the waste product of lanolin fed the growth of the Leeds soap and cosmetics industries – the remaining sludge being sold on as fertiliser and one of **Soapy Joe's** bi-products, glycerine, was sold on for explosives – or the wool trades more recent funding of Asquith's early mapping of DNA leading directly to the realisation of the proteins importance. The relationship between the woollen industry and the chemical industry went two ways and most of the many chemical companies in Leeds developed as a result of the demands of local industries. They made the dyestuffs for the woollen and leather manufactures, oils and lubricants for the engineering industries, fertilisers, medicines, cough balsam, metal and furniture polish, soap and cleaning materials, blackcurrant and glycerine, soap, baking powder, children's teething and cooling powders, many kinds of acids and assorted pharmaceuticals. My favourite examples of one invention or industry spawning another are the unexpected and unusual ones. **Wordsworth Donisthorpe**'s adapting technology from his father's inventions/wool combing machinery to create what could have produced the world's first moving pictures or James Longley adapting the equipment he had built for Le Prince for moving pictures to create some of the world's earliest **vending machines**.

It's well documented (and I've just reiterated it for the umpteemph time) that wool, cloth and their processing were central to the historical growth of Leeds but it was geographical position, smart people and diversity that has given its economy historical strength. In engineering Leeds really does seem to have made everything, just to take a couple of companies who will have innovated, developed and patented new products. **Thomas Green and Son** produced Britain's first chain driven grass mower, ornamental gates and railings, garden furniture, pub tables (which can still be spotted around Leeds), wheelbarrows, steam rollers, vehicles for sweeping roads, locomotives, food preparation machinery, they made portable lighting sets between 1895 and 1901), tram engines, lathes, bombs, mine sinker, mortar shells, artillery wheels and this was not one of the biggest Leeds companies. **Greenwood & Batley** were a big Leeds firm and I've lifted much of this straight off Wiki to save my fingers but it's well documented, when you get bored with the list move on, I'll keep going to properly illustrate the point. At the beginning of the 20th Century Greenwood & Batley's promotional material offered, 'every description of General and Special machine tools for Railway. Marine and General Engineers, including Hydraulic and other Forging and Stamping Machinery, Lathes, Punching, Shearing, Planing, Milling, Shaping, Drilling and Boring Machines. Bolt, Nut and Screw Machinery. Testing Machines for strength of Material. Wood Working Machinery. Special plants and machinery for making Armour Plates, Ordnance, Gun Mountings and Ammunition: also for Small Arms Cartridges, Gunpowder etc.

and every description of War Material. Rolling Mills for Metal Coining, Presses and Minting Machinery. The 'Albion', 'Leeds', and Anglo-American systems for Extraction of every kind of Vegetable Oil including Machinery for Preparing and Decorticating Seeds, Nuts etc. Presses for making Cattle Feeding Cakes, Seed and Grain Elevators and Warehousing machinery. – you still reading? I don't mind if you move to the next paragraph....it's a long list – Oil Refineries. Cotton and other Baling Presses. Improved Patented Machines for Preparing and Spinning Waste Silk, China Grass, Rhea, Ramie, and other fibres. Whyte's patent Cop Winding Machine. Frickart's Improved Corliss Steam Engines, single compound and triple expansion of the largest powers, for driving Factories, Mills, Electrical Installations, etc. Sole Manufacturers of The Brayton Patent Oil Engine. All kinds of Dynamos and Motors for Lighting or Transmission of Power. Speciality: Motors for electrically driven Machine Tools etc. De Laval's Patent Steam Turbine Motors, Turbine Dynamos, Turbine Pumps and Fans (for Great Britain and Colonies, China and Japan). All kinds of Military Small Arms Ammunition, Self-propelling Torpedoes (Whitehead's) for the Navy, and Horse Shoes for the British Government. Patent Platen Printing Machines. Patent Boot Sewing Machines. Cloth Cutting Machines. Patent Boot Sewing Machines. Cloth Cutting Machines for Wholesale Clothiers, etc.' And that's not to mention the battery powered *Greenbat* railway locomotives, the electric flat trucks for use in factories or the 25 electric tramcars for Leeds Corporation or the standard gauge locomotives – Armley Mills Industrial Museum has got one and Middleton Railway has a different model. Ey did I mention that in the late 19th century that they made their own electricity generating station for the factory and then started producing them for other people.

Again, you'd need a book to do justice to all the artisans, trades and crafts people and artists of the Leeds area, especially if you employed the layout, photograph and text size tricks that make 20 to 30 thousand word pamphlet/booklets into books costing over a tenner. From 21st Century artisans such as the woollen cups and saucers produced by **Emma Dolan** from Weetwood Studios in Far Headingley starting at £150 a pop (I'm guessing they're decorative) to the sole traders so crucial to the early development of the city, from the film makers to the plumbers and electricians, they all contribute to the fabric, culture and economy of the city.

In the title of this overview I've changed the tense of that well used phrase, to the past tense – in the past the phrase seems spot on. Leeds has produced all sorts of gizmos that can be found in obscure corners of the world, from pianos to binoculars to stone crushing machinery to big stone sculptures – I've got a Leeds built mangle in the shed, for example. Way into the 20th Century Marin Wainwright (*True North*) revels in Mikhail Gorbachev, during the height of Glasnost, appearing on TV in a Leeds made suit. Today, like the rest of the country, Leeds has moved into the service sector but we've done it well. Outside London, Leeds is Britain's largest centre for business, legal and financial services and has the largest number of people employed in financial and business services, with a total of 109,060 (2007). There are over 30 national and international banks based in the city. In keeping with its tradition, Leeds still has a relatively diverse economy which in 2006 generated goods and services to the value of £16.3 billion while the **Leeds City Region**, consisting of around 100,000 businesses, had an economy of £46 billion. Leeds is still the UK's fastest growing city and has the second largest employment total outside London with over 110,000 people commuting to work in Leeds from outside the district every day.

Leeds was named the best shopping destination in the UK by the Rough Guide to Britain (Aaron Lennon travels from London to shop in Leeds), so it's fitting the nation's current three most successful high street chains came out of Leeds, Burtons/Arcadia, Marks & Spencer and Next (Joseph Hepworth & Sons). Leeds city centre has approximately 3.2 million people within its catchment area, over 1,000 shops with a combined floor space of 2,264,100 square feet (210,340 m2) and there is over 1 mile of indoor shopping in the city centre. Leeds City Centre's shopping capacity is due to expand further with the £650m Eastgate Quarters retail development coming back on track and expected to provide another 130 stores and restaurants. Having said all that about the service and retail industries, Leeds is still the UK's third largest manufacturing centre. Right, I need to go fold some washing and throw some food at kids so I'll stop now.......s'pose I should do a conclusion first?... Can't you just do your own?... Ok, ok, Leeds and industry and business and creative thinking and that, we're right good at it and we always were.

I

Fiona May Iapichino (born 1969) was an athlete who competed for the United Kingdom and later Italy in the long jump. She attended and trained at **Trinity & All Saints College** in Horsforth while she was a World Junior Champion triple-jumper, studying Economics, Business Management and Administration. In 1994 she married Gianni Iapichino and became an Italian citizen and, feeling that there was insufficient support for athletes in the UK, began to represent Italy. At Gothenburg, in 1995, she became the first ever female Italian to become world champion in track and field and thus 'La Pantera Negra' (the Black Panther) became a national hero and, with her husband, the Italian 'Posh 'n' Becks'.

 She twice won silver at the Olympics, became World Champion a second time at Edmonton (2001) and controversially missed the gold at Seville (1999) when a Spanish athlete Niurka Montalvo beat her, only for TV replays to show that the Spaniard had crossed the board but had not marked the plasticine. In 2006 she retired from competitions and took advantage of her Italian celebrity status, modelling and starting a career in show business.

Icon A.D. I'm using as an example of a could've been band, there's more famous and successful Leeds bands that I haven't done but you can find out about those easily. They formed in east Leeds in 1978 and all attended Temple Moor High School, well the first line-up did – not sure how well the girls would have gone down at an all boy school – and gigged around for a while. They noticed an ad in the music press from **Crass** who were planning to release an album of 'unknowns' so they sent a rehearsal tape and the track *Cancer* was included on the first Crass compilation *Bullshit Detector*. They then sent some new recordings to Radical Change records who in September 1982 released the *Don't Feed us Shit* EP. The single was a big success, peaked at two in the 'independent' chart (a big deal in them days) and the band recorded a **John Peel** session the same month. They soon recorded their next single *Let The Vultures Fly*, also released on Radical Change in June 1983. It flew out, far out-selling the first. Both singles were released in the tradition of 'anarcho-punk' and sold at a 'pay no more than' price, lower than other singles and with the price printed large on the cover so that the shops couldn't up the price – 85p and 95p. The high sales and rosy future had Backs distribution (who funded Radical Change) encouraging the band to cross over into the more mainstream punk market with its full colour covers and full retail price so, in a *Complete Control* manner, they did a single called '*Backs To The Wall*' that was never released and ended the relationship with Backs. The band split soon after.

 I liked the male (Icon) lead singer, Dicki Walton (who was replaced by two women) but I don't suppose you can run a band if you're never sure if the singer's going to get too wasted to turn up to gigs as happened a couple of times, like at the F-Club, when Craig, the guitarist, had to do vocals. I'm not just doing them as they used to be old mates but the drummer and guitarist used to help out playing with me on my girly music before I got a band of my own together; tumbling, bouncing drummer full of energy and enthusiasm and Craig was the ultimate punky, chugging guitarist who nailed the brief, melodic, lead licks, although I saw a different side of their playing. Craig still plays with his son's band **Guns On The Roof** (not a Clash covers band) who are also managed by ex **Abrasive Wheels** guitarist Dave Ryan. Abrasive Wheels were another east Leeds punk band that had indi success and almost made it big; I heard them played a couple of times on the peak-time Radio 1 breakfast show. The Icon A.D. bass player Rog had his finest moments when he starred in goal as the one ringer in the triumphant **Hang The Dance** 5-a-side team.

  Lest We Forget, a retrospective album including all their recorded material was released in 2006 by Overground Records but unfortunately it hasn't got one of my favourites *Police Car* on it. After picking them out as there isn't likely to be that much info about them out there I've just found out that they've got a good chunk in *The Day The Country Died: A History of Anarcho Punk 1980 to 1984* by Ian Glasper.

Igloos are not really that common in Leeds on account that they'd probably melt. We prefer houses made out of more solid material, such as brick or stone or maybe steel and glass. But just double checking that people in Leeds don't tend to live in igloos I found.......

Igloo Thermo-Logistics. Do you remember them on Dragons Den? I was sure they were from Leeds and I've kept seeing the vans around Leeds ever since, which I thought tricked me into thinking that was the case. Do you remember? The first time they'd ever had a bidding war between all five of the Dragons. Anyway they run freezer/chilled transport including refrigerated Smart Cars, a selection of light goods vans, and multi-temperature HGVs. Their website says 'Igloo offers the widest range of high quality specialist refrigerated logistics services available in the UK and Western Europe' and they have two purpose built storage & distribution centres in Leeds and London.

Ilkley feels like a cheat, I mean, come on, is it part of Leeds? I don't feel like I should include it but it's got a Leeds postcode. Not that I've got anything against it, it's a lovely town and people from that side of Leeds will no doubt think of it as part of Leeds, as may half the residents. When I was a lad it meant you were almost there, or so Dad told us, and then on the way back it meant you were almost home. Never understood how that worked. Means I can't do Alan Titchmarsh or the Ilkley Literature Festival, the largest and oldest literary festival in the north of England, which can't be that good......they've not invited me yet. Have I mentioned that it's a beautiful town in its own right, well worth a visit? I could have mentioned the moor (where the ducks, apparently, play football) or the Bronze age carving, going on 4000 years old, or the druidical stone circle or maybe Charles Darwin again but I can't really, it's simply not part of Leeds – don't care what postcode it's got...although obviouslt it is. Fantastic, I've done Ilkley without mentioning a hat, or the lack of, once.

Ralph Ineson (born 1969) is an actor best known for playing the character of Chris Finch in the BBC TV programme *The Office*. He's obviously done loads of other stuff, I've heard him in plays on Radio 4 a couple of times, he's been in a few films, *First Knight*, *From Hell*, *The Damned United, Is anybody there?* and *Harry Potter and the Half-Blood Prince* and is the continuity announcer for the TV station Dave, the tenth largest television channel in the UK, he's also being used more by the BBC for the voice-over in documentaries.

The **Internet**. Again, this could be a book or an extremely large database. At the beginning of this century Leeds had Europe's biggest internet server farm, more ISDN lines per head of population than any other major city and handled over 33% of Britain's internet traffic making it the UK's biggest internet city. I can't find up to date info on this now and am suspicious that the sale of Dominic Marrocco's company, ISP Firstnet Services, may have sent the traffic elsewhere. Although it may not, the hardware may have stayed and the *186k* business on North Street sells commercial broadband. I'm also nervous of 'facts' in an industry that can change so quickly. After the sale of Firstnet, Dominic went and bought Mike Tyson's house in Las Vegas which he planned to put up as the prize in a reality TV poker tournament. Who knows how many it is now but before the recession Leeds had over 1,000 companies in the IT and software sector and one of the largest IT crowds outside London. The Leeds business sector was also an 'early adopter' and I started working for a company called Healthworks around 1995/6 who, as on online health information service, sold electronic newsletters such as *Health On The Internet* and *Disability Informer* – which also supplied content and information to a BBC disability based programme. These *electronic* newsletters also had to be distributed in print form as many people didn't understand the concept of clicking the links in the electronic version and going straight to the site concerned. I well remember having to explain to people what the internet actually was, never mind the mechanics of an electronic newsletter, and around the time that the company formed (1993/94) they were told by their bank manager that 'there is no future in the internet'.

There are many web-based companies in Leeds, I'm sure you'll have your own examples, and most companies will have a website – the **Hainsworth Textiles** site is an infomine – but I'll take txtttools with offices down by the river (employing 24 people) as an example of a small to medium-sized one. They developed software to allow people to send and receive text messages to and from multiple people through their computer using 'the most powerful text messaging platform on the planet'. They sell it into the public and private sector where people need to communicate quickly and efficiently with a group of people, so it can be used if a lecture has been cancelled or Sportscotland want to send out an avalanche report; according to their website 'over 45% of UK colleges and universities send critical messages every day with edutxt.' These are the basics of what they do but it has meant continually developing specialist software, so that they offer voting and surveying functions, software that instantly breaks down responses into percentages etc. This is just one example of innovative use of the internet in Leeds and I could have picked from many more traditional uses such as retroleeds.com with specially designed 'Leeds United Shirts, T-Shirts, Hoodies and Bespoke Leeds United Canvas Wall Art.' Which are 'retro, classic, contemporary, irreverent, funny and occasionally offensive.' The internet, Leeds gets it.

Interplay celebrated its 40th anniversary in 2010. It's a company/organisation based in Armley aimed at involving the disenfranchised in the arts. Moving from a predominantly theatre-based organisation it now involves 'theatre, film, music, visual arts, radio, literature – using the arts as a vehicle to help people re-engage with their local communities and in turn develop new skills and self-esteem...The company particularly engages with young people who experience economic, social and sensory barriers.' These include children who are severely disabled, young people having difficulties at school with behavioural/social barriers and less often adults suffering social isolation through disabilities or mental health. The people produce cultural artefacts and gain new skills.

Interplay's LS12 Film group won The First Light Movies Award 2010 for Best Film by Over 13s (under 19) with *One Man's Walk* about a man with Down's Syndrome showing the world through his eyes. The film has also been selected to appear in the 36th annual Seattle International Film Festival, the biggest in the US. This is just one example of the company's achievements. The organisation is heavily involved in the annual I Love West Leeds festival and Interplay Radio hits the air waves for the three weeks of the festival giving young people all sorts of skills and experience. To celebrate its 40 th Interplay revived the play **This Land** (the story of Woody Guthrie) which gained national attention when it was first produced. The production opened at the West Yorkshire Playhouse and went out on a national tour in the autumn of 2010.

Marian Ion Ionescu (born 1929) was a visionary, practical and pioneering cardiac (heart) surgeon and inventor who, with just a couple of suitcases, did a moonlit runner from Romania's communist dictatorship of 1965 and a year later found himself at the LGI, where he spent the most prolific and productive 25 years of life. His work at the fledgling department, with **Geoffrey Wooler** and team, developed into areas of world importance, putting the LGI and Leeds firmly on the map as a centre of pioneering heart surgery and excellence, at the forefront of global knowledge.

In February 1967, following extensive research in the LGI lab, Marian implanted, for the first time (in the mitral position in a person) a porcine aortic valve attached to a Teflon cloth collar. After adapting the frame of the valve he was able to implant the valves into all three cardiac locations (mitral, aortic, tricuspid). Ionescu kept experimenting and developing, changing the mountings and the substances he treated the valves with chemicals to improve their performance and longevity until in 1970 he achieved his goal of the world's first **pericardial heart valve**. This was a huge medical breakthrough which led directly to the almost perfect heart valves used today. Even though people mimicked his work to produce their own valves, a decade later there was only one that bore any comparison in positive outcomes.

Some of the rest has come pretty much straight of Wiki, the language is so specialised and precise that if I try to re-jig it, add my own thoughts and mix in other info I'd probably mess up the meaning. In congenital heart disease Marian 'was the first surgeon to successfully reconstruct a heart with a single ventricle, and continued to use various techniques for the repair of such a complex abnormality.' At his LGI lab he designed and built two original devices 'for the repair of congenital cyanotic cardiac diseases .... the 'mono-cusp patch' for the correct enlargement of the narrowed pulmonary artery and annulus and a valved conduit (a tube containing a three-cusped valve) for cases with discontinuity between the right ventricle and the pulmonary artery '

He was a prolific writer, publishing 242 scientific articles on various aspects of cardiovascular and thoracic surgery in medical journals, 37 chapters in books and treatises and was majorly involved in eight books including two of his own. The cardiac surgical unit in Leeds attracted a large number of overseas surgeons (and top students) for further training and knowledge and Marian accepted 122 invitations from various universities and medical centres to give lectures (making 22 visits for 'round table' surgical demonstrations) and presented 186 papers at different scientific meetings. He held six fellowships. He has a passion for high altitude mountain climbing and I'll give the last word to him; 'Sometimes I feel the impulse to scream: what the hell, let's try again, let's give it a roll, let's go for the hidden side of the moon.'....Which is a bit potty. Marian, I hope you know there's no oxygen in space.

Mohammed Iqbal was the 113th Lord Mayor of Leeds and the first Muslim Lord Mayor – full title 'The Right Worshipful the Lord Mayor of the City of Leeds'. During his time in office he represented the office at over 1,000 events. He came to Leeds from Pakistan when he was nine years old, attended various Leeds' school and thinks of himself as 'a Leeds man.' During his time as a businessman he found that many people were coming to him with their problems and decided to go into politics. He joined the Labour party and was elected to Leeds City Council in 1999 for the City and Hunslet ward and in May 2006 he became Lord Mayor of Leeds.

J

Erroll James founded the Leeds Caribbean Cricket Club in 1948, it travelled around playing the 'locals' of Yorkshire and played in the Leeds - West Riding Cricket League, winning the title in 2009, the last year of the league. He was also the co-founder of the United Caribbean Association and the Leeds branch of the International Council on Race Relations.

St James's University Hospital or **Jimmy's**, as it's more properly called, is known as the largest teaching hospital in Europe. It's also one of Britain's most famous hospitals, in part, thanks to the YTV documentary show *Jimmy's* which from 1987 to1994 was prime time, top-rating TV. In 2007 the NHS's first adult-to-adult live donor liver transplant was performed there and I'm sure there've been a theatre load more 'firsts' performed there that have disappeared into the ether, like perhaps **Bariatric surgery**.

Jo Lee I'm going to use as an example of artisans and artists that operate all over the city. I can't do them all. From the woollen cups and saucers produced by Emma Dolan to Casey Orr's photographs of inmates and their families blown up big and adorning the external walls of Armley prison or John Dace's metal work surrounding the sign at Leeds Market, these people are important to the economy and well-being of Leeds. Jo started out in her artistic (further) education at Park Lane College getting a distinction in a City & Guilds (B&W) photography course and later got a first class honours degree in ceramics. She supports her work by doing commissions, teaching and workshops in schools, Unis, colleges and selling privately as far afield as India and Australia – from a tenner for a mug up to quite a lot more.

Although she also does paintings and sketches, Jo works mainly in monochrome ceramics, sometimes with hints of colour, usually based around the human form, or elements of it, and she exhibits widely. On her website she says, 'core to my work is a fascination with the human form and the human condition. I am fascinated by the way in which people attempt to document their lives, retain memories, maintain histories and somehow try to make sense of their existence. My work is influenced by ordinary day-to-day events, life, living and ultimately our demise. I am interested by the ways in which a person's life can be acknowledged and validated.' She's an artist....they're like that, they think about stuff.

I'll concentrate on her piece *Wave* (previous page and detail pictured on cover) commissioned to celebrate The International Day of Older People and made by taking casts of the hands of people in care homes and the related generations that followed them. The hands hold photographs representing memories, stories and reminiscences, an exploration of identity and the connectedness of older people, if you will. I'll leave the next to last word to Jo. 'The manner of their display creates a wave-like effect, representing the wave of the generations. Young and old. Inseparable. Flowing into each other. Intermingled.... we are all old people in training.... A passing on of stories, histories and events from one generation to another. Combining all generations.' I'll just add the annoying comment that no doubt many people have made, it's also like they're waving to us and maybe even waving to each other across the generations. See what I did there? It was like a play on words.

Pauline Neville-Jones, Baroness Neville-Jones (1939). Now I've heard rumours that she was born in Leeds but as the former Chairman of the Joint Intelligence Committee, there's only sparse info on her background available. Wiki lists her birthplace as Birmingham but the former BBC Governor certainly attended **Leeds Girls' High School**. So if any of you know any spies can you check her SP and let me know? Ta.

Dorothea Jordan (1761–1816) was an Irish born actress using the name of **Mrs. Jordan** who was the mistress of **William IV** for twenty years before his seven years as King (prior to Queen Victoria) and was mother to his eight living, illegitimate children. Conservative Party leader David Cameron is one of their descendants. She apparently called herself 'Mrs' to conceal a pregnancy, which some sources attribute to rape, and as it was more acceptable for a married woman to be on the stage and used Jordan in comparing the escape across the Irish sea to that of the Children of Israel crossing the Jordan River and gaining freedom.

The first biography of her, *The life of Mrs. Jordan: including original private correspondence* (James Boaden, 1831, Edward Bull, London) starts her theatre career on the stages of Leeds in 1872 where, aged 20 she joined a theatre company operated by Tate Wilkinson. In July of that year 'she was put up, for the first time, in Leeds.' She became a great success in Leeds but when rumours spread of her proposed move to London her shows were less well attended and she left for London in 1785 'with no great cheer of mind' but was a huge success.

Virgil Craig Jordan. Tamoxifen has been found to be a safe and effective treatment for all stages of breast cancer. It is currently used in the treatment of both early and advanced ER+ (estrogen receptor positive) breast cancer in women and is the most common hormone treatment for male breast cancer. Originally used as a fertility treatment, it was Virgil Craig Jordan who first became aware of the substance whilst working on the structure-activity of anti-estrogens as part of his PhD at Leeds University and discovered its breast cancer prevention properties. Virgil arrived at Leeds Uni as an undergraduate and went on to gain his BSc and PhD here. He returned as a Lecturer in Pharmacology between 1974 and 1979; back to his alma mater, his nourishing mother, if you will, who awarded him a DSc in 1985. He also did crucial work showing the efficacy of using **Raloxifene** in the treatment of osteoporosis in postmenopausal women. He's obviously got a fist full of honours and awards and his work battling cancer continues. This is one eminent geezer who's given to humanity and I for one would like to say, nice one mi'old lad.

David Joy (1825–1903) spent much of his career with the Railway Foundry (E.B.Wilson and Company/Shepherd & Todd) in Leeds, where he worked on the design of the celebrated 2-2-2 **'Jenny Lind'** class of railway locomotive. With over 70 produced they set a long-lasting style for British locomotives. He developed the **Joy valve gear** extensively adopted by manufacturers. He developed an **assistant cylinder** for marine engines that was also widely adopted, eventually representing a total of more than one and a half million horse power. David designed engines for ships, a special form of steam hammer, a steam reversing gear, and took out three patents for hydraulic organ-blowers. The first large one was fitted to the organ in **Leeds Town Hall** and another was used at **Crystal Palace.** For more info search **David Joy Diaries** online.

The **Joy valve gear** was patented in 1870 and used extensively in the locomotive production until well into the 1920s. The gear valve regulates the steam entering and leaving a cylinder. It was adopted by most British railways including the Lancashire and Yorkshire, London and North Western, Midland, Manchester, Sheffield and Lincolnshire and was exported worldwide. He received various awards at Inventions Exhibitions and installed some to marine engines, providing a total of one million horse power.

K

Kaiser Chiefs need doing really don't they? Soz all you other Leeds bands I've ignored, but they're the biggest thing (with Corinne Bailey Rae) to come out of Leeds for years and I doff my cap to them. Brilliant and they're proud of their roots. I'll not get into stuff you'll know like the background to the name and all sorts of stuff easily found, but more reflect on the band. They confuse me because they're not for me and I find it hard to get a perspective. Not that I don't like them, it's just that I've been listening to guitar based bands for 40 years and have got a bit bored of the format. I grew up on Led Zep, Deep Purple, Wishbone Ash, Hendrix, The Doors, The Stooges, Be-Bop Deluxe, The Damned, The Clash, The Pistols, The Banshees, The Stranglers, Penetration, Magazine, Simple Minds, XTC on to New Model Army, The Pixies so I'm more likely to find my musical kicks elsewhere.

The guitarist reminds me of myself when I played; limited technical ability but intelligent, I wonder if, like me, he prefers playing rhythm. In fact the sound of the whole band remind me a bit of Hang The Dance (band I used to play in) 'cept they have better hooks and obviously, higher quality production with more time in the studio. There's other things I prefer about them as well but I'll not get into that here, it's way self indulgent.

Mrs Mick saw them live at some big festival during 2010 and thought they were absolutely outstanding live, blew all the other bands away, she was shocked at how good they were, not because she expected them to be bad but they were that good it was startling. Their first album *Employment* was short-listed for the Mercury Award, sold around four million (not bad in the days of downloads), the four (kosher) singles from the album went Top Twenty (three going Top Ten) and they won three Brits in 2006. Their second album, *Yours Truly, Angry Mob*, went to No. 1 in the UK and gave them their first No. 1 single (*Ruby*). The third album, *Off with Their Heads*, went to No. 2 in the UK album charts and the first single from it, *Never Miss a Beat*, entered the UK charts at No. 5.The second single from *Bad Days*, is about LUFC's League One Play-Off final defeat at Wembley Stadium. I should listen to some of their stuff really, shouldn't I?

The Kalee film projector. See **A Kershaw and Sons**.

John Keenan is a legendary music promoter on the Leeds scene probably best remembered by people of a certain age for the **Futurama Festivals** and **The 'F' Club**. He's been putting on gigs in Leeds for going on 40 years, at venues including: The Grand Theatre, Leeds Poly, The 'F' Club at the Ace of Clubs, Roots, Brannigans, The Leeds Queen's Hall, The Warehouse, Leeds University, The Fforde Grene, The Bierkeller, Tiffany's, Ritzy's, Leeds Irish Centre, Leeds Astoria, City Varieties, Leeds Town Hall, The Duchess, Rooftop Gardens, The Cockpit, Leeds Uni Stylus and his current venue **The New Roscoe**.

The **list of artists** John has brought to Leeds is way too big to provide but here's a small selection: The Police, U2, Human League, Joy Division, New Order, Radiohead, Coldplay, Nirvana, Oasis, Blur, Muse, Manic Street Preachers, PIL Ltd., Pulp, Wire, The B52s, The Stranglers, Siouxsie & the Banshees, The Damned, Killing Joke, Adam & The Ants, Toyah, The Cult, The Cramps, Echo & The Bunnymen, OMD, The Teardrop Explodes, The Birthday Party,

The Slits, The Adverts, Depeche Mode, Bad Manners, The Beat, The Specials, The Selecter, The Bodysnatchers, Prince Far I, John Cooper Clarke, UK Subs, The Vibrators, Ultravox, Johnny Thunders, XTC, The Psychedelic Furs, Mogwai, the Doves, The Fall, Half Man Half Biscuit, The Verve, Cast, Mudhoney, Hawkwind, Wishbone Ash, Mo Tucker, John Cale, Nico, Gong, Caravan, Fairport Convention, Maddy Prior, June Tabor, Loudon Wainwright III, John Martyn, Roy Harper, Christy Moore, Captain Beefheart & The Magic Band, Nils Lofgren, Al Stewart, Steve Earle, Joe Ely, Buffalo Tom, The Beat Farmers, Arthur Lee & Love, Lonnie Donegan, Chris Barber, John McLaughlin, Cowboy Junkies, Michelle Shocked, Elastica, Tanita Tikarum, Martin Carthy, Eliza Carthy, Norma Waterson, Lindisfarne, The Manfreds, They Might Be Giants, Bill Nelson, Inspiral Carpets, Richard Thompson, Bo Diddley, Stevie Marriott, Steve Harley, Ian Hunter, Ian Gillan, Georgia Satellites, Hanoi Rocks, Dogs D'Amour, The Quireboys, Wrathchild, Tiger Tailz, Napalm Death, Bolt Thrower, The Almighty, Judie Tzuke, Joe Jackson, Steve Gibbons, Bobbie Womack, Mary Coughlan, Mary Black, Francis Black, Moving Hearts, Capercaillie, Anne Peebles, Classix Nouveaux, Willie Mitchell, Gomez, Embrace, Green on Red, Robert Cray, Curtis Mayfield, Mary Black, Capercaillie, Eek a Mouse, Aswad, David Rudder, Gil Scott Heron, De La Soul, the Last Poets, The Beatnigs, The Beautiful South, Fishbone, John McLaughlin, Rik Mayall, Adrian Edmondson, Dawn French, Jennifer Saunders, Nigel Planer, Peter Richardson, Alexei Sayle, Craig Charles,Charlie Chuck, Frank Sidebottom, Wreckless Eric John Otway & Wild Willy Barrett, Mary Unfaithful, Ted Chippington, Joe Strummer, Jesus Lizard, The Jayhawks, Tom Russell, Chip Taylor, Jim White, Tony Joe White, Richie Havens, Taj Mahal, Orange Juice, Teenage Fanclub, The Icicle Works, Pete Wylie & Wah!, Del Amitri, The Raincoats, Wayne County, Billy Bragg, Space, Beth Orton, Suzanne Vega, Sam Brown, Kate Rusby, Kiki Dee, Shawn Colvin, Tina Dico, Sophie B. Hawkins, Laura Viers, Kate Rogers, Cowboy Junkies, The Eurhythmics, Steve Earle, Joe Ely, Donovan, Ramblin' Jack Elliott, Country Joe McDonald, Hubert Sumlin, RL Burnside, Honeyboy Edwards, Hubert Sumlin, Rufus Wainwright, Seth Lakeman, Glenn Tilbrook, David Gray, Damien Rice, Fion Regan, Iron & Wine, Geoff Healey, The Blockheads, Midlake, Richmond Fontaine, Tom Russell, Bob Brozman.

Geoffrey Anketell Studdert Kennedy nicknamed **Woodbine Willie** MC (1883–1929), was a writer, poet priest and social activist who gained the nickname 'Woodbine Willie' for giving Woodbine cigarettes with spiritual comfort to injured and dying soldiers during the World War I. Leeds-born and educated at Leeds Grammar School he won the Military Cross for running 'under murderous machine gun-fire into no-man's land, carrying a wooden cross,' to help the wounded of both sides at the Battle of Messines. He was a chain smoker who also gave out 'handfuls' of Woodbines to the troops with whom he'd pray, chat, joke, share a cuppa with and sometimes write home for. A committed pacifist, his poems after the war were influenced by his wartime experiences and published in the books *Rough Rhymes of a Padre* (1918), and *More Rough Rhymes* (1919). His stuff seems to have sold well, the 1919 published *Lies* reaching its 18th edition by 1937. He also seems to have held strong opinions that he didn't mind sharing if the chapter headings such as 'The Church Is Not a Movement but a Mob,' 'Capitalism is Nothing But Greed, Grab, and Profit-Mongering' and 'So-Called Religious Education Worse than Useless' from his book *Democracy and the Dog-Collar* (1921) are anything to go by. After the war he worked in the slums of London with the homeless and unemployed and carried out speaking tours of Britain as part of his work for the Industrial Christian Fellowship (ICF). According to the truly fantastic Spartacus Educational website a newspaper noted that at his public sermons 'women wept and men broke down', he was known throughout the land and at his funeral people covered his coffin and grave with packets of Woodbine as a mark of love and respect. He's also honoured with a feast day by the US Episcopal Church.

A Kershaw and Sons was set up in 1880s by **Abraham Kershaw** (1861–1929) producing electrical and scientific instruments, cameras, and later lanterns and projection equipment including the world famous Kalee Projector – named by reversing Abraham's initials and adding the first three letters of his home city. There are examples on display at **Armley Mills Industrial Museum**. It was Abraham who designed the camera that Scott (of the Antarctic) took on his ill-fated British Antarctic Expedition in 1910

There's little info that I can track down, so much of the following is from Gilleghan's *Leeds: An A-Z of Local History*. During the Boer War the factory made and repaired telegraphic and army signalling equipment and in World War II they made sights for bombs and guns (the telescopic sight/scope being invented in Middleton by William Gascoigne), tank periscopes and 250,000 pairs of prism binoculars. Kershaw's was bought by Gaumont-British in 1943, became part of the Rank Organisation in 1947 and looks to have closed in1980. Kershaw's manufactured the mythical Electrocardiograph for the LGI that I can find no info about. There's that and something to do with Ultrasound, that I keep hearing whispers about, being someway remarkable to Leeds but I can't find either and to make it more frustrating I half remember the Ultrasound one. I've emailed an eminent medic so let's see if he replies.

Martin Kettle (born 1949) is best known as a columnist for ***The Guardian***, where he is also the assistant editor. He attended **Leeds Modern School** and it looks like he'll have been born in Leeds as his dad, **Arnold Kettle**, was a lecturer in English Literature at the University of Leeds from 1948. Arnold was an author, Marxist literary critic, life-long member of the Communist Party and the first Professor of Literature at the **Open University**. Martin worked for various publications before moving to *The Guardian* such as *New Society* and *The Sunday Times* and before journalism he was a research officer for the **National Council for Civil Liberties.** He wrote regularly for *Marxism Today* and writes a column on classical music for *Prospect* magazine.

Kidney/Dialysis and **Frank Maudsley Parsons**, BSc, MBChB, MD (1918–1989). On the evening of 30th September 1956, **the UK's first dialysis** was performed by Frank Parsons at the LGI, after hearing from the Medical Research Council, that 'there is no place for an artificial kidney in British medicine.' This night marked the start of the first artificial kidney unit in the UK which saved many lives and put the LGI at the forefront of all British renal services. There was a period of time when the LGI provided the entire dialysis service for acute renal failure in the UK. Parsons maintained and continued to modify the prototype dialysis machines and the success at Leeds of dealing with this otherwise fatal obstetric complication led to other hospitals around the country adopting it. The 'Leeds' machine was still in use until about 1980. I like people who believe in something so much that they go against accepted opinion.

Old King Cole is an English language nursery rhyme. The historical identity of **King Cole** has been much debated and several candidates have been advanced as possibilities with my favourite being **Coel Hen** leader of the Hen Ogledd (the Old North, including Elmet of which Leeds is thought to be the last 'capital'). It has a Roud Folk Song Index number of 1164.

King's Mills were on Swinegate and link us back to Leeds' feudal past. There's a carved stone on the river bank marking the site of the oldest industrial site in Leeds going back, at least, to 1086. It was called King's Mills as the tenants of the manor were compelled to grind their corn here, at the lord's mill. They had to pay a percentage of the flour to the lord of the manor and were banned from buying flour produced elsewhere. Apparently some of Leeds City Train Station was built on part of the site. Right, sorry that this is a bit 'local history', I shouldn't have included it really but thought the carved stone on the river bank was interesting. So, let mi'off, go on, let mi'off, it was almost interesting and I promise I'll be disciplined from now on and not go off on one. Anyway, Priestley was a bit scatty as was Percy Alfred Scholes and Astbury, that's what us geanie-eye are like.

Red Kites were creatures of mythical beauty when I worra lad, a rare and exquisite bird with only a few breeding pairs clinging on in Wales. Now, you know that quite big bird with the forked tail that you keep seeing soaring high over the outskirts of North Leeds? That's a Red Kite. It's no exaggeration to say that as a young ornithologist I used to dream of seeing a Red Kite, I promised myself that one day I would, might have to wait until I was 11 and, like ar'kid, set off hitch hiking to Wales. When I could, I'd travel all over to see birds but Wales seemed too far away, I did make it to Blacktoft Sands on the East coast to see a similar bird, the Marsh Harrier, which at the time was extremely rare. Historically, Red Kites were so common that they could be seen daily, scavenging in cities and towns and were protected as they kept the streets clear of rotting food. However they had become extinct in England in the 1870s after years of persecution by humans as they were seen as competition for food and a threat to game birds. The truth is that their claws and lower legs are too weak to kill anything much bigger than small mammals and they're more likely to take the worms from the land than the grouse. They rely on carrion and will clean up road kill quicker than the council.

The reason why you can sometimes see them in the skies of Leeds is that a Red Kite project was set up in 1999 on the **Harewood Estate**, run by Doug Simpson, and over the next few years they released 70 birds. Uniquely, they had a breeding pair during the first year and by 2008 at least 430 young kites had been raised, Doug was rewarded with an MBE in 2007. The battle to save the Red Kite from extinction started over 100 years ago and is the longest-running conservation project in history. Beg, borrow or steal some binoculars and the next time you're going between Leeds and Otley or Harrogate, keep an eye on the sky, try and stop off and get yourself an eyeful, they are a stunning bird. Another good place is Harewood House itself. I recently went with a bunch of six and seven-year-old school kids. Just through the gates were a couple of kites hanging low in the sky. When we got to the place where the herons were feeding, the red kites were circling and swooping down to grab bits of fish. The kids who noticed it or had me shouting in their ears about it thought it was amazing. They weren't wrong, it was.

In a publication of 1835 the eminent Wakefield conservationist Charles Waterton, lamented the disappearance of large wild birds (excluding the Heron) formerly common in that part of

Yorkshire. 'The kite, the buzzard and the raven have been exterminated long ago by our merciless gamekeepers... kites were frequent here in the days of my father but I, myself, have never seen one near this place'. You can see one easily, don't miss the chance. For more info search 'Yorkshire Red Kites'.

James Kitson (senior) formed **James Kitson**, a locomotive manufacturing company based at the Airedale Foundry, Hunslet, in 1835 with Charles Todd (an apprentice of Matthew Murray) as a partner.

At first they built locomotive components for other manufacturers but in 1838 a wealthy businessman joined and they built their first six locomotives for the Liverpool and Manchester Railway, one of which can still be seen at the Museum of Science and Industry in Manchester. When Laird joined the company changed its name to **Todd, Kitson and Laird** and it was also later called **Kitson and Laird**, **Laird and Kitson**, **Kitson Thompson and Hewitson**, **Kitson and Hewitson**, and finally **Kitson and Company**.

As well as servicing the British market they were exporting locomotives to France, Germany, Ceylon, Argentina, Denmark, Australia, Japan, Spain, South Africa, Trinidad, Chile, Jamaica, Russia, India and Mauritius – this will not be a comprehensive list.

Kitsons entered steam tramway locomotive manufacturing in 1876 and two years later they started building to their own design. They made many improvements which became industry standard, such as boxing in and replacing many of the moving parts, replacing the vertical boiler with a horizontal design and Kitson's valve-gear that they held the patent for. They built over 300 units that were distributed all over the UK and abroad. The company won a gold medal at The Great Exhibition (1851) for their early tank locomotive and produced over 5,400 locomotives.

Kitson also had a type of articulated locomotive (that the company had developed) named after him, the Kitson-Meyer. One of the blocks of **Quarry Hill Flats** was called Kitson but I think that's more likely to have been named after his son.

Frederick William Kitson was a principal locomotive designer for the company and part-managed his dad's Monk Bridge iron and steel works, established in 1854. Although Wiki mainly credits his son (next) with this, James senior set it up as he required a source of good Leeds iron for the Airedale foundry and got his sons to manage it.

James Kitson, 1st Baron Airedale (1835–1911) became the first Lord Mayor of Leeds in 1896 and lived at Gledhow Hall in Little Switzerland which overlooks Gledhow. As just mentioned, he grew his wealth by managing and developing his dad's Monk Bridge iron and steel works with his elder brother and became a partner in the very successful business. This wealth left him free to pursue a political career and after working for the Liberal Party he became an MP in 1892 and 'served' for 15 years, supporting education, Irish home rule, and old age pensions. See **Herbert Henry Asquith**. Kitson financially supported the Leeds City Mechanics' Institute, the Leeds School of Medicine and the Yorkshire College, forerunner of the University of Leeds.

The Knights Templar. Around 1155, a half mile from where **Temple Newsam House** now stands, a Knights Templar preceptory was set up. The preceptory (part farmhouse, part monastery) was at the centre of their estate and will have been surrounded by a small settlement.

It is thought to have included a granary and there was certainly an early **Fulling Mill** on the nearby river Aire as well as two other mills for the grain they produced. They built a chapel at the now defunct Thorpe Stapleton (now part of Rothwell), a small settlement of which all that remains today is the wall of an Elizabethan manor house. The main site also contained a barn of almost 150 feet in length, one of the largest of its kind in England at the time. This was a money-making operation to support the cause of the Knights Templar.

The area was then known as Neuhusum (Newsam) and the Temple part of the name was added in honour of the Templars. The area had been inhabited at least as far back as Anglo-Saxon times as a ninth/tenth century toilet was found on the site and the land was part given to the Templars (usually in exchange for prayers for the souls of rich men), part exchanged for other land and part bought. They also acquired land at Skelton, Colton, Halton, Whitkirk, Osmondthorpe, and had holdings/tenants in the town of Leeds itself. A Templar cross can be seen on the side of The Pack Horse pub. The cross was used to identify the Templar's properties and as they and their tenants were exempt from tax some opportunistic scallywags also marked their buildings with the cross in order to avoid paying taxes.

The order of the Knights Templar was set up to defend Christian pilgrims travelling to the Holy Land. Although the knights will have learnt to fight here, this preceptory was primarily established to fund the Knights Templar movement. The knights, of what is now east Leeds, would more likely have spent time praying than they would fighting.

They made most of their money through their own and their tenants farming. The large barn described above will have stored feed (oats) for their livestock of mainly sheep. The fleeces were more profitable than cash crops and were exported to France, Belgium and Holland. It was unusual at the time to keep, rather than slaughter, livestock over the winter and the 'east Leeds' Templars kept over 1,000 sheep. They also kept cattle and a limited amount of pigs in the woodlands and are very likely to have 'farmed' fish in the river Aire.

I won't bang on too much about how the 'society' was ordered as there's plenty of material out there if you are interested but the King owned everything and then parcelled out large tracts of lands to others who parcelled out smaller and so on down to the peasants. Things were different in them days, a peasant could have his ear chopped off for not attending church and tenants of the Templars paid their rent from a combination of cash, crops, produce, livestock and labour.

Influential artist **Jacob Kramer**, (1892–1962) was born in the Ukrainian (Russian Empire), into a comfortable middle-class family. His father was a 'court painter' and his mother toured regional theatres singing traditional Slavic and Hebrew folk songs. A new Tsar came in, anti-Semitism grew and Jews were expected to 'assimilate' or leave so the Kramers left in 1900 to settle in Leeds.

Without reading the biography by David Manson, *Jacob Kramer: Creativity and Loss* (Sansom, 2006) it's hard to flippantly sum up a life but here goes. He seems to have had his demons and lived much of his life as an alcoholic in poverty. Perhaps some of these demons were connected to identity and leaving home at such a crucial age as, within two years of arriving in Leeds, the ten year old Jacob did a runner, working around the north of England and even going to sea for six months. Or this was the story that Jacob told, Manson reckons that Jacob made this up to enhance his crazy, rebellious artist reputation – good lad, I love a good myth. During this time he attended occasional art classes until returning to his family in Leeds and starting his formal education at **Leeds School of Art** (named Jacob Kramer College between 1968 and 1993) which he attended between 1907 and 1913. It was during his studies that he became involved in the **Leeds Arts Club** and developed the interest in Expressionism and spiritualism that defined his most important work and quest to get beyond the physical manifestations of subjects to their spiritual essence. Jacob won a scholarship to study for a year at the Slade in London, where he remained for a number of years, immersing himself in a hedonistic lifestyle.

He returned to Leeds and became a bit of a celeb in the local art scene and after the collapse of the Leeds Arts Club tried in vain to establish an artist group and meeting place until, finally, the **Yorkshire Luncheon Club** took off – no doubt with help of his close friend Herbert Read. With regular meetings at Whitelock's pub (just like the Leeds Social Realists today), leading cultural figures of the 1930s, 40s and 50s were invited to speak. On the planning of the new club Jacob said, 'There are plenty of vital people in Leeds. I believe [a new art] club would succeed here better than anywhere else. For myself, I find more stimulus in Leeds than in London and even in Paris.' (Ee Po or YEP 3 June 1931 – cited in *The Kramer Documents,* John David Roberts, ed.)

Jacob is best remembered for his early work and also did portraits of eminent people passing through Leeds such as Delius, J.B. Priestley, Gracie Fields and Mahatma Gandhi and it seems in later life he 'knocked off' sub-standard portraits for beer money. Mrs Mick has always liked a bit of Jacob Kramer of an evening and probably due to a (Bowie inspired) teenage fascination with expressionism, so (now I've had a proper look) do I. Jacob's work is on show widely but you're most likely to see him at Leeds City Art Gallery, the University of Leeds or maybe Tate Britain or the National Portrait Gallery.

The Kremlin or Quarry House, as it's less well known, is home to the Department of Health and the Department for Work and Pensions and was completed in 1993, taking eight years to build at a cost of £55 million. It's the big imposing building at the bottom of York Road – the largest building ever constructed in Leeds – and I love it. There's very little readily available info about the building but it's part of *the Leeds Looks* style of architecture typified by the use of dark red brickwork and steeply pitched grey slate roofs, intended to hark back to the city's Victorian past. Other notable buildings described as having the *Leeds Look* are 1 East Parade, Yorkshire Bank Offices (Wade Lane), Westgate Point (Westgate), HBOS Offices (Lovell Park Road), Leeds Magistrates' Court (Westgate), and the Crowne Plaza Hotel, (Wellington Street).

Having mentioned that the style is said to mimic the architecture of Victorian Leeds I'm not convinced that The Kremlin fits the bill. It reminds me more of the 1920s and 30s and brings to mind *Flash Gordon* or the film *Metropolis.* The **MI6 Building (SIS Building)** in London (they moved in two years after the opening of Quarry House) reminds me of The Kremlin. I think it's the tapering size of the round features, flat expanses and regular square/rectangular windows, symmetrically spaced and varying in size. The colouring's different but they're both government buildings and I'm sure they'll have had access to the Leeds plans. Ey, when, in the future, Leeds battles for its independence, you could make a camp, Art Deco feature film, with the goodies in The Kremlin battling the evil, dark government forces of MI6......sorry I'll take a break.

Right, if you're a stickler for specificity of genres in literature, move on and don't read this; it has no place in this book. It's a personal account of my relationship with LUFC, full of opinions and a lack of facts. Only someone a bit tapped would read such a thing in an encyclopaedia, so jump to the next entry and skip this superfluous waste of space. There are over 100 books on Leeds United so rather than repeat lots of stuff that's well covered, here's a personal reflection on what the club means to me, including life an'that.

I am Leeds United.

Football means many different things to different people; this is what Leeds United means to me. It's a feeling locked into my bones, an inherited emotional attachment that I can neither fully justify nor fight.....I wouldn't want to, I'd be fighting my soul. I'm doing this in the first person, it's football and it has to be in the first person. It's not abstracted, it's personal, sitting deep in the gut...........my gut and possibly yours.

Before I properly start I'd just like to say that people (women) have often levelled the accusation at working class men that they are not in touch with their emotions (and football is often an area of tension) whilst missing the fact that in football you see men fully in touch with their emotions – bare, naked and, at times, brutal emotions. I'd also like to add that football has long been slated for racism, sexism, homophobia etc. but I'd argue that football is the place where, in the more working class world, these issues are battled out, questioned and real social change occurs. Your 'average' football supporter doesn't read *The Guardian* or listen to Radio 4 and without football the prejudices would rarely be questioned. I'm also confident that throughout the days of racism the majority of the crowd was uncomfortable with the atmosphere. Good on *Leeds Fans Against Racism* who in the late '80s stood up for their beliefs and I'm sure they were the first fans to organise and do it.

Football, and for me LUFC, is about love, life, family, friendships and memories linking me intimately to shared moments and experiences in life. It's about bonding with your father, your son, your mother or your daughter, forging friendships and being part of a greater whole, something way-way bigger than you, your roots. It's about a passionate, emotional, one-way contract. Dedication in its true sense. Football is regular and dependable, like the onset of autumn, winter and spring, so if your life is falling to pieces it stands solid, always there, a distraction from your troubles. Even in the closed season it's still there. A solid emotional attachment that will remain in its basic form, rock solid, like the love you hold for your child. The emotional investment is all yours, you own it and you'll not find it snogging with another lad/lass or getting bored of you. It can't reject you as it punctuates your life with full-stops and new chapters, with regularity and routine.

I sometimes wake forgetting that my Dad is dead and think I'll see him later. Mindst you, it is only ten years ago – maybe more. The last game we went to together was at Elland Road, The European Championship, was it 1996? Who cares when it was? I hate dates, time and its poxy markers, although most of them in my life are football related. It was the 18th of June, 1996, Romania vs. Spain. Romania were still not mathematically out of it but played at a dawdle, we decided that this was simply how they played – this was not our football. Was I aware that he didn't have long left? Was he well?

Here it is, as life slivers through my being I can mark those moments in life, I can return there, I remember him, for example, telling me that Huddersfield Town were doing well. This can only have been '69 to '71. It strengthens the emotional bond with those I love or like and is intrinsically linked to them. Even if you didn't know each other at the time, the moments and the passion connect you. Football does connect, you could meet a complete stranger on holiday and end up discussing your love of Tony Currie or if it's a fan of another team have a bit of friendly banter or a serious discussion. Football can be a bridge. I well remember being in a bar on a Greek island with Mrs Mick and the kids, Leeds were playing Arsenal early season. There were a bunch of Arsenal lads and the banter between us started early doors, Viduka got a late winner and I started singing his name loudly (and to the tune of Kate Bush's *Babooshka* for some reason) there was no weird atmosphere and, in a strange way, over those 90 minutes we bonded and had a duelling laugh….obviously I was quicker witted than them.

Strangely, my Dad wasn't from around here, he was from Widnes so his local team should have been Everton or Liverpool, but sometime in the 1950s he started to go and watch and support Second Division Leeds. I think he'd left home and moved to Leeds. Over the years he classed himself as a Yorkshireman. I used to go regularly to Elland Road with mi'dad in the early '70s; he'd sit me on a barrier and stand behind it with his arms around me. Sitting on the barrier leaning back on him, the physical contact, the security was like being snuggled up in bed and knowing my parents were downstairs. Spending time with mi'dad, it was my time. No doubt I talked too much but he was patient with me, explaining the rules and tactics, pointing out the players and their strengths, telling me about the history and the hopes. Teaching me how to shout encouragement at the pitch and sharing those moments of frustration, despair and elation.

My first solid, Leeds United memory is listening to the 1969-70 European Cup semi-final against Celtic on the radio which, with a crowd of 136,505, means that Leeds were involved in the game with the highest ever attendance for any European club competition match – a record that will never be beaten. My first game attended is a mystery, all I know for sure is that it was with Dad. I could have sworn that the little cluster of fans were Turkish, red flags but the half moon could have been a sickle and the single star could have been more than one. I remember us winning 3–0 or do I? Yes I do. So logically it would have been Ferencvaros, a difficult name for a five-year-old brain to assimilate and store. Although in my head it was always Ujpest Doza, which looking at the dates, I'm fairly sure it wasn't. My youngest remembers his first game (Bristol Rovers) but as we didn't get promoted, in adulthood he may not be able to work out when it was or whether he was three, four or five, he was four. It's almost an act of cruelty giving your child a love of a football team, especially Leeds, but you can't hide them from life just as you can't stop them from having their hearts broken. They have to live and love and they have to experience passion to know that they are fully alive.

The following little section was omitted from *Coming Out As A Bowie Fan In Leeds, Yorkshire, England*, as it had no place in the book. The scene is The Millennium Stadium in Cardiff 2006 and the play-off final to gain promotion to The Premiership. My son had already been to watch Leeds RL lose two finals that year:

The main drawback to this passion is that it is an emotional commitment that can exact a high price.

Standing looking over at my 15- yr-old son, he has earlier, twice, stood up and sparked 50,000 Leeds fans into his searing chant. A lone voice catching across and up stands, spreading like a bush fire into the combined power and passion of 50,000 people committing themselves to the badge. His words spread because they were sung with conviction, they were his soul on show and had nobody joined in, he would have still been singing. As it was he was unaware that he had just inspired 50,000 people into reaffirming and proclaiming their pledge.

Leeds had gone three down in a 'cup final', the most lucrative single game in world sport, they have underperformed and will not return to the premier league of English football where their fans, undoubtedly, and club belong.

The Leeds fans were numb and quiet for the first time all day, the awful realisation that they could not inspire the team to come back from three down, as they had earlier in the season, there is no time. He stands, damp, pained eyes, throws his arms into the air and, with a grazed voice that feels like it will break at any point but there is too much power and sincerity to allow doubt, sings,

I'm Leeds until I die,
I'm Leeds until I die
I know I am, I'm sure I am,
I'm Leeds until I die

Had he been in the trenches he would have been the first 'up and over'. A raw statement of constant, unerring, steadfast love, non-negotiable and for life.

It was fitting that his voice stood alone, this was between him and his football team, a purely personal moment played out in front of thousands of people but nobody else was invited. The poignancy and raw emotion was a shave hook to my heart with paint stripper rubbed into the pumping scars via a brillo pad. I want to wrap my arms around him, cradle him in my arms and tell him that it's alright, but he's a man and knows that it is not. I cannot share his pain; I cannot deflect or distract just witness a heart in burning trauma.

I want to cry. Why didn't I get him into cricket? Why did I not break the cycle? We had no choice, he is alive and living and experiencing inevitably contains moments of despair. Despair often intensifies and sweetens joy, when joy arrives. We know what it is by what it is not, by its binary opposite.

I can still picture another scene, I'm eleven, and the whole family is there, even mi'Mum, the only time I can remember the whole family in the room watching telly. We are battering them, well what else would be happening? 'Lorimer, GOAL.' I launch the toilet roll into the air and run, I can hear voices but, in a dream, my head is crammed with joy that closes out all but the euphoria. Standing at the toilet, no memory of the journey, head exploding, heat dripping from my face, 'Michael, Michael, Mick, Mi-i-ick.' They are all calling to me, there's one word that is standing out, like a man with a bazooka at a Christening. *Off-side, no, that wasn't off-side.* That season, in which I'd been to every home game, except the European Cup semi-final (I was on my first ever foreign holiday in Majorca), ended in injustice, a riot and heartache.

Even now, my almost 80-year-old mother, who has no real interest in football, asks me every week how 'Leeds United' are doing. For her she must associate football mainly with a depressed household. But I recently discovered that it's deeper than that when she made the strange confession that she used to listen to all the home games on Radio Leeds. 'But I didn't think you were that interested in football?' 'I wasn't, I wanted to know you were safe.' With me first going to games under my own steam, from east Leeds, aged nine or ten with my class mate Terry Waite, football was also symbolic for my mother in letting go, allowing her youngest child to grow and move to the edge of the nest. So, although football in the early '70s was quite a dangerous environment she knew how much it meant. Dad had started doing a Saturday market in Otley and she allowed me the freedom even though she'd be worried sick, with her ear stapled to a radio, praying for no crowd trouble or incidents. It turned out fine, I'm still here and only nearly died two or three times. I know that she never mentioned her anxiety to me at the time as that may have clipped my wings. Maybe I'd feel guilty and go less. She'd suffer in silence not out of martyrdom but out of love.

Leeds and their fans have suffered more than their fair share of injustice. From badly called offside decisions cheating us out of the league title or European Cup to corrupt officials so bad that their own Greek crowd booed them and the European Cup 'Winners' Cup recipients AC Milan off the pitch, whilst insisting on Leeds United carrying out a lap of **honour** to a standing ovation, unheard of in world football. These injustices sit deep and give the experienced Leeds fan the intensity and commitment of a civil rights campaigner. I know fans of other clubs will feel like this but I think they'll struggle to compete with the injustices or heartache Leeds have suffered. Go to Anthony Clavane's book *Promised Land* and I'm sure you'll find the stats on our great Leeds team – one of the all-time great teams of world football – coming second. Then there's the bad luck, can you name me another club who, over an eight year period, came second in the league five times, including missing out to one of their biggest rivals on goal difference, or by one point two years in a row?

The idea of unconditional love for Leeds United is interesting. It can lead us to accepting abuse that we should not. When we were riding the crest of our early 21st Century wave, my best mate, **Dosher Dawson** told me he'd given up on football. I was amazed, he was a dyed in the wool, working-class, Leeds fan and he was giving it up when we were at last destined for greatness, again. His reasons were prophetic, logical and I now realise undisputable. It was too much of a business for him, the only loyalty he saw was from the fans to the team and the fans were simply consumers squeezed for every penny they would pay. Brutal capitalist economics and he, for one, no longer wanted to be exploited. During the 2009/10 season Leeds fans were charged the eighth highest prices in the country (probably the world) without the visiting 'big' names like Arsenal, Chelsea, Newcastle or Liverpool. We were watching third tier football. Still, way over 20,000 people would turn up week in week out, but with prices like that people like me could only afford to go to a handful of games.

Even when I was looking at a third season in (what I think of as) the Third Division, when you'd think the last five to six years of heartache would have dulled my senses, I still had a heavy lump of despondency in my gut when we lost and a fluttering heart after a win that stayed with me until the next game. It almost doesn't matter what happens on the pitch. We still hold our unconditional love, the type of love you hold for your child, your mother or your father. The first ever season in the third division (2007–2008) saw Leeds start with a 15 point deduction but the average Elland Road crowd of 26,040 generated a sustained passion like nothing else I've ever witnessed and which I'm sure will be unprecedented in English football. It's our club, just ours, not the players, not the 'owners', not the medias. We the fans are the club, we'll still be there when each person directly connected to the club is gone.

Since this book was first published there is a new regime at LUFC and at the time of writing I saw this is an extremely positive development, nobody could be as happy as me to see the back of Bates. The pricing structure at Elland Road has been greatly improved and me and my boys are now managing to get to many more matches. Thanks go to whoever implemented these changes and re-connected us fully to our club.

For my children Leeds United is all around them, it is above and below them and just like my father's, my life-giving sperm contained a spark of life and a love of Leeds United. This spark turns to a burning fire when it is fanned by peer approval, live games on TV, a sense of belonging, strangers, all around, who are just like you. Pick a Shakespeare play - any Shakespeare play - and I guarantee that football fans will have experienced the full range of dramatic emotions. The possible exception is the death of a loved one, although I can say I've been close to that emotion through football, it just doesn't last as long. Thanks for showing me I'm alive Dad.

L

Lads' mags. Although the London media village will tell you that **James Brown** produced the first Lads' mag (*Loaded*), the Lads Mag was actually the brain child of Dave Benson whose company produced the first example, *EX* magazine (see cover), in Leeds during 1991. Dave had been planning it, without the required finances, since the mid-80s. Obviously there will have been a difference in tone, *EX* gave itself an '18 certificate' and was more graphic than *Loaded* and James nailed the market but the basic concept of sex, beer, football, fashion etc. was the same. So the world's first Lads' Mag was conceived, written, printed and launched in Leeds and Leeds's own **James Brown**, using his publishing industry contacts, took the concept to a mass market releasing **Loaded** onto the world in 1994, which has since sold over 40,000,000 copies. See **EX, James Brown, Arkwright.**

John Anthony Lake has been publishing articles, reviews, poems and stories for over twenty years while teaching and lecturing in Greece, Japan, Finland and Britain. He started off on *Leeds Other Paper* and wrote for *Sounds* (extinct national music paper) for a few years, reviewing gigs and albums, writing features and carrying out interviews. He is the author of two novels, *Hot Knife* (Armley Press, 2008 available on amazon) and *Starchaser* (Scribd.com, 2009) and his story 'Hidden Among Leaves' was long-listed for the 2007 Fish-Knife Crime Short Story Award. He has played bass guitar in a number of Leeds bands including **Hang the Dance** and **The Butter Cookies** and is currently contributing to *Sabotage Times* whilst teaching at The School of Oriental and African Studies.

Laminated playing cards –Waddingtons of Leeds. I had reason to believe that the start of the Waddingtons games empire seemed to have coincided with a need for more durable playing cards for soldiers in the trenches of World War I. My story was that the old cards were just that, card, and disintegrated very quickly due to the wet conditions and that Waddingtons first came up with a way to put a light laminate coating on the cards, thereby winning large contracts from the British Government to supply playing cards.

I only think this because in the late '80s me and my mate went to interview a production manager at Waddingtons who had been working there since the 1940s and this story fascinated us and became the main thrust of our interview. Obviously, with me being a dope, I have no record of the interview but have corroborated the facts with my mate (who is now a very well respected Guardian journo and world expert on Kurdistan/Iraq) who said, 'Mick, I can hardly remember my name half of the time, it was 30 years ago, but yeh, it was something to do with cards.' Proof indeed and from a world expert.

I've searched for evidence of this, found nothing, and only have my primary source and a dodgy memory. He could have been mistaken, he could have told me that the number 189 bus is usually a single decker but the interviewee was a production manager at Waddingtons since the 1940s and knew what he was talking about. I've chased this further through **The Guildhall Library** (London) who passed me on to the **Worshipful Company of Makers of Playing Cards** who kindly contacted the retired Chairman of Waddingtons who said that the process of laminating cards **has been practised for literally hundreds of years** and way before

Waddingtons existed. So it appears that my memory is as full of holes as a trigger happy farmer's barn door and this laminated playing cards 'fact' seems not to be true and should not be repeated, we wouldn't want to create a myth. See how **Waddingtons** helped win the war with their ingenious (under) **Monopoly** escape packs and this one is absolutely true.

Pete Lapish produces water colours of Leeds scenes with a particular liking for trams. I can't find much about him but he certainly grew up in Leeds and researches his subject heavily to produce accurate studies of Leeds street scenes from different periods. Search him online or on Leodis to see his work.

Leeds Anti-Slavery Association was formed Feb 1853 and the first Anti-Slavery Association to have both male and female members – 110 female members and 77 male. This was a break with **all** voluntary societies (nationwide) before this time which were always single sex. Here, females were subscribers, committee members and officers, although the president and vice-president were always men, women outnumbered men on the committee and held the role of secretary.

  The association appears to have been set up by two women, **Harriet Lupton** (who had an interest in women's rights) and **Sarah Pugh** who had originally formed a committee to collect signatures. They planned a female association but then decided upon a mixed group. Harriet also gave a lecture in London, crossing the boundary of women not carrying out public speaking in the UK and in 1840 Sarah had led the American women's delegation to the World Anti-Slavery Convention. The Association also contained influential anti-slavery writer **Wilson Armistead**. (*Women Against Slavery: The British Campaigns, 1780-1870*, Clare Midgley, Routledge, 1995)

The Leeds and Bradford Boiler Company (LBBC Technologies) is a rare example of a manufacturing company that has lasted from Victorian days (founded 1876) to the present day. It has done this through adapting and investing in new technologies such as its most recent dead body disposal (the Resomator) an alternative to burial or cremation which places the body in a large pressurised cylinder that mimics and speeds up natural decomposition. It is already legal in some US states and Canada, where it has been exported to, but not yet incorporated into UK law.

  During the early 20th Century LBBC developed tar stills and tar distillation plants to help build the world's first **tar roads**. In 1934 and under commercial pressure, Maurice Pickard invented and patented the revolutionary Quicklock door – which is still the industry standard today. This was an easy to use fast-locking door for use in pressurised environments such as submarines, autoclaves (a device to sterilise equipment and supplies by subjecting them to high pressure steam) and pressure enclosures. Maurice's work led him to act as a consultant for the Health & Safety body that set the mandatory standards that are still present today.

  After World War II LBBC exported autoclaves and boilers around the world with the autoclaves having applications from vulcanising (converting rubber or related polymers into more durable materials) to timber impregnators (making them flame-resistant, fungi-resistant, or insect-proof) and textile steamers. The autoclaves are able to contain high pressures and highly corrosive liquids. During the 1960s the company expanded into the investment casting/lost wax process (for casting complex shapes), which was relatively new as a mainstream foundry process and was exporting autoclaves to over 100 countries, with over 200 vessels produced for the

Nestle Company alone. The company is still going strong today and its new cremation technology shows it to be still adapting and moving with the times.

Established in 1903 by **Alfred Richard Orage** and George Holbrook Jackson, **The Leeds Arts Club** was an important meeting ground for radical artists, thinkers, educationalists and writers. This centre of British modernist thinking was influenced by the progressive cultural, political and theoretical ideas coming out of Germany at the time and the closest England came to a genuine Expressionist art movement – the centre of English Expressionism. But it was a magpie of an organisation taking in the most revolutionary thinking of the day, mixing radical socialist and anarchist political ideas, the spiritualism of the Theosophical Society, Nietzschean philosophy, the notions of the Suffragettes and feminists and throwing it all up in the air at its weekly meetings. **Mary Gawthorpe** made her first speech there and **Isabella Ford** was on the committee. It also championed and inspired **Jacob Kramer**, Bruce Turner (1894–1963) (an expressionist artist of which there is little known) and the celebrated anarchist poet, critic of

Michael Sadler in 1914, photo by George Charles Beresford

literature and art Herbert Read, one of the earliest English writers to take notice of Existentialism. Members were central in providing **Henry Moore** with his first studio and prominent member **Sir Michael Ernest Sadler** gave Henry full access to his large art collection – he and his son were the first Brits to buy work by Wassily Kandinsky, known for painting the first modern abstract works.

Folk from the Arts Club were central in setting up The **Leeds Art Collections Fund** in 1912 to counter the more 'conservative' tastes of the day which dictated the art purchased. As one of Britain's oldest supporting art gallery 'friends' organisations, they concentrated on contemporary and historic works. The 'historic' works were often Leeds related such as **Thomas Chippendale**, **John Atkinson Grimshaw** or **J. M. W. Turner**. The independent charity still supports Leeds arts and is chaired by art historian **Benedict William Read**.

Leeds Castle dates back to 1119, is in Kent and has absolutely nothing to do with Leeds, Yorkshire, England. Not a thing. Nothing at all, no link. It is completely and utterly unrelated to Leeds, Yorkshire, England. Except, probably, people from Leeds have visited it. I bet they have, maybe out of inquisitiveness or perhaps out of a liking for castles and old stuff. So that's a small link but other than people from Leeds visiting it, it has diddley squat to do with our Leeds. Unless of course, maybe someone from Leeds was involved in the maintenance of the building or maybe fixed something but other than maintenance or visiting by Leeds folk there's no link. Well........there's the name, they share a name, so when some people hear the name Leeds Castle they'll think of a castle in Leeds but it isn't in Leeds, it's in Kent and has absolutely nothing to do with Leeds........that I know of.

Leeds Chamber of Commerce was established in 1785 and was the first body in this country to bear the name 'Chamber of Commerce.' It was refounded in 1851, since which time it has provided continuous service and support for industry, commerce and trade within the Leeds area, helping businesses address the changes in technology, working patterns and business processes that Leeds has witnessed over the last 153 years.

The Leeds Children's Holiday Camp Association. See **Mrs Helen Currer Briggs**.

Leeds City Station is the busiest station outside London with over 100,000 passengers a day. Leeds used to have three central railway stations, the Leeds New (the North Eastern Railway and London North West Railway), the *Central* (the Great Northern Railway station) and the Leeds Wellington Street station (Midland Railway). The one we know today is a combination of Leeds New (opened in 1869) and Leeds Wellington Street station (Leeds and Bradford Railway station which opened in 1846) – the two were combined on 2 May 1938. The station was completely rebuilt in 1967 and as a result the north concourse, built in 1937, was hidden. In 1999, during the £19.5 million renovation, the north concourse was restored and re-opened including the new entrance at the side that makes it so much easier to pick up and drop off from west and north-west Leeds. A planned £15 million southern entrance would enable people to get into and out of the station from both sides of the River Aire, connecting the station to the south side of the city (Holbeck and Little Neville Street) which has been experiencing commercial and residential growth in the recent years. It's projected that 20% of passengers would use the new entrance although at the time of writing the scheme, planned for 2012 completion, was in doubt, a statement saying: 'Following the Government's recent spending cuts announcements on 10 June 2010, we understand that the Department for Transport will not be in a position to make a decision for the new Southern Entrance until the Comprehensive Spending Review is complete in the Autumn (2010).'

Leeds College of Building is the only college in the UK which specialises in the construction industry. It was established in 1960 and has recently celebrated its 50 year anniversary. It currently has about 7,000 students, 11% of whom are full-time, and is spread over seven sites around the city.

On the 18th of September, 1963, the 1st **Leeds International Pianoforte Competition** was held at the Queen's Hall and it is now considered one of the world's greatest piano competitions. This event, jointly established by **Fanny Waterman** and **Marion Thorpe** (then Countess of Harewood), has become a successful triennial event and, with the Tchaikovsky competition in Moscow and the Van Cliburn in Fort Worth, is the world's most important, career changing competition for pianists under the age of 30. As it hugely raises the profile of the finalists, almost all go on to become successful concert pianists and recording artists, the most well known being Murray Perahia, Radu Lupu, Dimitri Alexeev, Andras Schiff, Peter Donohoe and Mitsuko Uchida. The competition takes place in the Great Hall of the **University of Leeds** and in **Leeds Town Hall** and is extensively covered by Radio 3, Radio 4, BBC2 and BBC4 – the next competition will be the seventeenth. It was originally the brainchild of **Fanny Waterman** who wanted to challenge the cultural dominance of capital cities.

The Leeds Library started in 1768 above a bookseller's shop as a subscription library and is now the oldest surviving example of this sort of library in Britain. Their website says, 'it boasts Joseph Priestley (1733-1804) as one of its original subscribers. The collections are particularly rich in travel, topography, biography, history and literature. There are long runs of periodicals, popular novels, children's books and Civil War pamphlets and Reformation Tracts. About 1,500 new books and audio/visual items are added every year and a large proportion of the Library's holdings is available for loan to its members. The Library became a charity on 1 July 2008' and has 'a wonderful collection of books and periodicals housed in a fine two hundred year-old building' on Commercial Street.

Leeds Other Paper (the LOP) started in 1974 to give an alternative view of the miners' strike. It was a cooperative which varied in size, had a circulation in 1989 of around 2,500 with 82% of its readership aged between 18 and 40. About half of its 24 - 34 pages were an extensive 'What's On Guide' and reviews of Leeds cultural events. Its editorial was left-wing and typically covered issues such as benefits, gender, sexuality, housing, policing and the environmental. It used commercial, low-rate printing to stay alive until it folded in 1991. Although I remember it carrying on as *The Northern Star* for a while but don't quote me on it.

On December 6th 1976 **Leeds Poly** (now Leeds Met) hosted the doomed **Anarchy Tour** featuring, **The Sex Pistols**, **The Damned**, **The Clash** and The Heartbreakers. This became the opening night of the tour as the previous three gigs had been cancelled. With the social uproar that the tour generated it became only one of three gigs that went ahead out of the planned 20 – the other two were played in Manchester and Plymouth. What makes the Leeds gig remarkable was that it was unique, after it happened The Damned left the tour. Now for me The Sex Pistols, The Damned and The Clash are the 'big three' of British punk and this was the only night of the tour at which all three played on the same bill. I'm sure they played together earlier in the year in London but I'm more than extremely suspicious that this was the only time the 'big three' played together outside London. So I've said it and if I'm wrong I'll find out soon enough and this bit will get cut – if it's here from 2011 it's true until shown otherwise. The concert was immortalised on a bootleg called *Anarchy in Leeds*. Anyhow, we liked them in Leeds and the Pistols did two encores. Last thought, I bet Mrs Mick's older sister was at this gig, she was weeeeell early on the Leeds punk scene but it's too late to ask her, my deadline is 5 minutes off.

Leeds RL/Rhinos like LUFC are well covered elsewhere, so it's a bit pointless me doing the club. Leeds are one of the oldest Rugby League clubs in the world and have been playing rugby at Headingley since 1890. In 1921 Harold Buck became the game's first £1,000 transfer with his move from Hunslet to Leeds and Leeds have broken the transfer record on numerous occasions. After winning the Super League Grand Final in 2009 the Rhinos became the first and, to date, only club to be Super League champions three seasons running. As I said, brief and a bit poor considering what a rugby city Leeds is but for the only ever all Leeds final see **Hunslet Cricket, Football and Athletic Club**.

In 1859 **The Leeds Rifles** were raised as a volunteer force to meet an invasion threat from France. They were titled 7th Yorkshire, West Riding, (Leeds) Rifle Volunteer Corps and many Leeds businesses raised complete companies, including Joshua Tetley who had a close link for over a century. With barracks next to the Town Hall, The Leeds Rifles, growing quickly to 1000 men, received little government funding and relied mainly on subscriptions. There was a bit of a kafuffle during the 1880s when the Corps was 'required' to become a Volunteer Battalion of The Prince of Wales's Own (West Yorkshire Regiment) and The Leeds Rifles refused the War Office. In 1887 they did become part of the regiment but did not bear the colours rather retaining their own distinctive Rifle Green uniform and regimental trappings and keeping Leeds Rifles as part of their name. By this time they had grown so big that they bought, refurbished and moved into Carlton Barracks, the old militia barracks at Carlton Hill.

During the Boer War the unit formed into two Companies resulting in their first battle honour, 'South Africa 1900-1902' for which a memorial of the killed can be seen in Leeds Parish Church. In 1908 the Volunteer became the Territorial Force and expanded to two battalions each of over 1000 men becoming the 7th and 8th (Leeds Rifles) Battalions. When the call to arms for World War 1 came, so many ex Leeds Riflemen and new recruits turned up at Carlton Barracks that two further (second line) battalions were formed, the 2/7th and 2/8th. As part of the Expeditionary Force from 1915, until the end of the war, the first line battalions served, holding the infamous Ypres Salient, and were involved at the Somme, Passchendaele and the final advance. The 8th received the French Croix de Guerre for gallantry (the highest French honour) in the capture of Bligny Ridge. Every year, 'Bligny Sunday' is marked with a parade through Leeds in memory of brave soldiers and wreaths are lain at the Bligny memorial outside the Parish Church. 2,050 members of the Leeds Rifles died in active service during WW1.

WW2 saw the 8th become a Heavy Anti-Aircraft Regiment as the 66th (Leeds Rifles) and the 7th become two TA Royal Tank Regiments the 45th (Leeds Rifles) and the 51st (Leeds Rifles) fighting at El Alamein and in Italy where the 51st were decorated with the emblem of the Canadian Maple Leaf, whilst supporting the Canadian Division. The Leeds Rifles have since gone through various changes and are now a platoon of the Imphal Company but retain the Leeds Rifles name, the proud traditions and the Croix de Guerre and Maple Leaf emblems. As I cannot cover all military connections, I took The Leeds Rifles as an example of our military past. The last British soldier to die in World War I, after four years at the front and just over an hour before the ceasefire (which was announced the previous evening), was George Edwin Ellison from Leeds who would never return to the city or his wife and their four-year-old son James.

Leeds School of Cookery and Domestic Economy/Yorkshire College of Cookery was founded in 1874, supported by **The Yorkshire Ladies' Council of Education** and was affectionately known as the 'Pud School'. It moved from Albion Street to Vernon Road in 1933 when it was known as the **Yorkshire Training College of Housecraft**. It was incorporated into Leeds Polytechnic in 1976 and today, shadows of the college can be seen around the Hospitality & Retailing Department at **Leeds Metropolitan University**.

Leeds United. Although these things shift and change Leeds are one of (if not **the**) the most reviled club in English football, at the time of writing we were the 'biggest rival' to more clubs

140

than any other side, as my oldest son has constantly chuntered on about in connection with his *Football Manager* digital game that lists clubs rivals. There are over 100 books on Leeds United so I'll not churn out lots of facts about the club, such as the badge introduced in 1984, and lasting until 1998, being the longest lived club badge of the modern era; or Leeds wearing the first visibly branded kit (Admiral) in English football during the 1973-1974 season, or in 1975 Leeds becoming the first club to design shirts which could be sold to fans in the form of replicas, with the club receiving a royalty for each replica sold, and thus starting the worldwide craze for replica shirts: or the first to wear lighter, 'breathable' nylon material rather than cotton. Neither will I get into the attached fact that Leeds also produced a replica 'away' shirt (the classic all-yellow with blue and white trim) that they wore in all their away games, regardless of whether the kits clashed, with the occasional 'change kit' rapidly replaced with the constant 'away kit,' which has now become almost universal as a result. I'll not explore the fact that **Albert Johanneson** was one of the first high-profile black players, of any nationality, to play top-flight English football and the very first to play in the F.A Cup final – he was also, according to Paul Harrison who is currently writing his biography, an accomplished harmonica player. I'll not mention that, before demolition, Elland Road had the tallest floodlights in Europe, which measured 260 feet (79 m), or that the first competitive football match at Elland Road, in 1898, saw Hunslet FC beat Harrogate 1-0 to win the Yorkshire Cup. Just forget that I said the East or Family Stand is noted by Clavane as the biggest cantilevered structure in Europe.

Here's a list of all Leeds born and played for United lads: David Batty, Len Browning, Walter Butler, Aiden Butterworth, Terry Carling, Terry Connor, Nigel Davey, Brian Deane, Martin Dickinson, Jack Duthoit, Tom Elliot, Gareth Evans, Harry Fearnley, Alan Fowler, Les Goldberg, Ernie Goldthorpe, David Harvey, Billy Heaton, Jonathan Howson, George Hutchinson, Rod Johnson, Dennis Kirkby, Aaron Lennon, Paul Madeley, Jack Marsden, James Milner, Richard Naylor, Mike O'Grady, Jack Overfield, Ben Parker, Lloyd Sam, Paul Shepherd, Alan Smith, Peter Swan, Nigel Thompson, Arthur Tillotson, Albert Wakefield, Simon Walton, Fred Waterhouse, Noel Whelan, Aiden White, Jimmy Wilson.

Obviously not stolen and updated off the WAFLL website where there's the same list with stats, although I've removed Paul Reaney as he moved to Leeds as a kid. Wait a minute, I've just realised, I did steal it off that cool website stuffed with LUFC stuff. See **Baroness Nicola Chapman**, **Ronnie Hilton**, **Arkwright**, **Marching On Together** and **I am Leeds United**.

Aaron Lennon was born in **Chapeltown**, played for Leeds United and was sold off (at a ridiculously low £1m) when it'd all gone pear shaped (2005) and returns to Leeds to shop rather than shopping in London. Making his debut for Leeds in August 2003 he became the youngest player ever to appear in the Premier League at the age of 16 years and 129 days. Two years earlier he set a record as the youngest ever player to have his boots sponsored – by Addidas.

While Aaron was still a junior ar'kid got a taxi driven by Aaron's Dad and when they inevitably started talking about footie, Lennon senior assured him that his son would be one of the greatest players to ever play for Leeds and that he would certainly play for England. I think that, with no major problems, Aaron could become a great England player – I really, really rate him.

A famous inmate of Armley Gaol was English dancer, suffragist and arsonist **Lilian Ida Lenton** (1891–1972) from Leicester. She vowed on her 21st birthday to burn two (empty) buildings a week until women got the vote. In February 1913 she was arrested on suspicion of having set fire to the Tea House at Kew Gardens – arsonists had some great excuses in them days.

In Holloway Prison she held a hunger strike for two days before being forcibly fed, which led her to become seriously ill with pleurisy caused by food entering her lungs. The case brought public outrage, especially as the then Home Secretary said that she had not been force fed but was ill due to her hunger strike. This brought about the hastily drawn Cat and Mouse Act of April 1913, where hunger-striking suffragette 'mice' could be released on temporary licence to recover and the security forces could then re-arrest them.

In June 1913 Lenton was arrested in Doncaster and charged with burning an unoccupied house; her accomplice, a local journo called Harry Johnson, received a year's hard labour in Wakefield Prison. She went to Armley but after the public outcry, only months earlier, and the politically sensitive situation, they did not try to force feed her. After a few days (under the *Cat and Mouse Act*) she was released into the care of a fellow (unnamed and unfound by me) suffragette in Leeds. Trapped in a through terrace, rossers (many detectives) covering front and back, a cart pulled up, with a young lad coming to deliver to the house, eating an apple and carrying a 'heavy hamper', he left a short while later.

Now don't try this today, if you've maybe got an ASBO and a tag, as I don't think it'd work but the delivery boy was actually renowned, militant suffragist Elsie Duval, who herself had been force fed many times. Here's the clever bit, they did a switch. Today it seems far-fetched but back in 1913 they hadn't watched hours of crap TV dramas and kids progs and Lilian simply put on the 'boys' clothing and left still eating the apple and carrying the hamper. They'd worked out 'a very elaborate escape scheme' but things went wrong, the police were soon on her tail and it took her days to shake them off. She says she hid at the house of a suffragette in Edinburgh but *The Times* and Wikipedia reckon she went to France, via Harrogate and Scarborough. I believe her. She returned to Armley Goal less than a year later but by then had been arrested and escaped at least two more times, becoming known as 'the tiny, wily, elusive Pimpernel'. Not a very catchy nickname, I could do better…. 'the constantly escaping scamp', 'Lil the Eel'.

So, she'd been repeatedly arrested for burning places down, repeatedly put in gaol, repeatedly released under the *Cat and Mouse Act* and repeatedly fooled the detectives and escaped. On May the 12, 1914, after being on hunger strike, she was again released from Armley, this time into the care of fellow suffragette **Leonora Cohen** who had, by this time, moved to Harrogate. As the cavalcade of 'cars' travelled to Harrogate, with Lilian in the middle, there was betting on the likelihood of her escape. At first the odds were evens but as people realised it was the same detectives who she'd previously escaped from the odds went out to 100/1. The house was again surrounded by detectives and a light placed in the garden of the neighbours to shine on the house through the night. Lillian's version (BBC Radio, 1 January, 1960, prog unknown) of the escape is that, on the day before she was to be returned to Armley, 50 'heavily veiled women' turned up at the front door and were allowed in one by one. Then the door suddenly opened and they all ran out and scattered, the police having no idea what to do or who to chase. The police continued to stake the house as they didn't know whether Lilian had scarpered or not. Guess what. She had.

Matthew Lewis (born 1989), aka Neville Longbottom of the *Harry Potter* films, went to St Mary's School in Menston and Helena Bonham Carter ruptured his eardrum when she stuck her wand in his ear. She was, of course, in character. He's been in all six films (maybe seven or eight by the time you read this) and had previously appeared in stuff like *Heartbeat, Dalziel and Pascoe* and *Where the Heart Is*, as well as the 2010 indie film **Sweet Shop** with Gemma Atkinson. He's the patron of **The Leeds Children's Holiday Camp Association.**

Theophilus Lindsey (1723–1808) was an **Anglican theologian**, who petitioned parliament against the *thirty-nine articles of religion* and became a **Unitarian**, he was educated at the Leeds Free School.

Live at Leeds is a classic 1976 **John Martyn** album, no, no, I'm joking (just trying to wind up Dock, never mind who Dock is.... nosy), well I mean it is a classic John Martyn album but it's best known as the classic live album by indie rock band **Shed Seven**. Ok, ok, I'm kidding, I mean, it is also an album by Shed Seven but it is best known as the classic live album by **The Who**. Variously described as the 'best live rock album of all time' and so important that a Blue plaque has been put up at the University of Leeds where it was recorded, the album has gone 'Multi-Platinum' in the US. All three albums were recorded at Leeds Uni and the John Martyn album cover mimics The Who cover.

Railway Locomotives. According to the Middleton Railway website Leeds produced more railway locomotives than any other town or city in England (over 19,000) and historically, I think we can stretch that to the world. Owners and engineers moved between Leeds companies such as Fenton, Murray and Wood - Fenton, Murray and Jackson - James Kitson (Airedale Foundry) - Hunslet Engine Co. - Todd, Kitson & Laird - John Fowler & Co - Charles Todd's Sun Foundry - Shepherd and Todd – Kitson - Thompson & Hewitson - Carrett, Marshall and Company - Fenton, Craven and Company - E.B.Wilson and Company - Manning Wardle - Hudswell and Clarke - Hudswell, Clarke and Rogers - Kitson and Company - Hudswell, Clarke and Rogers - Hudswell Clarke and Company. Leeds was the home of the first commercially viable steam locomotive, the **Salamanca** in 1812 which also featured in the first ever painting of a locomotive by **George Walker.**

Radio and television presenter **Gabby Logan** was born Gabrielle Nicole Yorath, in 1973. She's the daughter of ex-Leeds player **Terry Yorath** but scandalously doesn't support LUFC. She's got her chit-chatty show on Radio 5, does a lot of sport on TV and she wasn't the first female presenter of *Match Of The Day*. She attended Notre Dame Sixth Form College after Cardinal Heenan High School which is my old school but I wouldn't go out with her, which in some ways is connected to the fact that I was there 10 years before her. There's a studio load of stuff about her online so go search.

James W. Longley. See **Vending machine**.

Dame Kathleen Lonsdale was a PhD student of Sir William Henry Bragg and at Leeds Uni for three years in the late 1920s; she also studied with William Astbury so she was obviously a crystallographer. She had time out in the early 1930s to look after kids but went on to gain a number of firsts for a female scientist including first woman elected a Fellow of The Royal Society; University College London's first woman tenured professor; the first woman president of both the British Association for the Advancement of Science and the International Union of Crystallographers.

Lost in Austen, the critically acclaimed ITV drama included Leeds locations such as **Bramham Park**, **Leeds City Market** and **Harewood House** was the setting for Pemberley. **Screen Yorkshire** alerted the makers to some outstanding locations in Yorkshire where the series was filmed.

Lotherton Hall is a country house near Aberford and there's plenty of info about it online. There appears to have been a hall or manor house on the site since 1086 but the current building seems to be a bit of a confusing mish-mash of dates, the earliest I could find being 1828 and it was extensively rebuilt during the Victorian and Edwardian eras. I'm sure there will be people who understand the evolution of the building, I don't. Anyway, the house has a Bird Garden, activities for the public and the gardens have old varieties of plants to mimic an Edwardian garden. The house itself contains collections of fine and decorative arts from the eighteenth, nineteenth and twentieth century's such as furniture, fashion/costumes, sculptures, ceramics and paintings.

Love is the name of everyone who enters the boundaries of Leeds, you cannot fight it, just accept it, it's simple, you came to Leeds, you're called Love. Technically, it's a replacement name used by people who may not know your birth given name, but it's so widespread that it also used intimately between people who share unconditional love, such as mother and son, father and daughter. An example of the confusion this may cause and the complexity of the concept was shown at **David Bowie**'s 06/08/1997 gig at **Town & Country Club** (O2) where he became so perplexed he uttered the words no celeb should. An older member of the bar staff was in to change the barrels that day and, due the size of the 'star', the routine had been altered and the gentleman asked to stay for the sound check in order to man the bar and service the band with refreshments. Before the sound check, ar'David, with his Yorkshire roots, sauntered over to the bar in order to avail himself of this hospitality, the old bar man looked up and quickly muttered, 'Yes Love.' To which David (of a similar age) instinctively replied, through inquisitiveness rather than starryness, 'Do you know who I am?' And the old fella replied, 'Yes Love, what can a'get'y.' David later commented that he had wondered about being called Love, in a non confrontational way, ever since (24 years earlier) he'd played the **Leeds Rollerena** wearing all his makeup and gender-bending clothes and an old fella on the door had repeatedly called him 'Love '.

It's very possible that you think you've visited Leeds but have not. Officially, unless you've been called 'Love' by a stranger, you haven't actually visited the City, you just think you have......you have not. The 'Love' phenomena is spreading throughout the country and may have actually overrun it by the time you read this, so remember, it's a Leeds thing

Low Hall, Horsforth is a stone manor house built around 1575. In 1642 it was sacked by the Cavalier Army, who billeted it as lodgings for their soldiers. As it was being renovated for use as a restaurant in the 1960s the ancient **Cup and Ring Stone** was discovered. It was historically the home of the Stanhope family who moved to the purpose built **Horsforth Hall**, a much more impressive house and park, in 1707. In 1932 Horsforth Hall and park were donated to the people of Horsforth and the impressive hall was demolished in the 1950s. Low Hall is now used as commercial premises.

Lumiere is a mixed-use skyscraper proposed development that is currently on hold. The project represents the second phase to the redevelopment of a Royal Mail sorting office, which has already seen a 65 metres (213 ft) tall former Royal Mail office reclad to become apartments called West Point. The construction of Lumiere will consist of two towers of a height of 54 storeys/171 m (561 ft) and 32 storeys/112 m (367 ft), both of which are to be clad in glass, with the taller tower to be predominantly blue and the smaller tower a reddish hue. The company who had taken the project on went into liquidation meaning the building is unlikely to be ever built.

Charles Lupton (1855–1935) was Lord Mayor of Leeds in 1915 and from a 'prominent' Leeds family both before and after him – see Aunt Harriet under **Leeds Anti-Slavery Association**. He was instrumental in the expansion of the **Leeds General Infirmary** and, in 1924, announced the development of **the Headrow** as one of Leeds's major thoroughfares at a cost of £500,000 and was behind the creation of the **Outer Ring Road**. One of the 'houses' of **Quarry Hill** flats was named after him and he left his art collection to the city. His son Charles Roger Lupton was a World War I flying ace credited with five aerial victories between 1917 and 1918 when he was killed, and his brother, Francis Martineau Lupton, was Kate Middleton's (of will she marry Prince William fame – my God, I'm out of date already) great, great grandfather. Kate's father Michael was also born in Leeds as were her Middleton grandfather, great grandfather and four of her great, great grandparents.

M

The M1 motorway, London to Leeds, was the first full-length, inter-urban motorway to be constructed in the UK. Quick adjunct, the A58(M) Leeds Inner ring road appears to be the only motorway in UK with a junction feeding off the outside lane to North St. And yes, although it has a 40 mile an hour speed limit, 2.5 miles (4.0 km) of the road is classed as a motorway.

Owney 'The Killer' Madden (1891–1965). Top New York gangster involved in organized crime during Prohibition. He also started the famous **Cotton Club**, became one of the major bootleggers in New York and was a leading boxing promoter in the 1930s. Owen Victor Madden's nicknames were *The Killer* (after killing a notorious local, Italian gangster) or *The Duke*, and was described by fellow gangsters as "that little banty rooster from hell". At the time of his death he was said to have $3 million in assets, quite a lot in 1965.

Owen "Owney" Madden was born on December 18, 1891, at 25 Somerset Street, Leeds. His parents Francis and Mary (formerly O'Neil), were also born in Leeds, both of Irish ancestry. In 1901 Mary Madden sailed to New York on the *RMS Oceanic*, to stay with her widowed sister Elizabeth O'Neil, in Manhattan. Until 1903, when she could finally afford passage for them, Owen and his older brother, Martin, were left at a children's home, at 36 Springfield Terrace, Leeds.

He moved to the tough New York ghetto called **Hell's Kitchen**, and joined the **Gopher Gang**. He became known as a fierce and relentless fighter, quick to use a lead pipe, knife or gun. By 18 he had moved to the upper ranks of the gang, and was suspected by police of having murdered at least five members of the rival **Hudson Dusters gang**. He wasn't just a nutter, he had a business head and started a protection racket in which local businessmen were forced to pay money to the Gophers who threatened to firebomb their stores. His reputation soon saw him lead one of the three factions of the Gophers and Madden regularly earned $200 daily.

Full of bling, he liked women and was often accompanied by several. His violently jealous reputation was enhanced when store clerk, William Henshaw asked a girl on a tram, that Madden was interested in, for a date. Madden followed the man onto another streetcar and shot him, in front of dozens of witnesses. Before Henshaw died, he identified Madden who was arrested and tried for murder. The case was dropped when, spookily, no witnesses came forward.

You may have surmised by now that not only was he psychotic, he was also a fighter. As he recruited gunmen, he was encroaching further into rival gangs' territory. Over three years, the gang's influence rose until November 6th, 1912 when the drunken Madden was ambushed, outside the 52nd Street Arbor Dance Hall, by eleven members of the Hudson Dusters and shot eight times, gaining another nickname of 'Clay Pigeon'. He didn't die and refused to help the police, telling them from his hospital bed, 'Nothing doing. The boys'll get 'em. It's nobody's business but mine who put these slugs in me!' Within a week of his release, six members of the **Hudson Dusters** had been killed.

In 1914 Owney arranged the death of high level, rival gangster Patsy Doyle after a dispute over a woman. Doyle had also, against Irish etiquette, told the police of Owney's operations and then assaulted Owney's close friend. Owney Madden set up a meeting and killed Doyle, his two accomplices were later arrested and dobbed Madden in. He went to Sing Sing prison for 20 years but was out on parole after nine. Upon release he found that the **Gopher Gang** had broken up and, after a short while, began to work for the **Dutch Schultz** mob as a soldier in the 'Manhattan Beer Wars' fighting against **Jack 'Legs' Diamond**, **Waxey Gordon**, and **Vincent 'Mad Dog' Coll**. Madden rose quickly in the Schultz organization and in 1931 left to go out on his own and, with Schultz as his partner, soon became one of the major bootleggers in the city.

With his former gang rival turned partner **Big Frenchy De Mange**, Madden began to open/acquire some of the flashiest speakeasies and nightclubs of the era, most notably the legendary **Cotton Club** - see the **Cotton Club** entry, surprisingly, under '**C**'. It is rumoured that he had romantic ties with **Mae West** and bankrolled her career. When she was later asked to describe him, she replied: 'Sweet – but oh so vicious.'

Madden also partnered with two boxing promoters and soon the three controlled the careers of the top five boxing champions including **Rocky Marciano**, **Primo Carnera** and **Max Baer**. Madden took a special interest in Carnera, a crap boxer but a huge brute of a man, and after his previous opponent had died after their fight, he got a championship bout and took the heavyweight title in 1933, with a 'knock-out' punch that many believed did not connect. Suspicious reporters started digging around and asking uncomfortable questions so Madden stopped fixing his fights and quickly abandoned Carnera and he lost the title to Baer in a legitimate fight on June 14, 1934.

In 1932 his old rival **'Mad Dog' Coll** attempted to extort money from Madden, amongst others, only to die not long afterwards in a drive-by shooting. Madden was questioned but kept schtum although not long after he was arrested on a parole violation and briefly jailed. His power and influence sweetened his short stay in Sing Sing with dancers and strippers from the Cotton Club occasionally 'performing' for him. The police kept hassling Madden until, in 1935, he left New York, to open a hotel, spa and casino in Hot Springs, Arkansas – a place that welcomed gangsters. Although his hotel was a haven for wanted mobsters keeping their heads down – **Alphonse Gabriel 'Al' Capone, Charles 'Lucky' Luciano** (reputedly the most powerful criminal in the country) escaped justice until he was arrested there – Madden managed to stay out of trouble (while, obviously, still being involved in local crime) and the news. Madden married the daughter of the city postmaster and died there (Hot Springs) in 1965. Unlike most gangsters, he died quietly in bed, of old age. Hot Springs eventually became a national gambling Mecca, led by Owney and his Hotel Arkansas casino.

Mug shot of Owney Madden from June 1st 1931.

Madden had connections with **The Five Points Gang** (Scorsese's *Gangs of New York* film set 60 to70 years earlier) such as Al Capone and Charles 'Lucky' Luciano and I can see connections between Madden's life and **Francis Ford Coppola's** *The Godfather* and *The Godfather Part II*, but perhaps it's just chance and I'll leave it, although Coppola did also direct the 1984 film, *The Cotton Club*.

Mad Old Woman at the End. Childhood Leeds streets always had one, but they weren't usually mad and didn't always live at the end. You could tell they were mad because after you'd ran through their garden shouting and dived over their hedge they'd come out of their house to tell you off .....y'see, they were nutters.

A portable **magnetometer** has been designed at **Leeds Quantum Information Group** (School of Physics and Astronomy, University of Leeds). A **magnetometer** is a bit of kit, around 200 years old, used to measure the strength and/or direction of the magnetic field near the instrument and is traditionally large and bulky – the more sensitive the magnetometer the larger the apparatus that goes with it. Through a series of random occurrences **Ben Varcoe**, Leeds Uni's Professor of Quantum Information Science, and PhD Student Melody Blackburn have designed a smaller version that will be invaluable to cardiologists and you and me. See **Heart monitor** and **Melody Blackburn**.

Tom Maguire (1866–1895) Born into poverty in the **Bank District** of Leeds, according to Leeds City Museum, Tom was a poet, pioneering socialist and trade unionist. His working class background made him more of an activist than a theorist and he believed in action over words. In 1887 he wrote a handbill stating that the objectives of socialism were to 'put a stop to the mad competition for existence, which is the cause of poverty, and to establish a co-operation commonwealth.'

Not forgetting that he was a poet here's the second verse of *A New Nursery Rhyme*:

Sing a song of England,
Shuddering with cold
Doomed to slow starvation
By the gods of gold;
See her famished children
Hunger-marked, and mean,
Isn't that a dainty dish
To lay before the Queen?

He was a journeyman rabble-rouser and poet who helped found the **Leeds Socialist League**, one of the first socialist societies in northern England and co-founded the Labour Party's forerunner, the **Independent Labour Party**. He was also a founder of the Leeds Building Labourers' union, a Leeds branch of the Gasworkers and General Labourers' Union (he led the famous 1891 Leeds Gasworkers' Strike), a Labour Electoral League, and a Leeds branch of the Fabian Society. West Leeds MP **John Battle** (my MP) has written a book about him called, *Tom Maguire: Socialist and Poet* (Medium Publishing Co, 1997.)

He died of pneumonia in 1895 at only 30 years of age and I'll leave the last word to Tom: 'A few of us, green and tender saplings, started a society, the simple object of which was to nationalise the inherited world. We believed that the object of life was to be happy; the place to be happy, here; the time to be happy, now; and the way to be happy, to make others so - even at the risk of making ourselves intensely miserable.' Tom is buried in Beckett Street Cemetery and there was a rare red plaque commemorating him at Leeds Bus Station (put up by the Ford-Maguire Society) that disappeared at some point.

Makkah Mosque is on the corner of Thornville Road and Brudenell Road and visible as you drive up (or down) Cardigan Road. It's a stunning building and, nestled amongst the red brick, has made me stop and look on numerous occasions. It won the Model Mosque competition in 2008, beating over 1000 other mosques from around the UK. The competition was televised on the Islam Channel and was judged by viewers, over a number of months, by knock-out phone votes. The criteria were not just the building but more how they served their local community, engaged with Muslims youth, gave the mosque over to women for two days a week, their relationships with local agencies and non-Muslim communities. The imam sees it as a progressive, liberal mosque with a mission to encourage visitors to learn about the Islamic faith through connecting cultures events and exhibitions – they hosted Yorkshires largest ever Islamic exhibition which is now an annual event for which the Mosque is open to the whole community, faith or no faith. They encourage visitors to experience the unique interior, especially the beautiful hand painted internal dome....hand painted, that's a serious artist. The dome includes a lilac/pink colour used nowhere else, the amount of calligraphy in the dome is also unique and the theme of it is mercy. The mosque was built in 2003 (I watched it go up) at a cost of £2 million raised locally. Some gave £25,000, some a fiver. I love the tiles on the outside and the way that such a beautiful and colourful building manages to be sympathetic to its red-brick surroundings. In the national Brick Development Association awards the mosque won second place in the best craftsmanship category, fourth place in public buildings and was short listed for best building of the year for 2003. Look it up online.

The **Manchester and Leeds Railway** was a railway company which opened in 1839, connecting Manchester with Leeds via the North Midland Railway which it joined at Normanton. It was also the main constituent of **Lancashire and Yorkshire Railway (L&YR)** that formed in 1847 and its route is now the backbone of the **Caldervale Line**.

Marching On Together is the Leeds United (and Leeds RL) anthem and is actually entitled *Leeds! Leeds! Leeds!* with *Marching On Together* in brackets. It was written by **Les Reed and Barry Mason** (who also wrote *Delilah*, *It's Not Unusual* and *The Last Waltz*) for the 1972 (centenary) cup final in which Leeds beat Arsenal 1 – 0 and was in fact the B-side of *Leeds United*. The song spent around three months in the charts and rose to number ten. It rose to number ten again in 2010 as Leeds fans downloaded it in celebration of the team's promotion to the Championship.

Marine chronometer. When astronaut Neil Armstrong, the first person to stand on the Moon, was the guest of honour at **10 Downing Street** during the early '70s he thanked the British nation for this invention and it setting mankind on the journey to the Moon. 'This object…is considererably more important than the landing on the moon.' (*A History of the World in 100 Objects*, Radio 4, 11 Oct 2010) See **John Harrison**.

Married Single Other, is a six-part drama, which went out over six weeks in February 2010 on ITV1, was filmed at **The Leeds Studios** (formerly YTV on Kirkstall Rd.) and on location around Leeds, including such places as Millennium Square (Civic Hall), Hanover Square, Chapel Allerton, The Calls, Leeds City Centre, Victoria Quarter, Kirkstall Abbey, Clarence Dock, Roundhay Park, Harehills, Allerton High School. Screen Yorkshire provided locations and crewing support and invested £250,000 in the production.

Henry Rowland Marsden (1823–1876) has a statue on Woodhouse Moor (by local sculptor John Throp, 1878) and a large memorial (topped with a praying angel) in Holbeck Cemetery. He was born poor in Holbeck and after an apprenticeship as a tool maker/machinist emigrated to America where he patented and made his fortune with the Black's Stone Breaker, which produced material for new road building. He returned to Leeds a rich man in 1862, showed his stone breaking machine at the South Kensington Exhibition and set up his Soho Factory in Leeds. He won many awards and medals for engineering inventions, – unfortunately I haven't been able to track any others down so if you're aware of any please let me know. He also founded the Leeds Music Festival, last held in 1985, and was twice Lord Mayor of Leeds. There are a lot of examples of what a popular and generous man he was and the marble statue was funded by public donations of £1,000, following Marsden's sudden death on 19th January 1876.

John Marshall (1765–1845) was one of Leeds' and the world's pioneers of the first Industrial Revolution. Marshall's Mill (1792) was thought to be the biggest in the world, heralded the transition – with the help of **Matthew Murray** – from the cottage industry of hand driven spindles to a mill with 700 steam-powered spindles and was the first of the iconic Holbeck industrial buildings. It is still in use as office space for several companies, including Orange. John was behind the building of the world's first iron framed building, in Ditherington, which is considered the '**grandfather of skyscrapers**.'

Next to Marshall's Mill, he built what is currently the second favourite building in Leeds, Temple Works/Mills (opened 1843) based on the Temple of Horus at Edfu – flax-spinning was one of Egypt's most important industries. Temple Works (including ducts for air-conditioning) was the biggest single room in the world and an early example of a turf roof, cropped by half a dozen sheep until a daft one fell through a dome - I'm surprised the others didn't follow. Trevor Mitchell, English Heritage's head of historic properties (West Yorkshire), said Temple Works 'is unique in its elevational treatment and plan form, and is the most important symbol of the linen industry in West Yorkshire....probably the finest example of a carved stone elevation in the whole region.' (Evening Post, 10 December, 2008.)

Whilst we marvel at the birth of the modern world unravelling before us in Leeds let's not forget how it happened. 'In Mr Marshall's mill, a boy of nine years of age was stripped to the skin, bound to an iron pillar, and mercilessly beaten with straps, until he fainted.' (E.P. Thompson, *The Making of the English Working Class*, Penguin, 1991). Even in the later Temple Works 20% of the workers were under thirteen and further 40% were young women between 13 and 20 and they worked 72 hours a week. Having said all this, Marshall is considered to be one of the most liberal factory owners of the Industrial Revolution and it looks like the management techniques developed. Corporal punishment was banned, the younger kids encouraged to attend day school and the older ones given free education on Monday afternoons. Anyway, John helped fund Leeds Mechanics' Institute, Leeds Philosophical and Literary Society, gave money to Leeds Library, started a campaign to create Leeds University in 1826 and was Liberal MP for Yorkshire.

Marsh Jones & Cribb Ltd. was a firm of cabinet makers, decorators, artists and upholsterers. Known as one of the finest painting and decorating businesses in the country they had an international reputation, for example decorating many of the Tsarist palaces of St Petersburg during the nineteenth century. Originally set up in 1760 as John Kendall & Co. on Boar Lane, Edward Jones and Henry Cribb acquired the company in 1859. The firm of Marsh & Jones 'Medieval Cabinet Makers' of Leeds became Marsh, Jones & Cribb in 1868 and were also famous for the manufacturer of high quality furniture, with designs by Charles Bevan and B.J. Talbert in the 1860s. They later produced some well regarded early Art & Crafts furniture. During World War I they manufactured Camel bi-planes, in 1957 they painted the reconstructed West Stand at Elland Road and seem to be still operating as decorators from Cross Green Lane.

Kiran Matharu (born 1989) is a Leeds born and raised professional female British golfer currently playing on the Ladies European Tour. In 2006, at the age of 17 she was English Ladies Amateur Champion and went professional the following year, gaining three top ten finishes. She went to Allerton Grange High School and particularly likes R&B. I'm faced with one of those classic wishy-washy liberal dilemmas here. Her Wiki profile immediately says 'a Sikh of Punjabi origin' and I want to note the 'multicultural' nature of Leeds and that the city has been and will be shaped by people with roots all over the world and it's all the better for it. I love the fact of a young, female tyke with 'Punjabi origins' being ace at golf and travelling Europe making a career of it but then ask myself if I'd mention her religion or 'roots' if she were a white Catholic and feel, in some advanced way, racist. I know I could be being daft but I think I'd best bottle it, not mention her roots and just leave it as 'Leeds lass is ace at golf'. So anyway, Kiran Matharu, she's a young Leeds lass who's so good at golf that she's making a living out of it.....brilliant.

Professor John Maule is head of human decision making at Leeds University's Business School. Their website says, '**Decision Research** focuses on the way individuals, groups and organisations make decisions. It involves perspectives that are:
  Descriptive - why and how decisions are made the way they are,
  Normative - how decisions should be made in some ideal sense, and
  Prescriptive - how can decision making be made more effective.'

Phil May (1864–1903) was an extremely influential caricaturist, his main area of interest, mirroring his background, being 'street urchins'/'guttersnipe'. He was born on, Wallace Street (off Wellington Road), where artist **John Atkinson Grimshaw** had lived years earlier, and grew up in **Wortley**.

Like many at the time, he had a difficult childhood. Part of a large family, his father died when he was nine and having had little schooling he went out to work at the age of twelve. He began his working life as an errand boy in a solicitor's office, moved on to help in an architect's office until he spilt ink over a plan and ran away. He also worked as a time-keeper at a foundry, tried to become a jockey, went on the stage and by the age of 14 had drawings accepted for the *Yorkshire Gossip*. He eventually ended up mixing paints for the scene painter at the **Grand Theatre** where he began doing caricatures and portraits of actors for shillings and then posters for the theatre.

At 17/18 he set off to London with a sovereign in his pocket and ended up living rough, begging from pubs and sleeping under a market cart. He eventually obtained employment as designer to a theatrical costumier and drew posters and cartoons until he was commissioned to do a few drawings for the 1884 Christmas issue of *St Stephen's Review*, he continued working for the *Review* but life was still hard. His work was noticed by W H Traill, the managing director of *The Sydney Bulletin* who offered him £20 a week to work for him in Australia, which (also under medical advice, the streets having affected him badly) he did for three years, leaving Dec 1885 aged 21. During this time in Australia he had 900 drawings published in *The Bulletin,* around six per issue. Through his work and influence on prominent caricaturists and artists, Livingstone Hopkins, the five Lindsay siblings, and later David Low, he helped shape the 'Australasian style' which would sweep London.

His lack of formal training was central to his influential loose style, which contrasted with his British contemporaries. He would apparently start without 'roughs' and at any place in the drawing, moving to an unconnected place, perhaps draw the eye first, move to the shoe and then fill in the spaces. Others comment that his economy of line was sometimes due to a process of elimination from preparatory sketches and I personally wonder whether his early experience in the architect's office had an influence on his 'economy of line'. The central thing to his work was his affection and sympathy towards his main subjects, cheerful, cheeky street children drawn with wit and a sense of fun.

When he returned to London, via Rome and Paris, he gained almost instant success and fame working for the major publications and published many collections – *Phil May's Sketch Book* (1895), *Phil May's Guttersnipes* (1896), *Phil May's Graphic Pictures* and *Phil May's A. B. C.* (1897), *Phil May's Album* (1899), *Phil May, Sketches from Punch* (1903) In his later years his services were retained exclusively for *Punch* and *The Graphic*. In 1898 he was a founder member of the London Sketch Club.

The internationally celebrated caricaturist **Alan Moir** commented that by his death 'he was probably the most popular and imitated cartoonist and illustrator in England.'

A self portrait by Phil May.

Nell McAndrew. Using a self-designed electro spectrometer Nell broke the colour blue down into its constituent parts, winning the 2004 Nobel Prize for physics. Not really, blue is a primary colour and Nell is a model not a physicist. Born in Belle Isle, 1973, Nell first gained fame as the official **Lara Croft** model for the video game **Tomb Raider** between 1998 and 1999, but was quickly fired when she became the first British woman to pose nude on the cover of *Playboy*. She's appeared in many TV shows, presenting some, and I saw her on *I'm a Celebrity... Get Me Out of Here!*, where she came across as a nice, sorted woman. Her main work has been glamour modelling in **Lads Mags**, best selling fitness videos and calendars. She does a lot of charity work and while running for charity in the 2005 London Marathon (aged 31), she was so fast that her time allowed her to start with the elite athletes in future events.

Mick McCann is widely regarded as Leeds's greatest ever author/writer....ever. He was last seen wandering around Armley babbling to himself about the need for an encyclopaedia of Leeds.

Malcolm McDowell (born 1943, see back cover) is a serious actor. Lead in the iconic film of a dystopian future Britain *A Clockwork Orange*, one of the most controversial films of all time, in which his character is pure Leeds. The film (some of which was filmed in Leeds) was withdrawn soon after its release in 1971 (on police advice), rarely shown in public and unavailable on video/DVD for 27 years; the few places that broke the ban were prosecuted, sometimes leading to bankruptcy. The un-cut version wasn't shown until 2001. Malcolm also played the lead in *Caligula*, the first film to have famous actors in sex scenes, and his debut (where his scenes were retained), the classic, public school boys run amok with machine guns *If....*. He's obviously gone on to do all sorts of fabulous stuff.

Arthur Fergusson McGill was the first surgeon to carry out **suprapubic prostatectomy** (also called transvesical prostatectomy) shortly before he became Professor of Surgery in 1887. Apparently it happened by mistake, McGill was checking the size of the prostate inside a man's bladder with his finger and it simply came away. He understood how important this happy accident was and published his findings in the *Clinical Society Transactions 1887-8*. In 1869 he became residential medical officer at Leeds Infirmary, and in 1874 became surgeon to the Leeds Public Dispensary, demonstrator in anatomy and was later appointed lecturer in pathology and surgery at the School of Medicine.

Leeds born, bred and based writer **Frances McNeil** started her career writing for radio, has written scripts for TV and theatre and has four novels (as well as other books) published. See **Mrs Helen Currer Briggs**

Melbourne Brewery Ltd. Leeds (Kirk Matthews and Co) was established in 1875. In 1889, as Leeds and Wakefield Breweries, it was amalgamated with Carter and Sons' Victoria Brewery of Wakefield at a cost of £216,000. In 1935 the company acquired a further three breweries and in 1957 changed its name back to Melbourne Brewery Ltd. Leeds, before being bought, with its 345 (I've also seen the figure given as 245) licensed houses, by Joshua Tetley & Sons in 1960 when it ceased brewing – although some sources say it ceased brewing in 1961. In 1965 it went into liquidation. You can still see the **Melbourne Brewery Ltd.** logo of a courtier on signs, mirrors, windows etc. around pubs in West Yorkshire – the *Secret Leeds* website has a great thread on it.

The Beech Hotel on Tong Rd., Lower Wortley is a fine example and the pub retains much of its 1931 interior.

Kay Mellor (OBE) is an extremely successful TV, film dramatist and founder of Rollem Productions, Leeds. She's a script writer, actress, director, business woman, describes herself as 'Leeds born and bred' and has won a shed-load of awards. Blokes might think Kay's stuff is a bit girly with it being based around women, but its female outlook adds balance to our screens and I love her dramas. Her main characters are invariably working class, strong, Leeds/Bradford women, getting on with real life. She was herself pregnant at 16 and the child of a single mother who grew up on a Leeds council estate (Ireland Wood) in the '50s and '60s, she writes about what she knows and I like to know about it too. A consequence of this is that her dramas are full of strong women of different ages and in an era where roles are notoriously difficult to find when women get to a certain age. If you look at the lack of dramatic roles for the more mature women and the institutionalised sexism/ageism around newsreaders and presenters, (Moira Stuart et al) we don't like to see older or women on screen, or so TV executives believe, not that Kay agrees.

So out of Leeds, thanks to Kay, come dramas about real women, with real women in the leading roles and men, for a welcome change, take the supporting roles. Cutting her writing teeth in theatre and soap – **Coronation Street, Brookside** and the 90 episode children's series **Dramarama** – Kay learnt how to write quantity to deadline. She has been involved in hundreds of hours of prime time TV for both children and adults, **Children's Ward** that she conceived and co-wrote with Paul Abbott (although Kay went off to do other things) became around 70 hours of TV covering difficult and sensitive issues. **Families**, the daytime soap opera that Kay created, was over 152 hours of television. That's a lot of airtime. It also took on subjects that, at the time, were deemed controversial for prime time soap. Her stuff isn't typically 'gritty' but it's very real and that reality gives it the unforced, unclichéd grit of real life. **Band Of Gold** for example, a drama based around prostitutes, you couldn't get a much grittier subject matter but it's stuffed full of nuance and humanity, simple stereotypes are expelled. The series was prime time TV, attracting **15 million viewers** on a Sunday evening to 15 hours of real West Yorkshire people and drama.

I'd say that through reflecting real life and people Kay avoids a couple of nasty little TV stereotypes, the first of which is the constantly pristine and beautiful actress, whose prime purpose/role/priority in life is to look glam and with few distractions. Add to that the make-up artist, hair stylist, flattering angles, pampering, Botox, time in the gym and salons, the 'work' done to improve their bust or apish pout and we are constantly presented with an unreal version of femininity that is bound to have some effect on the self esteem of ordinary people. This obviously combines with other presentations of women in separate media where they are photo-shopped and reshaped as even the most perfect are not quite perfect enough. The characters in these 'serious' dramas are fantasy in so many ways, they are rarely 'plain' or even a bit ugly, perhaps over weight or maybe a tad out of shape, or just 'ordinary' as Kay's characters often are. The second daft TV stereotype that she avoids (which I'd argue is dangerous, bordering on racist) is the casting/characterisation of a three to four person professional 'team' with a white middle aged boss, a relatively young male, black side kick and a 'pretty' brown or 'Asian' young woman. I mean this is just an opinion but I'd love to know how many British born, young, black male or young, brown, pretty, female highly qualified forensic scientists, archaeologists, pathologists, MI5 agents, specialist police officers, nuclear physicists, space experts there are. It's not just simple demographics, it's also social barriers, and the likelihood of finding this combination in real life once, never mind every time, is so remote as to be only possible in silly, clichéd and patronising TV dramas. Oops, have I gone off on one? I try not to. Sorry, I promise to concentrate on Kay's fantastic, cliché avoiding career.

Ooh, wait a minute, before I go on, can I just point out that, on this thing of Kay showing/representing ordinary people and hiring people according to talent – and TV being dominated by the beautiful and thus excluding the ordinary and often more interesting/talented people – that *Fat Friends* starred both **James Corden** and **Ruth Jones** (writers and stars of *Gavin and Stacey*) as well as **Alison Steadman**, Gavin's mum. It was James's big break, Ruth contributed to the writing of *Fat Friends* – her TV writing debut as far as I can see – and I'd put 20 quid on it being where the two first met. Like *Fat Friends*, *Gavin and Stacey* is a beautifully observed, funny, real life portrayal of 'ordinary' people and a huge TV hit. Ey, and Ruth has moved to West Yorks and now lives just outside Wakefield.

Kay's TV drama *A Passionate Woman*, which she wrote and directed was a BBC 1 two-parter (180 mins), with Billie Piper and Sue Johnston in the main roles. The BBC drama was adapted from the play originally produced and staged at the West Yorkshire Playhouse in 1992 (where she also did a one woman show) and which ran in the West End for a year, followed by five national tours and has been staged in ten countries over four continents. The TV drama was produced and filmed in Leeds, featuring such places as Roundhay Park, the Hyde Park Cinema, Leeds Town Hall/the Headrow, Chapel Allerton and Woodhouse/Blenheim Square. I respect Kay Mellor for so many reasons and one is her pride and passion for her roots and her city, writing about Leeds people, setting up of Rollem Productions in Leeds, filming, providing employment in Leeds, helping keep Leeds as a centre of production and cutting the high percentage of TV productions being made in either Manchester or London. "I have to live in Leeds, I'm hearing brilliant things around me all the time, I love Leeds and it feeds my work." (Ee Po 16th of November, 2006.) Did you know that Leeds is cheaper to film in than Manchester or London? And it has all the required infrastructure and expertise? Did you know that Ofcom is supposed to ensure that broadcasting is representative of and reflects all the people of the UK and that this means a certain amount of 'regional' programming and not just local news? I've heard, from a reliable source, that one of the ways that Ofcom get around this duty is to classify 'the north' as starting just the other side of the M25 that circles London. Anyway here's a list of some of her TV stuff, mainly based in Leeds.

Strictly Confidential, writer and creator of this six part series (50 mins) from Rollem Productions for ITV1.

The Chase, writer, creator and executive producer of two series (20, 1hr episodes) from Rollem Productions for BBC 1 Sunday, 8pm slot, 2006-2007.

Gifted, writer, actress and executive producer of this single drama (95 mins) from Rollem productions for ITV1, 2003.

Between the Sheets, writer, creator and executive producer of the six part series (50 mins) from Rollem Productions ITV1 2003

A Good Thief, writer and actress of one-off drama (120 mins, although I suspect 95 mins if you subtract adverts) Rollem Productions for GranadaFILM/ ITV1, 2002.

Fat Friends, writer, creator and executive producer of the show that ran to four series (25, 1hr episodes) won Television and Radio Industry award and TV Quick award, was BAFTA nominated and winner of The Dennis Potter Award. (Rollem's Productions/Tiger Aspect/Yorkshire Television, 2000-2005.)

Fanny and Elvis, writer and director, 111 min film, won the Audience Award at Dinard and the Fort Lauderdale Festival Award, 1999.

Jane Eyre, writer, 108 min, adaptation for LWT 1997.

Playing the Field, Kay wrote the first 12 of the 29 episodes which made five series for the BBC. Ran from 1998–2002 and was BAFTA nominated two years in a row.

The Things You Do For Love: Sweet Dreams, writer, 60 min TV drama, 1998.

Girls' Night, 102 min, writer, one-off drama commissioned by Granada Films 1995 and winner of the Gracie Allen Award.

Some Kind of Life, 102 min, writer of single drama commissioned by Granada Films and Screened at the London Film Festival 1995, broadcast in August 1996 by ITV and nominated for BAFTA and winner of the Prix Niki Award.

Band of Gold, creator and writer (18, 50 minute episodes, 1995-1997). The first series was nominated for a BAFTA for Best Serial and the Prix Italia Award. Won the 1996 Royal Television Society Award, ITV Programme of the Year and the 17th American Cable Ace Award, aired on HBO.

Just Us, creator and writer and actress Yorkshire Television 1990. The third series won the 1993 Royal Television Society Award for Children's Drama and the 1994 Writer's Guild Award.

I'm not just saying it because of what she's done for Leeds or because she's from Leeds but I love her stuff....well the stuff I've watched anyway. Here's a list of actor's mouths Kay's put words into: Ray Winstone, Maxine Peake, Sue Johnston, Ciarán Hinds, Billie Piper, Gaynor Faye, Jennifer Saunders, Kerry Fox, David Morrissey, Ben Daniels, Nicola Stephenson, Julie Graham, Alun Armstrong, James Thornton, Norman Wisdom, Brenda Blethyn, Ralph Ineson, Alison Steadman, Julie Walters, Josie Lawrence, Ruth Jones, Richard Ridings, Jane Horrocks, James Corden, Barbara Marten, Samantha Morton, Gemma Jones, Geraldine James, Barbara Dickson, Mark Strong, Peter Firth, Nick Berry......that's not all of them obviously but I'm stopping now. Kay's cool, OK. Watch her stuff, she's a Leeds treasure.

The Middleton Railway founded in 1758, is the oldest continuously working railway in Britain, and the world's first railway line to be authorised by an Act of Parliament – England's first railway Act. Initially, the railway was a horse-drawn wooden waggonway linking the Colliery at Middleton with Leeds Bridge (Casson Close) but The Peninsular War (1808-14), The Napoleonic Wars and The French Revolutionary Wars caused an increase in the price of horses and horse fodder and **John Blenkinsop** (the manager) to look to cut costs. This economy led to the world's first working locomotive the *Salamanca* built by **Matthew Murray** of **Fenton, Murray and Wood** in **Holbeck**, although some sources have the same people and track using another locomotive *The Prince Regent* a couple of months earlier. This revolutionary technological development was also influenced by geography, the incline from Middleton to central Leeds making a canal unfeasible. David Goodman (*The Making of Leeds*) reckons the 1758 innovation was also the world's first horse-drawn railroad.

During the 1960s it was restored by enthusiasts and re-opened with volunteers (a group of Leeds University Students, led by Dr Fred Youell) operating passenger and freight services becoming the first standard gauge railway to be taken over by volunteers. From 2005 the line and site was re-developed, with the aid of chunks of money from the Heritage Lottery Fund. They re-laid track, demolished stuff built a new Engine House where the historic locos are on show, and a new station/platform. It puts on events, is available for parties (I went with a bunch of young kids and they loved it) and school/educational groups and is well worth a visit.

The micrometer (also known as a micrometer screw gauge) is a device for precision measurement and was invented in 1641 by **William Gascoigne** in Miggey (Middleton). The micrometer is crucial in engineering, machining and most mechanical trades. His original design, for telescopes, was adapted for the precise measurement of handheld (and other) objects and the ability to also measure small things and differences accurately – as Gascoigne would have done with planets, not that planets are small, obviously, but they will have appeared so through an early telescope. Micrometers and modern calliper design followed on from Gascoigne's work and they now come in various shapes and sizes for measuring all sorts of things such as wires, spheres, shafts, blocks, the diameter of holes, depths of slots and steps, inside diameters and the thickness of tubes.

The Mighty Boosh is a TV comedy series which started life in 2001 on BBC London Live and later transferred to BBC Radio 4 where it attracted the interest of the BBC television people. It's half Leeds and half London (Julian Barratt and Noel Fielding), with all the funny lines coming from Leeds and the fake glamour cheap laughs coming from London – I'm joking, I like Noel. It's not laugh a minute but it's very clever, hugely entertaining and I'm disappointed if I miss it. It's very 'off the wall' but if you see it on give it a go, although you'll also need to give it time. *The Mighty Boosh* won Best TV Show at the Shockwaves NME Awards in 2007, 2008 and 2009, their Best DVD award in 2010 and The Royal Television Society award for best Situation Comedy and Comedy Drama, 2008. See **Julian Barratt**.

Mill Hill Chapel Leeds is one of the oldest and most respected Dissenting congregations in England and there has been a **Unitarian** chapel on City Square since 1674, but the present building dates from the 1848 rebuilding of the chapel in Potternewton and Meanwood stone. The Mill Hill Chapel website says, 'the Unitarians are a liberal religious movement rooted in the Jewish and Christian traditions but open to insights from world faiths, reason and science.' The most well known Mill Hill minster was the Rev **Joseph Priestley**.

Monopoly is the most successful selling board game of all time, although I'm not sure how you collate figures for the amount of Chess or Backgammon sets that have been sold in the last five thousand years. It has been produced by **Waddingtons** of Leeds for over 70 years. Anyway, since its launch, Monopoly has sold an average of half a million pounds worth a year. Monopoly is licensed in over 80 countries, and more than 200 spin-off versions exist.

In 1935 Waddington's had sent a copy of their game *Lexicon* to Parker Brothers in the US to try and sort a licensing deal. In response the Parker Brothers sent *Monopoly* and the rest is history. Waddingtons had worldwide rights, other than the US and Canada, and adapted it to the British market by using London landmarks, although they recently saw the error of their ways and produced a Leeds edition. Parker Brothers later took the Waddingtons game *Cluedo* and changed its name to *Clue*.

How Monopoly helped win World War II

During the early years of the war (by request of the British Secret Service) Waddington's perfected the process of printing on silk to manufacture silk escape maps for British airmen – they were light, easy to handle, did not deteriorate in bad weather and were silent when used.

They were then approached again by the British Secret Service who wished to supply escape aids to prisoners of war. Waddingtons set up a secret group of four people in a small, secure, secret room even keeping its existence away from other employees. These were skilled craftsmen who set about lining the inside of the cardboard boxes with silk maps, marked with safe houses and specific to the area of the particular prison camp. Other aids were included in the box, as well as the standard playing pieces such as the liner, thimble, car etc... they included additional pieces, such as a metal file and magnetic compass. These 'special edition' games were made known to any frontline servicemen (who may be captured) and were delivered to the camp with the Red Cross parcels. They even included real German, Italian, and French currency simply placed underneath the play money for escapees to use for bribes, food or fares.

So how did you know if you had a 'special edition' set? They simply placed a red dot in the corner of the *Free Parking* space. Knowledge of the existence of these 'special edition' Monopoly sets has only recently emerged. After the war all remaining sets were destroyed and servicemen were sworn to secrecy in case the ploy needed to be used again in any future conflicts.

How Monopoly helped win the Cold War

During the Cold War the U.S.S.R., other Eastern Bloc countries and Cuba banned the game in case it corrupted their populations with positive ideas of a free-market economy. They had seen the popularity of the game explode and thought it was clearly pro-capitalist and anti-communist, the whole aim being to get rich and bankrupt your opponents. The game went underground and became a symbol of dissidence and the Communists brought out similar games to replace it with names such as 'Save' and 'Manage' in which the players were frugal and more supportive of each other.

The ban could not hold back the popularity of the game which came to symbolise the excitement and riches of the West and its playing showed opposition to the Communist state and life. The ban on the game was only lifted in 1987, four years before the collapse of the Soviet Union.

Henry Moore (1898–1986) was a sculptor and one of the world names of 20th Century art. He was born in Castleford, the seventh child of a mining family. I can't believe Cas has a Wakey and not Leeds postcode but, anyway, he has an extremely close association with Leeds. During World War I he was the youngest man in his regiment and got injured in a gas attack but, overall, didn't have such a bad war. After the war (1919) he used his ex-serviceman's grant to become the first student of sculpture at the Leeds School of Art (now Leeds College of Art), which set up a sculpture studio especially for him. He met Barbara Hepworth at college and began a friendship that lasted for many years.

Although he was a modernist he was hugely influenced by the over thousand year old Chac-Mool, a type of stone statue produced by a central Mexican civilisation. I didn't know that but could always kinda see it in his stuff, I knew it was 'modern' but it also has a solid, ancient feel to it, like it'd been there forever. Many people can see the undulating hills of Yorkshire in his work and I think they work better in a natural rather than built environment, I'm sure I saw some in the 1980s at The Yorkshire Sculpture Park (Bretton Hall) but can't see any reference to them on their website. Perhaps they wish to keep schtum considering the 2005 theft from the Henry Moore Foundation of a 2.1 tonne Reclining Figure sculpture worth £3m. Police reckon that it was melted down and sold for scrap at less than £1,500 even though the Henry Moore Foundation is thought to have offered £10,000 for its return.

Anyway Henry was world famous and a figurehead of British sculpture and modernism and received prestigious commissions such as the marble Reclining Figure (1957-58) for the UNESCO headquarters in Paris and his Knife Edge Two Piece 1962 in bronze which stands outside the Houses of Parliament in London. He was a war artist during World War II and some of his sketches of war-time London were absolutely stunning. Moore defined and dominated British sculpture and won the International Sculpture Prize at the 1948 Venice Biennale and at the 1952 Venice Biennale (Moore having also exhibited there the previous year) eight new British sculptors (including **Kenneth Armitage)** produced their *Geometry of Fear* works as a direct contrast to Moore's idea of *Endurance, Continuity*. Moore was given a block load of awards, seventy awards from over a dozen countries. He accrued lots of money, although he lived simply and saved the cash, which now runs the Henry Moore Foundation which in turn funds the **Henry Moore Institute** next to the Art Gallery supporting exhibitions and research in international sculpture.

Looks what's happened, I was supposed to be keeping this brief and I've gone and got all expansive on his ass. So there's a sculpture park load of material available about him online, go root or have a look at the reclining woman in bronze outside the Art Gallery. See white sculpture on front cover, **Barbara Hepworth** and **Leeds Arts Club.**

The **Moot Hall** was built in 1615 on Briggate for the Justices to hold their Sessions. They presided over more than just criminal law, regulating corn prices, deciding on paternity, fixing wages etc. It replaced the old medieval courthouse which had been in the floor above a 'comon oven' and the smoke, heat and smells were most disagreeable. The hall was re-built in 1710 and held court for over 100 years but in 1825, after a new courthouse was constructed and it was decided that the hall was too much of an obstruction on Briggate, it was pulled down. A statue of Queen Anne from the hall was passed around the fine buildings of Leeds until it finally arrived at the Art Gallery where it can be seen today. Oops, this is a bit 'local history'....soz.

Colin Stuart Montgomerie OBE (born 1963) is a fairly well known and successful golfer who went to Leeds Grammar School, supports LUFC and captained the European Ryder Cup team to victory in 2010. I've nothing more to say, go dig if you're interested.

Moortown Golf Club (established in 1909) hosted the first Ryder Cup match held on British soil in 1929.

Angela Morley (1924–2009) was one of the world's leading 'light' music composers, conductors and arrangers; she's done so much amazing stuff that I can't possibly do her justice here. Working in the commercial world, her early work was in cinema and she went on to work with John Williams on many films including the orchestration of his scores for *Star Wars*, *Superman* and *The Empire Strikes Back*, *E.T.*, *Hook*, *Home Alone I & II* and *Schindler's List*. Before this she had been a regular conductor of the BBC Radio Orchestra, wrote numerous film scores, notably *Peeping Tom*, *When Eight Bells Toll* and *The Looking Glass War*, *The Little Prince*, *The Slipper and the Rose*, most of *Watership Down*, wrote the theme tune and incidental music for *Hancock's Half Hour* and was the musical director for *The Goon Show*. She had a long association with the Philips record label, arranging for, accompanying and conducting the company's artists – a who's who of music. Scott Walker commented that 'Working with Wally Stott on *Scott 3* was like having Delius writing for you.'

Walter (Wally) Stott was born above his parent's watchmaker's shop in Leeds. The house was full of music; his father played the ukulele-banjo that (at a young age) he let Wally tune for him, using his pitch pipe and his mother sang. When Wally was eight he had piano lessons and practiced above the shop but due to the death of his father, they only lasted three months. Wally toyed with different instruments before settling on the saxophone. And here's a reason why Angela's work may not be as widely known outside the industry as it should be – she was born in Leeds as **Wally Stott**. In 1972, when Wally Stott went to Scandinavia on holiday, he came back as Angela Morley, a she, so prior to this gender realignment operation and treatments the work is credited as Wally Stott and post-op it's listed as Angela Morley. Her public profile meant that, after the operation, she attracted a lot of unwelcome publicity and press interest. This, and fear of the reaction of the musicians that she would have to work with on a daily basis, meant that she kept her head down for a while, thinking her career was over. To get it into perspective this was almost 40 years ago. Although people had been attempting it for around 40 years (often leading to death) the idea of a 'sex-change' was very shocking to many people. Society was different then. Only five years before, for example, homosexuality was illegal and still was in Scotland and Northern Ireland. (A personal study of the transgender issues can be found in the book by Leeds based transsexual Jane Preston with much of it set in Leeds, *Jane Preston: Pt. I and II*.)

Angela's work was often uncredited; she has scored for so many people that I can't list them but from Placido Domingo to Marlene Dietrich, Noel Coward to Shirley Bassey, Petula Clark to Dusty Springfield.

The work I know best is the stuff she did with Scott Walker. There were sometimes two or three arranger/conductors but Angela was the always the prime one. Have a look on YouTube (make sure you get a good quality version) for Scott Walkers, *Jackie* or *If You Go Away* which Angela certainly did or *Next* which should bring up a good version first and is one of the best bits of orchestration I've ever heard.

She moved to the US in 1980 and between 1979 and 1990 scored several TV films and many episodes of TV series such as Dallas, Dynasty, Falcon Crest, Cagney & Lacey, The Colbys, Wonder Woman and conducted at most of the Hollywood studios – Warner Bros., Paramount, M.G.M., Universal and 20th Century-Fox. She had two Oscar nominations, was nominated six times for an Emmy Award and won three of them. I feel like I've underplayed her more 'serious' stuff but go have a root, there's stuff out there about this amazing Leeds lass.

Bryan Mosley OBE (1931–1999) is best known as Corrie's **Alf Roberts.** Born in Leeds he attended Leeds Central High School and Leeds College of Art. His death followed just weeks after his screen death on **Coronation Street.**

Leeds born **Nevill Francis Mott** (1905–1996) was a physicist who won the **Nobel Prize for Physics** in 1977 for his work on the electronic structure of magnetic and disordered systems/the magnetic and electrical properties of noncrystalline, or amorphous, semiconductors. In the 1960s he studied the conductivity of amorphous substances (atomically irregular or unstructured) such as glassy materials. He devised formulas mapping the transitions that these amorphous substances can make between electrically conductive (metallic) states and insulating (non-metallic) states, thereby functioning as semiconductors. These glassy substances are cheap as chips to produce and replaced more expensive semiconductors in many electronic switching and memory devices, making stuff like computers, calculators, copying machines etc cheaper. That's good, I like cheap electronics, cheers Nev. He was knighted in 1962. A **Mott transition** is a metal-non-metal transition in condensed matter. The term **Mott insulator** is also named after him. For any of you who are particularly smart, go off and check **Mottness** and **Mott Criterion.**

Warning, don't read this next entry if you've just read Kay mellor, my two main rants are, by chance, within a few of pages of each other…it'll do your box in.
 Chris Moyles took over **Radio 1**'s flagship breakfast show in 2004. With audience figures falling, he increased the figures by one million listeners during his first three months in the slot, clearly justifying the nickname he gave himself of *The Saviour Of Early Morning Radio.* His listening figures steadily increased, his figures of 7.72 million jumped 600,000 to 7.88 million in 2010, and if you included under 15s they would've been well over nine million.
 When he left Radio 1 Chris was the longest running Breakfast Show presenter ever, filling the seat from the 5th of January 2004 until Friday the 14th of September 2012. He put a band together and went on tour with 'Chris Moyles Live' before taking the part of King Herod in an arena tour of the musical *Jesus Christ Superstar*, which he joined again for a tour beginning on 1 October 2013.
 The longest serving **Radio 1 Breakfast Show presenter** is a very funny man, using his typically blunt and direct Leeds humour to great effect. His show made me and my children laugh on average, 3.4 times a morning during our 8 - 8.50 a.m. journey, the laughter was often prolonged and we were a bit dozy having just woken up. I'd suggest that the show contained too much music and not enough babble/talking and I preferred it when it was just Chris and his team rather than when there are guests on the show. The humour also came out of his interaction with his 'team' Comedy Dave, Dominic Byrne, Rachel Mallender (formerly Jones), Aled Haydn Jones, Matt Fincham and sports reader Tina Daheley who replaced Carrie Davis (now Prideaux) who left the show to have a baby.
 He certainly served his apprenticeship, starting on hospital radio in Wakey and moving onto Radio Aire aged 16 and Radio Top Shop in the Leeds Briggate store, he also went onto do local radio all over the place. Chris has won lots of radio awards, although he quite rightly doesn't think it's enough. He has done boat loads of TV, currently (time of writing, not now, now could be anytime) presenting his *Chris Moyles' Quiz Night* (Friday night, Channel 4) and had a TV

show with Comedy Dave on SKY. He 'plugged' **Leeds United** all the time on his Radio 1 breakfast show, for example, before **Radio Leeds** lost the rights to **Leeds United** games under Bates, he'd tag on their live goal celebrations to the news and sport most Monday mornings and for weeks after we knocked Man U out of the cup, he'd randomly drop in a little celebration clip throughout the show.

  Although it may have rubbed some people up the wrong way, – who didn't listen to his show enough or understand the humour – he's got proper east Leeds humour, direct, cutting and blunt and, for me, it was like having one of my daft mates on the radio. I think he's very funny but he seems to be a love him or hate him figure. One last thing I've noticed is that, probably due to his huge popularity and saviour status, between 6.30 and 10 in the morning he used language that wouldn't've previously been acceptable but there were apparently few complaints. I reckon that **Richard Hoggart** might sigh if he heard it, but I've got my seven yr-old in the car, who's heard it since he was three, and it doesn't bother me. They'll hear it all around, you can't escape 'bad language'. What children need to know is at what age and in what situation it is acceptable to use certain words; that's a brilliantly complex and continuously shifting issue for them to get their fantastic little brains around and to deny them it is close to neglect. Sorry, I may have gone off on one there. He also actually wrote his autobiography *The Gospel according to Chris Moyles* (Ebury Press, 2006) which sold over two and a half million and *The Difficult Second Book.* (Ebury Press, 2007). His jokey album *The Parody Album* sold over 100,000 copies. Right that's him done so move on to the next entry while I stay here and have an overlong rant about accents and that. Seriously, it's rambling and opinionated in the extreme, go to Baron Moynihan, Chris Moyles has been done.

  I certainly remember a fuss from the chattering London-based media when Moyles first got the Breakfast Show gig. He 'wasn't appropriate for the peak morning slot', 'too abrupt, plain talking and rude to guests' they said, but that was just their soft, London, middle class bias, ignorance and regionalism. I don't think they liked the strong accent, they'd have preferred one of 'their own'. One of those awful characterless voices that cover the BBC, the type that are about class not place and have moved from Queens English (or Received Pronunciation) 40 years ago to that awful washed-out accent of nowhere but passed down elocution lessons and taught pretension, also paradoxically known as 'speaking properly'. I need to say, this is not about the people/presenters/commentators – they speak however they speak, no problem – this is about TV and radio not reflecting the character of the population and slowly leading a nation full of wonderful accents into a bland mush of an upgraded Estuary English. The media is full of people who try to sound ordinary but all sound the same, with no roots, just floating in the sky somewhere unspecified above a general southern space. The sad thing is when you hear one who recognises that they've – through no fault of their own – been stripped of roots, of accent, they try to develop one, dropping aitches and replacing *t* with *d*, so that 'dirty' becomes 'dirdy' and 'thirty' becomes 'thirdy'.

  Didn't I warn you to move onto the next entry? I haven't finished yet so you've still got chance. The one that is completely unforgivable and where over-prepped people simply can't speak proper, no excuse, they're simply developing their own language, and it's debilitating, a disability, it restricts them; they can't go under bridges or up stairs. They have to go ander bridges and ap stairs. The glorious round 'u', so expressive, so lyrical, so prevalent in the north and so necessary for words such as understand and ultimate, ditched for being too northern. What confuses me is how they differentiate between a close male relative and the bit of the body that links the foot to the leg, so easily sprained. On the path/parth, bath/barth thing, the only consolation I can find for the perversion of the English language is that the mythical 'extended A' (in parth) was, in the 17th Century, looked down on as working class. Ignoring that small comfort there simply is no *R* in path, bath, staff etc. and elocution lessons, run by me, should be forced on all people who insert *R*'s into words. I just need to make clear I have absolutely nothing against individuals who speak in these rootless voices – some of my friends can't talk right – it has been given to them and it doesn't mean they are bad people....well, not necessarily. What I don't like is the assumption that people with this voice are somehow superior to people with strong regional accents, more intelligent or acceptable. That's obviously nonsense but the BBC seems to have a preference, in presenters, for the non-accent. I love and can easily understand all regional accents and think it's a crime for TV and radio to prefer the non-accent and yes, I know there are some regional accents in national broadcasting, I'm talking about percentages. To finish my rant, I hate the lazy prejudice against 'posh' people just as I hate the fact that early in her career, Mrs Mick (with a 'well' spoken, very slight Leeds accent) was told by a high-up, 'I'd forget opera darling, you're accent is just not right.' To conclude, will I put my money where my mouth is? My youngest has developed a fantastic Armley twang which one of his older brothers encourages and the other corrects. Knowing that there are likely to be times when the accent will hold him back, where do I stand? Oh poo, I've just realised, I should have put all this under *accent*, I could maybe get away with it without you thinking I'm potty. Can't put it under *accent*, it'd be the first entry......maybe I'll put it under *arccent* or do a tenuous entry....ooh, I know, see the **Accent Revolt** of 1996.

Back to **Chris Moyles**'s choice as the breakfast show presenter whilst still in rant mode. The thing that the ivory tower commentators, locked into their SW1 bubble, didn't realise was that Chris Moyles dropped the pretention of the patronising presenter speaking to the 'ordinary' and spoke to them like he would a mate, teasing them if they said something stupid. He spoke to them like they were normal people, and we like real people. Anyway who was right? The Beeb execs that held their nerve, that's who. Listening figures revived and are steadily grew.

Last thing, on 16 March 2011 Chris and Dave Vitty began an attempt to break the Guinness World Record for 'Radio DJ Endurance Marathon (Team)' by continuously broadcasting for 51 hours 30 minutes which they achieved. The record stood until the 23rd of March, 2013, when it was broken by 20 hours, but it's still Radio 1's longest ever show. The marathon was to raise money for Comic Relief and raised a grand total of £2,821,831. With an audience of 2.84 million, the event was the most popular live BBC Red Button radio feature ever and 3.8 million people watched it on the Radio 1 Website.

Berkeley George Andrew Moynihan (1865–1936), **1st Baron Moynihan**, **Baron Moynihan of Leeds** was a noted and ground breaking British abdominal surgeon, President of the Royal College of Surgeons for six years, the first from outside London and the only one to be elevated to a Peerage. He was son of the Victoria Cross recipient Andrew Moynihan (who in one year taught his whole company of men to read and write) and the family moved to Leeds from Malta after the father's death when Berkeley was two. His early, primary school education was in Leeds and he later returned to the **Leeds School of Medicine** where he later taught, becoming lecturer in surgery until he took the role of professor of clinical surgery at the **University of**

Leeds. At a young age and after overhearing his mother speak of her fear of him joining the army and her wish for him to become a doctor, his decided that, 'the Moynihans have done enough of killing. It's time they mended their ways. I'm going to be the first to do it. I'm going to be a doctor.' He became a big, powerful man and a keen sportsman with 'fiery' red hair. Following the work of **Joseph Lister** and others, 'He was the first to break away from the old filthy traditions of the operation rooms by introducing, as much as possible, absolute cleanliness and sterility by using sterile towels, coats, caps, masks, rubber gloves, etc. This ritual is now universally practised and can be observed in all operation rooms........he was the first to use blood transfusion successfully as a routine.' (1)

During his *Harveian Oration* at the Royal College of Physicians of London, 1937, peer, eminent gastroenterologist and founder of the **British Society of Gastroenterology**, Sir Arthur Hurst (1879-1944) said of a clinical picture of a duodenal ulcer drawn by Moynihan, "It is as much a piece of original research as the discovery of a new element or a new star, and equally deserving of recognition". Moynihan published countless articles in medical journals around the world, following his ambition of having "one paper in print, one in the press and one in preparation", he also lectured around the world and was a particular hit in the US where his showmanship, oratory skills and confident attitude were seen as more American than the usual self-deprecating Brit. With his old boss, Mr. Mayo Robson, he wrote the book *Diseases of the Pancreas and their Surgical Treatment* (Messrs. W. B. Saunders, Philadelphia, 1901) and another *Diseases of the Stomach and their Surgical Treatment* published in 1902 by the same firm and his own *Gall Stones and their Surgical Treatment* was published in 1904 to much international praise. Although he lectured and published widely it was his book *Abdominal Operations* (published 1906) that cemented his international reputation.

His work being based in Leeds shaped his career and achievements in various ways. Historically, Leeds had been a centre of excellence in surgery but was also far enough away from London and Edinburgh to escape their influence and Berkeley had a brief apprenticeship as assistant to the pioneering abdominal surgeon **Sir Arthur Mayo Robson.** Berkeley was undoubtedly a great and visionary surgeon but it was his role in communicating, organising, spreading information and best practice that struck me. It was during his life that surgery, still performed by GPs, became a speciality and practices could be very different across Britain never mind the world. Throughout his adult life he travelled the world building bridges between surgeons of different countries and during his holidays, and whenever possible, he'd visit schools of surgery in Europe and the United States picking up tips and noting better practice which he'd nick and incorporate into his surgery. This novel behaviour came to be known as 'the Moynihan technique' and is the philosophy that all of modern medicine/science is based on.

In 1909 he wrote letters to 27 provincial surgeons suggesting that they meet up twice a year, share best practice and study the different techniques of each and received 27 letters of acceptance and thus started the *Moynihan Chirurgical Club*. On Friday, 23rd July, 1909 operations were performed in the Leeds General Infirmary by various surgeons (including an eminent American), observed by other surgeons and the 'club' was officially formed. As an extension of his provincial 'club' he founded **The Association of Surgeons of Great Britain and Ireland** (and The Dominions), and *The British Journal of Surgery* of which he was chairman of the editorial committee from its inception until his death. As president of the

Voluntary Euthanasia Legislation Society he introduced a Euthanasia Bill in the 1936 autumn session of the House of Lords.

Berkeley was knighted in 1912 and created a Baronet of **Carr Manor** (where he lived in Meanwood) in 1922. He received a hatful of awards including the Freedom of the City of Leeds. His portrait hangs in the 1st hall of Royal College of Surgeons where there is also a marble bust. Another bust stands on the main staircase (facing the main entrance) of the LGI, a bronze cast of his hands in the Leeds Medical School library with a replica in the City Art Gallery* and the Medical School also has a bronze bust of him. The family was asked if he could be buried in **Westminster Abbey**, but they declined and he was buried at **Lawnswood Cemetery** in the city he loved. 'It would not have been Berkeley's wish to have been buried elsewhere than in Leeds. Leeds had been his home, his love, and the scene of the long march of his endeavour from obscurity to fame.'

* Berkeley was known for gentle hands during surgery, seeing the body of the patient as a sacred vessel, this is thought to be part of the reason for his high success rate.

(1)*The Moynihan Chirurgical Club (1909-1959) Jubilee Meeting at Leeds: 24th and 25th September 1959*, Ann R Coll Surg Engl. 1960 March; 26(3): 180–194.

Matthew Murray (1765–1826) was a steam engine, machine tool and machinery for the textile industry designer/manufacturer. With **John Blenkinsop** he designed and built the first commercially viable steam locomotive, the twin cylinder **Salamanca** in 1812.

He started working in Leeds in 1789 and soon designed and patented new flax-spinning machines, saving the ailing flax industry. He made important improvements to the machinery for heckling and spinning flax, including the revolutionary new technique of 'wet spinning' flax. He put the British linen trade on a solid footing and helped create jobs in Leeds as he developed his ideas and large quantities of the machines were sold at home and abroad. By 1895 he'd set up a business with two partners and began building the world's first steam engineering foundry, **The Round Foundry**. The Round Foundry appears to be one of the first work places in the world to have been lit by gaslight and Murray's house in the complex (**Steam Hall**) was the first building in the world to be heated by steam and is an early example of domestic central heating. Wiki cites Angier March Perkins but his work was 30 years later.

Murray made many improvements to steam engines, was the first to place the piston in a horizontal position in a steam engine, patented an automatic damper that controlled the furnace draft depending on the boiler pressure, a box valve which simplified the movement of steam, and designed a mechanical hopper that automatically fed fuel to the firebox. He also designed a precision, mechanical plane for sliding valves that he apparently tried to keep as secret as possible, keeping it in a locked room with controlled access. In 1811 one of Murray's steam engines were fitted to a **paddle steamer** by John Wright in Yarmouth and was a great success. Five years later the **United States Consul** in Liverpool, Francis B. Ogden, bought two large twin-cylinder marine steam engines from Fenton, Murray and Wood, had the design copied, patented them in the US where it was widely copied and used on **Mississippi paddle steamers**. He received a gold medal from the **Royal Society of Arts** in 1809 for his heckling machine.

Myosin is a family of muscle proteins/molecular motors which 'motors' the contraction of muscle fibres in animals – it allows us to move. See **William Astbury**.

N

Nailed – Digital Stalking In Leeds, Yorkshire, England is a fantastic gritty, kitchen sink thriller by obscure Leeds writer Mick McCann. It's based on a true story (that he takes into fiction) of how he and his wife were arrested by CID and then on bail for a few months over a SIM card she had given away five years before. The fact that not enough people bought it is the reason you're reading this....and this....It's my book and my other book, I'll plug what I like, you can't stop me. Ey, have a look at the cover on Amazon, it's ace, and while you're there and your credit card details are already held....

Lilian **Adelaide Neilson** (1848–1880) was an actress who lived hard, died young and left a beautiful corpse way before James Dean or Marilyn Monroe even thought of it. She was born (out of wedlock) in St. Peter's Square and grew up in Guiseley where she worked in a factory and as a nursemaid. Aged 15 she left for London to pursue an acting career. There were many myths about her, for example the *New York Times* obituary (August 16th, 1880) says she was born in 1850 in Zaragoza, 'not of unmixed Spanish parentage, although in physique and appearance she was a true Spanish woman. Her father was a Spaniard but her mother was of English extraction, and as often occurs with those who mingle the blood and traits of two races, the result was a highly emotional and dramatic nature, combining the intensity of the swart Peninsular with the self-control of the colder English stock.'

Adelaide Neilson on Broadway as Juliet in the 1870's photo by SARONY.

She gradually built up a reputation in London, toured extensively and within ten years was highly acclaimed, making, amongst others, the role of Juliet 'her own'. She appeared to have put together a show in which she played various parts in one evening and was also a huge success in America and Canada. Of her death, the *New York Times* obituary put it down to a heart condition which had, in the past, led to fainting fits after demanding roles but in reality she died after horse riding in a Paris park, rupturing her 'broad ligament near the left fallopian tube' and bleeding to death. Her gravestone is a large white marble cross inscribed with the words 'Gifted and Beautiful—Resting.' I'll give the last word to that *New York Times* obituary; 'Her artistic method was simple, charged with emotion and passion, yet sufficiently tinged with imaginative grace to render it of very high quality, if not of the highest.'

Nesyamun, otherwise known as **The Leeds Mummy** is housed at Leeds Museum.

The New Penny in The Calls opened in 1953 as the Hope And Anchor and although it had to be a bit hush-hush, homosexuality being illegal in the UK until 1967, it was the first known gay venue to open outside of London and believed to be the oldest, continually running, gay pub in the UK. Wiki reckons that it changed its name to The New Penny in 1982 but I'm sure that it was called The New Penny way before that, although someone must have checked and posted that date. Anyway, back in the era of COAABFILYE, late '70s and early '80s, a couple of mates used to go down there and somewhere, we think, called Charlie's for the scrapping. With others, they'd look out for people going down for a bit of gay bashing or to hassle people and fulfil their wish for violence. Could I just add that back in them days some of the hardest people I knew could mince like a badger? Lastly, violence is bad and never, ever justified, so kids, don't hang about outside pubs looking for fights. The New Penny was always a lively pub but it has prospered under the new licensing laws and its mixed crowd of gay and straight welcome some of the best drag acts in the UK.

Next plc, the UK's largest clothing manufacturer, was founded in 1864 by **Joseph Hepworth** (1834–1911) in Leeds. Joseph left school in 1844 aged ten to work in the mills and in 1864 set up a tailoring business with his brother in-law. During the 1880s they opened shops to sell direct to customers and in 1881 their Wellington Street factory employed 500 people; by 1890 they employed 2,000 people and ran 107 shops. Joseph died in 1911 and within the next six years Joseph Hepworth & Son became the largest clothing manufacturer in Britain.

In 1982, Hepworth's chairman, Terence Conran, bought a Leicester-based woman's wear company and their 70 stores, recruited George Davies (of George at Asda fame) and reopened them, as Next stores, catering for men and women, by the end of the following year. Davies became chairman, converted the Hepworth stores to Next and in 1986 moved the headquarters from Leeds to Leicester, he continued innovating, adding 'trendy' children's clothes and introducing the 'coffee table' Next Directory. Next's high street operations have made them the third most successful high street chain in the UK behind Marks and Spencer and Arcadia Group/BHS.

William Gustavus Nicholson, 1st Baron Nicholson GCB (1845–1918) was a big cheese in the army, who, in a half-century of service defending and expanding the British Empire, rose through the ranks from Lieutenant to Field Marshall. Involved in India, getting whupped by the Boers (in South Africa obviously) and the nineteenth century Battle of Kandahar (sound familiar?) with a final hurrah in World War I. He was born on his family estate (Roundhay Park) and went to Leeds Grammar School and was awarded a Dutch settler's barn load of awards and medals.

Night-school. It's claimed that a wealthy, middle-class Quaker family in Leeds were responsible for the first ever night school. The parents of the Ford family (Robert and Hannah) were involved in radical, liberal politics and established the school at which their daughters Isabella (**Isabella Ford**) Emily and Bessie taught. It was established for local mill girls so that they could gain further skills, options and maybe escape the hard labour of the mills. I can't find a definite date but think, with good reason, that it was around 1871.

John Thomas North 'The Nitrate King' (1842–1896) A Leeds born investor and businessman, becoming known as **Colonel North** on 25 March 1885 when he became an Honorary Colonel. During the **War of the Pacific**, also known as the 'Saltpeter War' (1879–1883) between Chile and an alliance of Bolivia and Peru, North purchased large numbers of bonds (falling prices due to the war) in the Peruvian nitrate industry, obtaining a monopoly that he defended in court. This monopoly was very lucrative as the nitrates were used as fertiliser and he expanded into more monopolies in waterworks (distillation of sea-water) and freight railways, whilst he also owned several iron, coal fields and invested around the world. A new Chilean president (José Manuel Balmaceda) wanted to breaks North's monopolies and had to force through competition reforms against opposition in congress, one in a number of disputes which eventually escalated into the **Chilean Civil War** of 1891.

His nitrate business was the primary cause of the development of the towns of Iquique (the regional capital) and the, now deserted, port of **Pisagua** –from the Spainish words 'pis' and 'agua', roughly translating into 'pisswater' probably due to the water tasting of nitric acid. When back home in the UK he became a famous high society gentleman – described, by *The New York Times* as a 'lion' of the social scene – and was worth $10 million in 1889, with a huge estate and race horses, but his wealth dwindled by the time of his death, He bought and donated **Kirkstall Abbey** to the city of Leeds, as well as giving money to the **Leeds Infirmary** and the **Yorkshire College of Science** – later became the **University of Leeds**.

Northern Foods plc is a large food manufacturer, employing over 10,000 people, headquartered in Thorpe Park, Leeds 15.

Northern School of Contemporary Dance is an academy of dance with 200 students mainly doing three year professional dance-based degrees. The school was founded in 1985 and two years later moved to the current Chapeltown Road site in the old synagogue. It's a 'world-class' contemporary dance institution also providing taster sessions, evening, weekend and holiday classes for those with an interest in dance. All I can say is that everything I've ever seen by the school has absolutely blown my socks off and I want to see more.

The history is a mish-mash of different people but John Bramwell is a central figure, a headmaster in Harehills whose school had a lot of children whose first language wasn't English. John thought that dance may improve communication and inclusion, so he brought in dance teacher Nadine Senior. The success of the scheme meant that Nadine became one of the founders of the Northern School of Contemporary Dance as well as inspiring the three lads who went onto to form the excellent **Phoenix Dance Company** in 1981.

Northern Star and Leeds General Advertiser was a chartist newspaper published between 1837 and 1852. The Chartist movement of 1830s and 1840s was the first mass revolutionary movement of the British working class. The paper's most notable contributors were **Karl Marx** and **Friedrich Engels**.

Ex Chumba **Alice Nutter** is a Leeds based writer, more precisely she's a scriptwriter for theatre, radio and TV. She wrote *Foxes* for the West Yorkshire Playhouse performed in 2006 and *Where's Vietnam?* for Red Ladder theatre company in 2008. Amongst her radio and TV work is the afternoon play *Snow In July* (2008) for Radio 4, an episode of Jimmy McGovern's *The Street* and an episode of *Casualty*. She wrote an episode of *Moving On* for BBC 1 which aired in spring 2010 and an episode of Jimmy McGovern's series, *The Accused*. See **Chumbawumba**.

O

Richard Oastler (1789–1861) was a labour reformer and abolitionist. He fought for the rights of workers (particularly children) in the Factory Act (1847), was a prominent leader of the factory reform and anti-Poor Law movement and became known as the 'Factory King'. The 1847 Act meant that children working in mills could not work more than ten hours a day – the 1861 Act stretched it to children in all factories. It was after the 1847 Act that Richard retired from public life. From 1840 he spent over four years in prison after being, pretty much, stitched up by his boss over debts. He had given all his savings and a percentage of his income to the cause and his boss was annoyed due to his militant speeches urging workers to use strikes and sabotage. His friends and admirers started to raise funds to try to get him released and there were 'Oastler Committees', 'Oastler Festivals' and an 'Oastler Liberation Fund' (held all around the north) with the proceeds being forwarded to Richard. The previous decade, the first Short Time Committees (battling for children's rights, which Richard had helped fund) had been set up in Leeds and Huddersfield, quickly followed by most of the other large textile towns. Richard was instrumental in forming these committees and was the main speaker at many of their public meetings.

After reading much about Leeds' proud record on the rights of workers, especially children, it had occurred to me that conditions for workers were so bad that before the 1833 Slavery Abolition Act they were in a worse situation than slaves as they had no intrinsic value. I've read accounts of people having to work for four days with short breaks for sleep and the permanent, severe damage done by working conditions that left workers seriously disabled. This figure of four days is not as well documented as 12 to 16 hours a day (for children) and may be connected to the fact that many factory owners were unscrupulous and children sometimes lived at the factories. There was another scam some owners carried out which was to ban any kind of time piece from the factory and put the clock back on a morning and forward at night (if there was a clock there) Frank Forrest, in *Chapters in the Life of a Dundee Factory Boy* (1850) says:

'In reality there were no regular hours, masters and managers did with us as they liked. The clocks in the factories were often put forward in the morning and back at night. Though this was known amongst the hands, we were afraid to speak, and a workman then was afraid to carry a watch.'

Children as young as three are known to have worked in factories – although six or seven was a more usual age, with no proof of age required – and those who fell asleep would be beaten (see John Marshall). Many serious accidents occurred as children fell asleep around the machinery or tried to get their little fingers into the part of the machinery that adult hands could not reach. The Factories Act (1844) stated that, 'Accidental death must be reported to a surgeon and investigated.' Before this act what happened? Simply move the body out and move another in....'there's plenty more bodies where that one came from.' I was struggling with how and where to include the comparison to slavery but Richard's letter on *Yorkshire Slavery* to the *Leeds Mercury* newspaper has done it for me:

'It is the pride of Britain that a slave cannot exist on her soil. ... Let truth speak out, appalling as the statement may appear. The fact is true. Thousands of our fellow-creatures and fellow-subjects, both male and female, the miserable inhabitants of a Yorkshire town, (Yorkshire now represented in Parliament by the giant of anti-slavery principles) are this very moment existing in a state of slavery, more horrid than are the victims of that hellish system 'colonial' slavery.'

Frank Oates (1840–1875) was an explorer and naturalist, who mounted expeditions in the late 19th century into Central America and Africa collecting bird and insect specimens, making detailed descriptions and drawings of flora and fauna and detailed maps of the areas. Frank was born at a house and estate called Meanwoodside which is located in what is now Meanwood Park He was one of the first Europeans to see the Victoria Falls having battled to get there due to poor weather and the 'hostility' of local tribes. A book charting his work, based on a set of his journals and letters home, was collected and edited by his brother, Charles George Oates, and was published in 1881 as *Matabele Land and the Victoria Falls; A Naturalist's Wanderings in the Interior of South Africa.*

Lawrence in 1911, taken by Herbert Ponting during the Terra Nova Expedition.

Captain Lawrence Oates (1880–1912) (Frank's nephew) moved to Leeds – his parent's home city – as a young child. He is best known for his role on Captain Scott's British Antarctic Expedition 1910 (Terra Nova Expedition) and the manner of his death. He clashed greatly with Scott about the running of the expedition – although he also attributed this to stress – writing in his diary 'Scott's ignorance about marching with animals is colossal....Myself, I dislike Scott intensely and would chuck the whole thing if it were not that we are a British expedition....He is not straight, it is himself first, the rest nowhere...' On March 17th, 1912, Oates, nicknamed 'Titus', was aware that his ill health was reducing his companions' chances of survival and chose certain death, leaving the tent with the immortal, mumbled words, 'I am just going outside now and I may be some time' Search him on the Ee Po website where Neil Hudson has written an excellent article on him.

There are two memorials to Lawrence in Leeds, one can be found in the Lady Chapel at Leeds Parish Church and another on Memorial Drive in Meanwood. The Oates Collection at the Oates Museum at Selborne, Hampshire is dedicated to the lives and adventures (and exhibits artefacts connected) to these two members of the Oates family.

David Oluwale (1930–1969), was a Nigerian immigrant who, in 1969, looks to have been murdered by two Leeds policemen, they went to prison for it anyway. It was the first widely publicised case of racist police brutality leading to a death and the only example (at time of writing) of policemen being convicted after the death of a 'suspect'. There's so much more to this story but it's well documented, including a piece by **Caryl Phillips** and in **Kester Aspden**'s *Nationality: Wog – The Hounding Of David Oluwale*. For the paperback the title of the book was changed to *The Hounding of David Oluwale* after stupid people complained. Their sensibilities were offended by *Nationality: Wog* which is the perfect title for the book as it is taken directly from the racist police's charge sheet for David and powerfully exemplifies the institutional racism. The book also includes a poem by **Ian Duhig** whose collection *PANDORAMA* contains a further reflection on Oluwale. It was an absolutely shameful incident of repeated and sustained harassment and brutality.

The **Madness** video, **One Step Beyond** was part filmed in Holbeck, and inside and outside of the old Alex's barber shop near **Water Lane**, Leeds. The on stage scenes are not Leeds.

Alfred Richard Orage, (1873–1934) was born near Harrogate and as a Leeds school teacher founded **The Leeds Arts Club** with **George Holbrook Jackson** in 1903. The club became one of the most advanced centres for Modernist thinking in Britain and from what I've read I'd give the opinion that it was **the** centre of British Modernist thinking. After ten years of teaching, learning and lively debate Alfred moved to London and within a couple of years – with the funding of **George Bernard Shaw**, who had been championed by The Leeds Arts Club – acquired *The New Age* magazine. He turned it from a Christian Socialist mag into an extremely influential publication in which a wide range of intellectuals of the time (H. G. Wells, Joseph Belloc, George Bernard Shaw, G. K. Chesterton etc.) discussed radical, modernist theories. It was instrumental in defining, reviewing and developing Modernism in the visual arts, literature and music with a mixture of culture, politics, economics, Nietzschean philosophy and spiritualism. It was, for example, one of the first English forums in which Sigmund Freud's ideas were discussed. The American, Brown University, *Modernist Journals Project* states that '*The New Age*.... helped to shape modernism in literature and the arts from 1907 to 1922 under the direction of its editor A.R. Orage.' Tom Steele's 1990 book *Alfred Orage and the Leeds Arts Club, 1893-1923*, has been re-published in paperback (Orage Press, 2010). See **The Leeds Arts Club.**

Peter O'Toole doesn't even know himself where he was born in 1932 (Ireland or Leeds) but he grew up in Leeds and was mates with Keith Waterhouse and Willis Hall. Peter became a world famous actor and it's another of those entries that I'll keep brief as there's not much I can add to the material out there. After eight unsuccessful nominations for the Best Actor Oscar (in a Leading Role) he's the most-nominated actor not to win the award. I hope Anthony Clavane (*Promised Land*) included this in his Leeds 'nearly moments' of how the city often just misses out and punches below its weight.....Just checked and no he doesn't, the slacker, although he does note *Time* magazine featured him on their front cover, calling him 'Lawrence Of Leeds', which I can nick.....don't tell him, he's got a temper on him has that Clavane fella – I'm being ironic, he's a lovely, calm man. Back to Peter and his lack of an Oscar. He did receive an Academy Honorary Award for his lifetime's work which he initially turned down as he thought he still had a chance to 'win the lovely bugger outright'. Being a polite lad and after the

Academy wrote back to him saying that they'd award it whether he accepted it or not, he accepted it.

P

Tom Palmer is primarily a children's football writer although if you visit his website you'll find some of his writing aimed at adults. He's best known for two football fiction series for children, *Foul Play* which runs to over nine books one of which was selected as one of 2008's Booked Up titles and short listed for the 2009 Blue Peter Book Award. *The Football Academy* series is more than seven books based around an under-twelve Premier League academy. Tom was born in Leeds (1967), says that 'being a Leeds fan is a special destiny' and his favourite all-time player is Gordon Strachan.

Parks and Trees. Trees are everywhere and like really, really big plants, giant plants almost. Many people of a certain age will remember their parents (usually the dad) saying, 'Did you know that Leeds has got more trees per head of population than any city in Europe?' Now I can't find any reference to this but I remember hearing (I think during the 1970s) that another city had overtaken Leeds and I certainly remember reports that we had recaptured the mantle. It was my Dad who first mentioned this to me and I have other friends who were told the same thing. My dad wasn't born in Leeds and lived in a few cities, before he settled in Leeds in the 1950s. It wasn't just the amount of trees that struck him; he was constantly going on about the amount of parks and green space and was sure this was unique to Leeds. Martin Wainwright in his excellent *True North* points to three wedges of greenery/walks that make it 'possible to deceive yourself that you are still in the countryside......until you are less than half-a-mile from the town hall.' He's talking about the canal/river into Leeds from the west, Meanwood valley, and coming in from Seacroft hospital, through Killingbeck. Although you may not be able to walk it, I'd like to add the remarkable thing of getting into your car in Armley and within three to five minutes (going out toward Tong) you are surrounded by farmland, including the views from Wortley which are straight onto hilly farmland, with Beeston nestling over the hill. It was the number of parks that really sparked mi'dad and where ever you are in Leeds I bet that within five minutes (usually less) you could walk to a park. I'm guessing that this is to do with the development of Leeds and the Victorian/Edwardian-era love for parks and open space – most of the city's parks being acquired and developed from the 1850s onwards – where thousands would descend on them in their free time making the park an important leisure activity. Neil Hudson in the Ee Po (29 July 2010) notes that 'crowds of up to 10,000 people, most in family groups, would gather on Woodhouse Moor.' I'm not surprised that in the dirtier, more cramped city spaces of the time that people would 'escape' to these green spaces and maybe catch a concert or flirtatious glance.

Leeds has the large parks, such as Roundhay Park (over 700 acres/2.8 km^2), Temple Newsam (1500 acres /2.34375 sq mi/over 6 km^2), the 630 acres of Middleton Park (for you youngsters, that's well over 2.5 km^2, around 1 square mile in real money) and Golden Acre Park with 137 acres (around half a square kilometer) as well as over 20 other major parks – some of which are not much smaller than Golden Acre. This doesn't include the dozens of smaller green spaces (such as Charlie Cake Park), playing fields, allotments and unadopted woods/green spaces. Also, taking Martin Wainwright's 'western canal wedge' as an example, there are sections where it links to Gott's/Armley Park at around 24 acres and the attached golf course that stretches all the way down to the fringes of Kirkstall. Just popping back to trees for a moment, Middleton Park contains Middleton Woods which is the largest ancient woodland in Leeds (200 acres), and has been continuously wooded since before 1600 and there are also the scattered elements of the 1200 hectares making up the **Forest of Leeds**. So I'm going to say **Leeds is the greenest city in Britain** and wait for someone to contradict me, which I don't think they will. In keeping with the most trees in Europe 'fact' that I started with and which was passed down by our forebears, I'd guess that Leeds is the city in Britain, maybe Europe, with the largest proportion of green area, especially when you add the more spacious and green estates for the workers such as Gipton (Britain's first 'Garden suburb'), Halton Moor, Middleton or Belle Isle, but that's just a guess. Although I have read that over two-thirds of the Leeds District is open space, public parks, gardens and green belt land. Anyone know who the contenders are? Whatever, I bet we'd kick their butts, coming over here with their extreme areas of urban green space.

Charles Algernon Parsons isn't from Leeds and finally set up his company near Newcastle. He invented the **steam turbine** in 1884 which revolutionised sea transport and, over 100 years later, still generates about **80% of the world's electrical power**. After serving his apprenticeship Parsons took on his first proper job at **Kitson and Company** in Leeds, attracted by the fact that Kitson's were at the cutting edge of engine and steam technology. It was at their Airedale Foundry that he produced his first commercial engine and filed a number of joint patents with Kitson. He was also assigned the job of producing rocket powered **torpedoes** which must have alerted him to the need for another method of powering water-based crafts. Although he took his invention elsewhere, he later commented that it was his work in Leeds that made him realise that an alternative to pistons was required and started his search for an alternative. Considering he developed the steam turbine engine as soon as he left Kitsons I'd guess he was holding the idea in his head or maybe even discussed its development with Kitson – if Kitson rejected it that goes down with the publishers who rejected *Harry Potter*. I must stress that the last sentence is pure speculation. The idea of a turbine was not new; a gas turbine had been patented almost 100 years previously and the basic principle seems to go back to ancient Greece, although no-one noticed it was useful.

Jeremy Paxman has been a presenter of Newsnight since 1989 and I love him. There's a plain talking bluntness that comes out in his interviews that's a joy and that I think of as a Leeds trait. He's done all sorts of well documented stuff and was a journo based in Northern Ireland for three years and worked on Panorama before he got the Newsnight gig. He presented the flagship BBC Radio 4 show Start the Week from 1998 to 2002 and since hosting University Challenge in 1994 has become the longest-serving current quizmaster on British TV. He's written many bestselling books, presented TV documentaries and series and, most importantly, is a Leeds United fan. There's so much more that I could say but there's lots of info out there, so go and look or search him on YouTube. Jeremy's TV awards include:
Royal Television Society: Award for International Current Affairs, 1985
Voice of the Listener & Viewer: Award for best contribution to Television, 1993 and 1997
BAFTA: Richard Dimbleby Award, 1996 and 1999
Royal Television Society: Interview/Presenter of the Year 1997, 1998, 2001 and 2008
Broadcasting Press Guild: Award for best TV Performer in a non-acting role 1997
Variety Club: Media Personality of the Year, 1999

Billy Pearce was born in Kirkstall and is my alter ego, not only do we share looks and a sense of style regarding haircuts but I was recently told that the stuff I say was similar to him by someone who been to see him a few times. I've never seen him, but from that, I think we can safely deduce that's he's a comic genius. He's a comedian and big in pantomime – his 2009/10 panto at the Alhambra took a record-breaking £1.3m – and his big break came in 1986 when he got to the final of New Faces. First going on stage at the Empire in Leeds, aged 6, he's gone on to do loads of TV work as well as a few Royal Command and Children's Royal Variety shows.

Bob Peck (1945–1999) was a stage, television and film actor who had major roles in loads of stuff you've seen but may not have clocked him as an outstanding actor and in my world, that's part of his '**Leedsness**'. Born in Leeds he attended Leeds Modern School (became Lawnswood School) and got a Diploma in Art & Design at Leeds College of Art. He spent six weeks at the National Youth Theatre but didn't enjoy the experience and had trouble mixing. He was later spotted, whilst doing am-dram by **Alan Ayckborn** who took the teenager over to Scarborough to act and learn the ropes of an ASM (Assistant Stage Manager) and Ayckborn remembered finding an "actor of strength, extraordinary natural technical ability, wit and truth". Before his film career he was in theatre, including nine years at the Royal Shakespeare Company, with people like Ian McKellen, Donald Sinden and Judi Dench, McKellen commenting that Peck was the actor he 'learned the most from.' In the celebrated 1981 RSC production of *Nicholas Nickleby*, Peck played the hero John Browdie and the baddie Sir Mulberry Hawk. He played the same roles in Channel 4's adaptation of the novel which was screened when the channel was launched the following year.

Peck won the Best Actor BAFTA and the Broadcasting Press Guild television critics' Best Actor award for **Edge of Darkness,** the BBC's 1985 drama which also won both Best Drama awards. The series was one of the most talked about and successful of the decade and the corporation's fastest ever repeat when BBC1 started a rerun of the series just 10 days after the last episode on BBC2 but even with this breakthrough Peck preferred to keep himself to himself and not do many interviews. In 2010 **Mel Gibson** revived Peck's role in a Hollywood film remake of **Edge of Darkness** which also starred **Ray Winstone**. Peck has had too many stage, TV and film roles to list and is probably most recognised internationally for his role as **Jurassic Park**'s game warden Robert Muldoon who, as a raptor that has out foxed the wily hunter is just about to rip him to pieces, has the classic line 'Clever girl'.

I'll give the last word to Anthony Hayward who, in his obituary to Peck (The Independent, 9th of April, 1999) said, 'Bob Peck was an "unstarry" actor who brought a compelling integrity and authority to his many screen and stage roles.'

Peepal Tree Press, based in Burley, are thought to be the UK's leading publishers of Caribbean, Black British and South Asian fiction, poetry and academic books. Set up by Jeremy Poynting in 1985 they now publish around 30-40 books a year. Their website says that Peepal Tree Press really 'began in the ruins of the former Lusignan sugar estate on the East Coast Demerara in Guyana in 1984' and survives 'by running a parallel printing business, looking for jobs from other small publishers' Hats off to you Jez, well done, I know what risks you will have taken with your life to achieve this and I think you've done a belting thing. Search them online, there's a lot to see on their website.

The **pericardial heart valve** was invented by **Marian Ion Ionescu** at Leeds General Infirmary in 1970. He made his prototypes, which were tested on patients, at his Lab in the LGI made from chemically treated, bovine (family of animals including cattle) tissue of the sac that contains the heart. This major breakthrough in cardiac surgery was taken up by Shiley Laboratory in California, who began the manufacture of the 'Ionescu - Shiley Pericardial Xenograft' and distributed it worldwide. Between 1976 and 1987 they distributed and sold around 200,000 of these pericardial valves which were implanted in patients and saved many lives. The techniques and procedures for fitting the valve were developed by Marian and his team at the LGI, as were many of the valve's developments and improvements. It's very difficult to calculate how many implants (and lives saved) have taken place since, as other companies, quite rightly, mimicked, modified and improved Marian's invention.

Peppers (capsicums), green, for use in salads and cooking, were considered exotic in Leeds up until the 1980s. Red or yellow peppers were unheard of and we still don't trust the blue ones.

Caryl Phillips (born1958) is a successful author and academic, a professor, he's taught around the world and is currently at top American, Ivy League university Yale. He came to England as a baby and grew up in Leeds. Caryl is a prolific and celebrated writer having written nine novels, four works of non-fiction, two anthologies, four stage plays, two screenplays and the first of his, at least, eight plays for radio was published in *Best Radio Plays of 1984* (Methuen Publishing Ltd, 1985) and won the BBC Giles Cooper Award 'Best Radio Play of the Year'. His debut novel *The Final Passage* became a 'for TV' film which Caryl also scripted. He has a fist full of awards, both academic and literary, and has been translated into more than 13 languages.

Photosynthesis. Joseph Priestley discovered that when he isolated a volume of air under an inverted jar, and burned a candle in it, the candle would burn out very quickly, much before it ran out of wax. He further discovered that a mouse could similarly 'injure' air. He then showed that the air that had been 'injured' by the candle and the mouse could be restored by a plant, inadvertently showing that plants produced oxygen. His experiments also included the role of light. 'What Priestley found was that the quality of the air wasn't just improved by growing the plant in it, if you shone a light on the plant the air quality went shooting up. What it showed was that light, shining on the green matter, in plants, could restore the air to almost a paradisiac quality, where it would keep animals alive for unparalleled periods of time, where flames would burn with extraordinary life. Light and life went together. We now know Priestley's discovery as Photosynthesis.........Light is a powerful chemical, physiological and biological agent which can have the most huge effects on anything with which it interacts.' Simon Schaffer, *Light, the Universe and Everything*, BBC 4, 25.2.10

According to **Brett Harrison**'s *A Century of Leeds* **Charles Richard Hattersley Pickard's** 'business in Kirkgate was to dominate commercial photography in the city for most of the century' (20th). I have absolutely no reason to doubt this but can find few references to the business. There's one tag on the **Leodis** website, on a photo of Sheepscar Branch Library, that says 'Photograph: Chas R H Pickard and Son' and there was a postcard of **Temple Newsam House** for sale on eBay by 'Pickard and Son'.

Playing cards (see laminated playing cards) were found in China from as early as the 9th Century. UK interest in playing cards took a leap during the World War I and from 1921 the **Waddingtons** factory started production. After World War II they started to produce the cards for their main competitor (De la Rue who had been producing playing cards since 1832) leading to them becoming the UK's biggest producer. I've read that they became the biggest producer in the world, which is possible, but I'm guessing that **if** that was the case, it will have been for a limited period of time only. The design of the cards was crucial and they employed artists such as William Barribal, Lucy Dawson, Harry Rountree, Paul Brown and Tony Gibbons to give them an edge. In 1929 Waddingtons started the production of the very popular circular cards (Cir-Q-Lar) and when these were introduced into the USA, sales exceeded expectations. I should also mention that lots of companies and products liked to use playing cards as promotional material – I've got a Waddingtons set designed and produced for CONSETT Iron Company Limited, County Durham.

In 1962, market pressures led Waddingtons and De La Rue to join forces again and launch the Amalgamated Playing Card Co. Ltd. – which had been the unofficial name of their joint efforts for many years – and in 1971 Waddingtons took over De La Rue and as they'd bought **Alf Cooke Limited**, the previous year, they were Britain's sole manufacturer of playing cards. I should tell you a bit about Alf Cooke Limited as they were also Leeds-based (see **Printing**). Alf Cooke was a huge Leeds printer and an important producer of playing cards in the UK during the period 1920-1970, first labelling their cards as *British Playing Cards* and entering the market with a variety of unusual court card designs. In 1925 they changed the name to Universal Playing Card Company Ltd, so if you have cards marked with *Universal Playing Card Co.* (producers often mark the Ace Of Spades) they were made by Alf Cooke. As well as their interesting and unusual range of playing cards, Alf Cooke's also produced fortune-telling, tarot cards and card games for children and adults.

Waddingtons also made lots of other card games, including 1933's 'lunchbox' packaged *Lexicon* at 1/9d but sales bombed so they repackaged them at 2/6d and sold around 1,000 packs per week or *64 Milestones: The Game of Life*, *Kan U Go* and many more. They did *Top Trumps* and *Quiz Card Games* with topics such as Pop Music or London as well as TV-linked card games such as the *Teenage Mutant Ninja Turtles*, although *Sexis,* a 'psychedelic card game', was probably never issued.

According to Wikipedia the most commonly available pack of cards in the UK was Waddingtons Number 1, which comprised the 52 standard cards plus four others – two coloured jokers, a contract bridge scoring card and an advertisement card. The Guildhall Library (London) held, on deposit, two important collections of playing-cards, donated by John Waddington PLC. My intensive research shows that they have since passed this collection on to the Print Room Office of the London Metropolitan Archives. Anyway, to conclude with a conclusion of few words; Waddingtons and Cookes exported playing cards all over the world, if over the last (almost) century you've been playing cards in the UK the cards were most likely produced in Leeds. If you've been playing cards here in the last 50-odd years, they were almost certainly made in Leeds. *The World of Playing Cards* website has been most useful for this entry and has some lovely pics so if you're interested, go have a look.

Pop. All fizzy drinks, from Coca Cola (1.6 billion servings each day) to Tizer, the whole multi-billion pounds fizzy drinks industry has its roots in Leeds, see **Soda Water**.

The modern pram. See **Silver Cross**

Louis Aimé Augustin Le Prince (born 1842 and disappeared in 1890). I'm putting the amazing Louis here so that he doesn't get obscured by all the Leeds entries. Louis was well built and 6ft. 3 to 4in.tall – a ruddy giant in them days when people were much, much shorter....even I'd have been tall in them days. I think most of you will know that the first moving images captured on film were taken in Leeds, around three years before Thomas **Edison** and four years before the **Lumiere** brothers. Never mind Le Prince, another Leeds lad **Wordsworth Donisthorpe** also made moving images before them three but we are Leeds and we get cheated and ignored....I'm being ironic....almost. Le

Louis Le Prince, inventor of motion picture film. circa 1885. Courtesy of Armley Mills Industrial Museum.

Prince is well known and easily researched so I won't rattle on too much about him but, with the help of Frederick Mason and J. W. Longley, he created **Roundhay Garden Scene** in 1888 which is regarded as the first ever motion picture. Soon after he made his more famous moving picture, recording traffic on Leeds Bridge from the second window from the top, closest to the bridge, of No. 19 Bridge End, then Hicks the Ironmongers. There's another snippet of film, from an unknown date, called *Man Walking Around A Corner* filmed at his workshop on Woodhouse Lane.

I'm amazed that no-one has made a major film about this early period of motion pictures as it's stuffed full of intrigue such as Le Prince's mysterious disappearance on a train in France when, although in debt, he seemed to have the world at his feet. With him his films disappeared and the snippets we see now are not the whole films but parts of the original paper film strips remaining in his Leeds camera that were restored in 1931. There seems to have been an antagonistic battle to get the technology perfected and owned through patents (there would be wouldn't there? It's a huge and lucrative breakthrough for humanity) and it seems in America that they favoured their own, shown by the fact that a patent refused in America to Le Prince was granted, unopposed, to Edison years later. Louis' son, Adolphe, who had worked on the technology with his dad, was found shot two years after appearing as a witness in a patent battle questioning Edison's claims to have invented the moving picture camera, which Edison won. The death was recorded as suicide. Although they were exhibited in Hunslet and Roundhay and were about to be shown in London and New York (until disappearance) Le Prince's films were not distributed to the general public and his achievement was largely overlooked until recently. You may have deduced from his name that Louis wasn't from 'round 'ere but he moved to Leeds in 1866, married a Leeds lass, settled, worked and had children here. Away from inventing the moving picture he and his wife set up the Leeds Technical School of Art in 1871. They were experts in general photographic technology and became well-known for their work in fixing colour photography on to metal and pottery. They were even commissioned for these styles of portraits of Queen Victoria and PM William Gladstone which were included in a time capsule buried in the foundations of Cleopatra's Needle on the bank of a river known as 'the Thames' in a town called London – the time capsule was manufactured by Whitley Partners of Hunslet.

It seems that Louis was largely forgotten due to a lack of finance and influence but we in Leeds have kept his memory alive. As well as the blue plaque on Leeds Bridge, in 1930 the Lord Mayor of Leeds unveiled a bronze memorial tablet at 160 Woodhouse Lane, Le Prince's workshop and in 2003 Leeds Uni's Centre for Cinema, Photography and Television was named in his honour.

Anti-Priestley cartoon, showing him trampling on the Bible and burning documents representing English freedom. Circa 1780-1790.

Joseph Priestley (1733–1804) was an 18th-century theologian, dissenting clergyman, natural philosopher, educator, political theorist, not really an inventor more of a discoverer, who published over 150 works and was 'one of the greatest English chemists.' (*Light, the Universe and Everything*, BBC 4, 25.2.10). Joseph was born in Birstall, on the Leeds/Bradford border. He had relatives in Leeds, both his sons were born in the city, he was the first secretary of Leeds Library and was minister at Mill Hill Chapel, Leeds City Square from 1767 to 1773.

He was an amazing man whose impact and achievements have been well documented, information on him is easily accessible and I can't cover a quarter of his work here but the range was incredible – similar to David Hartley. For example he did important work in pedagogy (the study of being a teacher or the process of teaching) and published a seminal work on English Grammar – see what I did there? I gave grammar a capital when it shouldn't have one....what a wag. He's credited with the invention of Historiography (the study of the history) or the discovery of oxygen, hydrochloric acid, nitrous oxide (laughing gas), carbon monoxide, and sulphur dioxide, never mind his work on the history of electricity and major breakthroughs in the understanding of electricity. He led and inspired British radicals during the 1790s, championed the work of David Hartley, was a good friend of Benjamin Franklin (one of the Founding Fathers of the United States of America) and eventually moved to Pennsylvania in 1794. The move followed the **Priestley Riots** caused by his controversial publications and outspoken support for the French Revolution. The rioters first burnt down Priestley's church and home and then attacked or set fire to four dissenting chapels, 27 houses, and several businesses.

Priestley is scattered throughout this book but before I move on a few words on oxygen. Joseph is widely credited with the discovery of the gas and although Swede Carl Wilhelm Scheele actually discovered oxygen earlier than him, Priestley published his findings first. The thing that I think is relevant is that they discovered it independently; Antoine-Laurent de Lavoisier ('the father of modern chemistry') recognized and named it oxygen in 1778, after seeing Priestley's demonstration. This fella tried to take credit for a few of Priestley's discoveries, although he no doubt did important work. Anyway, oxygen is a snappier name than Priestley's 'dephlogisticated air' although I do like his term for it as 'a luxury air'. Priestley was also the first chemist to prove that oxygen was essential to combustion and life and was produced by plant growth.

Joseph was made a member of every major scientific society in the world and to commemorate his scientific achievements, The American Chemical Society in 1922 named its highest honour the **Priestley Medal**. I've got to stop now, there are a few biographies on the man and plenty online, so go dig. There's a Priestley Society, a charity dedicated to 'educating the public on Priestley's contribution towards education, science, religion and politics', might be a good place to start. Me, I've decided that he's one of them there 'great men of history' and I'm not sure he's as widely celebrated as he should be. Leeds is full of statues, plaques, colleges and University undergraduate chemistry labs named after him, so we obviously rate him. See **Greenhouse, David Hartley, Photosynthesis, The Rubber/Eraser, Soda Water**.

The Prince Regent locomotive is, according to some sources, the world's first commercially viable locomotive, built by **Matthew Murray** of Holbeck, in 1811/12 – seventeen years before **Stephenson's *Rocket*** in 1829. It is said to have started working on the Middleton to Leeds line on June 24th, 1812. **Richard Trevithick,** who should take a big dollop of credit, had been experimenting with locomotives for some time but they had flaws such as being too heavy for and damaging the track and being unable to go up gradients. **John Blenkinsop**'s twin cylinder design (I imagine with quite a lot of input from Murray and his engineers) was very different to Trevithick's. At a cost of £380 to build each of the engines they were also expensive to run, but it is thought they did the work of around 50 horses and 200 men.

Printing has been, and still is, an important industry in Leeds and there have been important innovations that came from the city. According to Gilleghan, John Hirst was the first printer in Leeds printing The Leeds Mercury in 1718, moving onto books within a decade. Leeds has always had a diverse economy, being known as 'the city that makes everything'. Many industries grew up to service this expanding local market, just as it did around the country, but towards the end of the 19th Century Leeds printing was said to be second only to that of Londons and had become one of the city's top four sources of employment.

The industry doubled in size between 1842 and 1861 and will have carried on expanding with developments such as the **Wharfedale Printing Machine** in Otley. Leeds seems to have specialised in the colour printing of posters, calendars, postcards and tinplate and companies like

Alf Cooke's expanded, leading to the building of his huge Crown Point printing works in 1872 that still stands along from the Crown Point shopping complex. Some of Alf's employees broke away to set up their own companies such as Chorley and Pickersgill who set up on Cookridge Street and Charles Lightowler of Joseph Street. Leeds was also a hub of book and music publishing with, according to David Goodman, important editions of The Pilgrim's Progress and Robinson Crusoe produced here.

E J Arnold, established in 1870, printed books for schools, railway timetables and HMSO work and was apparently bought and asset stripped by Robert Maxwell, who also tried and failed in taking over **Waddingtons**. Waddingtons initially specialised in printing programmes and posters for the theatre but expanded into a nationally recognised company through the printing of playing cards and board games. See, under **Monopoly**, how Waddingtons perfected the process of printing on silk and as a result aided the British/allied airmen of WW II.

The rise of printing in Leeds obviously led to a rise in industries to service it. As well as the growth of printing press makers coming out of Otley, a nationally renowned manufacturer moved into south Leeds to get close to its customers. There was a print ink manufacturer and the type foundries were joined by Taylor and Watkinson, printers' lead casters, who moved to Leeds 'to meet the requirements of the trade.'

Leeds is still the second major centre in the UK for paper, printing and publishing which have become the city's second largest manufacturing industry. Leeds Web (the printing arm of Yorkshire Post Newspapers) produces 125 million copies of publications a year with, as well as their own titles, other dailies including the Financial Times. Waddington's, who were Britain's biggest playing card printer, are now Communisis Chorleys and Alf Cooke's printing works on Hunslet Road is now owned by the printing firm Bonar Imca. Polestar Petty's place on Whitehall Road can knock out 8,000 four-colour 32 page sections a minute, 476,000 an hour, 11.4 million a day, or 520 million complete magazines a year and I think it's likely to be linked to Petty Printing that in 1900 employed 400 people at its Whitehall Road site. See **Waddingtons, Wharfedale Printing Machine**

Pulse is a 60-minute pilot, supernatural medical horror drama made for **BBC Three**, who screened it five times in early June 2010 featuring Leeds City Centre, Leeds Met and University of Leeds.

Pudsey Bear is the BBC's Children In Need yellow mascot with a handkerchief tied around the head and over one eye. The yellow bear was designed for the BBC by Joanna Ball a graphic artist. Joanna is from Pudsey which the national BBC refuse to describe as 'in Leeds' it's a 'Yorkshire market town' or, at best, a 'West Yorkshire market town.' Anyway, Joanna chose the name for the bear as she is Pudsey born and bred – her Grandfather was a Mayor of the Borough of Pudsey. In 1987 the Parks Department of Leeds City Council created a big Pudsey Bear made from thousands of plants in Pudsey Park.

Q

In my head **Quarry Hill Flats** will always be connected to the Second World War for a couple of reasons. The first is that I was often told that, when he defeated the British, Hitler had planned to use Quarry Hill as his British headquarters. Martin Wainwright (*True North*) has it as Hitler's northern headquarters so I'm torn. Mi'dad was usually quite good at war years stuff but Martin is a respected journo. I'd go with mi'dad but I bet Martin has a good source so who knows which is right. The second reason is that the flats were built on the verge of and during the early years of World War II causing corners to be cut and vital resources to be siphoned off elsewhere, ultimately leading, so it seems, to their eventual demolition. Roger Ratcliffe (*Leeds Fax*) says Quarry Hill Flats 'was the biggest public housing scheme in Europe by completion in 1940' and by their demolition in 1978 they were still the largest social housing complex in Britain - 938 flats on the 26-acre site housing over 3,000 people. What should not be forgotten is how revolutionary and life changing they were for the people who moved out of their cramped and ill-equipped back to back houses with as many as ten people sharing a bedroom. The art deco buildings were radical, modern and studied around the world; they had solid fuel ranges, electric lighting, hot running water, bathrooms and inside toilets, a state-of-the-art refuse disposal system and communal facilities including launderettes, shops and play areas. The complex was made up of 13 blocks (houses) named after Leeds worthies (other than Victoria and York – the house of) Jackson, Kitson, Lupton, Moynihan, Neilson, Oastler, Priestley, Rhodes, Saville, Thoresby, Victoria, Wright and York. Within ten years of their construction the structural problems started to manifest with damp, cracks, rat infestation and water seepage leading to rust in the prefabricated, pressed steel skeleton of the building.

Quebec Street which runs onto City Square seems a weird name for a street in Leeds. Maybe we're twinned with Quebec? But that's a large area like a county. Maybe there's a Québec City? Yes, there is but we're not twinned with it. Quebec Street was opened in 1872 and named after/in memory of General Wolfe who captured Quebec in Canada from the French in 1759; he doesn't appear to have any particular links with Leeds, more of a national hero. Unfortunately he was killed in the decisive Battle Plains of Abraham (also known as the Battle of Quebec) during the Seven Years War, which wasn't just between Britain and France but involved all the main European powers. The battle followed a three month siege by the British but only lasted around an hour. General James Wolfe's famous last words were not, 'Lordy-Lou that hurts' or 'what a ridiculous time to need the toilet' or 'bugger, I wanted to learn how to knit' but something akin to, 'What? We've chinned the French? Now I can die a happy man.' I don't think spin had been invented back in them days so it's obviously true, those were his very last words. The actual siege and battle are quite interesting, just look up James Wolfe on Wiki. There's a small yard/houses off Quebec Street, which used to be known as Eyebright Place the name apparently taken from the old healing well which was opposite, where Aire Street now begins.

Quebec House is a truly stunning building and appears to have been named for the same reason as the street. Leeds is full of buildings with beautiful architectural details; I've stopped and stared at this one a couple of times and am using it to say look up and look around when you're walking in town. It was opened as the Leeds and County Liberal Club by Sir James Kitson on 12 March 1890. The stunning terracotta work is described as 'Welsh terracotta' but I've also read descriptions of it as 'Burmantofts terracotta' which I take to mean that the Burmantofts (Pottery) produced the tile cladding and decorative details out ot Welsh terracotta. The building underwent a £6 million renovation when it was acquired by The Eton Collection in 2000 who opened it 2001 as Quebecs, an award winning, 4 star hotel. A blue plaque on the building reads:

'From Parliamentary and Municipal reform in the 1830s to 1894 The Liberal Party dominated Politics in Leeds. This splendid club in Welsh terracotta opened in 1891. Crowds were addressed from its balcony 'on occasions of political excitement'. Chorley & Connon Architects' – William Gladstone definitely spoke to the crowds from the balcony and I'd be amazed if Leeds' own Liberal Prime Minister Herbert Henry Asquith didn't also. See back cover detail.

Not that I'm struggling for 'qs' obviously but **Quebec Mills/Works** is where William Waites Sons and Atkinson Ltd established themselves in 1922. The firm manufactured twine and cordage in Hunslet. The factory, at the junction of Houghton Place with Ashford Street, was known by the locals as the 'Band Mill' and was apparently hugely noisy. Both streets seem to have disappeared and apparently Peter O'Toole used to knock around in the area with Willis Hall and Keith Waterhouse and I know that Keith was re-housed in Halton Moor after 'slum clearance'. Anyway, the company was still going into the '60s and I think it's likely to have been part of a Manchester company of the same name, established in 1895, who were flax and hemp spinners, manufacturers and bleachers, specialising in yarns, twines, lines, ropes and cords made from flax, hemp, cotton, jute etc... I'm also suspicious that the building is now used by **The Works Skatepark** but I could well be wrong.....anyone know?

Queenies Castle. Lebowski off Regdafish, an expert in such matters, says, 'I believe that The Cardigan Arms was used to film an ITVseries in the '70s, might have been Queenies Castle which was based in the old Quarry Hill Flats and starred Diana Dors.' The series, produced by YTV, ran from 1970 to 1972 with scripts by Keith Waterhouse and Willis Hall and plenty of early '70s footage of Diana Dors walking through Leeds market. I can see a lot of comparisons with *Only Fools and Horses*. Both series were about people living in council blocks/flats were about 'ducking and diving', not always strictly legal activities (always a strong element of the script), will they get caught, 'colourful' characters, had question marks over the father, relationships in close family networks and the battle to survive/come good in difficult circumstances.

The Queen's Hall (Sovereign Street) was a building which was originally a tram and then a bus depot and latterly became a venue hosting events such as circus's exhibitions, flea markets and numerous concerts/gigs from The Beatles to Megadeth. The Queen's Hall was demolished in 1989 and the plot is currently a car park although there are plans to turn it into a green space with a footbridge over the River Aire. It was to be the site of the 'Kissing Towers' of Criterion Place until the project was cancelled. See T**he Futurama Festivals.**

The Queens Hotel is that rather large, white building that sits on City Square near the Railway Station. It was opened by the Midland Railway, in 1863, and extended twice – 1867 and 1898. It was rebuilt by the London Midland and Scottish Railway in 1937.

Quincey Jones has probably never been to Leeds, although you never know, he may have visited to watch Michael Jackson at Roundhay Park or visit family....if he has any here, which I doubt.

Quizzical Looks can be seen throughout Leeds when someone says something daft, confusing or hugely complicated or when an author writes something weird. It's a centuries old tradition probably going back before the Romans.

R

Radio Asian Fever on Roundhay Road has been broadcasting to South Asian communities in Leeds since 1999 and ten years later it received a five-year Community Radio License from OFCOM. It broadcasts at 107.3FM and is available through the internet. Putting out programmes in English, Urdu, Punjabi, Kashmiri and Mirpuri it aims to get people talking 'across the cultures, faith groups and their many denominations.' It also 'recruits and trains volunteers in the use of broadcasting equipment, IT and vocals. It supports these volunteers (through training, mentoring and supervision) to research, produce and present their own radio shows. Programming 'by the community – for the community' is a core value of the station.'

Corinne Bailey Rae (born **Corinne Jacqueline Bailey**, 1979) is a singer-songwriter and guitarist whose first album sold over four million copies making her only the fourth female British act in history to have a debut album at number one in the UK. It's too early to get proper figures for her second album *The Sea* but it entered the UK charts at number five, the US Billboard chart at number seven and was nominated for the 2010 Mercury Prize. She's been nominated for and won a soul load of awards including MOBOs, Brits and Grammys.

Again she's well documented so I'll leave you to search and I'll give opinions and an anecdote. First the anecdote. Someone had scandalously copied her first album for me and at the time I was mates with one of the backing vocalists on her first album, who had also written one of her B-sides and was good mates with her. I was in the middle of flogging *Coming Out As A Bowie Fan In Leeds, Yorkshire, England,* and for purely cynical reasons thought I'd get one passed on to Corinne. I feel a bit daft signing books but do it when asked and was told I should sign it. So I was in the middle of putting a little message in when Mrs Mick and the friend said, 'Woah. Woah, what y'writing?' I'd half written my message which was, 'Corrine, a mate illegally copied your album for me, so you can have a free copy of mi'book to make up for it. Anyhow, you've got the best of the deal, my book's way better than your album, Regards Mick.' No matter how much I argued my corner and spoke about upholding my artistic principles, they made me scribble it out. They wanted me to start again but I refused to waste two books. Anyway, our mate passed over the book and Corrine was trying to work out what had been scribbled out and when the mate told her she laughed heartily and was disappointed not to have the original, honest message. So it just goes to show, not only is she beautiful and massively talented but she's got a sense of humour and doesn't take herself seriously – we've got a lot in common me and Corrine.

Ooh, one last 'off on one' before the opinions. I got a copy of *Nailed* to Ian Rankin in which I'd written, 'Here y'go Ian, this'll learn'y how to write proper. Take Care, Mick.' Shockingly, I never heard anything from him. A short while later I heard him talking on Radio 4 about the future of thrillers and that no author had yet taken on elements of modern technology and connected identity theft, all of which were in *Nailed*. So not only had he missed my literary genius and failed to plug it to his hundreds of thousands of readers, (meaning that *Nailed*, the greatest thriller of the 21st Century was a complete flop) he obviously hadn't even looked at it. Not that it matters. Although he shouldn't go on Radio 4 spouting off.... 'HEY, Ian, all that stuff you said hadn't been written about.....you were wrong, it had and I did it first.' (At this point, on the time-space continuum, Mick childishly sticks his tongue out at a famous and talented author).

Brilliant, try to do an entry on Corrine and end up writing more about mi'own books......egocentric, moi? Never. Anyway, I'll stop and get onto Corrine's albums but when you're the world's greatest author and your top seller only shifted a couple of thousand it's hard....Actually, I'm upset now, I'm off to chop sommat off mi'face like that Dutch, messy painter lad. Right opinions, I love both Corrine's albums – even though it's not stuff I'd usually listen to. I can honestly say that when *Put Your Records On* and *Like a Star* (re-release) were played on the radio they made my soul skip and that was before I knew anything of her association with Leeds. I'd describe both her albums as uplifting and I happily paid full price for the second one. Now I hate musicals with a passion, but Corrine's songs sometimes remind me of show tunes but the classic ones before they turned crap, like *Let's Go Fly A Kite* or *Somewhere Over The Rainbow*. I don't think her songs are *like* songs from musicals, just sometimes remind me of them, but that's just me being daft. *The Sea* is a brave album, it's rawer and more stripped back than her debut with an extreme live feel that gives it a vital edge and vulnerability. What strikes me with her stuff is that the songs are beautifully written and constructed and I love the understated and clever arrangements on *The Sea* – the arrangement of her first album is also excellent. I guess most people would describe her music as soul with a soft jazz edge. She has a masterful control of voice and marvellous precision. I'm waiting for her to let rip and go to the edge of her voice, move beyond the controlled delivery (which is no doubt part of the exquisite nature of her music) and if/when she does I think she'll be a historically important singer-songwriter who'll sing directly to your soul.

Harry Ramsden's is the oldest and largest fish and chip chain in the UK and according to the Guinness Book of Records the Guiseley branch is the largest fish'n'chip shop in the world, seating 250 people and serving nearly a million customers a year. In 1952 the restaurant served a world record 10,000 portions during a single day in celebration of its 25th anniversary and Harry Ramsden's have broken this record three times, serving 10,182 portions in Guiseley (1988), 11,964 in Glasgow (1992) and 12,105 in Melbourne (1996). It's now an international brand with 35 outlets and is about to expand further. Their website also reckons the fish are made with a secret batter recipe.

Harry Ramsden (1888–1963) opened his first fish'n'chip shop in 1928 in a wooden hut by a tram stop in White Cross, Guiseley. It proved so popular that within three years he moved into larger premises, opening a sit-down 'fish and chip palace', complete with fitted carpets, oak panelled walls and chandeliers modelled on London's Ritz Hotel. The original hut is still there adjacent to the main restaurant and when I was a kid (I think on the way to or from the dales) mi'dad used say, 'See that? Most famous fish and chip shop in the world is that and y'see that hut? That's where it all started.' To which I'd reply, 'so can we get our fish'n'chips from there then?' 'Don't be daft,' he'd reply, 'we're not tourists, we'll get some proper fish'n'chips and I know just the place.' He'd then pull over down the road at what is now Westfield Fisheries (I can't remember the name back then) where the scran was better, there was no queue and crucially, you didn't pay 'tourist prices'. He knew about fish'n'chips did my dad, he grew up in a fish'n'chip shop and used to tell us about riding a big, old dog around the shop when he was a nipper. Can you imagine that being allowed nowadays, with our hygiene obsessions and Health and Safety culture? A kid in a fish'n'chip shop? It'd never be allowed.

In the last 80-odd years Harry Ramsden's has passed through a few hands but is now owned by a private investment vehicle of Ranjit Boparan, BVL. Judging by his business empire Ranjit (from West Bromwich) is a shrewd cookie and plans to open another 100 Harry Ramsden's over the next five years. In 2002 Ramsden's got through 10 million pounds of potatoes, 2.5 million pounds of fish, 46,000lb of salt and 16,000 bottles of vinegar. Harry Ramsden, 'the king of fish and chips'.

Andrew Rawnsley (1962) is an influential political journalist, notably for *The Guardian*, more recently *The Observer* and on TV. He worked at the Guardian from 1985 from until 1993 spending six years as the newspaper's parliamentary sketch writer. Andrew has been Chief Political Commentator and Associate Editor at *The Observer* since 1993. He was co-presenter of *A Week in Politics* on Channel 4 from 1989 to 1997, the main presenter of Radio 4's *The Westminster Hour* from 1998 to 2006 and has co-presented ITV's *The Sunday Edition* since 2006. He's written two books, both best sellers, *Servants of the People* (2000) is an account of the early years of New Labour in government and *The End of the Party* published in 2010 which was a No.1 best seller in its first week of release.

Sophie Raworth is one of the main faces of BBC news. In May 1995 she got her big TV news break becoming the regular joint presenter of BBC's Look North programme in Leeds until she moved to BBC Breakfast News in 1997.

Red Hall was reputed to be the first red brick house built in Leeds (just off the Headrow) and was completed in 1628. Early in the 17th Century wealthy people were moving away from oak frame, wattle and daub, thatched roof construction and into brick and stone. The Hall contained a room that became known as the **'King's Chamber'** after it was used to imprison **King Charles I** in 1647 – he was beheaded in 1649. **Snowden Schofield** bought **Red Hall** 265 years later and used the room, with its figured plaster ceiling, as a restaurant for Schofields. This captivity of the King was remembered by the naming of the King Charles Hotel which was demolished in the 1970s, the naming of part of the garden as King Charles' Croft and the only thing, which I can find, remaining today, King Charles' Street. Although an episode where John Harrison took the King a tankard of nut brown ale laced with several gold pieces, should he escape, is commemorated in stained glass at **St John's Church**.

The house passed through the hands of various 'worthies' and was briefly used as business premises until, in 1911, it was bought by **Snowden Schofield.** Snowden gutted the ground floor and turned it into his shop front, ripping out walls and fundamentally altering the building. Whilst this 'renovation' was happening, the building gave a reminder of its history when a small cannon ball from the English Civil War was pulled out of the wall. In 1960-1 the last remnants of Red Hall were demolished to make way for the construction of the new **Schofields** store – the new structure didn't even last 50 years.

So whilst you're your perusing the glass fronts and 21st century shops of **The Core** remember that almost 400 years earlier, the last English king to realistically try to be an absolute monarch, a 'little God on Earth', was being held captive, roughly where you're standing, awaiting his death. In the space of **The Core** was a small moment in the creation of our **constitutional monarchy** and the establishment of our **parliamentary democracy**.

Now, forget all this big history malarkey whilst I lurch off into some conjecture – and if someone knows this to be wrong I'd appreciate an email. Leeds is a largely red brick city and I'm **guessing** that Leeds is the most red brick city in Britain. My theory is to do with Leeds's comparatively late growth as a city and the fact that in the late 18th and early 19th Centuries bricks were more expensive than most stone. At this time Leeds was not a large town or city, like most other major UK cities, and so did not have the amount of buildings or new builds happening compared, for example, to Liverpool. It was in the 19th and 20th Centuries that Leeds grew from a population of 53,162 in 1801 to 428,572 in 1901 and to 715, 402 in 2001 and I'm **guessing** that through this time more red brick building will have occurred. So, if **Red Hall** was the first red brick house in Leeds, the loss is even sadder as it's central to the very fabric of Leeds.

Vic Reeves (James Roderick Moir) was born in Leeds in 1959 and his family moved to Darlington when he was five. Probably best known for ***Shooting Stars*** (with Bob Mortimer) there'll be shed loads about him on line but I think he is very funny and in a 2005 poll (The Comedian's Comedian) Vic and Bob were voted the ninth greatest comedy act ever by fellow comedians. Sorry but that's impressive.

According to Anthony Clavane, **Louise Rennison** was born and brought up in Seacroft.....he's sure of it. Her most recent book (at time of writing) *Withering Tights* is partly dedicated to Leeds United FC. A lot of her books, aimed at teenage girls, are based on growing up in Leeds and some have been thought a bit strong for the American market. Author of 16 books (2010), she's extremely successful and sells shelf loads of books.

Replica football shirts/strips are a worldwide football craze and industry worth billions of pounds and it's one of the major revenue sources for football clubs and it started in Leeds. We've all watched the news and even in the most remote part of the world there's often a kid (or adult) in the background in an Arsenal or Barcelona shirt. See **Leeds United** for the first replica shirts.

The Resomator produced by LBBC Technologies in Pudsey for hi-tech dead body disposal which hasn't yet been okayed in the UK. See **The Leeds and Bradford Boiler Company**.

The **Retrospective Usage of Door Handles** is a concept developed by sociologist, psychiatrist, author and compendium compiler Mick McCann to describe a psychological illness that he encountered during his studies; 'most people have mastered the pre-emptive use of door handles, illustrated by the fact that they are able to open doors, but many of my patients have failed to master the retrospective use of door knobs and are unable to close them after moving through the frame of the door.'

  The condition was first noted by Mr McCann on observing his mother-in-law's ability to enter and leave the house and her inability to close the door behind her. 'She's not yet mastered the retrospective use of door handles,' he exclaimed and quickly calculated the amount of hot air escaping and snow rushing into the previously warm house to be around £5 of gas per visit. This situation also led directly to the widely used, sarcastic expression 'do you think it may be possible to heat the house and not the street?' He developed his theory to include children/teenagers and noted that when an adult is nearing a relaxed state which is reliant upon an auditory experience (such as music, radio or television) the child has an uncanny knack of coming in and out of the room (three times an hour) and on each occasion leaving the door to two rooms open. The first room is the room in which the adult is listening to a programme or music and the second room is one where the child is listening to an electronic device at approximately twice the volume of the adult's electrical appliance leading to 'dual (triple or quadruple) sound source anxiety'. The result of the child/teenagers inability to grasp the concept of **the retrospective use of door handles** is that the adult's relaxed auditory state is replaced by a cacophonous noise emanating from the other room with the associated anxiety and need to, first, shout to the child a number of times and then go to close both doors saying for the twelfth time that evening 'I'm sick of telling you, can you get a grip of your retrospective use of door handles?'.

The theory is particularly relevant to households in which adult smokers have a 'smoking room' in which they try to contain the smoke through a 'closed door policy'.

Joseph Rhodes (1782–1854) is a Leeds artist that I can find little about, although **Leeds Art Gallery** lists four of his works. They look kinda 'pastoral' to me.

Diana Rigg (Dame Enid Diana Elizabeth Rigg, born 1938) attended Fulneck School, Pudsey. An actress probably best known for Emma Peel in The Avengers, her appearance in the *Morecambe and Wise* 1975 Christmas Special and her role in the1969 James Bond film *On Her Majesty's Secret Service*. She's become a top theatre actress, I saw her early '90s in *Medea*, she was fantastic and (with *Shock Headed Peter*) it was the best theatre experience I've ever had and I've had too many. Although, in case we should forget her talent, and celebrate her real achievement, in 2002 she was voted joint first (with George Clooney) sexiest stars in television history by readers of the U.S. magazine *TV Guide*.

Sam Riley (born 1980) is, at the moment, best known for playing the lead role of Ian Curtis in the feature film *Control*, a biopic about the lead singer of the 1970s post-punk band Joy Division. His performance in the role won him the British Independent Film Award for 'Most Promising Newcomer' and a Kermode for Best Actor 2007 for the film.

Rising Damp, was produced by YTV in Leeds, it ran from 1974 to 1978 and was the highest-ranking ITV sitcom on the 100 Best Sitcoms poll run in 2004 by the Beeb. Although its setting was never specified the Tetley's drinking Rigsby was a Leeds fan who apparently smashed his TV when Leeds lost the '75 European cup final. I think the character Philip was quite groundbreaking (and I'd be interested in any reflections or info on this) as representations of black people were not always that positive in the 1970s. Philip was the antithesis of most cultural representations of the time and questioned these stereotypes; he was extremely 'well-spoken', sophisticated and suave and easily the most well educated and intelligent character in the show. I know it seems a bit daft now but in 1974 this was quite important and the show constantly and explicitly de-bunked the stereotypes and it wasn't tucked away where few people would see it, this was a one of the most popular sitcoms of its day. If you've never seen it, I'd recommend that you check it out.

Rob DJ is a Leeds DJ and the 'presenter' of *The Monday Night Pub Quiz* on **The Chris Moyles Show** – although he's not really in the studio, they play loads of pre-recorded sound bites of him and pretend he's there, anyway it's funny.

Sir Robert Robinson (1886–1975). An ex-pupil of Fulneck School, he was an English chemist and awarded the **Nobel Prize in Chemistry** in 1947 for his research on plant dyestuffs (anthocyanins) and alkaloids. In 1947, he also received the Presidential Medal of Freedom with Silver Palm, the highest civilian award in the U.S..

The Nobel Lectures, Chemistry 1942-1962 (Elsevier Publishing Company, Amsterdam, 1964) states, 'Robinson's extensive researches in organic chemistry dealt not only with the structure and synthesis of many organic bodies, but also with the electrochemical mechanism of organic reactions. His interest in the chemical constitution of plant dyestuffs (anthocyanins) soon extended to another group of vegetable bodies, the alkaloids, where the whole series of his researches are remarkable for their brilliant syntheses. He contributed greatly towards the definition of the arrangement of atoms within molecules of morphine, papaverine, narcotine, etc. These discoveries led to the successful production of certain antimalarial drugs.' His synthesis of tropinone, a precursor of cocaine, in 1917 was not only a big step in alkaloid chemistry but also showed that tandem reactions in a one-pot synthesis are capable of forming bicyclic molecules. He is also known for discovering the molecular structures of morphine and penicillin. Not to be confused with **the** Robert Robinson off **Regdafishthinktank.**

Rothwell Temperance Band is a brass band with roots going back to the mid 1800s and the Rothwell Model Band. The Rothwell Temperance Band was founded in 1881 by a breakaway faction of eight men after a dispute over whether to spend a good payday on beer or split it and allow the men to take the windfall home for their families. The amount (between £2 and £4) split between the 24 men would give them spare cash they'd struggle to earn in the local pits where most worked. The band had strong links with Rothwell's Temperance Hall which was built in 1904 and one of the four corner stones was inscribed with: 'Laid by Thomas Blackburn in the name of the Rothwell Temperance Band.' – Thomas being one of the main shakers in the formation of the band.

I've chosen to do this small entry on The Rothwell Temperance Band to cover brass bands as I have little knowledge of the subject and my mate who used to play in them and tried to get me into them when I was too young and ignorant has moved to New Zealand. Anyhow, the Rothwell band appear to be the most successful Leeds based brass band, currently ranked ninth in the world, although the rankings are controversial and may be skewed by the amount of times a band plays and the competitions they enter. They are a championship band (top league) and came third in the 2010 England final and in 2009 won the Yorkshire Area Championship Section beating some of the giants of the brass bands world, Grimethorpe Colliery, Black Dyke, Brighouse and Rastrick. Seems to me that's some achievement. I'm sure there'll be a few Leeds brass bands but I think they often evolved out of pits which tended to be around Leeds rather than in Leeds – see **Coal**. But I've also found the Kippax Band, Horsforth Leeds City Band (formed from Horsforth Brass and Leeds City Bands), Tingley Brass Band, Lofthouse Brass Band*,

190

*Don't know if Lofthouse should be included as it's in the City of Leeds metropolitan borough but with a Wakefield postcode, similar to Ilkley which has a Leeds postcode but is part of Bradford Metropolitan Borough.

Roundhay Garden Scene was the first ever motion picture. See **Louis Le Prince**

Roundhay Park, more commonly known as **Roundi Park**, is one of the biggest city parks in Europe. It has over 700 acres (2.8 km^2) of parkland, lakes, woodland and gardens which are owned by Leeds City Council. It may be third biggest (behind Richmond Park and one in Dublin) but if you think I'm going to check the size of all the large municipal parks in Europe you've got another thing coming, what we need to do is deal with the problem. Now Leeds folk* are a proud race and, if we pull together, we have two realistic choices to get Roundi Park to the top of the British chart. The first, and my preferred option, is that we compulsorily purchase all the Roundi Park surrounding houses and demolish them, thus extending the park – I'm sure, given the importance of the task, that the householders, full of civic pride, would be only too willing to sacrifice their homes and anyway, they're loaded, they can get another. The second is that we go one evening, en masse, to Richmond Park, London, remove the boundary wall and re-establish it well within the existing boundary. We then need to commandeer that land, we may even be able to sell it and make a bit of a profit, I reckon that such prime London space may be worth up to a third of the Leeds equivalent. But crucial to this plan is that we place buildings on the re-claimed land to establish 'precedence and proof of use' and I suggest terrapins placed at 30 metre intervals. My main concern with this second scheme is gloves. Health and safety would dictate that we have to supply gloves for all people working with stone work, that's a heck of a lot of gloves and I fear it may render (sic) the project unworkable. Anyway, going forward, at least we've got a plan.

The park is visited by nearly a million people each year and was the destination of my first independent trip out, as a seven or eight-year-old kid, and I also remember visiting the open air swimming pool, the lido, just the once – you know the North Pole? It's warm there in comparison. The Roundhay Park website says, 'In June 1907 an open air swimming pool 'lido' opened, at a cost of just over £1,600, it was built mainly by unemployed citizens. During the 1950s and 1960s about 100,000 people a year visited the 'swimming baths'.

Back in the days when winters were winters and autumns were proud of them, people used to skate on the lake no probs. Talking of the lake, the 33 acre Waterloo Lake – named after the soldiers, back from the Napoleonic wars who built it – is around 60 feet deep and World War I munitions were dumped in it after the war. In the 1880s it was also the site for testing steam driven torpedoes – see **James Kitson.** Check out **Robert Blackburn** for the parks central role in the history of aviation. The park is now home to a number of attractions including a train ride to the mansion and the fantastic **Tropical World**, always a nice place to take kids.

*I'm not going to use the descriptions loiners or tykes, they are sooooo 20th Century.

The Roundhouse on Wellington Road, currently home of Leeds Commercial (Van Hire) Ltd., is the oldest example of this type of building left in England.

The **Royal Armouries** has got a website or you could take a day out to go visit it and still come away thinking you've skipped a lot.

Royal Exchange Chambers was on Boar Lane cornering onto City Square. The building closed in January 1964 and was demolished and replaced by the controversial tower block we see now, Royal Exchange House, opened in 1966. The earlier Royal Exchange was built between 1872 and 1875 (although I've also seen a date of 1829). All this information has come from the infomine that is **Leodis** and one contributor was doing some building work on the site and discovered a plaque commemorating the opening of the original building by Prince Arthur – son of Queen Victoria and Prince Albert – which would support the later build date. It originally contained an exchange room, newsroom, shops, a club, restaurant, offices and went on to house all sorts of stuff including the Leeds Chamber of Commerce.

The large clock on the tower of the Royal Exchange was installed by William Potts & Sons (Potts of Leeds) in 1877.

The Rubber/Eraser. On April 15, 1770, **Joseph Priestley** recorded his discovery of Indian gums ability to rub out or erase lead pencil marks. He wrote, 'I have seen a substance excellently adapted to the purpose of wiping from paper the mark of black lead pencil.' These were the first erasers which Priestley called a 'rubber'.

Rude Utilities Ltd. is based at **The Round Foundry** Media Centre in Holbeck and **Sarah Shafi** is the Founder and Managing Director. In 2008 she went to the House of Commons to collect her IAB Award for Highly Commended Business Entrepreneur of the Year and was a finalist in Asian Brand of the Year 2009. Rude is a specialist leather goods design company and their current ranges are aimed at the hairdressing industry, high end leather tool belts and holsters which Steve Strange described as 'the most cleverly designed bag I have ever had.' Sarah appeared on the kids version of *The Apprentice*, *Beat The Boss* and also works as a business coach in Leeds.

Paul & Barry Ryan (twins born 1948, Paul died 1992) were a successful singing duo from Leeds, with Paul writing the songs. They attended Foxwood School and lived near Dib Lane, Easterly Road. In 1965, aged 17, they signed to Decca records and performed at the London Palladium but within a short time Paul had decided that the bright lights and fame thing wasn't for him so he continued writing the songs for Barry, who went solo. Their biggest hit was the melodramatic *Eloise* (1968) which was heavily orchestrated and sold over one million copies, going gold. The following years *Love is Love* wasn't a major hit in the UK but sold over a million in Europe.

I must admit, with a smidgeon of embarrassment, that I hadn't heard of these two but I was talking to a mate last night about the electrics on a moped when I asked him if he'd heard of them, 'Oh yeh, my older sister used to love **Barry Ryan**, posters on her wall and everything, he was a real heartthrob.'

Being only two when they started putting their stuff out it's hard for me to retrospectively get an angle on them but I think one of the most important things to say is that they were a songwriter and a singer not a band. In bands there's a few ways that songs come together.

Someone may turn up with the whole thing or a couple of riffs or you may just start jamming and something happens but ultimately you mess around with the bass, drums guitars and vocals until it takes shape and this process shapes the song. It's different when you write the song and have the freedom to develop it however you like. Think of different instrumentation and arrangements and that's what shaped **Paul Ryan's** songs. They're definitely interesting; most of them have unexpected and clever changes, from chords to tempo, time signature or feel and arrangements. It's a different school of music to bands and I'm not surprised that Frank Sinatra's 1971 album *Sinatra & Company* contained a couple of Paul's songs including the UK hit single *I Will Drink the Wine* and the same year Dana took Paul's *Who Put the Lights Out* into the top 20, it stayed in the charts for eleven weeks. In 1986 The Damned's cover of ***Eloise*** got to number three in the UK Singles Chart.

Prof Tony Ryan, OBE. Tony hails from Croggie (although I think he may have been born on Halton Moor) and delivered the 2002 Royal Institution Christmas Lectures on the science and technology of everyday things. The lectures, on materials, covered subjects such as 'The spider that spun a suspension bridge' and 'The ice-cream that will freeze granny'. They were broadcast to audiences of nine million on Channel 4 and prompted feature articles in the national press. The lectures have also been broadcast in Europe, Japan and Korea but unfortunately I couldn't find them on YouTube. He's done various media work, I heard him talking polymers on Radio 4, for example.

Tony is ICI Professor of Physical Chemistry and director of the Polymer Centre at the University of Sheffield. The common theme in his research is phase transitions in polymers, leading to the development of the new field of Soft Nanotechnology. Developments in polymers responsive to their environment have lead to research into molecular machines, specifically the fabrication of molecular valves and motors.

His main contribution to the field has been the development and application of the techniques of time-resolved structural tools to polymers. He's had a small submarine (built in the 1960s) load of awards and published extensively in the academic press – co-author of over 200 papers, and the author of a book on Polymer Processing, *Emerging Themes in Polymer Science,* Royal Society of Chemistry; (2001). I think nanotechnology is fascinating and mind boggling. I heard a discussion on the radio about creating nano gear that could go around your body checking everything's ok and repairing damaged material. Material....that's a technical term us scientists use, just think of it as like stuff and that.

Sue Ryder, Baroness Ryder of Warsaw and Baroness Cheshire, CMG, OBE, was born in Leeds during 1923 and was founder of the **Sue Ryder Foundation** charity – later renamed Sue Ryder Care. At the age of 16, during the Second World War, she volunteered for the **First Aid Nursing Yeomanry** but was soon assigned to the Polish section of the **Special Operations Executive**, driving agents to the air field. In 1943 she was posted to Tunisia and later to Italy. After the war she worked as a volunteer amongst displaced and stateless refugees on the continent of Europe. The first home opened by Sue Ryder was St Christopher's in Germany, designed as a haven for the people she'd met in Europe, many of whom were survivors of concentration camps. The first home to be built by Sue Ryder was in Konstancin in central Poland.

In 1953 she established the **Sue Ryder Foundation** to provide help for the elderly and disabled and said that it should be "a living memorial to the victims who suffer and die as a result of persecution." It operates more than fifty projects across 12 countries in Europe and southern Africa, 14 Care Centres in the UK (including six hospices and seven neurological centres), has about 350 high street charity shops and more than 24,000 volunteers. They provide 1.4 million home visits to people in need, four million hours of care per year to people living with cancer, multiple sclerosis, Huntington's disease, Parkinson's, motor neurone disease, stroke and brain injury.

Sue wrote two autobiographies: *And Morrow Is Theirs* (1975) and *Child of My Love* (1986) and with her husband Leonard Cheshire *The hope of the disabled person* (Royal Society of Medicine, 1983). She died in 2000. There are parks in both **Warsaw** and **Gdynia** (Poland) named after her.

S

Mohammed Saddique from Roundhay was invited down to Ministry of Defence, London during 2009 to pick up a veterans prestigious lapel badge that had been awarded to his father **Goolam Hussein Bawa**. According to the **Asian Express** (Feb 09) Goolam was one of the first Asians to come to England when he joined the merchant Navy in 1909. He served in the First World War and joined the Royal Navy to serve in the Second World War being awarded, amongst other things, the Atlantic Star for his role in the Battle of the Atlantic where he was sunk at least once. Goolam died in Karachi 1949 whilst still serving.

Waseem Saeed, an Honorary Senior Lecturer in Plastic Surgery at St James's Hospital, is also a superhero waiting for the next world disaster to hit so that he can fly out and help save lives. He works for **Merlin** (an acronym for 'Medical Emergency Relief, International') and is an expert in reconstruction for limb paralysis and spasticity, children's hand surgery and microsurgery. He's become a bit of an expert in treating earthquake victims after flying out to the earthquakes in Indonesia, Pakistan, China and the last one in Haiti. I'm glad someone did something useful with their life.

Salamanca, according to some sources, is the world's first commercially working locomotive, built by **Matthew Murray** of Holbeck, in 1811/12 – **Stephenson's** *Rocket,* 1829. Named after a recent British victory in Spain, it made its first public run on the **Middleton – Leeds** line during the official opening of the line on August 12th, 1812. Other sources name the five ton *Prince Regent* locomotive, set to work on the same line (June 24th, 1812) as the first. When its boiler exploded *Salamanca* was destroyed in 1818, George Stephenson told a committee of Parliament that the driver had tampered with the boiler safety valve.

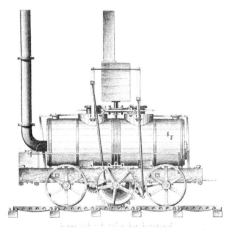

Salamanca, 1829 original engraving published in The Mechanic's Magazine.

Sir Titus Salt, 1st Baronet (1803–1876) a manufacturer, politician, philanthropist and creator of the stunning **Saltaire** is more associated with **Bradford**, so I'll keep this brief and just say he was born in Morley, Leeds.

Salvo's Restaurant, Otley Road, won Best Local Italian Restaurant on Gordon Ramsay's *F Word* television programme. I've eaten there a couple of times, nom-nom-nom.

Saturday Night is a 50 minute documentary about night-life in Leeds with poetic commentary written and narrated by Huddersfield poet **Simon Armitage** (Century Films, BBC2, 1996). It was directed by Brian Hill and broadcast by the BBC in 1996 as part of the 'Modern Times' series. I've not seen it but one of my mates (with taste) says it's absolutely outstanding. Simon Armitage also lectured on creative writing at the University of Leeds.

Savage Pencil/Sav X is a kinda grotesque pop-art/cartoon artist who currently contributes the monthly Trip Or Squeak strip to *The Wire* magazine. He got his first break in 1976 contributing his Rock 'N' Roll Zoo punk strip to *Sounds* and has also done work for the *NME* and *Kerrang!* He's produced album covers, posters, T-shirts etc for bands, including covers for The Fall and Sonic Youth, and characters such as Dead Duck, Mr Inferno and Wolfink as well as stuff for his own Sexy Swastika imprint.

Jimmy Savile, (31 October 1926 – 29 October 2011) We are now all fully aware of the crimes carried out by JS which I won't go into, other than to condemn them. This was an extremely difficult decision but I felt uncomfortable re-writing (or simply removing) this entry and air-brushing history, so I've decided to leave the entry largely as was. Obviously it should be read with his heinous crimes firmly in mind.

Not only did he complete the 2005 **London Marathon** at the age of 81 but he's also more influential than you think. He held the world's first ever (recorded) **disco** in Leeds and introduced the basic tools of all **DJ**'s, **two turntables and a microphone**, to the world. He opened and presented the first ever **Top of the Pops** on 1st January, 1964 and closed and presented the last ever Top Of The Pops on 30th July, 2006 when the last shot was of him turning off the lights of the empty studio.

Most important to me, Jimmy shaped our lives by spearheading the future of our nights out; he moved the world away from the dance band to the DJ, to relatively cheap discos and dances held all over the place. After his early experiences of the 'effect' on people and easy money to be made holding discos he moved into dance hall management with the Mecca. Between 1952 to 53 he was DJing at records-only dance sessions at large dancehalls such as the Palais in Ilford, Essex which the teenagers flocked to. His nights were such a hit that he 'finished up running 52 dance halls and employing 400 disc jockeys. They made me a director of the company and I left my DJing thing and looked after the whole shebang, the whole of Mecca Ltd.' He was the first to realise the full power of the record and made dancing to records mass market, cheap and available, just a shilling to get in. According to djhistory.com, 'it was Jimmy Savile who revolutionised British nightlife by spearheading the Mecca organisation's move from dance bands to DJs at the end of the '50s.'

Jimmy devised and hosted *Jim'll Fix It*, the iconic, long-running, prime-time British television show (1975 until 1994) broadcast by the BBC. The show was aimed at children and gave them a chance to fulfil a dream. Fix-Its ranged from dropping and smashing a supposedly valuable vase on the *Antiques Roadshow* to drumming with **Adam and the Ants**. The show which has entered the national psyche and has been referenced all over the place in popular culture and everyday life was a successor to Jim's Saturday night TV chat/variety series *Clunk, Click* which ran from 1973 until 1974. He still makes occasional TV appearances and recently had **Louis Theroux** over to stay for the programme *When Louis Met Jimmy*, which, watching them sparring, was fantastic television.

Jim started his working life as a Bevin Boy coal miner during World War II but he was 'blown up underground in the pits', quite seriously injured and on the sick he started to experiment with

DJing to earn extra money and then moving on to his early '50s ballroom management. He began his broadcasting career as a DJ on Radio Luxembourg in 1958 and was headhunted by Radio 1 in 1968, spending over 19 years there and remembered mainly for Jimmy *Savile's Old Record Club* – the first radio show to play chart hits from previous years. He started his TV career in 1960 on the Tyne Tees music programme ***Young at Heart***, dying his hair a different colour each week even though the show went out in black and white. He went on to front TV advertising campaigns for products such as **Green Shield Stamps**, Bisto Gravy (with his mother), Startrite Shoes and Dale Farm Yoghurts. Back in the days when people had the freedom to be catapulted through their car windscreens due to not wearing seatbelts Jim fronted a series of hugely successful public information films. The ***Clunk Click Every Trip*** campaign (1971) encouraged people to use seatbelts at a time when it was very unusual to do so and was sponsored by the Royal Society for the Prevention of Accidents. It was a series of quite graphic films and paved the way for the 1983 law that made seatbelt wearing compulsory. During the early 1980s he also fronted British Rail's long running series of ads with slogan such as 'This is the age of the train' and 'Let the train take the strain'.

Many of his catch phrases, that people enjoy mimicking so much, are pure Leeds, 'Now then, now then, now then', 'ow's about that, then?, 'as it 'appens', 'Goodness gracious', 'Guys and gals'. But my favourite can't really be written down, as it was simply him looking at the camera making an undulating **Tarzan** type call whilst tapping his cigar in perfect rhythm, sheer brilliant madness. Can you imagine him explaining it to the producer? 'Well I'm just going to stare at the camera, make a daft noise and tap my cigar....people will love it.' 'Yes Jim, the acid, you must leave it alone.'

Although we, of a certain age, probably see him as a flamboyant, slightly embarrassing uncle there's certainly an argument to be made that he's the most influential DJ of all time, not just because of his music, that comes down to taste but because he defined, created and popularised what a DJ is.

Here are some more random facts about the man.

When Louis Met Jimmy was voted one of the top fifty documentaries of all time in a survey on Channel 4.

Jimmy has raised over £40 million for charity.

He competed in the 1951 **Tour of Britain** cycle race and over 300 professional bike races.

Jim is a member of MENSA.

Jim'll Fix It featured him smoking a big fat cigar on children's TV with an ashtray built into his chair.

By the year 2000 he had run 212 marathons and was still running them five years later.

A range of licensed Jimmy Savile fancy dress costumes were released in 2009.

He won the New Musical Express award for top DJ for eleven consecutive years.

He worked for many years as a volunteer porter at the Stoke Mandeville Hospital in Bucks mimicking his earlier life working as a hospital porter at Broadmoor Hospital.

He is only one of two civilians to ever complete the Royal Marine Commando speed march, 30 miles across Dartmoor carrying 30lb of kit and was awarded honorary **Commando Green Beret** by the Royal Marines.

Jim was named as one of the *Radio Times* 'Top 40 most eccentric TV presenters of all time' in July 2004

He's appeared twice on *This Is Your Life*.

He wrestled professionally, with many fights at **Leeds Town Hall**, losing 35 of his first 35 fights and saying 'from start to finish I got a good hiding. I've broken every bone in my body. I loved it.' He improved and competed in 107 pro fights. See, **Disco, DJ (Disc Jockey)** and **Hip-Hop.**

Schofields was a department store that operated on (or near) The Headrow from 1901 to 1996 and expanded to open stores in Harrogate, Skipton and Sheffield. It was considered the pinnacle of Leeds shopping.

Dave Simpson was born in Tinshill 1963 and has written on music for the Guardian for 15 years. He's written two books, the first, *The Stone Roses: The Illustrated Story* was written in nine days and is now out of print. His second, *The Fallen: Life in and Out of Britain's Most Insane Group*, was *The Times*, *Sunday Times* and *Observer* music book of the year for 2008. He tracked down all the ex-members of The Fall (over 50) for the book and collected stories and anecdotes. He began writing in 1989 putting The Stone Roses on the cover of issue two of his *Avanti!* fanzine, dubbing them 'the best band on the planet'. He did this just as they were breaking and before the music press had picked up on them. He wrote reviews and articles for the Melody Maker from that time until 1998.

In May 1901 **Snowden Schofield** (1870–1949) opened a 'Fancy Drapers and Milliners' in the entrance to the Victoria Arcade. It thrived and by1906 Schofield's also filled Nos. 2 and 3 and 4. The store used a variety of promotional devices although, traditionally, drapers did not advertise in the press and Snowden broke with this by having the first business in Leeds to place ads on the front page of local newspapers. The store continued to expand buying Nos.5 and 6 in the arcade (occupying six shops in a row) and in 1911 bought the Red Hall. Snowden restored the building and converted the King's Chamber, where King Charles I had been imprisoned, into an oak-panelled restaurant with its own quintet of musicians, the *All-Star Versatiles*. The Headrow frontage and Red Hall courtyard were bought in 1921 and by 1926 Schofields had 300 staff. Through the following years there were various acquisitions, expansions and extensions, pausing for the war and by 1947 Snowden Schofield owned the whole of the Victoria Arcade (as well as other sites) where he had once rented a small shop for £50 a year. He died on 24th March 1949.

In 1962 Schofield's newly built store was completed which, for the first time in England, included the installation of three 'packaged' escalators into an occupied building. Although I can find very little info about it, in August 1964 Schofield's had a zoo exhibition on the roof to attract more families, amongst other animals, it included a baby elephant, a baby polar bear and an orang-utan.

The family connection with the store ended in 1984 when it was sold. In 1988 the new owners reconstructed the original building and created a shopping centre (the *Schofields Centre*), the same year selling Schofields and the various sites to the Al Fayed brothers, who also owned Harrods and House of Fraser, for £4.7 million. The Schofields Centre subsequently became known as *The Headrow Centre* and after further recent renovations has again reopened as *The Core*.

I find it a bit sad that in this story all the history of the **Red Hall** and the **Theatre Royal** on Lands Lane (amongst other buildings) were demolished.

Percy Alfred Scholes (1877–1958) is best known for conceiving and writing the first edition of, *The Oxford Companion to Music* (Oxford University Press, 1938). He was a musician, journalist and prolific writer (over 30 books) who helped popularise classical music. Over a million words, The Companion took him six years to write and is longer than the Bible. He had various clerical assistants but the only bits of The Companion he didn't write were on **tonic sol-fa**, the process for sight singing that encompasses **do re, mi, fa, so, la, te, do** made famous by *The Sound of Music* – as he wasn't happy with his attempt – and the synopses of the plots of operas, which he thought were simply too boring. His edition (it has been twice revised) was considered as knowing its stuff but at times a little eccentric/idiosyncratic as it went off into personal anecdotes or gave strong opinions rather than being neutral. Imagine a reference book written by a Leeds lad going off into personal anecdotes and giving strong opinions. As I was saying to ar'lass this morning, 'he must have been crazy.'

His opinions, sometimes unusual and elitist, were wittily expressed; harpsichord music sounded like 'a toasting fork on a birdcage'; describing a certain religious composer's music, his pieces 'long enjoyed popularity, and still aid the devotions of undemanding congregations in less sophisticated areas.' He also wrote for the *Radio Times, The Observer* (1920-1927) and the *Evening Standard.* The National Library of Canada got his 'professional' library of research files and correspondence, which (in the days before computers) stretched to around 50 metres in length. His book *The Great Dr Burney* won the **James Tait Black Memorial Prize** (the oldest and one of the most prestigious literary awards) for biography, the same year that Graham Greene's, *The Heart of the Matter* won the award for fiction

Schrödinger's cat. An experiment at Leeds Uni led by **Ben Varcoe** into this conundrum led directly to the invention of a portable **magnetometer** through fluctuations in one of the lasers leading to noise that complicated the experiment. See **Heart monitor** and **Magnetometer.**

Screen Yorkshire is the Leeds-based agency which supports media output in Yorkshire. Based in The Calls they have put money behind productions like *Red Riding* and *The Damned United, A Passionate Woman, This Is England '86* and much more. Their website states: 'Screen Yorkshire's mission is to inspire, promote and support the development of a successful long-term film, broadcast, games and interactive media sector to grow the economic, social and cultural wealth of the region.' I worry for their existence and for the future of Yorkshire as a media-based area given the cuts going on.

Frances Segelman, FRSA, ARBS. Sculptor in bronze, steel & terracotta – '**sculptor to the stars'**. Not that it matters but in a break with the sculptor stereotype of mucky blokes with beards, Frances is a woman (like **Barbara Hepworth**, another Leeds-related, female sculptor), a leggy blond. Her most famous work is the statue of some bloke called **Billy Bremner** that stands outside one of my favourite places on earth, Elland Road. Which must have been a dream commission for a Leeds lass. She has also sculpted Vinnie Jones. Her website says (and from looking into it, I don't think they're over egging the pud), 'Frances has become one of the most successful professional sculptors in Britain. Often working in front of an audience, Frances is a fast and naturally creative sculptor.

Frances is an established sculptor of personalities from the world of entertainment, politics and sport, whose recent clients include Her Majesty The Queen, H.R.H The Duke of Edinburgh, Sven Goran Eriksson, Jack Rosenthal, Terry Venables, Clive Anderson, Bob Wilson, John Profumo CBE and Sir David Frost. She is a fellow of The Royal Society of Arts and an associate of The Royal Society of British Sculptors.

Seven Arts can trace its roots back to 1997 when a group of local people set up the Chapel Allerton Arts Festival. The festival began in 1998, with a few musicians performing on an open-truck stage in Regent Street and has become a week-long, annual event. Their long-term aim was to create a venue for arts activity. The building of Seven and initial set-up was supported by funding from the European Regional Development Fund – you see the EU does do some good stuff as well as all the tittle-tattle you read in the papers. It's a lovely space with an open, airy café/bar and a 100 seat venue, which puts on all sorts of interesting and diverse stuff. It opened in 2007, hosts 'film, theatre, dance, music, words and comedy'. Highlights have included sought-after touring artists from Japan and USA attracting three live BBC broadcasts. It is well worth a visit or keeping an eye on what's coming up because there is usually something interesting. It's not-for-profit so any food and drink you buy subsidies the arts programme.

Aryan Shimpi was a beautiful intelligent, talkative and friendly little two year-old boy who lost his life on the 24th of June 2009 in a tragic accident on the way back from registering at a local nursery. In a city the size of Leeds there will be personal tragedy on a daily basis and I cannot cover so much experience but I imagine that no grief can compare to that of losing a child. At the very core of the history of Leeds is a concern and campaign for the welfare, rights and safety of children, it's part of the fabric of the city.* I write this entry as a memorial to all those people of Leeds who died too young, to the city for losing the immense potential of the children but primarily to all those who have lost a child. I cannot even imagine their pain, although the thought of their loss fills me with sadness.

(* see, **Charles Turner Thackrah, Mrs Helen Currer Briggs, The Leeds Children's Holiday Camp Association, Herbert Henry Asquith, Tom Maguire, Richard Oastler etc**)

Silver Cross, the pram makers, was set up by Leeds postman **William Wilson**, although we know little about him. He was a prolific inventor and engineer who filed over 30 patents in his lifetime and, with his wife, started his own business making postal carts and perambulators at **Silver Cross Street, Hunslet,** Leeds. William got the idea for designing prams and postal carts from using a cart delivering post through the cobbled streets of Leeds and by 1877 William had finished his first 'perambulator' which he patented. It was groundbreaking for its day, having the first reversible folding hood and heavy spring suspension. William basically invented the modern pram.

In the late nineteenth century William backed two purpose-built factories, the first one burnt down leading to the second, called the 'Silver Cross Works'. In 1936 the growth of production led to another move to an old silk factory in Guiseley where, during World War II, most of the factory was requisitioned by the Air Ministry and produced over 16 million parts for airplanes such as Hurricanes and Spitfires.

They moved with the times and their lightweight, collapsible pushchair, the Wayfarer, launched in the early 1980s, sold over 3,000 units a week for several years. Silver Cross's headquarter are now at Broughton Hall near Skipton and the traditional prams are made near Bingley, while the rest of their stuff is made abroad.

John Simm was born in Leeds in 1970, although his family moved around a lot. He's a top actor, appearing as Sam Tyler in the iconic BBC detective drama *Life on Mars,* as well as the excellent *Clocking Off* but he's done loads of TV and film and is easy to find out about so go and look.....if you want, if you're not bothered, don't look, do something else like design a quick dry swimming costume or sommat.

Sky Plaza (also known as **The Plaza Tower**) is a 105-metre (344 ft) tower block, in Leeds, Yorkshire, England. It is the second phase of a development in Leeds city centre, consisting of 572 student apartments. It is the second tallest building in Leeds, after Bridgewater Place, and (according to Skyscrapernews.com) is also the world's tallest student accommodation building. Here's a thing, its roof is the highest point in Leeds although the building is not the tallest..... how can that be? I know, so don't email me.

Samuel Smiles (1812–1904) started his life in Leeds as a surgeon but packed it in for literature becoming editor of the *Leeds Times* in 1838 and in 1859 he wrote a book called *Self Help*. Now there's little information for when 'Self Help' books started but I'd suggest this may be an earlier one, unless of course it's about physics or 13th Century glass-making. If that's the case I'd best shut-up.

Richard W Smithells (1924–2002) MD, FRCPCH, FRCP, FRCPE, FRCOG, DCH. In his time as Professor of Paediatrics and Child Health (1968-1988) at Leeds Uni Richard highlighted the importance of **folic acid** in the prevention of **spina bifida** and other malformations of the spine and brain. In the late 1960s he established a laboratory in Leeds to study the effects of drugs and nutrition on the early development of the embryo and foetus and the links between poor nutrition and vitamin deficiency and conditions leading to malformed babies. In 1991 the MRC concluded that 'public health measures should be taken to ensure that the diet of all women who bear children contains an adequate amount of folic acid.' He also showed that through the rubella vaccination preventing German measles in mothers you reduced the incidence of handicapped babies. He received various well regarded national and international awards for his work and co-author *Lecture Notes on Paediatrics* which ran to seven editions.

Soapy Joe's – Joseph Watson and Son started production in 1861 and by 1906 were producing 500 tons of soap a week (*A History of Modern Leeds*, Fraser), that's a heck of a lot of clean people. Now I've done a quick calculation and in today's money (weight of a bar of soap which I've just weighed) they produced around 3,360,000, over 3.3 million, bars of soap a week. This can only be an estimate as I don't know how heavy a bar of **Soapy Joe's** weighed but soap is a pretty basic substance and more specialist soaps that are slightly denser/heavier tend toward a

Joseph Watson, 1st Baron Manton. Portrait sketch by John A M Hay, 1923.

smaller bar. We should also bear in mind that some of the soap will have been in the form of flakes. **Joseph Watson and Son** began life as dealers in leather, skins and hides but in 1861 moved to a site between Whitehall Road and the river, branching out into fats and soaps at the Whitehall Road Soapworks. One of the by-products of their work was glycerine which they sneakily sold on for the production of dynamite/explosives.

The **Leodis** website contradicts Fraser slightly and reckons that by 1893 **Soapy Joe's** were producing 600 tons of soap per week, which equates to over 4 million bars. Now obviously they were one of the biggest soap manufacturers in Britain, employing around 750 people to produce brands such as 'Watson's Matchless Cleanser' (see back cover), 'Nubolic', and 'Venus Soap'. At a time when the population of the UK was around 30 million people that's a bar of soap a week for every seven and a half people in Britain or, if my maths aren't awry, a bar of soap, per person every 7.5 weeks – Lordy Lou I'm confusing myself now, that's a, four letter word ending in 'ck'*, of a lot of soap.

I do the shopping in ar'ouse and, for five people, I buy a couple of bars of soap every few months and the people I live with wash way too much. It's ridiculous. Mrs Mick, for example, washes her hands every time she handles fresh meat. I think her wanton waste of soap is based on the fact that she forgets that she lives with four Leeds lads. Fair enough, each time she does it she's saving us from a week of chronic diarrhoea, violent vomiting and possible death but we're lads from Leeds, Yorkshire, England, we're hard, we'd just get on with it, without whinging, as we lay on our death beds. I think at most our eyes would water but that'd be unavoidable and we certainly wouldn't cry. Now, at this moment I think I should stop babbling semi-related nonsense and make a point to render this paragraph largely irrelevant. They didn't just wash their bodies with the stuff, they washed their clothes with it too, and in grimy Victorian Leeds that'll have been a lot of washing, without washing machines.........ey, did you know, I've got a big, old mangle made in Leeds? Anyway, **Soapy Joe's**, they obviously exported large amounts of soap around the world and supplied soap to **Lever Brothers** for them to rebrand.

Joseph Watson got together with William Lever (founder of **Lever Brothers)** in August 1906 to set up a 'Soap Trust' which would merge the major soap manufacturers into a monopoly, increasing economies of scale for advertising and production and cutting costs/increasing profits. Due to American examples, there was a media and public backlash leading to boycotts of their products and in the initial arrangements of the 'Soap Trust' Soapy Joe lost much of his shareholding to Lever who bought the remainder of his shares in July 1917. After the Second World War the soap production ceased and they concentrated on toiletries: toothpastes, shampoos, and shaving creams and in 1962 merged with D & W Gibbs. The company (although still known as 'Soapy Joe's) became **Elida Gibbs** in 1971 when they merged with Austrian firm Elida. Which lasted until all production was moved to Coal Road, Whinmoor in 1987, with the new name of **Elida Faberge**, where it still operates under the name **Lever Faberge** who employ over 500 people at their Leeds production, research and development centre.

Anyway, Joseph Watson didn't retire when he sold up – he'd also sold his half share in the **Planter's Margarine Co Ltd.** to Lever a few years earlier – he got involved in pioneering industrialised agriculture, was asked by the government to help in the setting up and running of national munitions factories, bought a proper mansion (Compton Verney) and race horses. In 1921 his horse **Love-in-Idleness** won the **Epsom Oaks** and **Lemonora** won the **Grand Prix de Paris** also coming third in **the Derby**, and by chance getting immortalised through the character 'Mr Memory' in the 1935 film *The 39 Steps* who has to recite the first three placings of the 1921 Derby. In 1922 he was made a peer, **1st Baron Manton**, and there's a bust displayed on a wall at **Leeds General Infirmary** and a department named after him as he gave them vat-loads of money in 1921.

*Heck

Soda Water/Carbonated Water was invented by **Joseph Priestley** when he first discovered a method of infusing water with carbon dioxide in 1767, producing the first drinkable man made glass of carbonated water (soda water). Joseph published a paper called *Directions for Impregnating Water with Fixed Air (1772)*, which explained how to make soda water. However, Priestley did little with it, other than show the crew of Captains Cook's how to make carbonated water to avoid Scurvy on their voyage of discovery. They needed fruit not pop, even I know that. So Joseph didn't exploit the business potential of soda water products but just over a decade after Priestley's work, Johann Jacob Schweppe did – he made a fortune – and more than 225 years later as soon as I read that I went 'Ahh, Schweppes.'

Sooty and Sweep was a children's puppet-based programme produced by the BBC which, although it was known as that by kids, doesn't ever appear to have borne that name. Through its various incarnations – The Sooty Show (1955–1992), Sooty & Co. (1993–1998), Sooty Heights (1999–2000), Sooty (2001–2004) – it's the longest running children's programme in the UK. Martin Wainwright in his excellent *True North* (Guardian Books, London, 2009) reckons that 'the two famous puppets (were) invented in Guiseley' and he's about right. Harry bought the 'Sooty' puppet for 7s 6d as a present for his son Matthew from a stall in Blackpool; he took it back to Guiseley and began to practice his routine on Matthew, checking for the bits that tickled his audience of one. Isn't it interesting that the characters sold in 1996 to a Japanese-owned merchant bank, for more than £1.4 million were simply picked up off a market stall almost 50 years earlier? Martin Wainwright also notes the names of the puppets and links them to the state of Leeds, commenting that 'even in 1971, 25 tons of soot fell every month on every square mile of the city south of the river Aire,' mindst you 'it was good for the roses.' Sooty was originally all yellow but Harry put soot on the ears and nose so that he stood out on black and white TV* and it was at this point that he was named Sooty. His big break came in 1952 on the BBC's *Talent Night* – a show which was broadcast live; Harry won the whole thing by public vote and, as it was the only channel available in Britain, became famous overnight. Sooty didn't speak, well he didn't to us, he whispered into Harry's ear and mimed actions. Most of the humour of the show/routine came out of Sooty being naughty or mischievous, although we were never quite sure if he maybe didn't understand, or was just a bit daft.

*Hey kids, Sooty is so old that when he first came out we didn't have 3D televisions, not even widescreen. It was worse, all televisions had no colour, just black and white – my Mrs didn't have a colour TV until 1979 – and the TVs were small and the pictures would often go fuzzy so that you had to move it around or fiddle with the aerial. And you couldn't sit around watching telly all day in your jim-jams, there was no daytime TV, it didn't come on until the afternoon. And right, listen right, y'know like if you didn't like what was on, right and you wanted to turn over? Well, like, you couldn't, there was no other place to go, just BBC1, just one channel. In't that like, well minging?

George Sorocold ensured in 1694 that Leeds became one of the first places in Britain to have piped water to housing.

Wole Soyinka (Born Akinwande Oluwole Soyinka in 1934) is a Nigerian writer, poet and playwright. In 1986 he became the first African to win the **Nobel Prize** for Literature. In 1954 he moved to Leeds to study English Literature, mentored by Wilson Knight. He gained a first class honours degree in English Literature from the University of Leeds. Whilst studying he started writing literary fiction, published several pieces of a comedic nature and worked as an editor for *The Eagle*; a satire-based mag. He stayed in Leeds to take an M.A. and in 1958 wrote his first major play *The Swamp Dwellers*. In 1959 he wrote *The Lion and the Jewel*. Both these plays were performed in Nigeria, to where he returned in 1960.

Back home, he became more politically active and spoke out against Government censorship, he continued to write and released a feature film, *Culture in Transition*. He was first imprisoned in Nigeria in 1964 for political reasons but was released after a few months due to national and international pressure. As the Nigerian Civil War approached (1966/67), Wole tried to mediate and was finally imprisoned for another 22 months until the Civil War ended. In 1998/9 he was offered the **Presidency of Nigeria** (and the 155 million people) 'on a platter', 'guaranteed I didn't need to campaign.....to accept something like that would be contrary to everything I've ever believed in.' He turned it down because he didn't like the involvement of the military in the state/civilian life and thought it was anti-democratic.

He's written over 20 plays, seven novels/memoirs and eight collections of poems as well as essays. In 1972 he was declared an Honoris Causa doctorate by the **University of Leeds** and in 1986 he became the first African to win the **Nobel Prize** for Literature for his 'prolific store of words and expressions which he exploits to the full in witty dialogue, in satire and grotesquery, in quiet poetry and essays of sparkling vitality'. He delivered **The BBC Reith Lectures** in 2004, entitled *Climate of Fear,* returned to Leeds Uni in 2007 to mark the 40th anniversary of the university's Workshop Theatre and according to Wainwright's **True North** has 'returned repeatedly to give readings, encourage young playwrights and premiere work at the West Yorkshire Playhouse, rather than London or New York.'

He annoyed 'influential' people by writing against corruption, speaking up for human rights and for trying to encourage people to learn from past mistakes and move forward. He has spoken out against various administrations in Nigeria and still does. I've seen him on *Newsnight* and other TV news programmes a few times and he's an intelligent, straight talking man of the people and his blog spot is well worth a visit.

Stead & Simpson was established in Leeds during 1834 as a footwear manufacturer (making boots and shoes) with retail outlets. It opened outlets throughout the country but ceased production during the 1960s when the company moved its headquarters to near Leicester. Stead & Simpson still has 276 stores in the UK under a deal with Shoe Zone.

St Ives Mount (Upper Armley) won the accolade of Friendliest Street in Britain in a 2006 Radio 5Live poll. A *Daily Mirror* reporter visited the street to follow up the story and was surprised as he walked down the street that people smiled and said 'good morning.' He was also surprised by tales of local resident Abdul Qayam scraping ice off neighbour's windscreens of a morning. He commented on the street, 'I'm left in no doubt why....people voted the street....the nations friendliest. It's not just tea and gossip these neighbours share. They help each other out with anything from DIY to relationship disasters, money problems and motoring mishaps.' (17 Jan 2007) Apparently Ricky Wilson, front man of the Kaiser Chiefs and a man of money and taste, bought a flat just around the corner.

Celia Stone, a retired teacher from Guiseley, invented, patented and created the **Addacus**, a tool/machine used to help people with **dyscalculia,** which is related to dyslexia but concerning numbers – 40% of dyslexics have dyscalculia. Celia was a 'coal-face' teacher specialising in dyslexia for over 25 years and, with Myra Nicholson, she is co-author of **Beat Dyslexia** a multi-sensory synthetic phonics course used in schools for over 15 years which has sold over 40,000 copies. She created the Addacus after requests from teachers for resources to help children who struggled with maths; it helps the understanding of basic number concepts and the significance of place value. Both her course and the Addacus helps children understand number concepts by incorporating bright colours, and by being multi-sensory and tactile.

Stuntmen, see **Roy Alon** for the world's busiest.

St John the Evangelist church (New Briggate) is the oldest church in Leeds city centre. The main body of the church was built in 1632-34 and retains many of its original features, most interesting are probably the Jacobean (Carolian) fittings. The cost of building the church was borne completely by **John Harrison**, the wealthy wool merchant. Worth a visit I'd say and there appears to be a knowledgeable curator on site.

Subbuteo (Waddingtons). The brain child of Peter Adolph, his final patent went through in 1947 and the first sets were available the same year. They were not what we would recognise today as Subbuteo. The original sets, known as the Assembly Outfits, had goals made of wire with paper nets, a cellulose acetate ball, cardboard playing figures with bases made from buttons weighed down with lead washers. The story is that Peter Adolph found one of his mother's coat buttons and used Woolworth buttons for the early set bases.

There was a pre-existing rival to Subbuteo called Newfooty, a very similar game, invented in 1929 by William Keeling. Newfooty ceased trading in 1961 after a failed TV advertising campaign which coincidently corresponded with the development of the 3D Subbuteo players that we would recognise today. It wasn't easy to pin down exactly when Waddingtons obtained the rights and brought Subbuteo to the mass market but Mike at the subbuteoengland website was very helpfully and said 'I have a feeling it was 1971' and sent the following quote from elsewhere, "In 1971 Mr Adolph sold Subbuteo to major toy firm Waddingtons for £250,000 and soon afterwards manufacturing was moved to a larger building." However during a visit to Leeds City Museum I've seen a Subbuteo box marked *Copyright Waddingtons, 1965* and their factory at Tunbridge Wells appears to have been producing Subbuteo in 1960.

Suffragettes fought for the rights of women, particularly the right to vote. The first example of an organisation I can find – **The National Society for Women's Suffrage** – was formed on 6 November 1867 by Lydia Becker who also founded and published the *Women's Suffrage Journal* from 1870. Emmeline Pankhurst and her husband Richard created The Women's Franchise League in 1889 and in 1903 the more famous Women's Social and Political Union in 1903. The **Leeds Women's Suffrage Society** was formed in 1890 by **Isabella Ford,** her sister Bessie and sister-in-law Helen. Although it seems to be a quiet history, Leeds has its fair share of strong and powerful women fighting for the right to vote. Jill Liddington's *Rebel girls - their fight for the vote* (Virago, 2008) covers the movement in Leeds and Yorkshire. See **Isabella Ford**, **Leonora Cohen**, **Mary Gawthorpe** and **Lilian Ida Lenton.**

Sunday excursions. In 1841, according to ***Francis Frith's Leeds Pocket Album***, a train of 40 carriages took 1,250 passengers on the earliest known **Sunday excursion**. The trip from Leeds to Hull was organised by Thomas Cook. Might seem a bit weird clambering to go on a trip to Hull but for many it will have been the experience of a lifetime and a first sight of the sea. I joined the cubs for a few weeks when I was a kid simply to go on a trip down the Humber.

The Switched Reluctance Motor/Drive (or variable reluctance motor) is an electrical techy thing very hard for you and me to get our heads around, unless you're an expert and you'll probably know all this anyway but, amongst other things, it appears to markedly reduce carbon emissions. It's described by the **Institute of Electrical and Electronics Engineers** as 'the only radically new family of machine drives in a century, (they) operate entirely on magnetic attraction, and offer an ideal fit for the electronically controlled drive systems used throughout industries and products today,' and '**Dr. Peter Lawrenson** is widely known as the father of the switched reluctance (SR) drive.'

This description, from their website, describes why **Peter John Lawrenson**, previously dean of engineering at the University of Leeds had been awarded the **Edison Medal** 'for a career of meritorious achievement in electrical science, electrical engineering or the electrical arts.' The medal is the oldest and most coveted medal in this field of engineering in the United States and in his time at Leeds Peter also won the British equivalent the **Faraday Medal,** as well as the ESSO **Energy Gold Medal** of The Royal Society and the J.A. Ewing Gold Medal of the Institution of Civil Engineers.

Peter was at Leeds Uni from 1961 until 1991, although in 2005 he was still Emeritus Professor in the Department of Electrical Engineering, University of Leeds and it appears that he now operates as a private consultant connected to Leeds. As a leading world expert in electrical and electromagnetic devices, he left his post as Dean of Engineering in 1991 to create (according to the Emerson Electric Company) a global business in Leeds. The business spawned SR applications in market sectors ranging from automotive, household, mining and textiles to earth-moving equipment, industrial pumps, medical equipment and high-performance servo systems. This business, SRD, Ltd., was acquired in 1994 by the huge multinational Emerson Electric Company, the world's largest producer of electric motors. **Switched Reluctance Drives Ltd.** is still operating and based in Harrogate producing for a whole range of applications but it seems that transport, and carbon reduction through electric motors and pumps, used in planes, cars, buses, trucks and trains is central to their business.

The Symphony for Yorkshire was commissioned by the BBC, written by Benjamin Till and released on Yorkshire Day (August 1st) 2010 on Radio Leeds (and other Yorkshire-based local BBC radio stations) featured on Look North and big screens around the region. It was laid down at a recording studio in Leeds, in separate sessions, performed by 250 musicians with different levels of experience some professionals, some school kids, and some amateurs. It incorporated different styles of music, folk, brass bands and Leeds rock band **Luver Gunk** for example.

T

T2 is a 'young' in-demand Leeds producer who has worked with Craig David, Kelly Rowland and Platinum and produced remixes for the likes of Kate Nash and J Holiday. He's worked on a track featuring Dizzie Rascal and his biggest track *Heartbroken* featuring **Jodie Aysha** reached No. 2 in the UK Singles Chart. He is reported to be soon working with Alesha Dixon, Cheryl Cole and Madonna.

Tar Roads: According to the company website, in the early 20th Century, LBBC Technologies **The Leeds and Bradford Boiler Company** specialised 'in tar stills and tar distillation plants to facilitate the building of the world's first tar roads.' I think they should have inserted the word 'modern' into that sentence as there is evidence of its use in Baghdad in the 8th century. No doubt a different technology that disappeared.

Taylors Drug Company's building can still be seen towards the top end of Burley Rd. Established in 1862, by the 1890s it was a chain chemists with over ten branches (only three others in the UK), including Leeds, Harrogate, London and Sunderland. In 1902 it was bought by **Chas F. Thackray Limited** who diversified hugely and in 1935 the drugs section, **Taylors Drug Co. Ltd,** merged with Timothy Whites to form **Timothy Whites & Taylors** with 614 branches, this was taken over by **Boots Pure Drug Co.** in 1968 to offer cut-price medicines.

The **telescopic sight/scope** (see **William Gascoigne**) allows an instrument to be pointed at the centre of a distant object with use of magnification. It is most often seen in popular culture when a soldier or hunter is accurately pointing a gun (or projectile) at its quarry. Wiki reckons that it's just weapons that use telescopic sights and doesn't credit Gascoigne but he invented it for use with telescopes and I've seen them used in other ways, on camera lenses for example. And there must have been other scientific uses of 'crosshairs'. Anyway, the telescopic sight was invented by **William Gascoigne** in Middleton during the 1630s when he realised that a placed wire running vertically on the lens could be used as a guide to point the telescope more accurately. By then introducing the horizontal wire (meeting at the focal point) he defined the centre of the field of view and gave the sight pinpoint precision. Now if that isn't a telescopic sight I've got a skipping tree I'd like to show you.

Top lad **Charles Turner Thackrah** LSA, MRCS Eng. (1795–1833), the father of **Occupational Medicine** and **Preventive Medicine** studied and fought for Public Health and the medical/welfare rights of workers through studying workplace conditions. He was a humanitarian, anatomist, experimental physiologist, clinician, teacher, and a founder of the Leeds Medical School.
  According to the **Leeds Institute of Medical Education** (University of Leeds) website Thackrah has a 'reputation as the **father of Occupational Medicine** in the English speaking world' and it is well-earned – an opinion enhanced in an article for *The Oxford Journal of Occupational Medicine* by J. Cleeland and S. Burt, Vol. 49. No.6. pp. 285-297, 1995.

His major work was *The Effects of Arts, Trades, and Professions, and of Civic States and Habits of Living; On Health and Longevity – With suggestions for the removal of many of the agents which produce disease, and shorten the duration of life.* (Charles Turner Thackrah, Longman, Rees, Orme, Brown, Green, & Longman, 1831, London) – I mean, I like a long title as much as the next man but this lot were ridiculous.

To imagine how bad factory conditions were, from the 1830s, there was a series **Factory Acts**, the third in 1844 stating that, 'Accidental death must be reported to a surgeon and investigated.' (This leaves me wondering what they did before the act, should someone die at work, just chuck the body out of the door and get someone else in?) The ground breaking work of Charles Turner Thackrah affected each of these acts. In the Houses of Parliament before the Second Reading of the Factories Regulation Bill (16 March, 1832) Michael Sadler, a radical British Tory Member of Parliament and leader of the factory reform movement, said "I hold in my hand a treatise by a medical gentleman of great intelligence. Mr Thackrah of Leeds"

Thackrah studied the working conditions of over 100 Leeds trades and, amongst other things, he examined the following topics; Agents Injurious to the Digestive Organs, Agents or States Injurious to the Respiratory System, Agents Injurious to the Circulatory System, Agents Affecting the Nervous System in General, Agents Injurious to Vision, Agents Injurious to the Hearing, Agents Injurious to the Bones, Agents Injurious to the Muscular System, Agents Injurious to the Skin.

Again, amongst other things, he considered ventilation, lead in glazes for pottery, children's rights, posture, fumes, diet, standing for long periods, pressure of the chest on the stomach, steam, great muscular effort, high temperature, common atmospheric impurity, dust and gaseous impurity of the atmosphere.

In the book Thackrah wrote, "No man of humanity can reflect without distress on the state of thousands of children, many from six to seven years of age, roused from their beds at an early hour, hurried to the mills and kept there with an interval of only forty minutes till a late hour at night - kept moreover in an atmosphere impure not only as the air of a town, not only as defective in ventilation, but as loaded also with noxious dust. Health! cleanliness! mental improvement! How are they regarded? Recreation is out of the question. There is scarcely time for meals. The very period of sleep, so necessary for the young, is too often abridged. Nay, children are sometimes worked even at night."

How bad must working conditions for children have been, if the **1833 Factory Act** improved the lot of children at work via the following?

No child workers under nine years of age

Employers must have a medical or age certificate for child workers

Children between the ages of 9-13 to work no more than nine hours a day

Children between 13-18 to work no more than 12 hours a day

Children are not to work at night

Two hours schooling each day for children

Four factory inspectors appointed to enforce the law throughout the whole of the country.

There was the *Report of the Factories' Inquiry Commission of 1833* which noted some of the conditions, which bordered on or were, perhaps worse than slavery – slaves had a value. Children as young as five worked shifts that often lasted 14 to 16 hours, discounting breaks, whilst others worked thirty to forty hours solid, a number of times a week, and were only allowed a couple of hours sleep. A Leeds doctor noted over 300 cases where the long working hours had led to distortion of the spine and a 'peculiar twisting of the ends of the lower part of the thigh bone.' For me, Thackrah's work is huge. How many lives were saved or lengthened as a result of it and how many people's working conditions improved?

Published on the properties of blood in 1819

Established private School of Anatomy in 1826

Co-founder and member of the Leeds School of Medicine in 1831

The Thackray Museum is Britain's premier museum for the history of medicine. Located in a grade II listed building (originally Leeds Union Workhouse) in the grounds of St James's Hospital, it's named after **Chas F. Thackray** (below) and has a collection of the firm's surgical instruments. It opened in 1997 and has a lot of interactive stuff and exhibits that will interest children such as a reproduction of Victorian Leeds with the sights and sounds of 1842. It's won Museum of the Year and my son's visiting with his school in a couple of weeks but it'll be too late to get his feedback....ooh, wait a minute he's been before.

I've checked and the conclusion was, 'it was kinda interesting....a bit,' which is high praise considering he was six and it was around eight months ago – equivalent to three years ago for an average adult. Don't forget, it displays the skeleton of **Mary Bateman**.

Chas F. Thackray Limited is a Leeds company that is now a subsidiary of DePuy Orthopaedics (Johnson and Johnson). It is best known for sponsoring the **Thackray Museum** (medical museum in Leeds) and through its partnership with **Sir John Charnley** the orthopaedic surgeon who pioneered hip replacement.

In 1902, Charles Frederick Thackray and H.S. Wainwright bought **Taylors Drug Co. Ltd** with plans to expand the business beyond pharmaceuticals and in 1905 bought a sterilizer for dressings, probably from **the Leeds and Bradford Boiler Company**. From 1918 they focussed on surgical equipment, including making surgical instruments for the legendary **Baron Moynihan of Leeds**. In 1934 Chas died and his two sons C. Noel and W.P. (Tod) took over the commercial and manufacturing operations. Their world and life changing work with Sir Charnley started in 1947 when they began developing and producing his instruments. In 1963, after work between Sir Charnley and Arthur Hallman, they produced the first low friction arthroplasty devices for hip replacements. Arthur Hallman was the head of development at Thackrays and an excellent instrument maker/craftsman who taught Sir Charnley about the production process and possibilities and worked with him on the practicalities and mechanics of the devices.

Sadly they didn't patent the invention – although a patent probably wouldn't have protected it in those days anyway – and it was copied around the world, Sir Charnley's interest being more about the progression of medicine than money. He was even happy to let other manufacturers put his name to their product. They were unable to compete on a world stage with companies using their innovations, although by 1990 they still had 50% of the UK market and still funded the research at Charnley's laboratory. In 1990 the company 'merged' with DePuy International (who had prospered from Sir Charnley's work) and were ultimately owned by Corange, parent company of Boehringer Mannheim/DePuy. DePuy International Ltd still has a number of sites in Leeds including its international headquarters. From the sale/merger sprung the Wetherby-based company **Kapitex** specialising in Laryngectomy, Tracheostomy and Airway Management, Dysphagia and Oral Motor Exercise. The company has many ex-Thackray managers and two of the directors carry the Thackray name. Another splinter seems to be **Seward Thackray** based in Gwent, 'one of Britain's principal surgical instrument companies.' There's a comprehensive book on the company, *Opposite The Infirmary: A history of the Thackray Company* (Medical Museum Publishing, 1997) by Penny Wainwright which I've only had chance to skim. I was drawn to her description of 'inventive instrument-maker' Arthur Hallam's (OBE) Second World War 007 work of fitting scissors, saws and wire-cutters into the heels of boots and secreting comapasses on buttons and flexible saws into coat collars for servicemen dropped behind enemy lines. I like a bit of intrigue me. See **Hip replacement** and **Taylors Drug Co. Ltd.**

John Philip **'Jake' Thackray** (1938–2002) was a singer-songwriter, poet and journalist who made over a thousand radio and TV appearances and seems to have come to a bit of a sad end. He's difficult to generalise about but live it's usually him with an acoustic guitar and minimum accompaniment (often just an upright bass) although his studio albums are orchestrated as the record company didn't think the audience would be able to handle just his voice and guitar. He's best known for his comic, satirical, wry, real life, often bawdy songs and was influenced primarily by Georges Brassens, Charles Trenet and Jacques Brel. I don't know the first two but although Jake is much lighter – and I'd argue more down-to-earth – I can certainly hear Brel in his stuff, in the colour and tone of the songs, the lyrical twists and graphic language. Having said this he sounds like himself, especially lyrically, and the Leeds accent and vernacular come through thick and strong. He in turn has influenced many people including, Jarvis Cocker, Mike Harding, Momus, Ralph McTell, Morrissey, Alex Turner (lead singer and songwriter of the Arctic Monkeys) and Nick Drake. Jarvis says 'Go and download Jake Thackray now — relive, or discover, *Lah-Di-Dah*. It's brilliant' and Mike Harding reckons 'there's more comedy and more humanity in one Jake Thackray song than the entire series of *Friends*.'

He was born in Leeds but I haven't been able to work out where, although I have read somewhere (that I can no longer find, so I won't mention it) that it was quite a 'rough' area and he certainly attended St. Michael's College. The French influence on his song writing came when he discovered the chansonnier tradition whilst teaching for a few years in France during the early 1960s after he'd graduated. Jake even had six months teaching in Algeria during the later stages of the war for independence (1961–62). He later commented 'I missed out on rock and all my influences were French.' Now, I can hear these influences but feel it's more a musical influence/tradition. His lyrics are wordy but concise, have a lovely pace and some ace rhymes, they are satirical, extremely clever with a very dry wit, but most importantly for me they cover 'real life'. He said of his songs, 'I think it is best to take the piss out of things and then when they are laughing, lob in a hand grenade.'

His first television appearance was on **The Good Old Days** from the **City Varieties** (Leeds) in 1966 and he made regular appearances on the regional *Northcountryman* programme. He became best known through his performances on *The Beryl Reid Show*, *The Frost Report*, *On the Braden Beat* (13 slots) and had a residency, every other week, on its successor show *That's Life* with Esther Rantzen (11 slots). He wasn't really into the fame and carried on teaching. He commented that on Monday morning 'the children were terrific. I'd walk into the class and they would say, "You were rubbish last night, sir."'

Thackray was most at home in small folk clubs, normal clubs, community halls or pubs and didn't like the larger theatres such as the London Palladium, the distance between him and the audience or the idea that people had paid a lot of money to see him. He was apparently modest, shy and self deprecating (see Leedsness) and didn't like being 'a performing dick', – that he thought came with the success – although at smaller venues he could usually be found at the bar chatting away with the punters, at larger venues he often didn't want to go on. Spencer Leigh in *The Independent* obituary (Saturday, 28 December 2002) notes this during a concert at the Queen Elizabeth Hall, London, 1971, the place was rammed but Jake 'felt he had no right to entertain them. Norman Newell persuaded him to perform and the resulting album, *Live Performance!*, is his best.' He hated the pomposity of showbiz and self important 'luvvies', the falseness, and refused milking the audience at the end of gigs with the pretence of walking off and the crowd baying for an encore, preferring instead to tell them: "That was mi last song and I'm going to do three more". He commented on his new notoriety by saying 'People come to see me because I'm on the telly. They would go and see Michael Fish the weatherman if he went on tour.'

Jake had four studio albums released, five live and five compilations. In the late 1970s/early 1980s he was turned against by some for being old school and faced accusations of sexism (which is clearly ridiculous). Look up the most 'guilty' song *On Again, On Again* on YouTube and make your own mind up. During this time he supported himself by touring in Europe, North America and the Far East but he returned to TV in 1982 with **Jake Thackray and Songs**, a six-part series on BBC2 with featured guests. He retired from gigging during the 1990s and suffered from ill-health, drink and financial problems and was declared bankrupt in 2000; on Xmas eve 2002 he died of heart failure. In May 2002 a group of fans had formed the Jake Thackray Project with the intention of making more of his work available to the public.

Now I heard tell of somebody who actually worked at the same school as Jake. Excited by the idea of maybe getting some original insights and getting closer to the real Jake I went through a series of clandestine meetings to try to make contact with the source, one of them in a supermarket car park, late at night, incorporating a scarf obscuring the face, for another I suffered the blindfold. We negotiated confidentiality through third parties, ensured that any responsibility was mine and that I would protect the source. Starting to worry that I was getting out of my depth and that there was perhaps an Al-Qaeda connection, I finally secured the phone number. Imagine my surprise when my father in-law answered the phone but never mind, his insight was quite startling, 'No, you can't use this. Honestly Mick leave it, because it was Harry Patterson (a.k.a Jack Higgins) that I worked with, not Jake Thackray........although he was definitely a teacher.....used to work at Intake.'

I must admit to being ignorant of Jake's work before writing this and it's been a revelation, I'd urge you to check him out on YouTube. There was a documentary on him by satirist, producer, critic and prankster Victor Lewis-Smith called **Jake on the Box** which first aired in October 2006 and has been repeated numerous times on BBC2 and 4 so keep an eye out for it. I'll leave you with a bit of the blurb from the BBC2 airing: 'Exploring the life and work of Jake Thackray, the undervalued genius famous for his biting satire and understated irony. A rare example of a British singer-songwriter in the troubadour tradition, Thackray could be darkly vicious, but was also able to write haunting and romantic songs. His words and music have influenced a generation of musicians and writers.'

The **Thoresby Society** is a Leeds gem and the city's historical society named after its first recognised historian, Ralph Thoresby. It formed in 1889 and published its first work two years later. The Society thrives to this day, continuing to publish essential material about our fair city.

Thrift Stores were started in 1881 by Wright Popplewell and J. W. Jessop and by the 1960s there were 150 stores across Yorkshire.

Thurstons Bakers, based in Leeds was taken over by Greggs (Newcastle-based) in 1974 and rebranded as Greggs in 1999.

Sally Timms is a singer and songwriter. She's had a long involvement with **The Mekons** whom she joined in 1985. Five years earlier she recorded her first solo album, *Hangahar* (an experimental improvised film score), at the age of nineteen with Pete Shelley of the Buzzcocks. Prior to joining The Mekons she was in a band called the She Hees. She has released several other solo CDs. According to Bloodshot records biog page, 'Sally was born in Leeds, grew up in the Yorkshire dales, sang in the church choir and performed in poetry recitals as a child. In 1985 she joined the **Mekons** as a full-time member and has regretted it ever since. Unfortunately, the only way out of the Mekons is in a box, so she's still there.

 Known as one of the laziest women in show business, she frequently calls in favours from her more talented and successful friends so that she can dedicate more time to watching television and eating bananas. She has blonde hair, grey eyes, and appalling mood swings.'

J. R. R. Tolkien (1892–1973) took up a post as Reader in English Language at Leeds Uni in 1920, staying until 1925. He was made a professor whilst at Leeds and produced *A Middle English Vocabulary* and collaborated on a definitive edition of *Sir Gawain and the Green Knight*, both academic standard works for many decades. He's best known for *The Hobbit* and *The Lord of the Rings*. I've heard and read online that the **Parkinson Building** was the inspiration for the 'White Tower' and that **Armley Gaol** (which can apparently be seen from the Parkinson Building) was the inspiration for the 'Black Tower'. This may be true but I've found absolutely no evidence of it, not a sausage and suspect, very strongly, a myth. It's a long time since I've read it and certainly remember a black gate but I'm not sure there are a Black and White Tower in the book, although the films show them. There's also chatter that some of the landscape of *The Hobbit* is based on Meanwood Valley/Park but I've found no evidence. I'm not going to say it isn't true as I don't know and I love a myth.

Top of the Pops was an iconic television chart show, featuring the hits of the week, which ran for over 42 years. People throw around the term iconic but if ever a TV show was iconic *Top of the Pops* was and it ran for around 2, 200 shows. The programme's roots are set firmly in Leeds, the first and last show being opened and closed by Jimmy Savile. More than this, in 1963 **Barney Colehan** had the idea of mimicking Jimmy Savile's hit Radio Luxembourg show *Teen and Twenty Disc Club* and adapting it for TV. Barney went on to produce the pilot which later became *Top of the Pops*. The last song before the credits was always the chart No.1 of the day – a big deal at the time. An appearance on *TOTP* could make a band and most people mimed 'live' on the show leading to many historic performances. See **Barney Colehan** and **Jimmy Savile**

Top Trumps. As a kid we used to play Top Trumps on the bus on the way to school. A set of themed cards – cars for example – with the attributes printed on each card (speed, weight, cost etc.), the person with the highest amount winning, until someone takes all the cards. Originally produced by Dubreq in 1977 (taken over by Waddingtons in 1982) manufacturing continued until the early 1990s. The packs from this period are now collectible.

Torpedo. C. A. Parsons designed, developed and manufactured steam-powered torpedoes, while working at **Kitsons**, which, during the 1880s, he tested on **Roundhay Park**'s Waterloo Lake. They had a range of 200 to 300 yards and a speed of nearly 20 knots. **Greenwood & Batley** also produced torpedoes in Leeds, the Whitehead's self-propelling torpedo for the British Navy.

Trams. William Turton ran horse-drawn omnibuses in Leeds from 1866 and first introduced horse pulled trams during the early 1870s. On major routes, they gradually replaced the horse-drawn omnibuses as the tracks enabled two horses to pull carriages twice the size. The first steam-powered **Trams** were introduced in Leeds in the 1880s but damaged the lines and in 1891 Europe's first over-head electric, trolley system, public tramway opened between Roundhay and Sheepscar – although Blackpool had a conduit line running from 1885. The Leeds Corporation took over this system in 1894, spreading the service and reducing fares and by the early 20th Century trams ran from 4.30 in the morning until 12.30 the following morning. The low cost of fares and speed of the electric trams meant the city rapidly expanded along the lines and by 1914 (20 years later) the track had grown from 21 to 114 miles in length, at a cost of £1.5 million.

At the time of writing Leeds has been given the go ahead (government support and funding) to develop the first modern electric trolleybuses service in the UK, echoing 1891. It is a cheaper alternative to trams that run in many British cities and the government has agreed to provide £235m of the £254m costs. The **Yorkshire and Humberside** region has traditionally had much lower governmental investment in transport than the national average. In 2006 approximately one third the amount of money was spent per person than the amount spent per person in London.

Illuminated tramcars Describing a photo from 1911 Brett Harrison in *A Century of Leeds* says that 'this enterprising development by Leeds City Tramways Department, of illuminating tramcars, was an inspiration for other municipal departments throughout the country.' I've had a look around and found a much more basic, illuminated tram from 1904 in Sunderland (spookily on a postcard being sent to Leeds) but Leeds may have had them earlier; I'd be interested if anyone knows. These brightly coloured, illuminated tramcars must have looked amazing coming out of a dark night.

I found a postcard of an illuminated Leeds electric tram commissioned to mark the occasion of the royal visit to Leeds of King Edward VII and Queen Alexandra to open the new electrical engineering wing of Leeds University on 7th July 1908. The side is decorated with ribbons and flowers and Union Jacks and the postcard states that the tram had '3,000 electric lights' and that it 'requires 150 horse power to run it'. For the week after the visit the illuminated tram visited every part of the city.

In **transport** Leeds has provided a few notable moments:

The world's first horse-drawn railroad.

The world's first functioning, commercial locomotive.

The world's first rack and pinion railway.

The largest producer of locomotives in Britain, probably the world.

Railway engine design that powered much of British rail during the mid to late 20th Century.

Revolutionary corrugated flue systems that greatly increased the efficiency and speed of 19th Century shipping.

A marine steam engine that was copied to power American paddle steamers as used on the Mississippi.

At 127 miles (204 km) long the Leeds and Liverpool Canal is the longest single canal in England.

Britain's first Sunday excursion with a day out in Hull.

Europe's first overhead electrical tramcar, popular around the world to this day and for avoiding the electrocution of dopey pedestrians.

Britain's first train dining car, between Leeds and London, 1879

The first flying plane in Britain.

Britain's oldest, still functioning plane.

Britain's first ever scheduled passenger flight

The first permanent traffic lights in Britain – Park Row, 1928.

The M1 motorway, London to Leeds, was the first full-length, inter-urban motorway to be constructed in the UK.

Herbert Hall Turner (1861–1930) was a Leeds-born astronomer and seismologist who has a crater on the moon and an asteroid named after him. He's credited with the discovery of deep focus earthquakes, coining the word parsec. He was awarded the **Bruce Medal** (one of the highest honors in the field of astronomy) in 1927 for an outstanding lifetime contribution to astronomy as well as a galaxy load of academic awards.

J. M. W. Turner (1775–1851) was a hugely influential and still world renowned artist of the 18th and 19th Century, one of arts big guns. Some think of him as the first *Impressionist* and a precursor to the French artists like **Monet** who carefully studied his techniques. He had close and important links with Leeds completing over 150 paintings and umpteen sketches of the City and surrounding area. Leeds was one of the most important cities to Turner (second only to his home town of London) and for around 30 years he mapped its development.

He had two Leeds patrons, Edward Lascelles of Harewood House, who commissioned paintings of the stately home, and Walter Fawkes and his family of Farnley Hall outside Otley. Aged 22 he first visited Otley in 1797 and was so into the area that he returned throughout his life, at least once a year before Walter Fawkes' death in 1825, painting Leeds, the hall, the house and the Wharfe Valley. Can anyone who has travelled from Leeds to Otley truly say they haven't gazed across the valley and thought, 'that's stunning'? One of Turner's most famous works, *Snow*

Brougham Castle sketch, J. M. W. Turner (1775-1851), engraved by William Say. Made during a visit to the castle in 1809 it provided the starting point for a later watercolour.

Storm: Hannibal and His Army Crossing the Alps (back cover), was assumed to have been based on a visit he made to the Alps but the inspiration for the setting was in truth a thunderstorm over the valley he witnessed while staying at Farnley Hall.

The blurb to David Hill's book (Professor of the History of Art at the University of Leeds) on the subject says that the painting of Leeds from Beeston Hill was 'the first industrial cityscape by any nationally recognised artist, literally the prototype image of industry' – see back cover. Apparently Turner used to sit outside The Old Bridge Inn (formerly known as the Horse and Jockey and renamed the Bridge in 1847) at the side of Kirkstall Bridge. Examples of his work can be seen at Harewood House and Farnley Hall, the latter containing about two hundred of the artist's works. For a heck of a lot more info, knowledge, images of Turner's paintings and sketches check out **Turner and Leeds: Image of Industry** by David Hill (Jeremy Mills Publishing, 2009).

As a quick footnote to the valley, according to Martin Wainwright, between Otley and Wetherby it's 'fertilsed with gold' in the form of Nultramulch a product of withdrawn and mulched banknotes. My mate Leigh used to work in the Nat West 'bullion centre' on Geldard Road, where the sad banknotes used to be processed. Each of the big four banks used to have such a centre in Leeds but only two remain.

William Turton (1825–1900) was the person who first introduced **trams** to Leeds. He set up his corn and hay business in Leeds, aged 19, and soon expanded it to include coal and cattle feed. It was later that he expanded further into horse drawn omnibuses and then trams but not only in Leeds, he set up horse drawn trams across Northern England. In 2007 a Leeds Civic Trust plaque, was placed on Turton's Wharf and Warehouse (now known as The Chandlers) it says:

"WILLIAM TURTON: Corn and hay merchant here at Turton's Wharf and Warehouse rebuilt 1876. He pioneered horse drawn tramways across northern England. From 1866 he ran omnibuses in Leeds, becoming a founding director, then chairman, of Leeds Tramways Company 1872-1895. Councillor and Poor Law Guardian."

U

The Ukrainians grew out of a John Peel session by The Wedding Present. Their Ukrainian-descended guitarist Pete Solowka instigated a session for the band (with the help of Sinister Cleaner Len Liggins) which went down a storm. Peel repeated the session on a number of occasions and quickly invited them to do another, on which Roman Remeynes joined them. The Ukrainian Peel Sessions – Ukrainski vistupi v Johna Peela – went to number 22 in the British album charts in the spring of 1989 and sold almost 70,000.

Peter, Len and Roman went on to form The Ukrainians proper and in 1990, within months of the fall of the Berlin Wall, they went to Kiev (properly called Kyiv) in the still Soviet controlled Ukraine to film the first ever Anglo-Soviet Ukrainian pop video and the first to be produced entirely in the east for a western band. A self-written first album followed ('The Ukrainians') and the band made major bucks by recording the soundtrack for a 30-second TV advertisement for NIKE training shoes featuring Sergey Bubka, the Ukrainian world champion pole vaulter which was shown worldwide.

In 1993 they made their first tour of Ukraine as guests of Ukraine's Ministry Of Culture. The tour culminated in a performance in Kyiv's Independence (ex-Lenin) Square in front of over 50,000 people, at the internationally-televised event organised to celebrate the 2nd Anniversary of Ukraine's independence from the Soviet Union.

Umbilical cords, we've all had them – as has every one who's been to or even thought about Leeds.

The **University of Leeds** is referenced throughout this book and there's plenty of available info so I'm going to concentrate on **The Parkinson Building** which was named in honour of **Frank Parkinson** (1887–1946) who donated £200,000 to the building which was started in 1938. The landmark tower has been a defining feature of the University (appearing on the logo) since its opening in 1951. Frank was a major benefactor of the university, there is still a The Frank Parkinson Scholarship offered for post-graduate research. Frank 'Yorkshire's quietest millionaire' made his money in electrical engineering and was known for early electric lighting installations, such as light bulbs and electric motors, he built a factory in Guiseley and also took over Crompton Lighting, one of the oldest lighting companies in the world, in 1927. In 1968 his company was taken over by Hawker Siddeley one of the founding companies of British Aerospace. Following Frank's death a couple of trusts were set up in his name which still give money to worthy causes.

One of the things you need to know about The Parkinson Building is that the bells play the wrong tune...well they did, I don't know if it's been sorted. 'The Leeds Quarters' were commissioned and chime out every quarter hour but were/are incorrect, which I discovered when viewing artist **Dan Robinson**'s *A Building Speaks* at the University of Leeds, MA Fine Art exhibition in 2003. In the immortal words of Eric Morecombe they are 'playing all the right notes but not necessarily in the right order'. After checking the score, musician Dan states on *A Building Speaks* (see back cover) that 'all four phrases were wrong....The first quarters started five notes too early and then went over for five notes too long. The second quarter did not chime at all. The third quarter started five notes too early. The hour chime started six notes too early. I wonder if it matters?'

A quick word about Leeds artist Dan Robinson, to mask the fact that I haven't included enough contemporary Leeds artists. He taught at Leeds Uni for a while and now teaches BA (Hons) Art & Design Interdisciplinary at Leeds College of Art & Design whilst also completing his PhD. I always find it difficult summing up artists so I'll let the web do it; 'His projects involve dialogues with specific sites and contexts. He makes photographs, drawings, texts, websites, events and installations. Longer-term work includes education projects, semi-fictional organisations and the ongoing renovation of a Cumbrian farm: these projects develop collaborative spaces for creative and critical thinking.' He's also got a recent commission to do a similar thing at a farmhouse in France. Exhibitions include Lucy Mackintosh gallery, Lausanne; Castlefield Gallery, Manchester and at Rennes Biennial. PM Gallery, Zagreb; Rosamund Felson Gallery, Los Angeles; the 51st Venice Biennale; Liverpool Biennial and Leeds City Art Gallery.

V

Frankie Vaughan (1928–1999). 'Mr Moonlight' attended the **Leeds College of Art** and sang 'Abide With Me' at the **1973 FA Cup Final** between Leeds and some other team – I remember one of my older brothers setting off to Wembley knowing that Leeds were going to win. He had eight top ten hits and a couple of number ones in the 1950s and 60s – Frankie Vaughan that is, not my older brother, he can't sing for toffee. I'm a bit confused about where he grew up (Frankie Vaughan, not my older brother); Wiki seems to describe a Lancashire upbringing and yet Gilleghan says he was 'raised in Leeds starting his professional career at Leeds City Varieties.' I don't mind ambiguity; I can live with it, if you really want to know buy *The Frankie Vaughan Story* by Frankie Vaughan for £60 on amazon. Anyway he had a great career, had hits on both sides of the Atlantic and made a couple of films including the 1960, *Let's Make Love* starring alongside **Marilyn Monroe**. He's also fondly remembered in Easterhouse, Glasgow where in the 1960s he did youth work to deal with gang culture.

The **Vending machine.** Leeds looks to have been one of the first places in the world to use vending machines and is the first place in the world to have coin operated ticket dispensing machines (*The Shell Book of Firsts*, Patrick Robertson). A patent published in 1885 (without the application date) filed by **James W. Longley** was for a machine for 'improvements in the Means or Apparatus for Checking Tickets Disposed of at Theatres, Concert Halls' with a diagram of how the machine worked – a machine that was widely used.

   The history of vending machines isn't very clear, and after one case from ancient Greece the next appears to be 'in the early 1880s' to dispense postcards – but I can't find specifics. The first US example was for chewing gum in 1888 so Longley was certainly before that. Longley was a skilled mechanic who helped Louis Le Prince produce cameras and projectors for the world's first moving pictures but Longley adapted the technology to produce this extremely early example of a vending machine. His machine was for the automatic delivery of tickets for trams, theatres, concert halls, and similar places utilising aspects of Louis' design with tickets rather than photographic plates pushed forward and then dropped into a spout for collection. References to Longley and his work are sparse but Raymond Fielding in *Technological History of Motion Pictures and Television* (University of California Press, 1968) says James, 'made his first machines to deliver tickets automatically with coin freeing mechanisms. They were used at the Leamington athletic ground, Leeds.' This machine was installed in 1886 but I'd like to be sure of when his first vending machines were installed and if this was it – it's always possible that he didn't wait for the patent to come through before flogging them – so if anyone knows, please email me. **See Louis Aime Augustin Le Prince.**

Ventura developed in 1968 out of Hepworth's (see Next) desire to offer their customers credit and, fittingly, their HQ is still at Hepworth House on Claypit Lane. Their website now describes themselves as 'one of the UK's largest customer management outsourcing companies....trusted to manage over 80 million customer contacts each year for 28 clients from the private and public sector through our contact centres. Having gone by the name the company is still register as, Club 24 Limited since 1977, they were providing credit for over 3,000 high street shops by 1984.

In 1988 they formed a joint company with the Kingfisher Group called Time Retail Finance and in 1991 they started to develop their 'Customer Service Management'. Again from their website, their 'contact centre (provides) outsourcing services to 28 blue chip and government organisations....We work across a broad range of sectors including Public Sector & Charities, Telcos, Technology & Media, Financial Services, Utilities, Retail and Automotive & Travel.' Y'see, Leeds even pioneered modern credit and call-centres.

Vesta Victoria (1873–1951) was a music hall comedienne and singer whose comic laments delivered in deadpan style were weirdly done in a cockney accent even though she was Leeds born and bred. She had her first big hit in 1892 with *Daddy Wouldn't Buy Me a Bow Wow* and became just as popular in the US as she was in Britain, touring the US in 1907 as one of the most highly paid vaudeville stars. She retired after World War I but returned in the 1930s to appear in a Royal Variety Show and to do three more films to add to the two she'd done around the turn of the century.

On 18th May, 2010 **The Victoria Quarter** claimed to be the first shopping centre in the UK to launch an **iPhone application** to promote itself. Once downloaded the centre manager John Bade claimed it to be the quickest way to communicate with its customers and that customers would get instant updates on offers and events.

Vue cinema out competing local cinemas all over the country and creating an Americanised experience of cinema. I prefer **The Hyde Park** and **Cottage Road** and would urge you to use them as often as you can, they are beautiful old cinemas and Leeds is a better place for them.

Carol Vorderman MBE (born 1960) Media personality and mathematician Carol lived in Leeds with her mum, found her first job in the city and in her spare time was briefly a backing singer in Leeds-based pop group Dawn Chorus and the Blue Tits, fronted by radio DJ Liz Kershaw. She came to fame after getting the job on **Countdown** (that her mum applied for on her behalf) and gradually became central to the programme. According to Carol on The Richard Bacon Show (R5L, 20.9.10) the programme sat in the top five places of Channel 4's ratings 'week in, week out....for over a decade.' This success led her to becoming one of the highest-paid women in Britain, earning over £1m a year. She had 26 continuous years with the show until in 2008 her contract offer included a 90% pay cut that she interpreted as a P45 and left Countdown. I'm sure I once heard Carol say that there were more individual Stock Exchange transactions in Leeds than London but I could be wrong....ooh could you ask for me and let me know? Ta.

The Leeds Social Realists: From muck to fantasy.

*(Being aware of Martin Wainwright's point that all is not dark and gritty in Leeds (the north), with his example of Lettice Cooper, and that **writers** can fall into cliché, I thought it best to completely ignore his perspective and hope no-one notices. They won't notice it y'know, people are daft like that.)*

Almost 50 years ago, at the Old Bailey, a jury was left to decide whether a book, previously banned from publication for over 30 years, was suitable to be read by the general population. Along with the graphic sex scenes, one of the main reasons for the books 30 year ban was the frequent use of the 'f' word and its derivatives. The 'star witness' in *The Lady Chatterley* trial, sociologist and academic **Richard Hoggart**, was born and bred in Leeds, he came from a working class background and was educated to degree standard in the city. During the trial he pointed out that, on the way to court, he'd heard the 'F word' used three times on a building site and that it was common parlance, also arguing that the book should be available to 'ordinary people'. The winning of this famous case brought increased freedom of expression to the UK publishing industry.

Leeds has a deep and, to my knowledge, much ignored literary history – hands up who heard of **Isabella Ford**'s novels, steeped in social realism and 'ordinary' people, *Miss Blake of Monkshalton* (1890), *On the Threshold* (1895) or *Mr Elliott* (1901). Writers from the city have provided some telling contributions to the freedom of authors and broadcasters to express themselves however they choose in pursuit of the 'authentic', of the 'real'. In modern Leeds writing there's a rich seam of gritty, working class life chronicled, and often defended, as the authors map out worlds of survival, drugs, crime, underclass's, battles with the police and 'the authorities', it's often laced with a blunt, brutal colloquial humour and the fierce resilience of ordinary people. This interest in real, gritty crime has deep roots; while researching this piece I discovered *Murder Ballads of Old Leeds*, a self published pamphlet from 1923, produced by **Miss Olive O'Grady-Burt**. In the introduction Olive states, 'I suppose my interest in murder ballads was first awakened in my infancy & on my mother's knee.' In opposition to this bleak cityscape is the more gentle, often positive and playful Leeds outlook, captured by writers such as **Alan Bennett** and **Keith Waterhouse** whose characters are nonetheless 'real'.

To give an example of the extent of Leeds writing, I was invited to attend a book day at a West Leeds arts event and to provide a comic, mock literary photo of myself. I captioned the photo 'Mick McCann, Armley's Sixth Most Successful Author'. People laughed, which pleased me, but I was only partially joking. Armley is an 'inner city' area of Leeds but on taking and collecting my son to his primary school we daily pass through gates that both **Barbara Taylor Bradford** (last count, 81 million books sold) and Alan Bennett passed through. **Peter Robinson**, who regularly lurks in the top sellers lists with his Inspector Banks novels, is also from Armley. I've discussed the idea of this article a couple of times with **Boff Whalley**, an Armley resident and playwright who, a few years ago, had his autobiographical novel *Footnote* published, including tales of his life in Chumbawamba and squatting in Armley. Now I'm a better writer than that lot, obviously, but I reckon they may have shifted more units.

Alan Bennett has, at times, nailed a sometimes gentle but still blunt humour, also found in *Billy Liar* by Keith Waterhouse, that Boff, as an outsider, thinks pumps through the cities heart. Boff (from Lancashire originally but transplanted to Leeds in 1982) believes that 'there *is* a unique character to Leeds writing; a grim and sullen bluntness coupled with a down-to-earth, no-frills sense of humour. If there's a wry smile to be got out of tragedy, then Leeds is the place.' Boff also suggests that what sometimes seems to be missing (and which becomes a trait of Leeds writers) is a sense of hope, of optimism. 'Strange that so many Leeds writers end up living in London but that their own protagonists and heroes are noted for being unambitious, homely and 'local'. ' Boff touches on something that is very hard to define here, which I recognise, I'm not sure it's a lack of optimism but there's certainly an attitude of 'keeping your feet on the ground' of 'not getting ideas above your station' amongst the people of the city which, as much as anything, is a celebration, an affirmation of the ordinary.

There's a much darker, grittier side that has fascinated many more writers. When the poem *V* by Leeds poet and playwright **Tony Harrison** was due to be aired by Channel 4 in 1987 there was press outrage at, in the words of the poem, 'a repertoire of blunt four-letter curses' including repeated use of the 'C word'. A group of Tory MPs also put forward a Commons Early Day Motion in response, entitled *Television Obscenity,* to try to stop the broadcast, the poem was aired and the boundaries stretched.

Tony Harrison is concerned with something that also permeates many Leeds writers, capturing and protecting an 'authentic' Leeds voice and character. In *Them & [uz]* he studies the hegemony of working class artists by the 'establishment' which is also connected to his experience as a working class lad attending Leeds Grammar School, where his Leeds accent would be fought over. He believed his accent to be as, if not more credible and worthy than Received Pronunciation and fiercely defended it. Harrison has battled lifelong to establish the legitimacy of working class/ordinary people and their expression, pointing out that people like Keats and Wordsworth were ordinary people with pronounced, regional accents.

It's not just Peter Robinson, and his Inspector Banks novels, there's a preoccupation with many modern Leeds writers with authority, law, crime and the interaction between 'under classes' and the police leading to a gritty 'real life' drama. **David Peace**, from Ossett, 10 miles outside Leeds – also the former stomping ground of Stan Barstow, author of *A Kind of Loving* – plumbed these themes in his hugely successful Red Riding Quartet, dramatised by Channel 4. **Kester Aspden**'s critically acclaimed novel *Nationality: Wog - The Hounding of David Oluwale* documented the late 60s murder of David by two Leeds police officers, preceded by his brutalisation at the hands of the police and the authorities. My last, flopped novel, *Nailed - Digital Stalking,* had as its starting point the real life arrest of myself and partner by Leeds CID due to a SIM card given away on a message board five years earlier and is a dirty, gritty thriller with suspect police, an unpleasant protagonist and immersed in the nature of Leeds.

Bernard Hare's hit novel *Urban Grimshaw and the Shed Crew* chronicles the real life experiences of a gang of young (many not even in their teenage years) children who are so far outside society that to describe them as marginalised is to underplay their abandonment. It's a tale of exclusion, car TWOCing, drugs, nonces, battles with the police and the authorities as the children simply try to survive and, maybe, one day escape their awful circumstances. In *A Fair*

Cop, **Michael Bunting** comes at the topic from a different angle, with the true tale of a police officer wrongly imprisoned. **John Lake**'s novel *Hot Knife* follows a group of Leeds ne'er do wells in drug debt visiting petrol stations and post offices with a gun, culminating in gangland killings, it drips with authentic colloquial Leeds colour and diction.

What Bennett and Waterhouse often share with the more modern, 'urban' Leeds writers is the sense that this place is our whole world, that trying to escape it is useless – Billy Liar, for all his ambition, doesn't get on the train. Leeds United fans will attest to this sense of chip-on-the-shoulder 'digging in', a fierce loyalty to the team/city, that can't help but come out. Although some Leeds writers leave, they return often through their writing.

Billy Liar, by the late Keith Waterhouse, is a seminal work to many Northern people of a certain age, ingraining a certain attitude and playful, trapped, bitter sweet, fantasist comedy in their psyche whilst nailing, for some, the crucial attribute of bullshitting (the film also contained one of the first times the word 'pissed' was heard on screen and said by a woman). Morrissey, for example, was heavily influenced by the novel, using many lines from it, see The Smiths song 'William, It Was Really Nothing'. Consciously and sub-consciously, the attributes of *Billy Liar* certainly influenced my first book, *Coming Out as A Bowie Fan In Leeds, Yorkshire, England.* Alan Bennett has also recorded this gentle but still blunt, tell it how it is, Leeds humour, which rears up unexpectedly into poignancy or tragedy. From his acclaimed *Talking Heads* to the more recent *A Life Like Other People's*, *Untold Stories* and production of his early '80s play *Enjoy,* much of Bennett's work is submerged in the characters, wit and insights of Leeds.

Keith Waterhouse went on to collaborate with his childhood friend **Willis Hall**, another Leeds writer who drew inspiration from his working class, Leeds roots. Together they wrote many stage and screen plays, from *Worzel Gummidge* to the seminal 60s, study of northern life, *A Kind of Loving,* from the popular 70s ITV series *Budgie* to the, children finding Jesus in a barn, film *Whistle Down the Wind.* While I'm discussing film and TV material I mustn't forget one of my favourite Leeds dramatists, **Kay Mellor** and her passion for the city and its people, 'I am Leeds born and bred, and the city, both architecturally and socially, feeds my creativity.' Her output stinks of the 'authentic' and of ordinary Leeds/Bradford folk through popular television drama serials, including *Band of Gold, Fat Friends, Strictly Confidential* etc. she straddles the space between the dark and gritty, Peace, Hare etc. and the gentler Bennett, Waterhouse etc. Returning to Willis Hall, he also wrote radio plays, musical and straight theatre, nonfiction (with people like Bob Monkhouse and Michael Parkinson) and a successful series of children's *Vampire* books, following in the footsteps of famous Leeds children's author Arthur Mitchell Ransome and his classic *Swallows and Amazons* series, written 50 years earlier.

Childhood and adolescence, unsurprisingly, is another theme that travels across many of the Leeds writers and a sense of losing/preserving something. Like Tony Harrison's work scattered with memories of his working-class childhood, **Barry Tebb**, author and poet, repeatedly tried to capture childhood and its 1940s Leeds backdrop in novels such as *Margaret* and *Pitfall Street* and throughout his extensive poetry. Leeds-born dramatist (and currently head writer for TV's 'Casualty') **Mark Catley** once remarked that he bases almost everything he writes on his childhood years growing up in Beeston, since that time was so ripe with both stories and characters. Bennett's *A Life Like Other People's* and *Untold Stories* chronicling the sensitive, awkward, loner child and adolescent in 1940s and early '50s Leeds. Keith Waterhouse painting his '30s/40s childhood and early life through his novels *There is a Happy Land* and *City Lights:*

A Street Life. In my first book (COAABFILYE) 1960s childhood is considered while I also try to pin down and dissect the freedom of 70s childhood/adolescence. My experience of an expansive, easy, loving childhood was in stark contrast to the 1990s, excluded childhoods cut brutally short or murdered in Hare's *Urban Grimshaw and the Shed Crew.*

As Bennett had done with *Beyond the Fringe* and the BBC television comedy sketch series *On the Margin,* Waterhouse and Hall also collaborated on and made a crucial contribution to British satire with programmes such as *That Was The Week That Was, BBC-3* (where Kenneth Tynan uttered the 'F word' for the first time on British television) and *The Frost Report.* Leeds people aren't renowned for their comic nature in a way that, say Liverpudlians are, but humour pulses through the city and its famous writing, comedic sons include **Barry Cryer** (also *The Frost Report*) whose writing credits are for a who's who of British (and American – Jack Benny, Bob Hope, Richard Pryor) comedy from Dave Allen and Tommy Cooper through to *The Two Ronnies* and *Morecambe and Wise.* **Ernie Wise** is another son of Leeds along with **Vic Reeves**, **Jeremy Dyson** of *The League of Gentlemen*, **Julian Barratt** of *The Mighty Boosh*, **Leigh Francis** creator of *Bo' Selecta!,* Avid Merrion, and his pure Leeds character and humour of Keith Lemon.

Why does any of this matter? Well, it notes that there is a Leeds literary scene; it's just that we're too 'down to earth' to mention it, it's part of the fabric of Leeds not to blow its own trumpet. It helps to explain to me, and thousands like me, part of who I am. It's also an opportunity to doff my bipperty-bopperty hat at Leeds writers for keeping it real and in the process helping to shape the more realist, reflective and edgy strands of British literature, drama and comedy.

W

WACCOE – derived from the LUFC chant denying the result of the 1975 European Cup Final 'We are the champions, champions of Europe,' – is an internet forum for Leeds United fans and supposedly the second biggest football internet forum in the world.

Steven Waddington (born 1968) is a well known actor who you'll recognise if you saw him. He went to Lawns Park Primary School, Farnley and Intake High School. He's currently playing Adam Fleet in *Waterloo Road* and has had major roles in *Robin Hood* (Beeb 1), *The Tudors* (Beeb 2), Garrow's Law (Beeb 1), the ITV drama *Vital Signs* and lead roles in the films *The Last of the Mohicans, Ivanhoe, The Parole Officer, Frost Giant* etc.

Waddingtons. Spreading fun throughout the world from their Leeds headquarters and factory, the company was a leading producer of playing cards, cards and board games during the period 1922-1995. Set up around 1896 on Wade Lane (with another factory on Great Wilson Street in 1902) by Mr John Waddington and Wilson Barratt as Waddingtons Ltd. the company was renamed John Waddington Ltd in 1905. Initially established as a small, family, printing business getting most of its work from theatre, by 1923 it was a nationally renowned company. The adoption of playing card production was what catapulted the firm to another level starting in 1921, the same year that the company became a plc.

I've done separate entries for their top, iconic games such as Cluedo, Monopoly and Subbuteo but, being a bit sad and finding my anorak for the first time in my life, I've counted and cross checked lists and found a total of **152 board games** produced by the company – I'm positive that's not extensive. Many of the board games were linked to TV shows and they also produced many different types of games, card games, Painting by Numbers sets and went on to make early 'electronic' games.

Over the years Waddingtons diversified – with several factories including one in Tunbridge Wells and another at Washington (Tyne & Wear) – and along with games and cards specialised in particular areas of printing: packaging (cartons, light bulb boxes), stationery, advertising, greetings cards, plastics, security printing, postage stamps and Green Shield Stamps. The company was bought by Hasbro in 1994. See **Cluedo**, **Monopoly**, **Playing Cards**, **Printing**, **Subbuteo** and **Green Shield Stamps.**

Martin Wainwright is the Leeds born northern editor of the **Guardian** and has been for yonks *waits to see if he gets a response to give the date*.....thanks Martin, since 1995 and lives in Leeds. Just as a gauge to his output, he has written over 900 hundred articles since the middle of 2007, the same period as he was writing his excellent book ***True North***. Now people are slightly disparaging about this book on Amazon but whilst I was skimming it I kept getting sucked into reading it – the selfish get....making it interesting. Yes, there are a couple of errors but in such a wide ranging project there are bound to be and in the big scheme of things they are minor things that don't alter his central points. I know that in this book there will be errors and I have spent ridiculous amounts of time checking and double checking the smallest things. He's written quite a few books (nine or ten or eleven or twelve) and **True North** is an extremely ambitious, insightful and courageous piece of work.

George Walker (1781–1856), an artist who started his career with local, rural landscapes, was born at Killingbeck Hall, Seacroft. When, in 1814, he was commissioned to carry out a series of 40 pictures for the book *The Costume of Yorkshire,* (Robinson and Son, Leeds, 1814) and included one called *The Collier* (sometimes called *Middleton Railway*) which shows **Salamanca** travelling from **Middleton Colliery** to Leeds. This was the first ever painting

The Collier by George Walker

of a locomotive. His work is sometimes credited to the engraver who worked on the book, Robert Havell the Elder, who I suppose 'created' the prints. Search him online and you'll see examples of his work. After much travelling, he returned to Killingbeck where he died in 1856.

Wallace Arnold was one of largest tour operators in the country. Based and founded in Leeds during 1912, it was named after the men who started the company, Wallace Cunningham and Arnold Crowe. In time, the company operated nationwide and was one of the first to develop the classic British coach tour and seaside break. From small beginnings, its business model proved highly successful until over 200 Wallace Arnold coaches could be seen at bus and coach stations up and down the length of the country. In 2005 Wallace Arnold merged with Shearings to become WA Shearings and two years later the Wallace Arnold name was dropped and the company is now known as Shearings Holidays. Quite sad really, I used to see WA coaches all the time on the motorway and travelled on them quite a few times. See Roger Davies, *Wallace Arnold (Glory Days),* Ian Allan Ltd, Hinckley, 2007.

Kimberley Walsh (born 1981) of **Girls Aloud**, from Bradford, went to **Leeds Trinity University College** in **Horsforth.** In 2006 she publicly apologised after being caught on camera smoking a spliff, commenting that it hardly makes her Pete Doherty. In 2009 she climbed **Mount Kilimanjaro** with Chris Moyles, Gary Barlow et al for Comic Relief. Kimberley won the Yorkshire woman of the year award 2009 due to her professional success and her role as celebrity ambassador for the **Breast Cancer Haven** charity with its Leeds branch. She now also presents TV programmes for SKY 1.

Sayeeda Hussain Warsi, Baroness Warsi, was the first Muslim woman to be selected by the Conservatives and the first ever female Muslim minister when she was named Minister Without

Portfolio on 13th May, 2010. She was made a life peer in 2007 and was named **Baroness Warsi of Dewsbury** where she was born, a few miles from Leeds) and attended the University of Leeds where she read Law.

Keith Waterhouse CBE (1929–2009) was a novelist, writer of television series, TV and feature film screenplays and a newspaper columnist. He's probably best known as a columnist, author of *Billy Liar* and his ability to drink huge amounts without falling over. I can't cover him properly here – no doubt someone will do a book – but a word I'd pick out to describe him would be prolific, he wrote shed loads and in different genres. He liked plain, clear language (so I would've done his head in) and in 2004 was voted Britain's most admired contemporary columnist by the British Journalism Review, which is well impressive. He's scattered through this book so I won't rattle on too much about him.

  Billy Liar is stuffed full of moments which straddle the space between comedy and pathos that Boff refers to in the Leeds Social Realists bit and in 2004 the magazine *Total Film* ranked it twelfth in their list of the greatest British films of all time. Have a look on Internet Movie Database where there's a list of 43 films and TV things he wrote (or co-wrote) with many of them having multiple episodes such as *Worzel Gummidge*, 29 episodes in two years for example. You can't easily sum up his years as a columnist and I've not read all his work but his style was pithy, musey, and opinionated, with a bit of a trad Labour, civic pride, cynical take on modern life and decline in manners outlook. See 'essay' on **Leeds Social Realists/writers.**

Dame Fanny Waterman, **DBE** (1 up from a **CBE**, 2 up from **OBE**, 3 up from **MBE**), was born in 1920 and, according to *The Guardian*, is 'the most legendary piano teacher in the world'. She jointly founded the **Leeds International Pianoforte Competition** in 1961. Her Russian, Jewish father emigrated to Britain/Leeds, I'm guessing, to escape the pogroms (large-scale, targeted, and repeated anti-Semitic rioting) which were comparatively common in Russia. For example, in the anti-Jewish riots that accompanied the Russian Civil War (1917–1921) an estimated 70,000 to 250,000 civilian Jews were killed.

  She had a brief but promising career as a concert pianist which was stopped by World War II and children. She taught at Allerton High School and gave private lessons, her piano pupils all started getting distinctions and she developed a reputation. She developed five prodigies who all started to play concertos with renowned conductors, (Carlo Maria Giulini, Sir Charles Groves, Sir John Pritchard, Sir Malcolm Sargent, Sir John Barbirolli, Harry Blech) and all received national acclaim. With it being pure chance that five child prodigies simultaneously emerged from a large northern cityat the same time, all taught by the same teacher, Fanny lost her star pupils as, one by one, their parents moved them to 'more experienced' teachers. This enraged Fanny who was determined to show that Leeds could be a centre of excellence so she decided to start an international piano competition based in Leeds. She was further annoyed and motivated by the opinion that international piano competitions could only be based in capital cities. I love regional stubbornness. With **Marion Thorpe** she set up the **Leeds International Pianoforte Competition** at the **Queens Hall** to encourage young players and the rest is history.

  Co-authored with Marion Thorpe (then Harewood), Fanny's piano tutor series *Me and my piano* passed two million sales in 2009 and is the standard piano textbook around the world. Her *Piano Lessons Book 1* was one of the first modern piano tutoring books and started Faber

Music's educational list. In the 1980s her series of ten piano master-class programmes entitled *Fanny Waterman's Piano Progress* was screened on **Channel 4**.

She's a busy woman who travels the world giving 'master classes', sits on the jury at a number of international competitions, is President of the Harrogate and Dublin festivals, and still Chairman and Artistic Director of The Leeds. She's got a soundboard covered in awards, her most prized being the **Freedom of the City of Leeds** – directly following Nelson Mandela's award in 2001. So when you're caught up in a Leeds City Centre snarl up, chill out, it's just Fanny shooing her sheep over Leeds Bridge.......and she's earnt the right.

The Western Cinema used to be on Florence Street, I'm using this **cinema** as my mate Joe's father-in-law gave some first hand info but it's symbolic of the cinemas that used to be strewn across the city in the days before Vue and 'home entertainment' – Armley had at least five cinemas and eight were built in Hunslet between 1910 and 1914. Robert Preedy's book *Leeds Cinemas Remembered* notes that in 1939 Leeds had 68 picture halls. Joe's father-in-law went to **The Western** during the 1940s, it was nicknamed **The Bughutch** (as they often seemed to be, or **The Fleapit**), it cost tuppence to get in, this was known as the tuppeny rush. All the kids scrounged jam jars from the cupboard or from neighbours, a large 2lb jar or two 1lb jars got you entry which were apparently passed on to a jam factory on Florence Street. At the end of the feature they played '**God save the Queen**' and at this point everybody scarpered. The Western was refurbished and renamed the **Vogue Cinema** and reopened in 1954 until it was destroyed by fire around 1961.

If you search **Cinema Treasures** online, get to England, list them by location and flick through to Leeds, there's great info on some of our old cinemas, some of which is included below. The best places for stuff like cinemas, theatres, swimming pools, pubs etc. are the **Leodis** and **Secret Leeds** websites. I found an ace thread called *Leeds lost cinemas* on SL with reminiscences from the 30s and 40s onwards. I've lifted the cinemas and some of the insights such as arry awk's on **The Majestic**. I won't have all the cinemas here but there are a couple of books you could look out for, Robert Preedy's *Leeds Cinemas* (or the original *Leeds Cinemas Remembered*) and for more of the reminiscing *My Life in the Silver Screen* by Gerald Kaufman. It's interesting what a glamorous thing the cinema used to be with many, in the silent cinema days, having their own tuxedo wearing orchestras. The heyday of British cinema was in the 1940s when attendances peaked at 1,640 million a year, over ten times the number of visits today. These cinemas were often the iconic building and landmarks of the areas and a look on **Leodis** makes you wonder why the buildings were often demolished. I've always know going to the flicks as 'off to the pictures'. Here's a list of old Leeds cinemas.

Abby Picture House, Abby Road, Kirkstall. Opened 1913 and closed in 1960. Is now a centre for Leeds MIND.

ABC Leeds, Vicar Lane, opened as the **Ritz Cinema** in 1934 and re-named **ABC** from 25th May 1959, becoming a twin screen cinema in 1970 and by 1974 the cities first triple screen cinema. It closed on 17th February 2000 and was demolished in 2006.

Alhambra Picture Palace, 94 Low Road, Hunslet, opened in 1913 and closed in 1914 when the owners took over the **Pavilion** just over the road.

The Alexandra, Camp Road, Little London.

The Atlas, 249/251 Kirkstall Road, Burley, opened in 1912, was renamed **The Embassy** in 1935 and was apparently very plush. It closed to become a Woolworths store in 1956 and was later demolished.

Beech Hill Cinema/The Star, Beech Hill, Otley, opened in 1930, changed its name to the Star in1945, closed in 1968 before being taken over by bingo and demolished autumn 1999.

The Burley Picture House, sat between Wordsworth Street and Roberts Place, Burley, opened in 1913 closed in 1959. Again there's mention of (pre-1950s) paying for the Saturday matinee with two washed jam jars or an empty pop bottle.

Burras Lane Picture House/Picture House, Otley, opened 25th November 1912 closed in 1922 as the owners opened the **Picture House** (Kirkgate) but re-opened, re-named, the same year. Likely to have closed in 1931 due to road widening. I've also heard that it first closed because of the introduction of the 'talkies.' It had a corrugated iron roof and when it rained the audience couldn't hear the words.

The Capitol Cinema and Ballroom, Green Road, Meanwood demolished in 1980.

Carlton Cinema, Carlton Hill, Little London/Woodhouse, opened in 1920 and closed in 1963.

The Carr Croft Cinema, 43 Carr Crofts, Armley, opposite and down from the new sports centre, opened in a pre-existing building (Sunday School) during 1912, closed in 1931 and now used as a small clothing factory.

The Classic Cinema, basement of the **Queens Hotel** (under where the obelisque is), City Square, started life as the News Theatre in 1938 lasting until 1966 when it started three years as a regular cinema before going erotic as **the Tatler**. It closed in the 1980s.

The Clifton Cinema, 377 Stanningley Road, Bramley opened in 1939 and closed in 1961. Used to be where the tram route stopped, it was gutted by fire and demolished in 2001.

The Clock Cinema, 247-249 Roundhay Road, opened in 1938 with a spacious foyer, cafe and a small parade of shops. It closed on February 28, 1976 and is now an electronics store.

The Coliseum, Cookridge Street opened as a cinema in 1906. North British Animated Films screened films there from 1907 until 1938 when the company was taken over by Gaumont Ltd, with the name change to the Gaumont - Coliseum. It closed as a cinema in 1961.

The Headingley Picture House opened on 29th July 1912 and its name was changed to **Cottage Road Cinema** in the mid 1950s. The building began life as a stable in 1835 and the cinema is certainly the oldest operating cinema in Leeds and thought to be the oldest in the UK, except that Brighton's Duke of York's Picture House and the Phoenix (East Finchley) – featuring a pair of Kershaw Kalee II arc film projectors made in Leeds – opened around two years earlier ....I should have just said one of the UK's oldest cinemas and you'd have been right impressed....soz. Mindst you, the first cinemas to open in Leeds were The Assembly Rooms (now part of the rehearsal rooms for Opera North) and The Picture House in Briggate (demolished), both opened in 1907, 3 years before them soft southern ones, with their weird records.

The Crescent Cinema, Dewsbury Road, Beeston Hill, opened in 1921 with the full title of the New Crescent Super Cinema and, apparently, had a 'first class orchestra' and a £3,000 organ. The cinema closed in1968 and is now a health club.

Crossgates Picture House, Station Road became **the Ritz** in 1938 and closed in 1965.

The Crown Cinema, 22 Tong Road, Wortley, built in 1916 – replacing the first Crown on Oldfield Lane which opened in 1911 – opened in 1919 closed on 21st September 1968 when it switched to bingo with **Elsie Tanner** (Pat Phoenix) again turning up to open it. Apparently there was quite a crowd and she arrived in a limousine, looking like a film star, in a sparkly dress, waving to the crowd. One five year old wondered that evening how she could be in Coronation Street and Armley at the same time.

The Electra, Craven Road, Woodhouse.

The Embassy Cinema, 281 to 285 Kirkstall Road, Burley was converted to a Woolworths.

The Gaiety Cinema, Roundhay Road opened in 1921.

The Gainsborough Picture House, Domestic Street, Holbeck was a conversion of the Unitarian Chapel carried out in 1931. The cinema closed in 1966 and converted into a warehouse which was demolished in 1981. In the early 1930s it had a brief time as a film studio producing mainly music hall sound-on-disc films.

The Gaumont (now the **O2 Academy**) opened in 1885 as a concert hall. It was converted into a theatre in 1895 and then into a cinema in 1905 (called **Coliseum Cinema**) – apparently an early date for such a large hall, 1746 seats. It closed in 1938 for a refurb, reopening as **The Gaumont,** until bingo took over in 1961. See **The Coliseum**.

The Gem built into one of the railway arches on Domestic Street. Old, old cinema.

The Glenroyal, New Road Side, Horsforth opened in 1937 and closed in 1964.

Greengates Picture House, Yeadon, looks like it's now **The Aviator** pub

The Haddon Hall Cinema, Bankfield Terrace, built in 1914 and closed in 1960, bingo, now warehousing.

The Hillcrest Picture Lounge, Harehills Lane opened in 1920 with a fine orchestra and a cafe, it closed in 1963 and has been demolished.

Hunslet Picture Hall, Hulland Street, opened in 1911 closed in 1918.

The Hyde Park Picture House, 73 Brudenell Road, opened on 7th November 1914, and has shown films ever since. It caters for the large student population and the films are often independent and some stuff you won't get at the multiplexes. It's a beautiful cinema, a Grade II Listed building, and has often been used in TV drama and film, **Kay Mellor**'s *Fat Friends* for example or more recently, *A Passionate Woman* broadcast in 2010 featured it heavily. The 1985, David Hare film *Wetherby* starring Vanessa Redgrave, Ian Holme, Judi Dench, Joely Richardson, Tom Wilkinson and Suzanna Hamilton featured the **Hyde Park**. **Munki**'s excellent thread on **Secret Leeds** unearthed the fact that in August 1928 the cinema began use as a church as Wrangthorn Church/St Augustine of Hippo (just off Hyde Park Corner) was being decorated, so the vicar and congregation held their services there. It apparently has a large gay and lesbian following which is central to the annual Leeds Film Festival. I'd say use it don't lose it and have been twice in the last six months.

The Imperial, Town Street, Horsforth (**The Tin Tabernacle**) demolished in the early 1920s when a permanent building was built.

The Imperial Picture House, 79 Kirkstall Road, opened on 1st September 1913, due to the war it closed on the 22nd of May 1940 and never re-opened.

The Kings, Holbeck Lane/Springwell Street, became Maenson House clothing factory, who look to still run a business on Meanwood Road.

King's Hall/The Kings, Station Road, Otley, opened 1911 closed as a cinema 30th April 1927 and went on to host various entertainments and is currently in industrial use.

Leasowe Picture Palace, 2 Leasowe Road, Hunslet, opened in 1910 and closed in 1917

Lido Cinema, Bramley Town Street, formerly the **Bramley Picture Palace** (until 1931), opened in 1912, closed 1961. There was an external staircase/ fire escape up to the projection room and the projectionists often let kids who couldn't afford to pay in to sneak a peek.

The Lounge Cinema, North Lane, Headingley opened in 1916 and closed in January 2005, like others, slaughtered by the multiplex.

The Lyceum Picture House at the junction with Thornville Road and Cardigan Road, Burley, was built in 1913 and known as 'the Loppy Lyo'. According to the boards in the early 1960s Brooke Bond tea did a promotion where, with an empty tea packet, you got free entry and the glamorous, fur coated, Coronation Street actress, Pat Phoenix (Elsie Tanner) came to either re-open it after renovation, or open it as a bingo hall, which happened in 1968. It was demolished and is now the site of the Spar petrol station.

The Lyric Cinema, Tong Road, Armley was opened in 1922 and finally shut in 1988. The boards reckon it's now used for lap dancing and a school for lap dancing.

The Majestic Picture Theatre, City Square, opened in1922 with its own Symphony Orchestra and a £5,000 organ. It closed in 1969, and has been a bingo hall and nightclub and was recently refused plans to turn it into a casino.

The Malvern 82 to 86 Beeston Road, opened on 23rd December 1912 and closed in 1971, demolished.

One of the lasses there was so inspired she went on to be a screenwriter and one ex-patron has a memory of the manager stopping the show to announce that JFK had been assassinated.

Newtown Picture Palace, Cross Stamford Street, Sheepscar, opened in January 1913 with a film accompanied by the Newtown Orchestra and closed in 1953.

The Paramount Theatre, the Headrow, first opened in 1932, with a £20,000 Wurlitzer that rose up 'out of the floor' during the interval. It had 1.2 million customers in its first year and was the last word in luxury. It was re-named **The Odeon** in April 1940 and **The Beatles** played there twice in 1963. It closed on 28th October 2001, the last picture palace in the city centre, gone.

The Odeon Merrion Centre Leeds is our shortest lived proper cinema and the first cinema built in Leeds since the 1930s, it opened in 1964 and closed in 1977

The Palace Picture Hall, Eyres Avenue, Armley opened on 26th August 1912, the building had originally been Armley Skating Rink, and closed in 1964. It was converted into an independent club which still operates as the **New Western Bingo Club**. The former dance hall/skating rink section became a squash club and bar and is now a gay sauna called the **Steam Complex Sauna**, which contains a licensed, 20 seat cinema. It describes itself as the North's largest, licensed, all male, gay and bisexual sauna.

The Parkfield Picture Palace, 60 Jack Lane, Hunslet opened 1914 and closed on August 3, 1946 when an engineering firm moved in.

The Pavilion Cinema, Stanningley Road, Stanningley opened in 1920 and closed in 1970 becoming a bingo hall. It has now been very sympathetically spruced up as a business centre, showing how beautiful these old cinemas could become, it looks ace.

Pavilion Picture Palace, 50 Low Road, Hunslet, opened 1913, closed in 1959 and a car dealer moved in carrying on the name the **Regal** which the cinema had adopted in 1930.

The Pavilion Cinema, corner of South Queen Street and High Street, Morley, was built as the **New Pavilion Theatre** in 1911 and originally put on variety shows, becoming mainly a cinema in 1915. The cinema closed in 1968 and became a bingo and social club; in 1990 it was turned into the nightclubs After Dark and Orbit which have now closed.

The People's Picture Palace, Meadow Road, Holbeck opened in 1915, became **The Palace** in 1932 and closed in 1961.

The Pictodrome, 12 Branch Church Street, Hunslet opened in 1912 and closed in1956 – also known as the Picturedrome.

The Picturedrome, (some insist it was called the Pictodrome) Wortley Road, Armley opened in 1913 closed in 1958, later demolished. **Alan Bennett**'s local and there's a funny section in his *Untold Stories* of actually meeting some of the stars (Lauren Bacall, Gene Tierney, Laraine Day) he'd last seen aged eight at the Picturedrome and being sometimes unable to stop himself from mentioning it.

The Picture House, Station Road, Crossgates opened on 5th August 1920, name changed to **Ritz Cinema** in 1938 and closed 1965, later demolished.

The Picture House on Harehills Corner opened in 1912, closed in 1963 and was demolished in 1968.

The Picture House, Kirkgate, Otley, opened in1922 and closed 1966, as Otley's last cinema. Has been demolished.

Plaza Cinema, Wellington Road, Wortley opened in 1930, and until the equipment for talkies was installed it had a symphony orchestra and soloists. The cinema was gutted by fire in 1937, but the outer shell remained and, ironically, the locals remember it being used as a fire station during the war. It was used for factory premises.

The Plaza Cinema, 32 New Briggate, opened as the **Assembly Rooms Concert Hall** in 1898 becoming a cinema in 1907 and changing the name to the 'Plaza' in 1958, closed in 1985. The Assembly Rooms were (2007) restored as part of the major Grand Theatre refurbishments.

The Princess Cinema (now Princess Fisheries), 84a Pontefract Lane, opened 1923, closed in 1965.

Premier Picture Palace, 37a South Accommodation Road, Hunslet, opened 1912, closed in 1952.

Queen's Hall Picture House, 4 Norfolk Street, Hunslet, opened 1910, closed in 1915.

The Rawdon Empire Cinema, known as the Temp as it was in the building of the Temperance Hall demolished 1964. There's a history of this cinema by David M. Ryder and Reg Wood available called *The Rise and Fall of Rawdon Empire; including Growing up in the Dark* (Cinemuseum Publications, 1995 – ASIN: B0014DMFS2). I don't know if those are also Bowie/Ronson references in the title but anyway, the book doesn't look to be widely available, no doubt Leeds Library will have copies.

Regal Super Cinema, 40 Crossgates Road, opened 1936 (taking just 27 weeks to build) and at the time had the largest cinema car park in the country, closed 1964, the building was later demolished.

The Regent Picture House, 3-15 Torre Road, Burmantofts, opened 1916 closed 29th May 1971 and the building is now a tile emporium.

Rex Cinema near Tommy Wass, Beeston, closed in 1976.

The Rialto Cinema, Briggate, (formerly the **Briggate Picture House**) opened in 1911 and the name was changed in 1927. The cinema was closed in 1939 and demolished. The site is the location of a Marks and Spencer store which although it didn't open until 1951 was completed in 1940 and used as an air-raid shelter.

Rothwell Empire Cinema opened in 1921 and closed in 1964. After years as a bingo hall it became a fish and chip shop in 2006

The Savoy Cinema, 72 Bradford Road, Stanningley opened 1937 closed 25 September 1965, demolished in November 2004.

The Scala Cinema, 12 Albion Place, 'Yorkshire's Wonder Cinema' was opened by the Lord Mayor of Leeds in 1922. It had a dancehall upstairs and closed in 1957, becoming a furniture showroom.

The Shaftesbury Cinema, (off York Rd) opened October 20th 1928 and closed on 25th June 1975, the auditorium was demolished in July 1980 leaving just the entrance. The cinema had a ballroom attached and was equipped for stage shows and is the cinema I went to most as a youth.

The Star Cinema, 5 Glenthorpe Crescent (off York Rd) opened 1938 closed November 1961. The Star Snooker Hall and Gym on York Road opposite the Irish Centre, Victoria Picture Hall. Opened 1912, closed 1937. The Star cinema was built on the same site.

The Strand Cinema, 122 Jack Lane, Hunslet, opened 1931 closed 1961, becoming Strand Bingo. Similar to collecting jam jars to go to the Western, **Secret Leeds** has tales of kids collecting old news papers and selling them to a waste paper merchant on Meadow Lane to raise the money to get in.

St. Patrick's Picture Palace, (New) York Road, Quarry Hill was a cinema in a church and ran from 1910 until 1924, only ever having an 'occasional' licence. It was 400 seats in the part of the building adjoining the church. A crucial bit of info is that in 1918 its telephone number was 5125. From the 1950s the same building was used by **St Patrick's Amateur Boxing Club** until in 2002 it was bought by **West Yorkshire Playhouse** who kicked them out to sell it to a local arts group, whilst WYP kept the church bit for storage. I can find no contemporary record of **St Patrick's** Amateur Boxing Club. Interesting that the 'arts' (I'd argue middleclass and exclusive) got funding when a club set up to help young, working class lads had to battle for 50 years without funding and was then closed by the surplus funding of 'the arts', who'd no doubt witter on about 'connecting with the community'. Us middle class tend to be better at politics don't we? Do y'know, it's really annoyed me has this.....anyone fancy starting a revolution? Having said all that, I've just realised that I've been to the 'arts space' I'm discussing and they've included a book of mine and related material in a exhibition/cultural exchange with a European city (I think Berlin) so we don't need to worry about it now....I'm part of the injustice and conspiracy.

The Tivoli Acre Road, Middleton, looks like it switched to bingo in 1961.

The Victoria, Peel Place; Victoria Hall in Burley-in-Wharfedale was used as a cinema. It was also known as the Drill Hall as it was used for training volunteer soldiers before World War I.

The Wellington Cinema, Wellington Road/Town end of Kirkstall Road.

The West End ('the Cosy'), north side of the viaduct, Burley, built in 1911 the cinema only lasted a year.

The Western (Pictureland) Branch Road, Armley, **Pictureland cinema** opened in 1910, was a converted Primitive Methodist Chapel, the name changing to **Western Talkie** in 1933, the **New Western** in 1957 and closing in 1960 – guess what? It was converted into a bingo hall. It now houses an amusement arcade, cafe and launderette.

Westgate Cinema, Westgate, Otley, demolished in 2005.

For more info on Leeds cinemas check out Robert Preedy's *Leeds Cinemas* (Tempus Publishing Ltd., 2005) or his original Leeds Cinemas Remembered (Netherwood Dalton & Co, 1980). Or, alternatively, there's *My Life in the Silver Screen* by Gerald Kaufman (Faber and Faber, 1985).

Boff Whalley (Born 1961) was a founding member, guitarist and vocalist of **Chumbawamba** and still plays in the band. He's also published an autobiography, ***Footnote**** (Pomona books, 2003), which charts his life, part interwoven with the history of Chumba and is about life and that. It's a good read with interesting reflections on life and a lovely, gentle, underplayed humour which left me thinking, 'Why's my humour so often a sledgehammer nailed to a hummingbird's wing? And why can't I build tension and fear through carefully constructed scenes but rather rely on hiding at the bottom of the stairs and jumping out on my seven-year-old screaming BOOOOO with a hideously distorted face?' He's also co-written (with Dom Grace) or written solo the following plays that have all been performed at places from **The West Yorkshire Playhouse** to **Armley Mills Museum**:

It's A Lovely Day Tomorrow. (With Dom)

Armley – The Musical. (For West Leeds Festival)

Play Up, Play Up. (For West Leeds Festival, with Dom)

Riot, Rebellion & Bloody Insurrection. (For Red ladder Theatre Company with Dom)

Sex & Docks & Rock 'n' Roll (Musical for Red Ladder Theatre Company)

The **Wharfedale Printing Machine** changed the face of printing during the latter half of the 19th Century. Little had developed in the world of printing since 1454 when Gutenberg printed his famous Bible on a wooden press in Germany and people around the world were looking for ways to modernise the printing press as a better educated public cried out for more periodicals and newspapers. The introduction of the cylinder and steam power at the beginning of the 19th Century provided major breakthroughs and it was in developing the cylinder and flatbed technology that 'the Otley machine set the pattern for printing machines...........for some time.' The Otley machine first emerged in 1859 and in the book just quoted (*Printing Presses: History and Development from the Fifteenth Century to Modern Times*, University of California Press, 1978) James Moran quotes an old timer comparing one of the originals he worked on to the more modern Wharfedales used in 1922.

The Wharfedale, as it became known, was invented by David Payne of Otley incorporating the innovation of a static cylinder and moveable type bed, giving a crisper impression and quickening the printing process. His most important advancement was the stop-cylinder principle creating a 'push back motion' which revolutionised productivity and quality, creating perfect register. It was the first machine to use the travelling bed which delivered the print without stopping the machine – the paper feeder could stay in constant motion. Payne worked as foreman for William Dawson, who started as a joiner and whose firm had built up a national reputation for manufacturing print equipment. They called this first machine '***Our Own Kind***' but did not take out a patent and with Otley and Leeds already having a vibrant printing press industry his design was widely copied and drew to/created more manufacturers in Otley and Leeds. Skilled men tended to leave Dawson's and in time many new firms employed people who had previously worked for him and making Otley a hive of production and innovation. By 1911 between two and three thousand men were engaged in building this type of press along the Wharfe and it was copied around the world.

Engineers from other firms (such as Samuel Bremner with inking) also made improvements and the machines became more sophisticated and diverse. Two to three thousand prints per hour were possible which, at the beginning of the 19th Century, would have taken two men a day and a half and they had a precision and sharpness that had previously only been thought possible through printing by hand. All these new machines were called all sorts of things by their manufacturers but they gradually came under the banner 'Wharfedales' and were all based on the 'Otley principle', as it was known, of the stop cylinder. It appears that Payne had been storing the idea for a while. In 1851, according to his son, he was shown a diagram of the Wharfedale stop-cylinder principle on the head board of a bed, which had always been kept carefully covered. The Wharfedale was used in all kinds of printing but it perfectly filled the demand for a machine to churn out high quality periodicals, magazines and newspapers at a fast rate and quenched the thirst for information of readers around the world. **Otley Museum** keeps an early example of a Wharfedale.

I should mention that James Moran's book on the history of the printing press reckons that Payne actually did patent his stop-cylinder in 1867 and that other aspects of the Wharfedale were copied first and a mad rush to incorporate the stop-cylinder by all other manufacturers happened as soon as his patent expired.

Lucy Watmough (born 1991) is a rock chick, classical soprano singer from Leeds who attended Prince Henry's Grammar School, in Otley. She seems to be going places and in 2010 performed at The Last Night of The Proms Concert at The Royal Hall, Harrogate. Keep an eye (or ear) out for her.

Marco Pierre White (born 1961) was the youngest, and first British-born, chef to win three Michelin stars....until he gave them back that is. He is classically trained – under Albert and Michel Roux – renowned for his contributions to contemporary international cuisine and noted as the first celebrity chef of the modern era. Wiki says White grew up in east Leeds but he attended Allerton High School (leaving without any qualifications) and certainly lived much of his young life in Cranmer Bank, Moortown, son of a Leeds chef and an Italian mother. In 1999, after becoming an internationally celebrated chef with many business interests, Marco retired from cooking saying, 'I was being judged by people who had less knowledge than me, so what was it truly worth? I gave Michelin inspectors too much respect, and I belittled myself. I had three options: I could be a prisoner of my world and continue to work six days a week, I could live a lie and charge high prices and not be behind the stove or I could give my stars back, spend time with my children and re-invent myself.' Many sources say that for a long period he 'never cooked again' but I'm sure he'll have got himself some toast at home. In 2007 he returned as a chef in *Hell's Kitchen* on ITV which, at time of writing, he still presents. He's trained many renowned chefs including TV celebs Gordon Ramsay (who he doesn't get on with) and Heston Blumenthal.

Tom Wilkinson OBE (born 1948) is a hugely successful actor that if you saw him you'd go, 'Oh, it's him, he's really good him.' Mainly doing US TV and film roles he's won an Emmy and a Golden Globe in the Best Supporting Actor category and he's quality. Search him online there'll be loads of stuff.

Ernest Wiseman better known as **Ernie Wise** OBE (1925–1999) was born in Bramley and grew up in East Ardsley (Morley). According to Graham McCann (*Morecambe & Wise*, 1999) he was half of the 'the most illustrious, and the best-loved, double act that Britain has ever produced.' Don't think anyone over a certain age would argue with that. Around half the UK population, 28 million viewers, watched the 1977 *Morecambe and Wise Christmas Show* – they were what the expression 'British institution' was penned for. If you don't know their stuff, keep an eye out for repeats or look them up on YouTube.

Penny Woolcock was born into the British community in (1950) Buenos Aires, Argentina and is a screenwriter, opera and film director who moved to England in 1970. Our main interest in her are the three gritty Leeds films she wrote and directed, *Tina Goes Shopping* (1999), *Tina Takes a Break* (2001) and *Mischief Night* (2006) set around several different areas of Leeds including Beeston, Tingley, Belle Isle and Middleton. The first two of the trilogy were Channel 4 films for TV, whereas *Mischief Night* was made for general release by the people who made *Shameless*. This is interesting as the trilogy is a more realistic, Leeds version of *Shameless;* although really, *Shameless* is a version of this trilogy as the first one was made 5 years before *Shameless* hit our screens.

Geoffrey Wooler (1911–2010) was a cutting edge heart surgeon who helped develop the heart-lung machine and was largely responsible for making Leeds a world centre in cardiac surgery. Geoffrey was born into money as his grandfather, a sanitary engineer in the 19th century, set up a business (that Geoffrey's father expanded) testing and servicing drains. Their horse-drawn carts, and later lorries and vans, could be seen around Leeds with the words 'We Test Drains' in huge letters on the sides. He was educated at Leeds Grammar School and after serving as a surgeon (mentioned in dispatches) during World War II he spent the rest of his working life in Leeds. He's largely ignored by 'popular culture' and hasn't an entry on Wiki, for example, who give over 4,000 words to Jordan. Mindst you I've done a bit of that in here so I should shut mi'gob.

Geoffrey was responsible for spotting the brilliance of **Marian Ion Ionescu** and attracted him to Leeds. He was also closely involved in the development of the 'heart-lung machines' which vastly improved the scope of open heart surgery and allow heart and/or lung transplants. Hammersmith Hospital, which used to send Geoffrey patients (with portal hypertension and varices) requiring particularly complex surgery, developed three prototype heart-lung machines. They kept one, sent one to Moscow to sweeten East-West relations and sent the last to Geoffrey and his team to tinker with and improve. These prototypes, funded by the Nuffield Foundation, were already a vast improvement on the technology that had first been successfully used, the previous year, in Philadelphia. In 1958 the BBC screened *Your Life In Their Hands* from the LGI including a demonstration of the heart-lung machine which had attracted worldwide interest.

He supported Marian Ionescu in his world changing development of animal-based heart valves and was sometimes seen, in his chauffeur-driven Rolls Royce, collecting fresh supplies of offal from a Leeds abattoir. I'm taking it for granted that you've realised he was eminent so I'm not going to list his posts and accolades but fellow cardiac surgeons formed the Wooler Society for meetings and exchanging information. He was also a renowned teacher with many surgeons sending him their pupils. Quite a few of his former students around the world will be dissecting hearts as you read this. The author of the definitive *Pioneers of Cardiac Surgery* (Vanderbilt University Press, 2008) not only included a section on Geoffrey but wrote in his a presentation copy: 'For Geoffrey Wooler FRCS – thank you for being my mentor and inspiration to pursue a life doing cardiac surgery.'

In his obituary The Yorkshire Post said, 'in 1957 he spearheaded one of the world's greatest surgical advances, when his team performed a successful open-heart operation, the repair of a mitral valve' (8 January 2010). The British Medical Journal obituary said 'he treated portal hypertension, helped in developing a heart-lung machine by ameliorating its excessive haemolysis, and co-developed two biological replacement mitral valves. Geoffrey was well loved and a mentor to many in open heart surgery, nationally and internationally.' (BMJ 2010; 340:c1929) I feel I should add my own reflection, from reading a bit about him, he also sounds like he was a right laugh.

The Works is 'the leading **Skatepark** in the UK, catering for skateboard, BMX and inline skating' based in Hunslet at Airedale Industrial Estate, Kitson Road. There website says 'we host an Extreme Sports Academy with the NHS which is the first of its type in the UK.....The main attraction of the Works is a massive, well equipped indoor Skatepark split into several sections catering for both beginner and advanced riders and skaters. The park features 25,000 square feet of high quality ramps and obstacles built to the highest standards by professionals.' How cool is that? Makes me wish I wasn't 40-odd with a fear of all them new-fangled, wheel-based activities.

XYZ

X-ray: There has been a couple of extremely important contributions by Leeds folk to the field of X-rays, **William Henry Bragg** and **William Lawrence Bragg** gave birth to the field of **X-ray crystallography** which determines the arrangement of atoms in solids and were duly awarded the Nobel Prize in Physics. **William Astbury** (who had in the past worked with Bragg) carried on this work in X-ray crystallography and in the 1930s, with his student **Florence Bell,** took the first X-ray images of **DNA**.

X-treme Vaccing is an event that Mrs Mick would like to see introduced at an Olympic level. Not that she vacs very much really, just when she's going up mountains or canoeing.

The Yorkshire Ladies' Council of Education (YLCE) has its roots in Leeds during the 1860s through a group of prominent women but it was not formally established until 1876 and for 27 years (1885-1912) Lucy Cavendish was President. Their website says that, 'the early Council members recognised the need to help other women living in overcrowded and unhealthy conditions in the industrial city. They also realised that to be effective such immediate help should be accompanied by improvements in educational opportunities for girls.' Traditionally the Council developed and supported certain causes until another organisation could take it on, an approach it maintains. It currently 'offers educational awards towards fees only to British women aged 21 or over who have been offered a place at a British educational institution and do not qualify for LEA support.'

The Council's main projects:

1918 Foundation of Yorkshire Ladies' Secretarial College (closed 1989)

1960 Opening of Forest Hill Residential Home for the Elderly (now sheltered housing)

1989 Start of The Educational Awards Fund

Other projects in which The Council was influential:

1874 Opening of Yorkshire College of Cookery

1870s Opening of Leeds Girls' High School, Wakefield Girls' High School and Bradford Girls' Grammar School

1903 Start of Yorkshire Training Fund for Women

1909 Establishment of Leeds Babies' Welcome Clinics

1937 YLCE lobbied Parliament on the Factory Bill

1944 Beginning of Meals on Wheels Service

The Yorkshire Planetarium was based at Harewood House and only lasted from May 2007 until 2008 when it was bailed out with a £1.2 million grant from Yorkshire Forward, it has now closed. Between February and October 2009 only 28,360 people visited – at a tax cost of £11 per head. I find that annoying because if I'd known it was there I'd have certainly taken the kids up and I've asked a few people and not one knew of its existence. It was three 'space-age' domes next to each other and the YEP (27 February 2010) described the attraction: 'The Star Chamber allowed visitors to explore the night sky with an introduction to its constellations and planets; the Hubble Space Dome brought images directly from the Hubble telescope and The Rocket provided the fun of an eight- metre climbing frame for all ages.' Live images from Hubble, how cool is that? It makes me angry that it's been stripped, not because of the cash spent but because of the apparent lack of publicity, had the people of Leeds known about it I'm positive they'd have gone and had a shufty. I went with a bunch of school kids in July 2010 and the end dome still had a space based film where you lay back on deck chairs and watch the dome around you, it was well impressive. Right I'm stopping before I swear; this should have opened up the horizons of d'yoof. Should we get cross, demand its re-installation and get loads of publicity for it?

Yorkshire Relish was produced by Goodall and Blackhouse who had a large factory east of Victoria Bridge (now offices). The company started out as manufacturing grocers (baking powder, powdered eggs, custard powder etc.) and the relish was based on Mrs Goodall's homemade sauce. The sauce sold 6 million bottles a year in the 1880s and its advertising material from 1885 claimed that Yorkshire Relish had 'The largest sale of any sauce in the world' and was 'sold by all grocers, druggists and Italian warehousemen.' Anyway the biggest selling sauce in the world, I believe them, obviously, and am sure they will have done extensive research before coming up with that fact. **Abbey House Museum** has a bottle of Yorkshire Relish on display, the 1885 vintage. I don't want to get into the relationships between Mr Goodall, Mrs Goodall and Henry Blackhouse, it seems way too *Bouquet of Barbed Wire* for me, so I'll end with the fact that the business was bought by Hammonds Sauce Ltd. in 1959.

Yorkshire Television Programmes:

3-2-1
Adam's Family Tree
Airline
Animal Kwackers
At Home with the Braithwaites
Bad Influence!
The Beiderbecke Affair
The Beiderbecke Tapes
The Beiderbecke Connection
The Beiderbecke Trilogy
Beryl's Lot
The Big Bang
A Bit of a Do
Calendar
Countdown
Cybernet
The Darling Buds of May
Duty Free
Emmerdale
Fat Friends
Flambards
The Flaxton Boys
Follyfoot

Get Lost!
Hadleigh
Hallelujah!
Harry's Game
Heartbeat
Home to Roost
How We Used To Live
In Loving Memory
Joker's Wild
Junior Showtime
Movies, Games and Videos
My Parents Are Aliens
The New Statesman
Oh No, It's Selwyn Froggitt!
Only When I Laugh
Parkin's Patch
The Price Is Right
Queenie's Castle
The Raggy Dolls
The Riddlers
Rising Damp
Round the Bend
The Royal

The Royal Today

The Sandbaggers

Stay Lucky

Through the Keyhole

A Touch of Frost

Winner Takes All

Alex Zane (born Alexander Laurence, 1979) is a television presenter, comedian and DJ who attended Boston Spa Comprehensive School. He's done script loads of TV presenting, helped write *The 11 O'Clock Show*, *Smack the Pony*, *Brain Candy,* is the film reviewer for The Sun newspaper and has had small parts in a few films. You can find him everywhere if you're interested.

Arnold Ziff (1927–2004) was educated at Roundhay grammar school and Leeds University. Stories of how well his Russian family had been welcomed into the city fed his later urges to support good causes in the city, to which he donated millions of pounds.

In 1948 Arnold joined the family firm, **Stylo Shoes** and became Chairman in 1966, with more than 400 retail outlets, and formed the Town Centre Securities property company in 1959 which, amongst other projects, developed the Merrion Centre – claimed by Clavane as 'the first shopping mall in Europe' – and reached a market value of £160 million. Stylo operated under several brands including Barratts, Shutopia, Shellys and Priceless. Stylo also acquired Saxone (& Sorosis Shoe Co. Limited) shoe company which looks to have been set up in Leeds (although I can't trace it) and was trading in the city from, at least, 1908. In 2009 Stylo went into administration and many stores were closed but 160 stores and 165 concessions remained open after being sold to the management of Stylo led by Arnold's son Michael and which employed around 6,500 staff.

Arnold's philanthropy is commemorated by the Marjorie and Arnold Ziff Community Centre in Moortown, his gifts to Leeds Uni are commemorated through the Marjorie and Arnold Ziff building which opened in 2010 and Tropical World in Roundi Park was renamed *The Arnold and Marjorie Ziff Tropical World* in July 2008 due to a generous donation. The list of his donations and work for the city is large, for example, raising £1m for one of the country's first body scanners at St James's University hospital. He was given the Freedom of the City of London in 1979, awarded an OBE in 1981 and spent a year as High Sheriff of West Yorkshire.

Zips....we've all seen them.

Zzzzzz.......**Wake up!**

Bibliography.

I've listed many titles within the book but here are some of the titles that I used and thought may be of interest.

Stephen T Anning, *The History of Medicine in Leeds*, WS Maney, Leeds 1980.

Derek Fraser, *A History of modern Leeds,* Manchester University Press, 1980.

David Thornton, *Great Leeds Stories*, Fort Publishing Ltd., Ayr, 2005.

Brett Harrison, *A Century of Leeds*, The History Press Ltd, Stroud 2007.

John Morgan, *A Celebration of Leeds*, Great Northern Books Ltd., 2006.

John Gilleghan, *Leeds: An A to Z of Local History*, Gilleghan John, 2001.

Richard Vickerman Taylor, *The Biographia Leodiensis*, Simpkin, Marshal & Co., London, 1865.

Martin Wainwright, *True North*, Guardian Books, London, 2009.

Diane Holloway and Trish Colton, *The Knights Templar in Yorkshire*, The History Press, 2008

David Thornton, *Leeds: The Story of a City*, Fort Publishing Ltd., 2003.

Ernest Kilburn Scott, *Matthew Murray: Pioneer Engineer. Records from 1765 to 1826*, E. Jowett Ltd., Leeds, 1928.

John Goodchild, *West Yorkshire Coalfield*, Tempus Publishing Ltd., Stroud, 2000.

Cathy Hartley, *A Historical Dictionary of British Women*, Routledge, London, 2003.

June Hannam, *Isabella Ford, 1855-1924*, Blackwell, Oxford, 1989.

Roger Ratcliffe, *Leeds Fax: The Complete Handbook to Life in Leeds*, Aire Press & Publishing, Leeds, 1992.

David Goodman, *The Making of Leeds*, Wharncliffe Books, Barnsley, 2004.

Compiled by Julia Skinner, *Did You Know? Leeds: A Miscellany*, The Francis Frith Collection, Salisbury, 2008. Not recommended.

Noel Proudlock, *Leeds, A history of its tramways*, J.N.D. Proudlock, Leeds, 1991.

Lynne Stevenson Tate, *Aspects of Leeds*, Wharncliffe Books, Barnsley, 1999.

Christopher Winn, *I Never Knew That About Yorkshire*, Ebury Press, 2010.

Robert Preedy, *Leeds Cinemas Remembered*, Netherwood Dalton & Co, 1980.

Francis Frith and Clive Hardy, *Francis Frith's Leeds Pocket Album*, Frith Book Company Ltd., 2004.

Lesley Richmond, Alison Turton, *The Brewing industry: a guide to historical records*, Manchester University Press, 1990.

Also available from Armley Press:

Coming Out As A Bowie Fan
In Leeds, Yorkshire, England
By Mick McCann
ISBN 0-9554699-0-2

Hot Knife –
Love bullets and revenge
in Leeds, Yorkshire, England
By John Lake
ISBN: 0-9554699-1-0

Nailed – Digital Stalking
In Leeds, Yorkshire, England
By Mick McCann
ISBN: 0-9554699-2-9

Blowback
By John Lake
ISBN 0-9554699-4-7

Speed Bomb
By John Lake
ISBN 0-9554699-5-3

Lightning Source UK Ltd.
Milton Keynes UK
UKHW031043071220
374769UK00008B/449